TO YOUR ETERNITY

YOSHITOKI OIMA

2

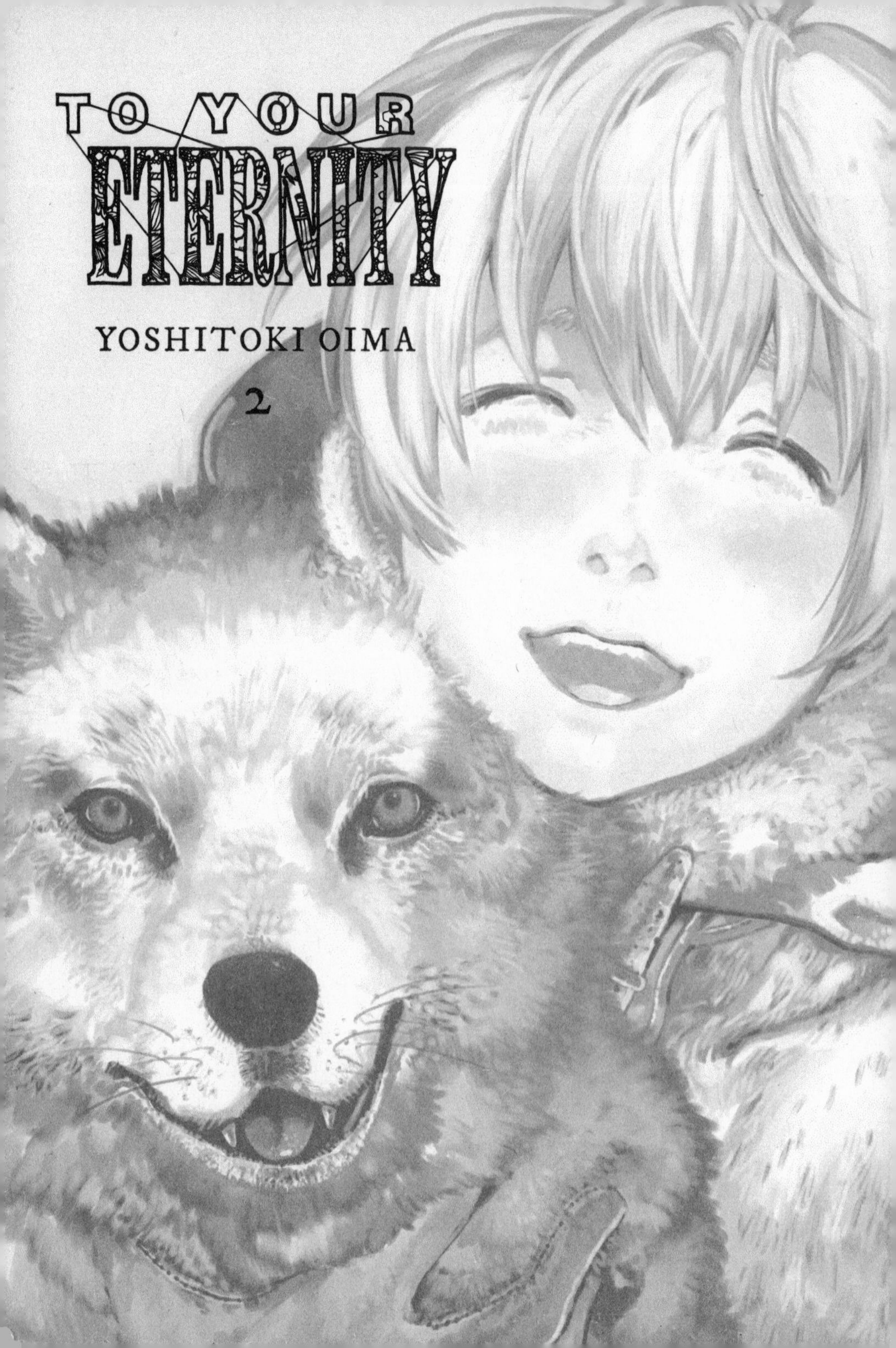

THE STORY SO FAR

An orb was cast unto the earth.
The orb transformed from rock, to moss, to wolf, reaching a snowbound tundra,
where It made human contact for the first time...
The boy lived alone, and yearned to learn more of the world beyond his home.
When the days they spent together came to a close, It obtained the boy's form.
Seeking more stimuli, It set off on a journey.
The next person It met was March,
the maiden from Ninannah who was chosen as the offering for the Oniguma.
It, as the boy, showed up at the altar where March rested,
and transformed into a wolf, defeating the Oniguma.
In order to cover up the failed ritual,
Hayase decided to return to the land of Yanome with everyone in tow.

CHARACTERS

FUSHI

Consumes knowledge through stimuli;
an undying being. If It meets all the
requirements necessary, It can
metamorphose into different forms
It has obtained. During Its battle with
the Oniguma, It transformed from boy
to wolf.

Fushi continues to grow while taking many forms.

MARCH

A maiden from the Ninnanah region who dreams of becoming a grownup. She was chosen as an offering to the Oniguma, but on the day of the ritual, escaped.

THE BOY

The first human Fushi ever met. He yearned to learn more about the outside world, but lost his life before fulfilling his dream.

JOAAN

The boy's pet Reshy wolf. The first animal that Fushi obtained.

PARONA

Like an older sister to March. She went into the forest to save March.

HAYASE

An official from the land of Yanome. She was dispatched to the Ninannah region to oversee the ritual offering.

SHAMAN

Chose March as the offering.

ONIGUMA

Revered as the god who grants peace and prosperity to the Ninannah region.

CONTENTS

#5 Journey of Memories

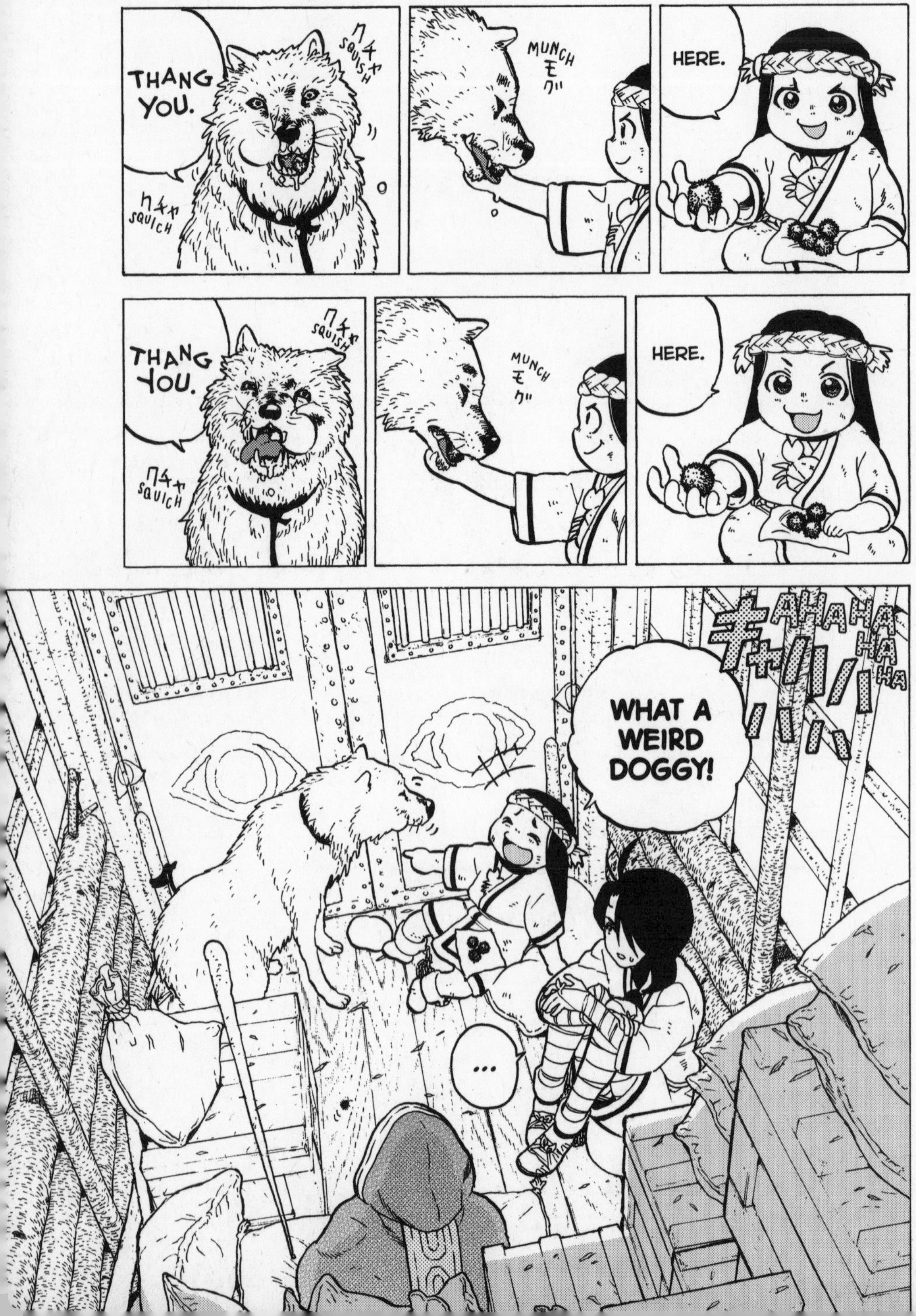
HERE.
MUNCH
モグ
THANG YOU.
SQUISH
SQUICH
HERE.
MUNCH
THANG YOU.
SQUISH
SQUICH
AHAHAHAHAHA
WHAT A WEIRD DOGGY!
...

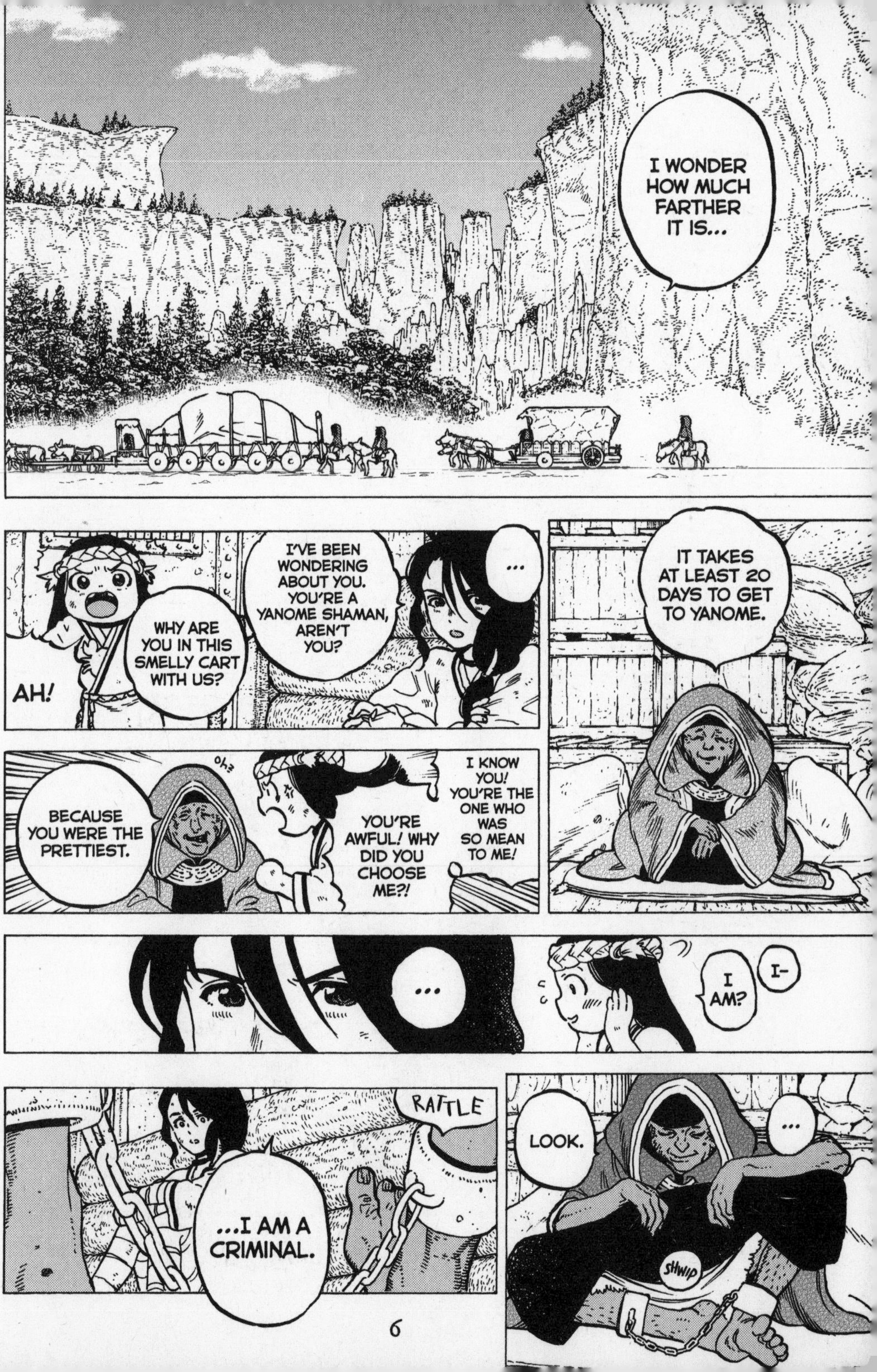
I WONDER HOW MUCH FARTHER IT IS...
IT TAKES AT LEAST 20 DAYS TO GET TO YANOME.
...
I'VE BEEN WONDERING ABOUT YOU. YOU'RE A YANOME SHAMAN, AREN'T YOU?
WHY ARE YOU IN THIS SMELLY CART WITH US?
AH!
I KNOW YOU! YOU'RE THE ONE WHO WAS SO MEAN TO ME!
YOU'RE AWFUL! WHY DID YOU CHOOSE ME?!
BECAUSE YOU WERE THE PRETTIEST.
I-
I AM?
...
...
LOOK.
SHWIP
RATTLE
...I AM A CRIMINAL.

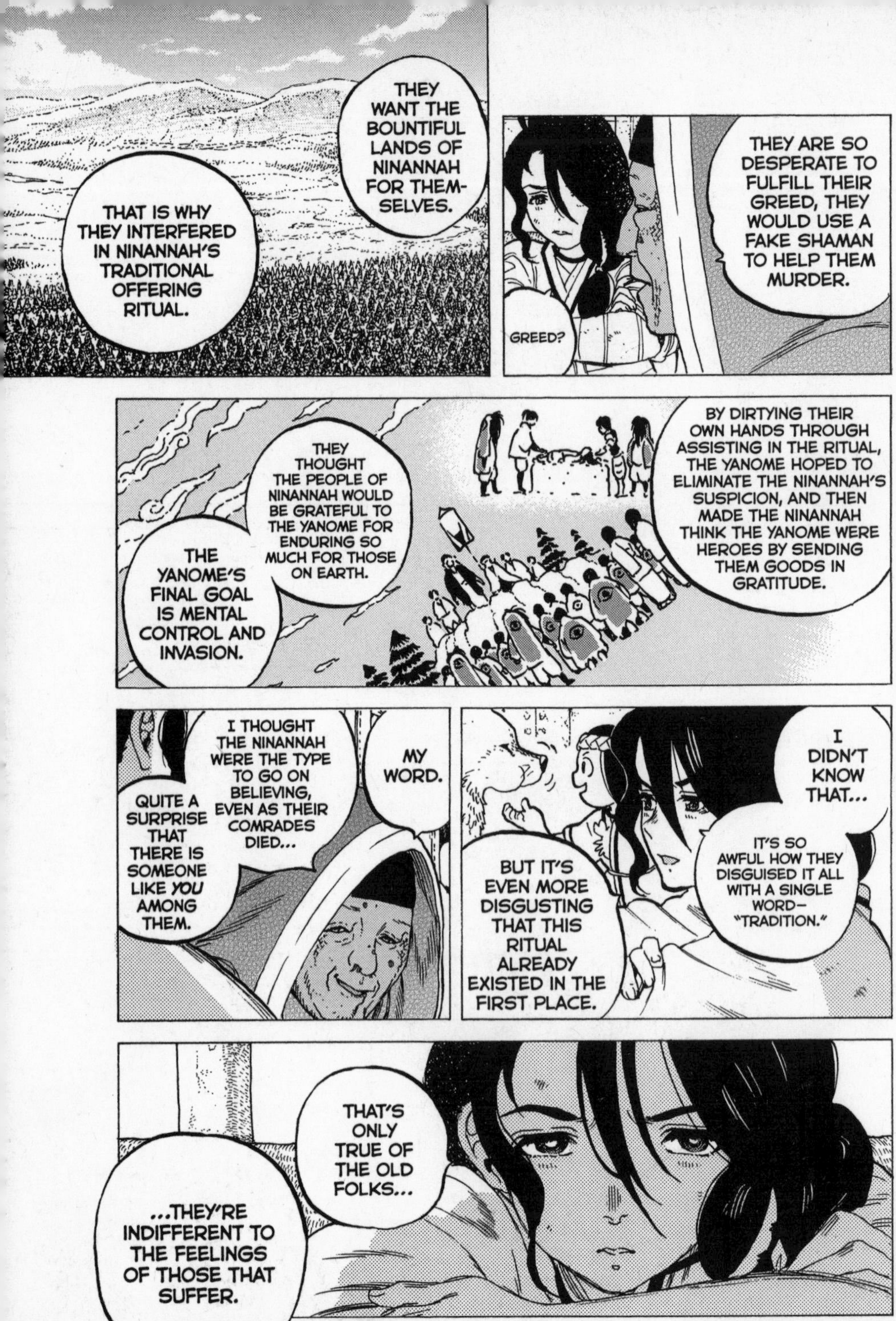
THEY ARE SO DESPERATE TO FULFILL THEIR GREED, THEY WOULD USE A FAKE SHAMAN TO HELP THEM MURDER.
GREED?
THEY WANT THE BOUNTIFUL LANDS OF NINANNAH FOR THEM-SELVES.
THAT IS WHY THEY INTERFERED IN NINANNAH'S TRADITIONAL OFFERING RITUAL.
BY DIRTYING THEIR OWN HANDS THROUGH ASSISTING IN THE RITUAL, THE YANOME HOPED TO ELIMINATE THE NINANNAH'S SUSPICION, AND THEN MADE THE NINANNAH THINK THE YANOME WERE HEROES BY SENDING THEM GOODS IN GRATITUDE.
THEY THOUGHT THE PEOPLE OF NINANNAH WOULD BE GRATEFUL TO THE YANOME FOR ENDURING SO MUCH FOR THOSE ON EARTH.
THE YANOME'S FINAL GOAL IS MENTAL CONTROL AND INVASION.
I DIDN'T KNOW THAT...
IT'S SO AWFUL HOW THEY DISGUISED IT ALL WITH A SINGLE WORD— "TRADITION."
BUT IT'S EVEN MORE DISGUSTING THAT THIS RITUAL ALREADY EXISTED IN THE FIRST PLACE.
MY WORD.
I THOUGHT THE NINANNAH WERE THE TYPE TO GO ON BELIEVING, EVEN AS THEIR COMRADES DIED...
QUITE A SURPRISE THAT THERE IS SOMEONE LIKE *YOU* AMONG THEM.
THAT'S ONLY TRUE OF THE OLD FOLKS...
...THEY'RE INDIFFERENT TO THE FEELINGS OF THOSE THAT SUFFER.

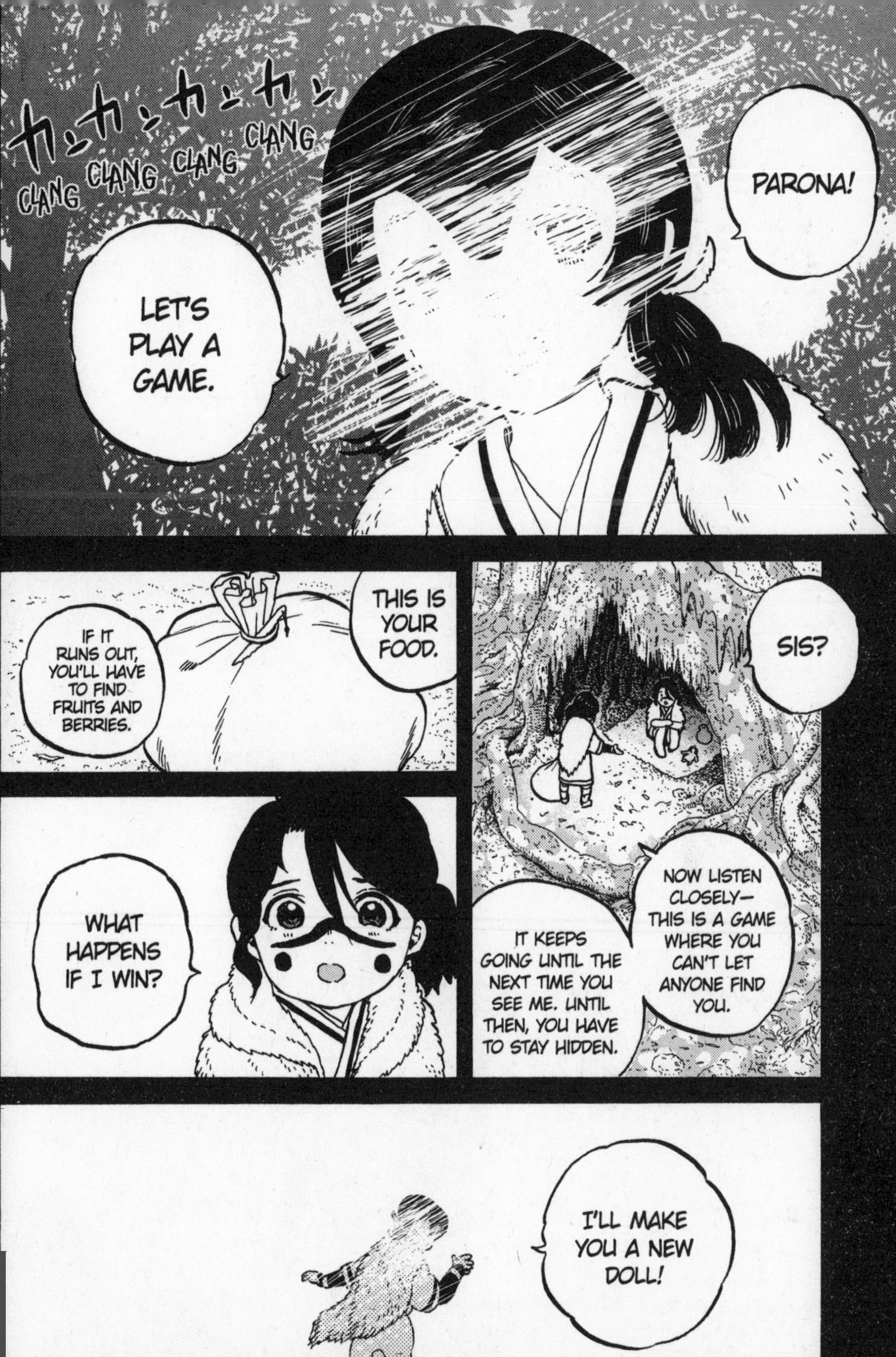
PARONA!
カンカンカンカン
CLANG CLANG CLANG CLANG
LET'S PLAY A GAME.
SIS?
NOW LISTEN CLOSELY— THIS IS A GAME WHERE YOU CAN'T LET ANYONE FIND YOU.
IT KEEPS GOING UNTIL THE NEXT TIME YOU SEE ME. UNTIL THEN, YOU HAVE TO STAY HIDDEN.
THIS IS YOUR FOOD.
IF IT RUNS OUT, YOU'LL HAVE TO FIND FRUITS AND BERRIES.
WHAT HAPPENS IF I WIN?
I'LL MAKE YOU A NEW DOLL!

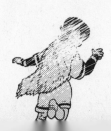

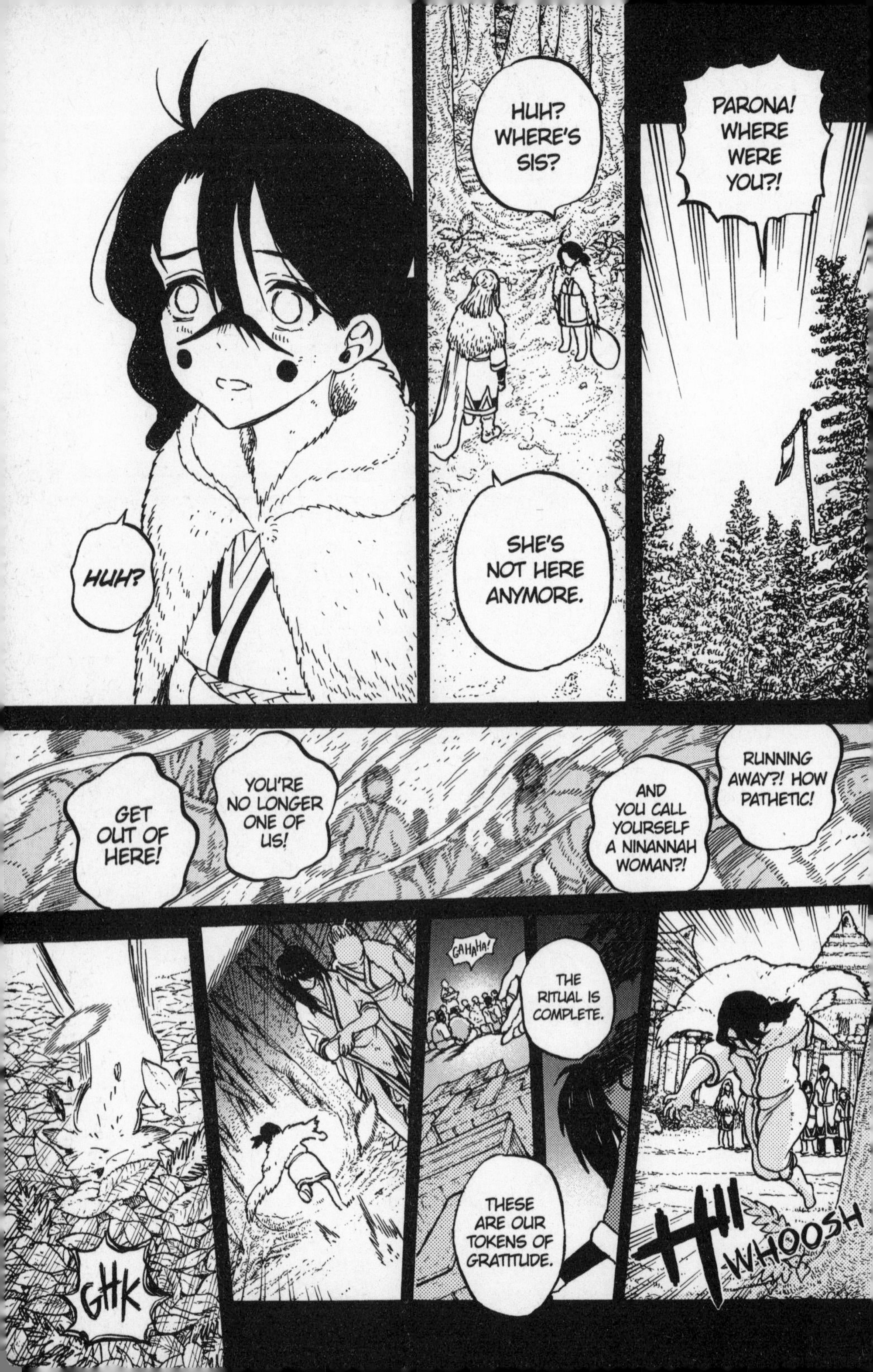
PARONA! WHERE WERE YOU?!
HUH? WHERE'S SIS?
SHE'S NOT HERE ANYMORE.
HUH?
RUNNING AWAY?! HOW PATHETIC!
AND YOU CALL YOURSELF A NINANNAH WOMAN?!
YOU'RE NO LONGER ONE OF US!
GET OUT OF HERE!
WHOOSH
GAHAHA!
THE RITUAL IS COMPLETE.
THESE ARE OUR TOKENS OF GRATITUDE.
GHK

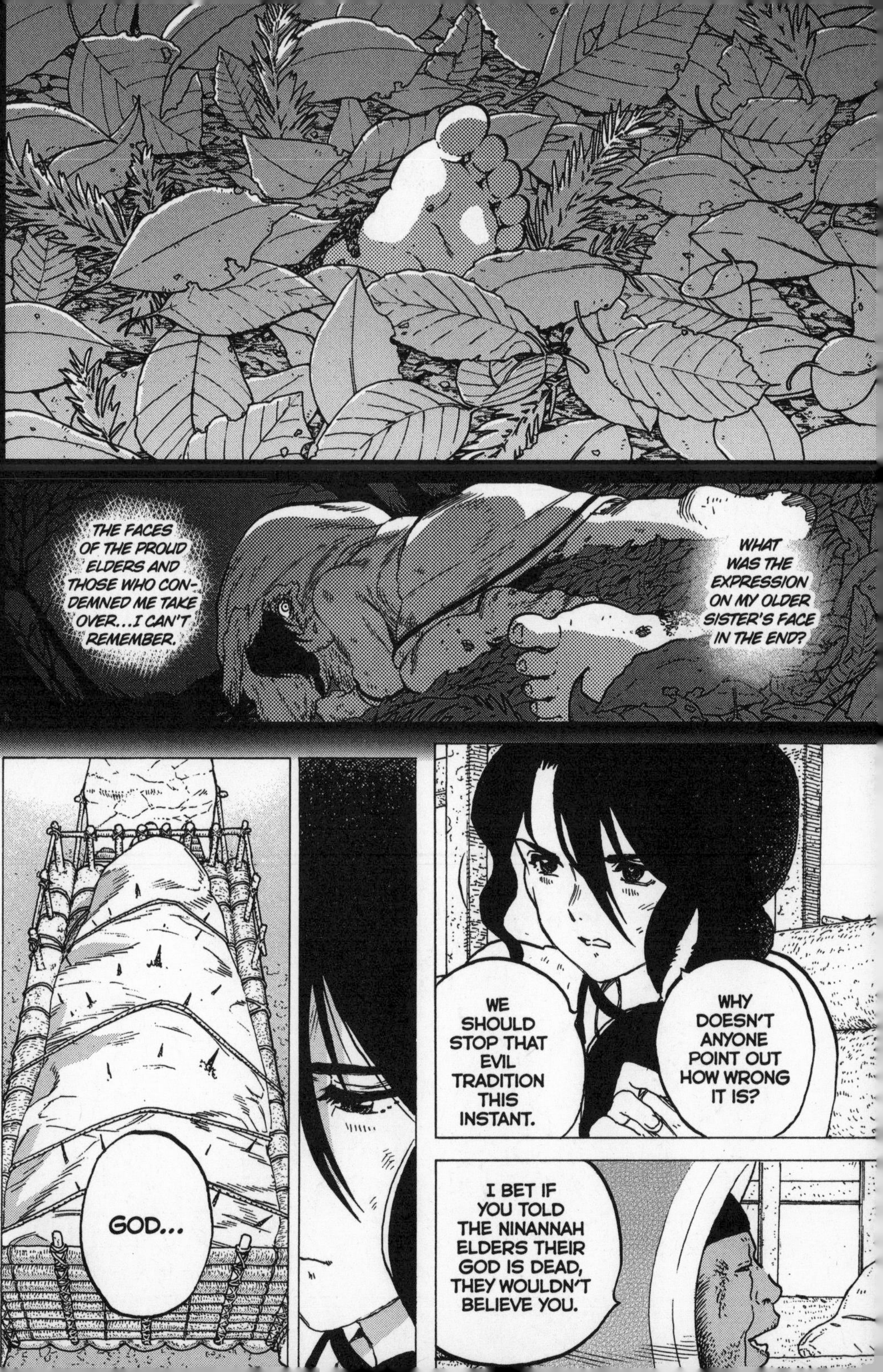
WHAT WAS THE EXPRESSION ON MY OLDER SISTER'S FACE IN THE END?
THE FACES OF THE PROUD ELDERS AND THOSE WHO CON-DEMNED ME TAKE OVER...I CAN'T REMEMBER.
WHY DOESN'T ANYONE POINT OUT HOW WRONG IT IS?
WE SHOULD STOP THAT EVIL TRADITION THIS INSTANT.
I BET IF YOU TOLD THE NINANNAH ELDERS THEIR GOD IS DEAD, THEY WOULDN'T BELIEVE YOU.
GOD...

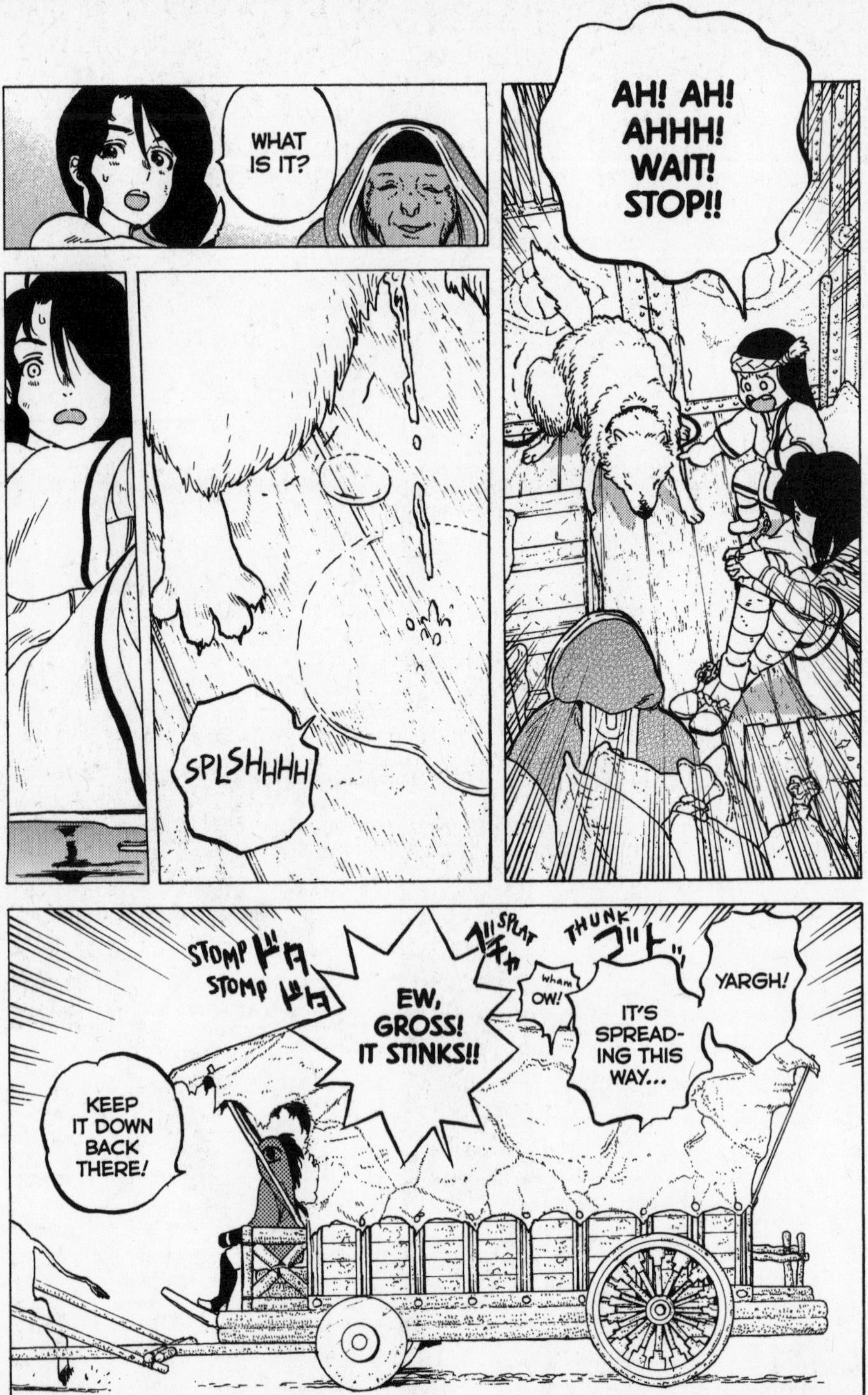

AH! AH! AHHH! WAIT! STOP!!
WHAT IS IT?
SPLSHHHH
YARGH!
IT'S SPREADING THIS WAY...
THUNK
wham
OW!
SPLAT
EW, GROSS! IT STINKS!!
STOMP
STOMP
KEEP IT DOWN BACK THERE!

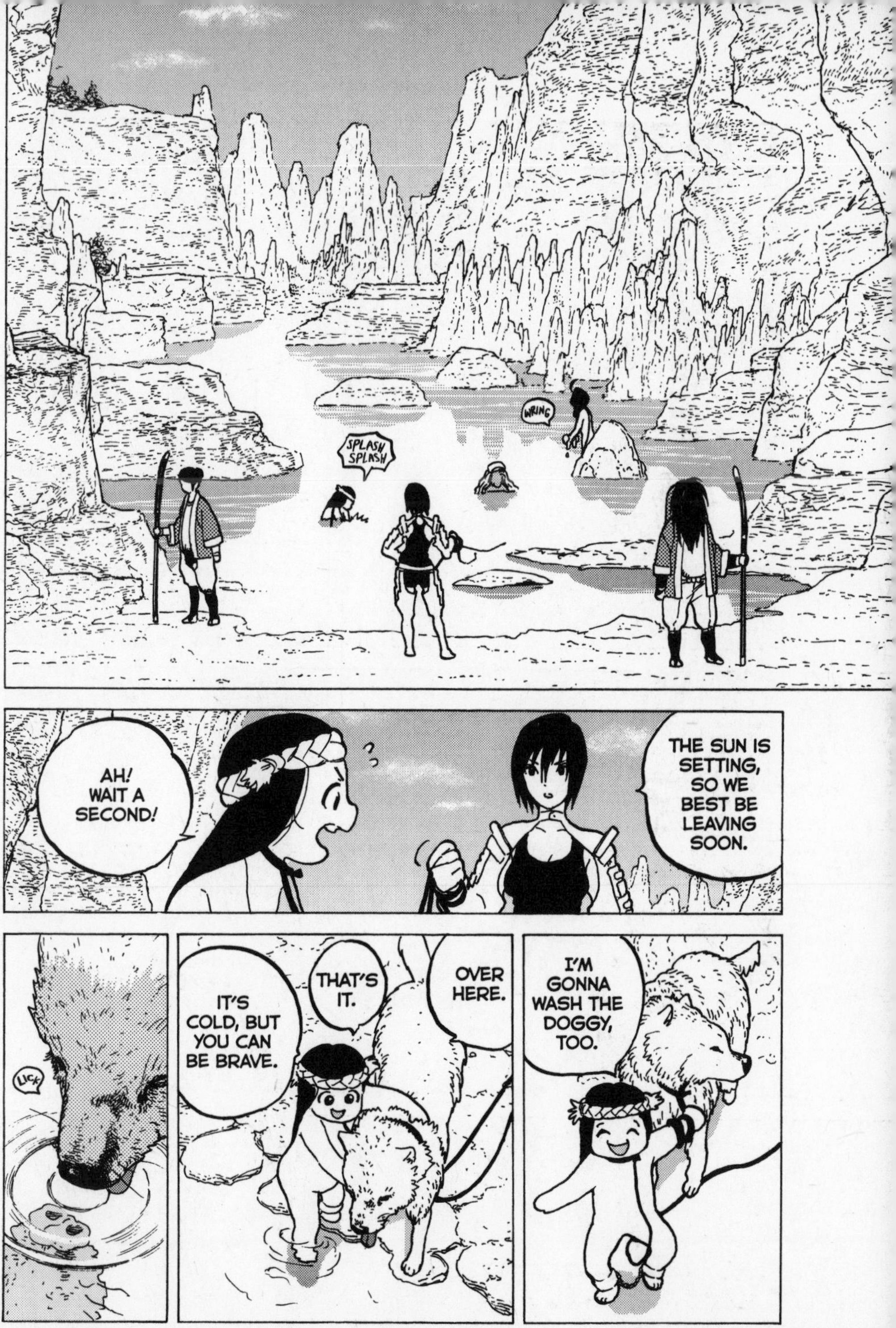
WRING
SPLASH SPLASH
THE SUN IS SETTING, SO WE BEST BE LEAVING SOON.
AH! WAIT A SECOND!
I'M GONNA WASH THE DOGGY, TOO.
OVER HERE.
THAT'S IT.
IT'S COLD, BUT YOU CAN BE BRAVE.
LICK

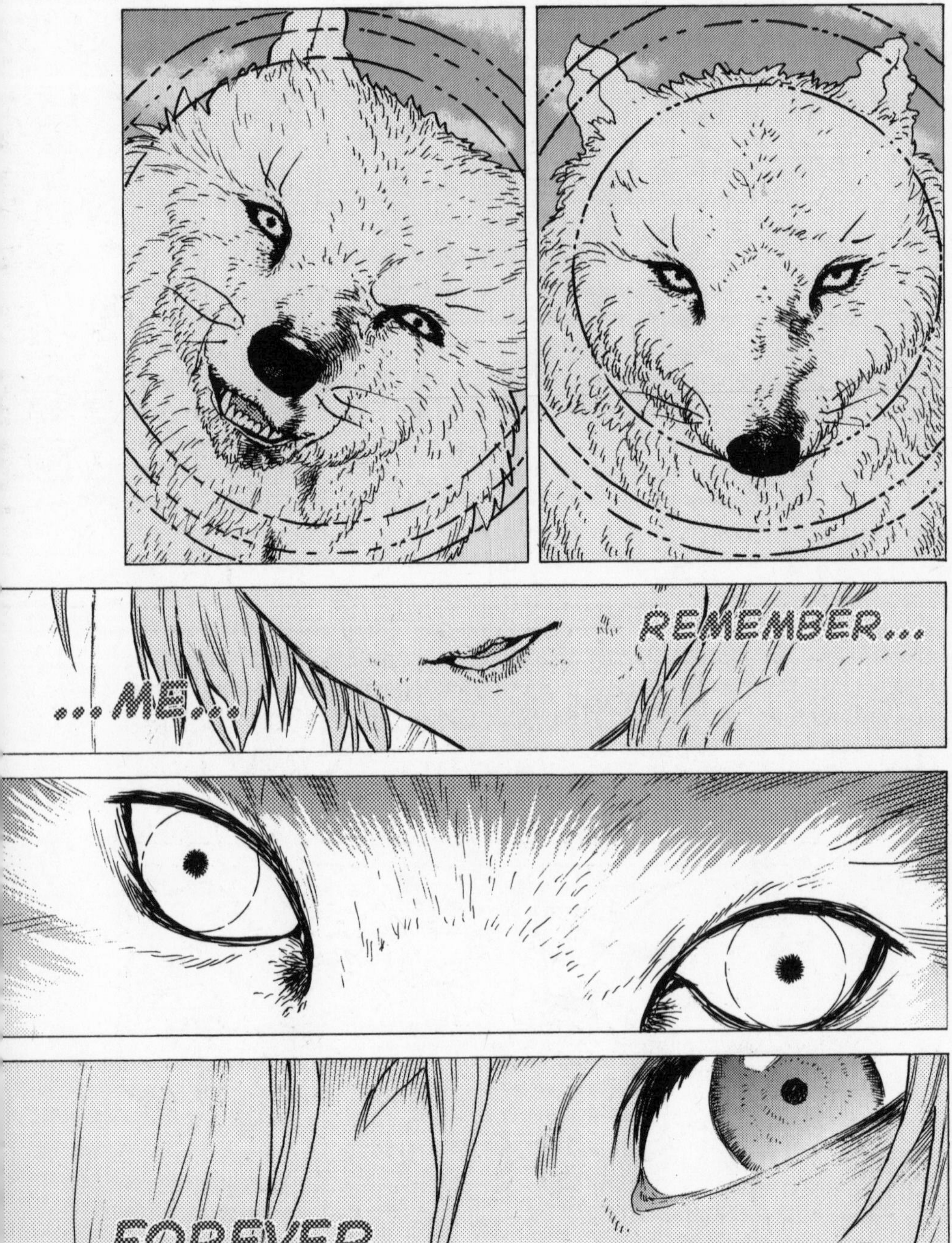
REMEMBER...
...ME...
...FOREVER.

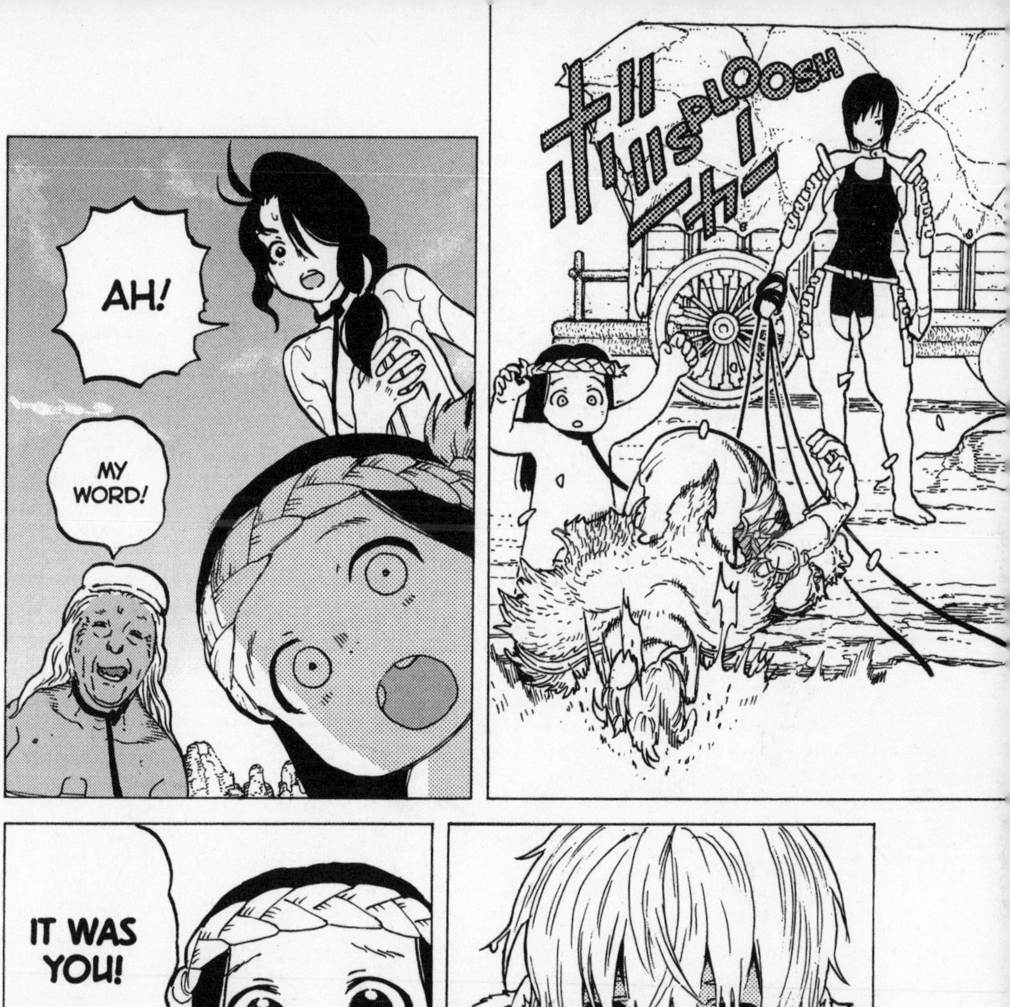
SPLOOSH
AH!
MY WORD!
IT WAS YOU!
I MISSED YOU, FU!
WH-WHOA, MARCH!
YOU KNOW THAT GUY?

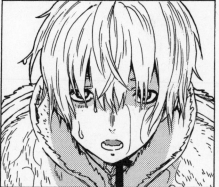

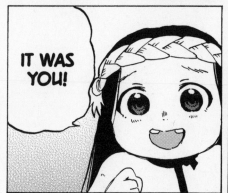

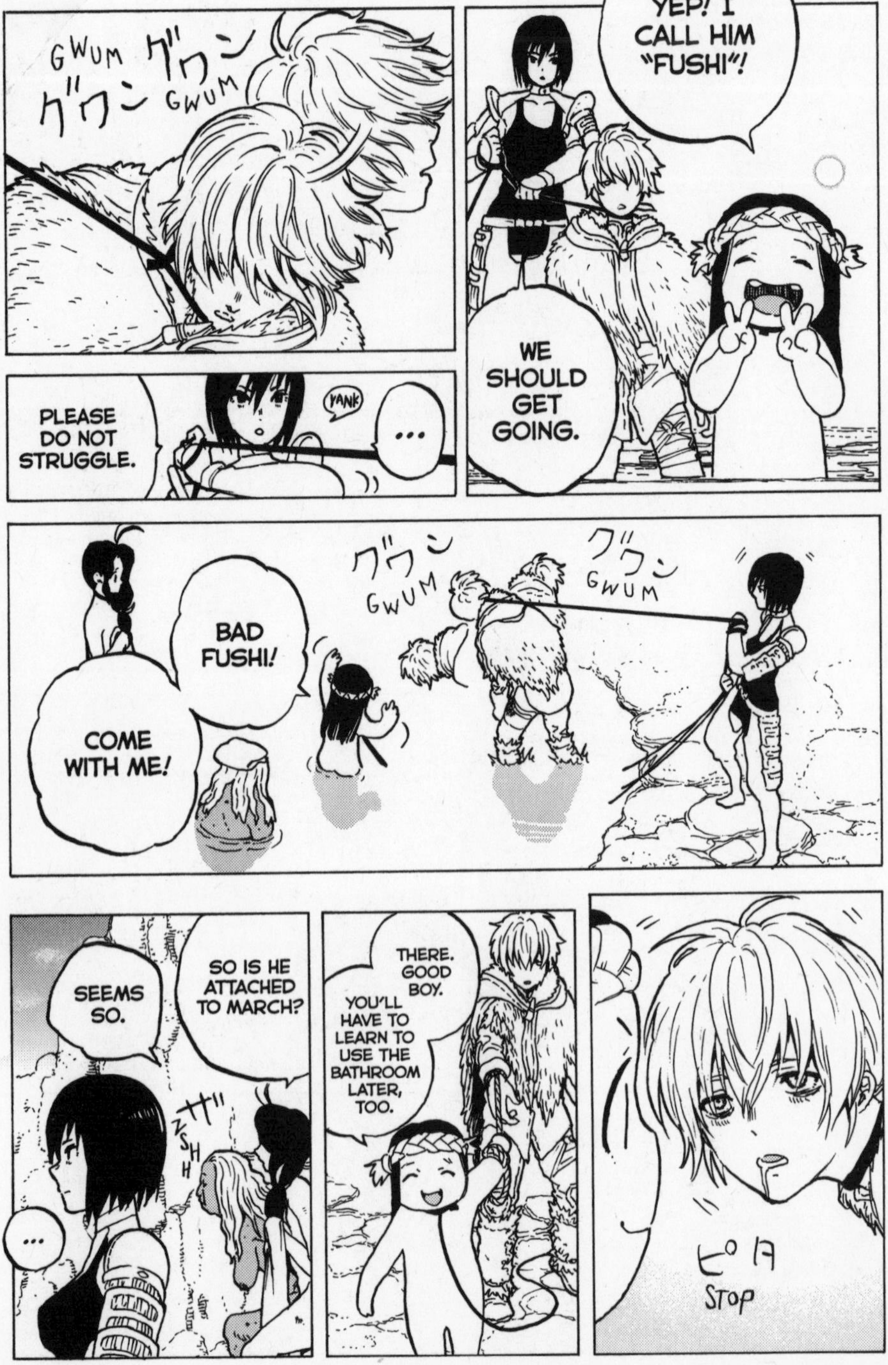

YEP! I CALL HIM "FUSHI"!
WE SHOULD GET GOING.
GWUM グワン
グワン GWUM
YANK
...
PLEASE DO NOT STRUGGLE.
グワン GWUM
グワン GWUM
BAD FUSHI!
COME WITH ME!
ピタ STOP
THERE. GOOD BOY.
YOU'LL HAVE TO LEARN TO USE THE BATHROOM LATER, TOO.
SO IS HE ATTACHED TO MARCH?
SEEMS SO.
ザッ ZSHH
...

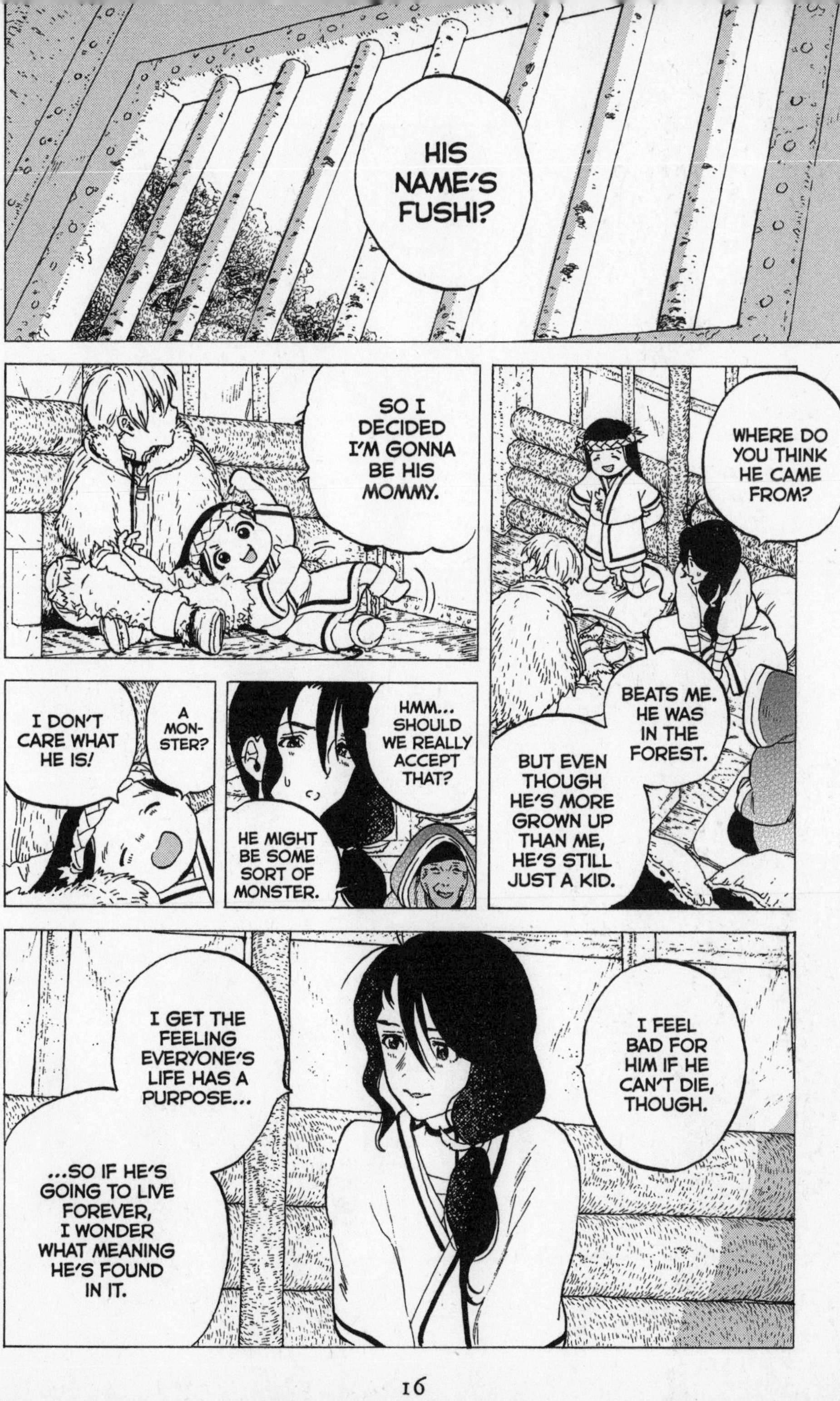
HIS NAME'S FUSHI?
WHERE DO YOU THINK HE CAME FROM?
BEATS ME. HE WAS IN THE FOREST.
BUT EVEN THOUGH HE'S MORE GROWN UP THAN ME, HE'S STILL JUST A KID.
SO I DECIDED I'M GONNA BE HIS MOMMY.
HMM... SHOULD WE REALLY ACCEPT THAT?
HE MIGHT BE SOME SORT OF MONSTER.
A MON-STER?
I DON'T CARE WHAT HE IS!
I FEEL BAD FOR HIM IF HE CAN'T DIE, THOUGH.
I GET THE FEELING EVERYONE'S LIFE HAS A PURPOSE...
...SO IF HE'S GOING TO LIVE FOREVER, I WONDER WHAT MEANING HE'S FOUND IN IT.

I'M SORRY, MARCH.

IT'S WRONG LOOKING FOR MEANING IN PEOPLE'S LIVES AND DEATHS.

OH.

MEANING?

...

PAT

I DON'T REALLY GET IT, BUT I'M REALLY HAPPY RIGHT NOW.

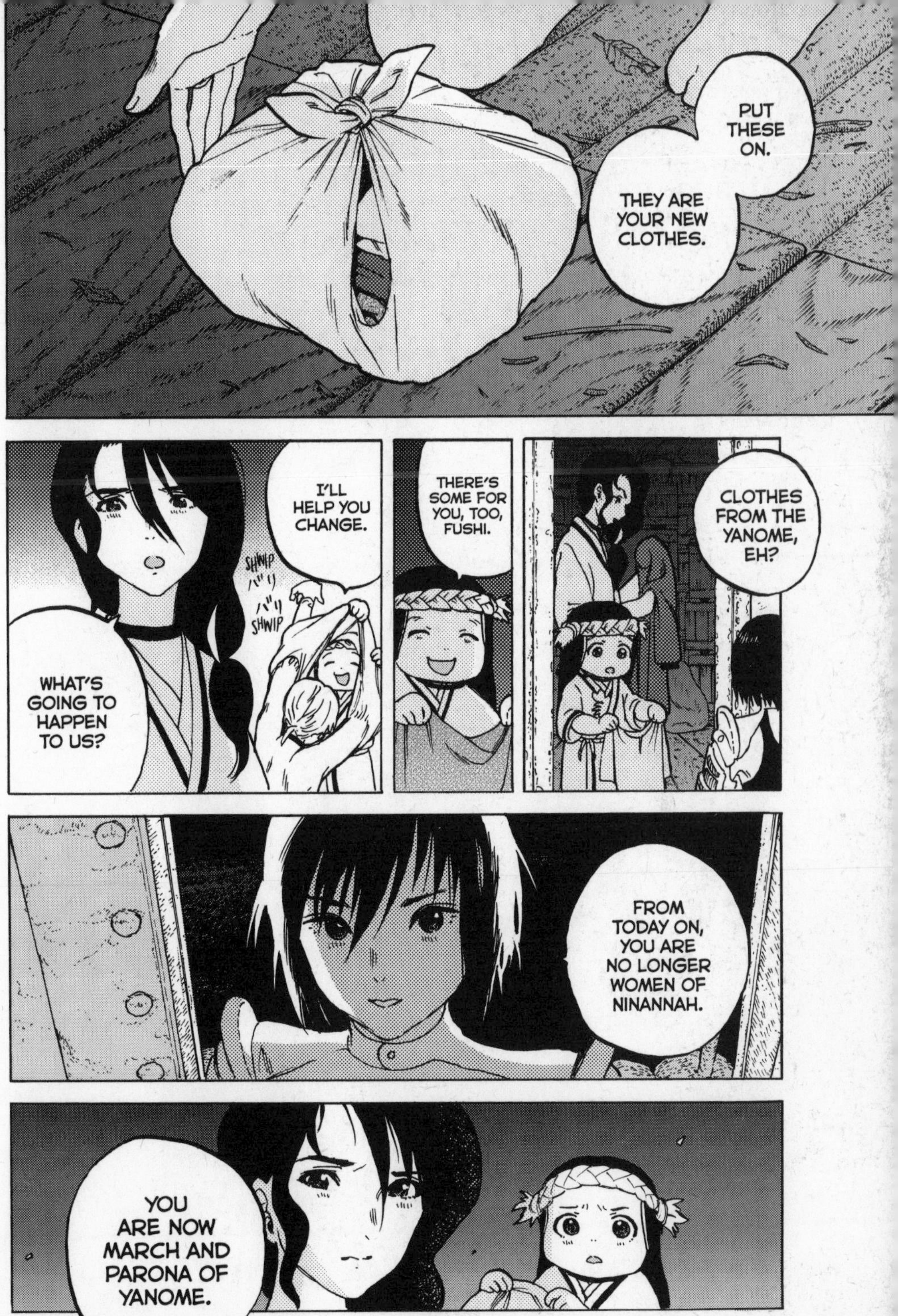
PUT THESE ON.
THEY ARE YOUR NEW CLOTHES.
CLOTHES FROM THE YANOME, EH?
THERE'S SOME FOR YOU, TOO, FUSHI.
I'LL HELP YOU CHANGE.
SHWIP バリ
バリ SHWIP
WHAT'S GOING TO HAPPEN TO US?
FROM TODAY ON, YOU ARE NO LONGER WOMEN OF NINANNAH.
YOU ARE NOW MARCH AND PARONA OF YANOME.

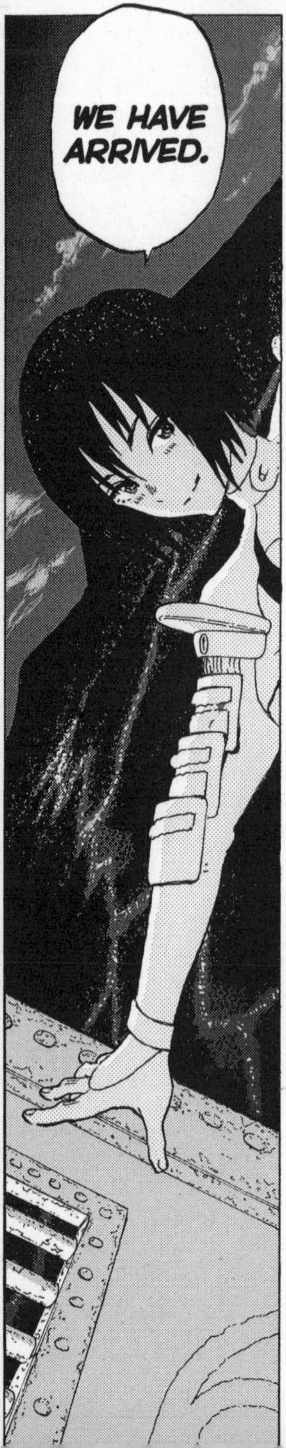
WE HAVE ARRIVED.

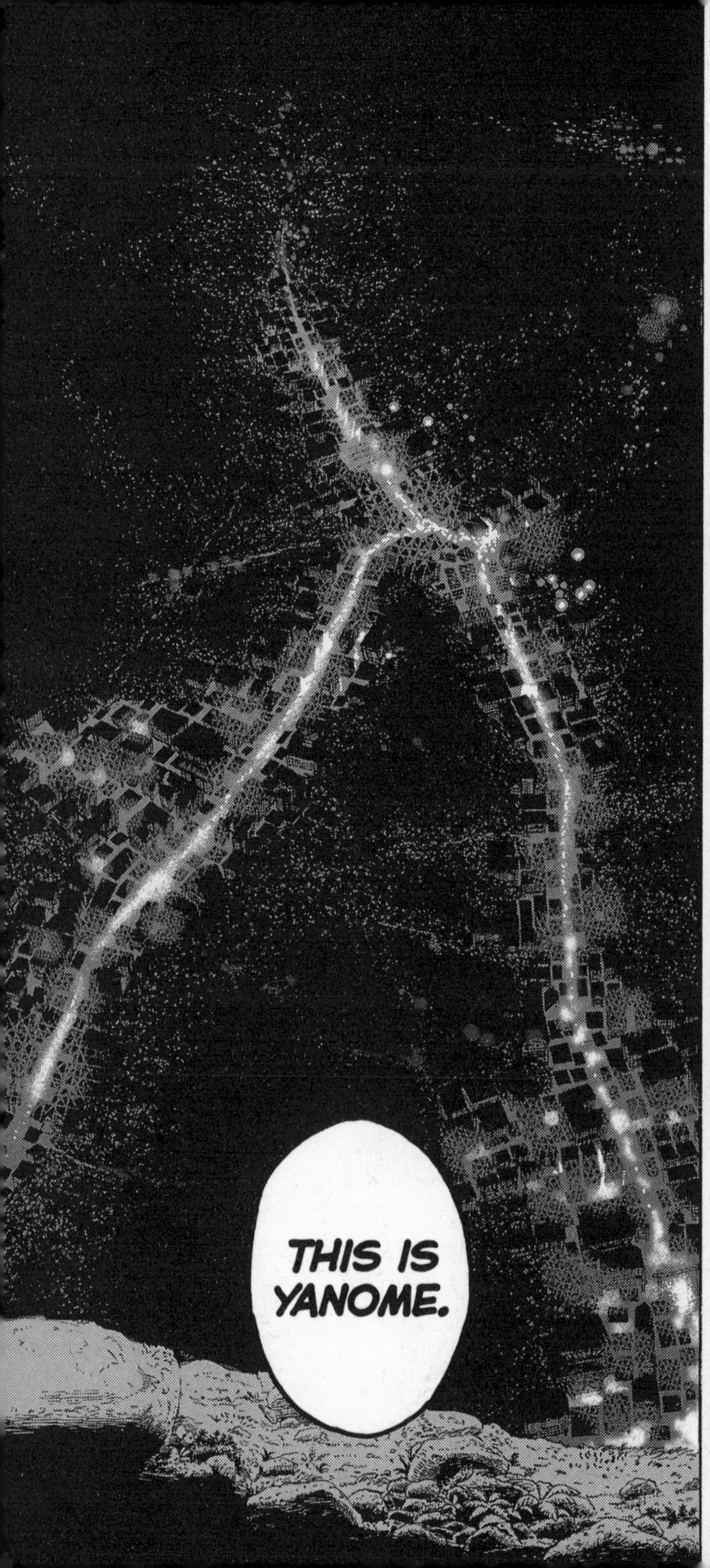
THIS IS YANOME.

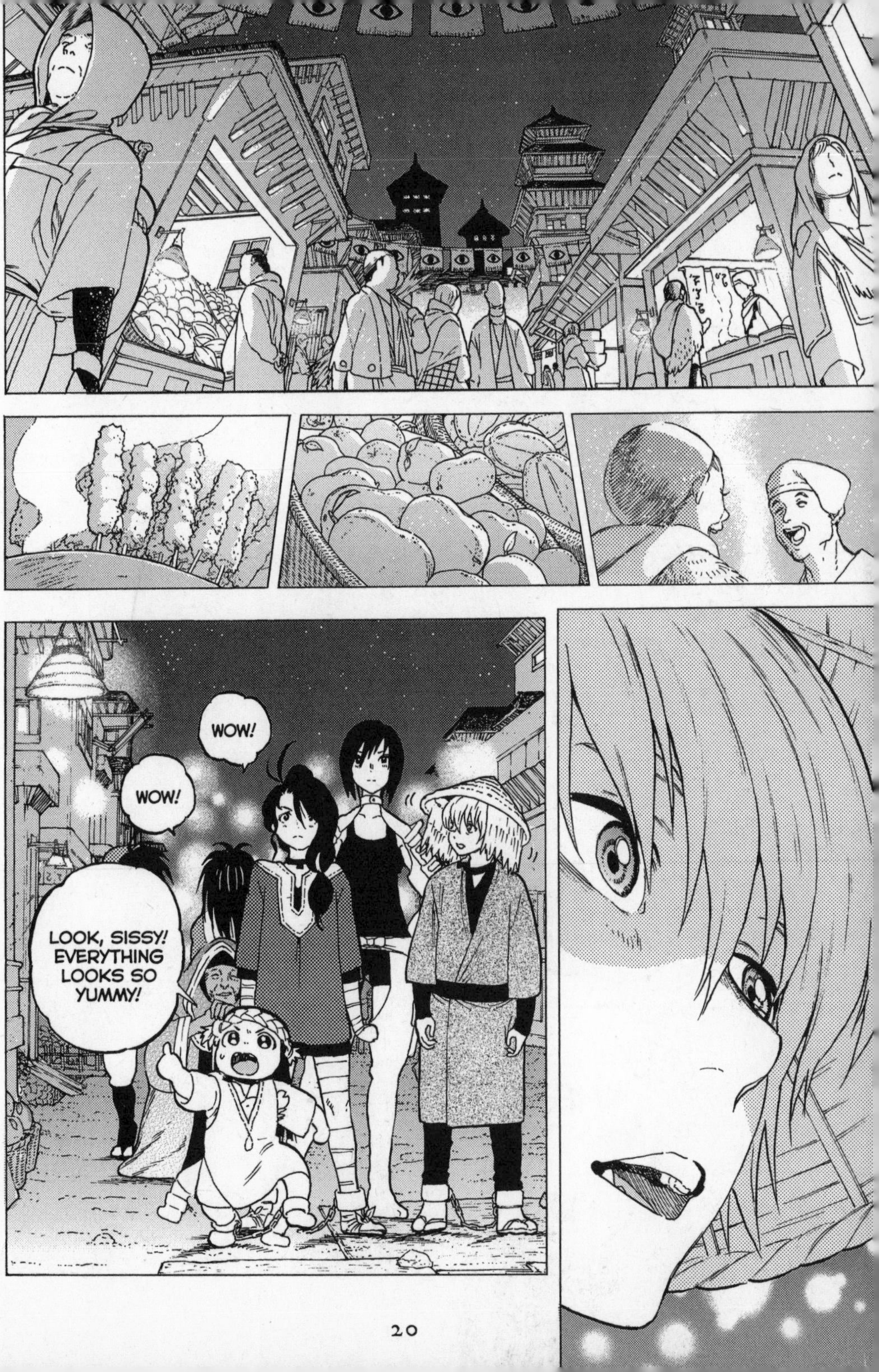
WOW!
WOW!
LOOK, SISSY! EVERYTHING LOOKS SO YUMMY!

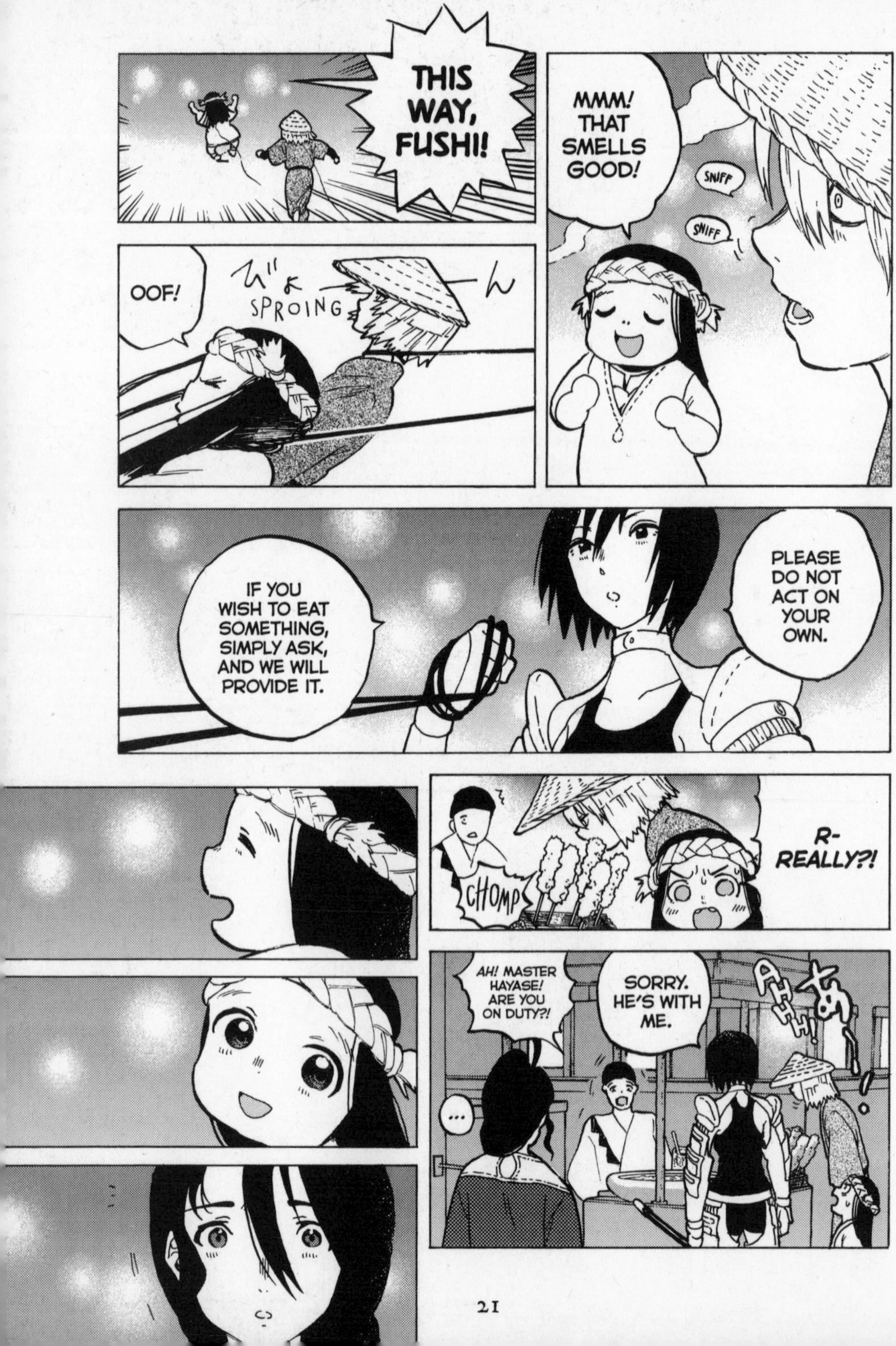
MMM! THAT SMELLS GOOD!
SNIFF
SNIFF
THIS WAY, FUSHI!
OOF!
SPROING
PLEASE DO NOT ACT ON YOUR OWN.
IF YOU WISH TO EAT SOMETHING, SIMPLY ASK, AND WE WILL PROVIDE IT.
R-REALLY?!
CHOMP
AHH!
SORRY. HE'S WITH ME.
AH! MASTER HAYASE! ARE YOU ON DUTY?!
...

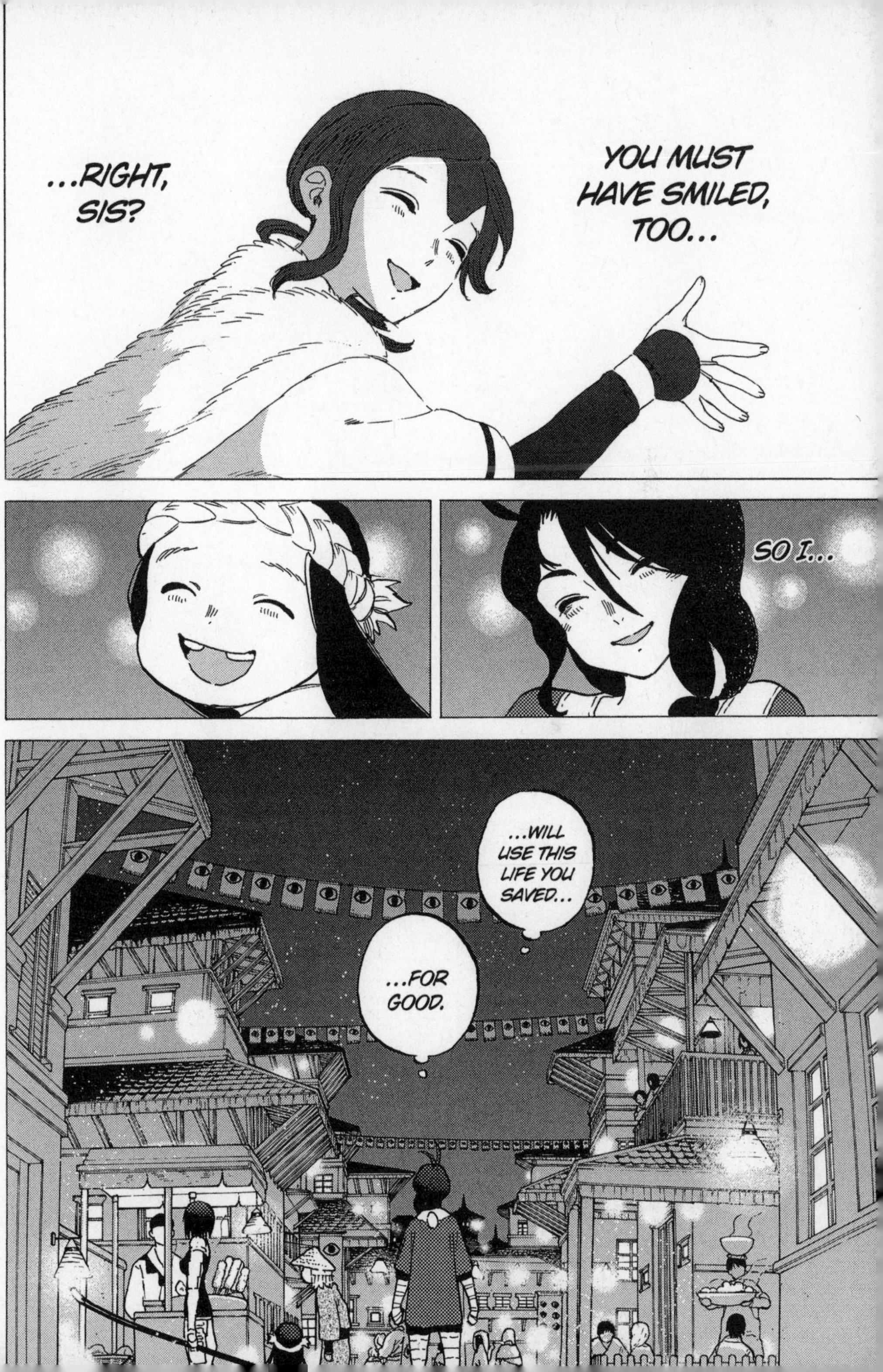
YOU MUST HAVE SMILED, TOO...
...RIGHT, SIS?
SO I...
...WILL USE THIS LIFE YOU SAVED...
...FOR GOOD.

TO YOUR
ETERNITY

TO YOUR ETERNITY

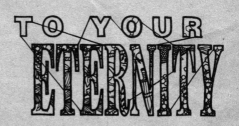

#6 The Comfortable Land of Yanome

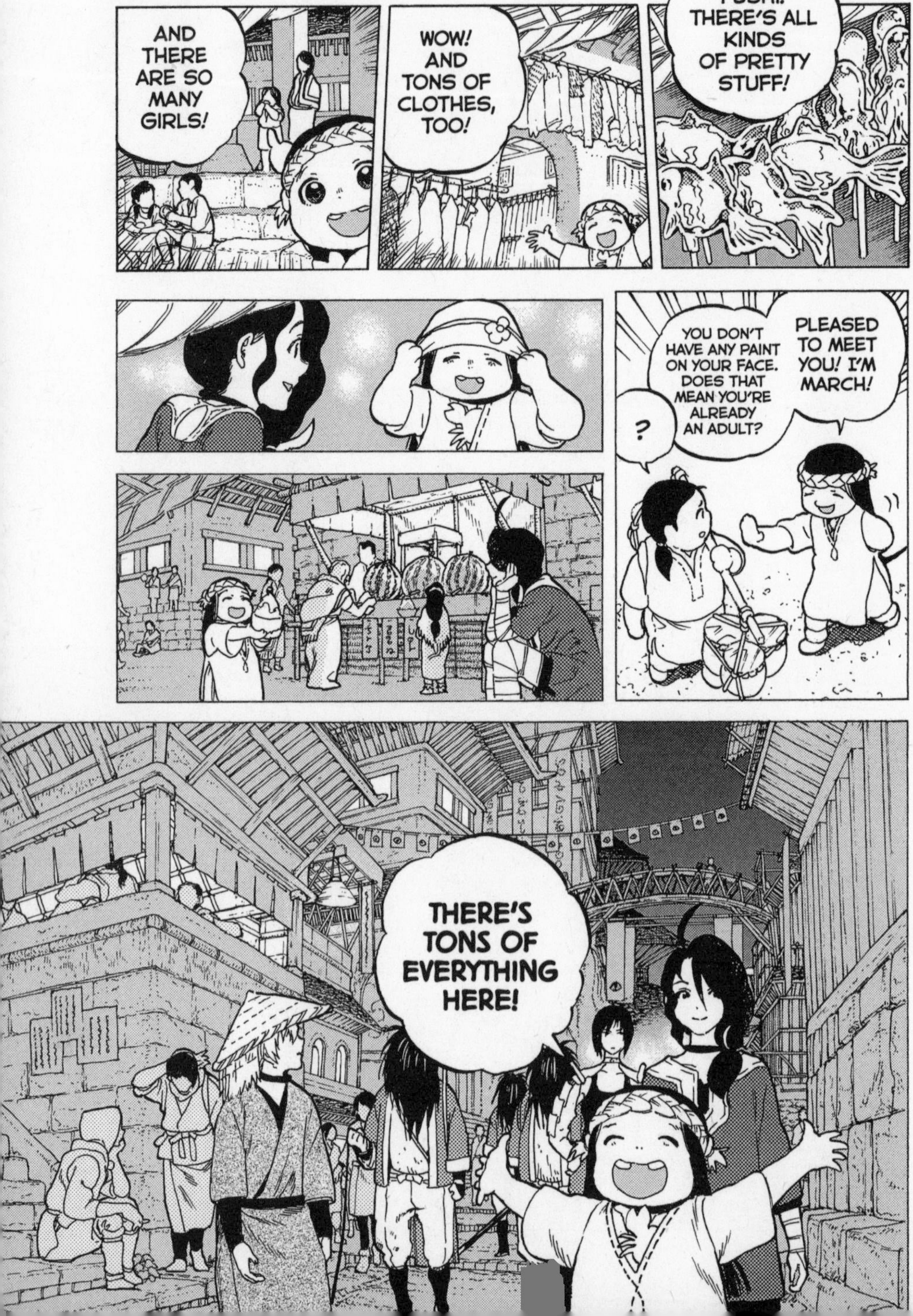
LOOK, FUSHI! THERE'S ALL KINDS OF PRETTY STUFF!
WOW! AND TONS OF CLOTHES, TOO!
AND THERE ARE SO MANY GIRLS!
PLEASED TO MEET YOU! I'M MARCH!
YOU DON'T HAVE ANY PAINT ON YOUR FACE. DOES THAT MEAN YOU'RE ALREADY AN ADULT?
?
THERE'S TONS OF EVERYTHING HERE!

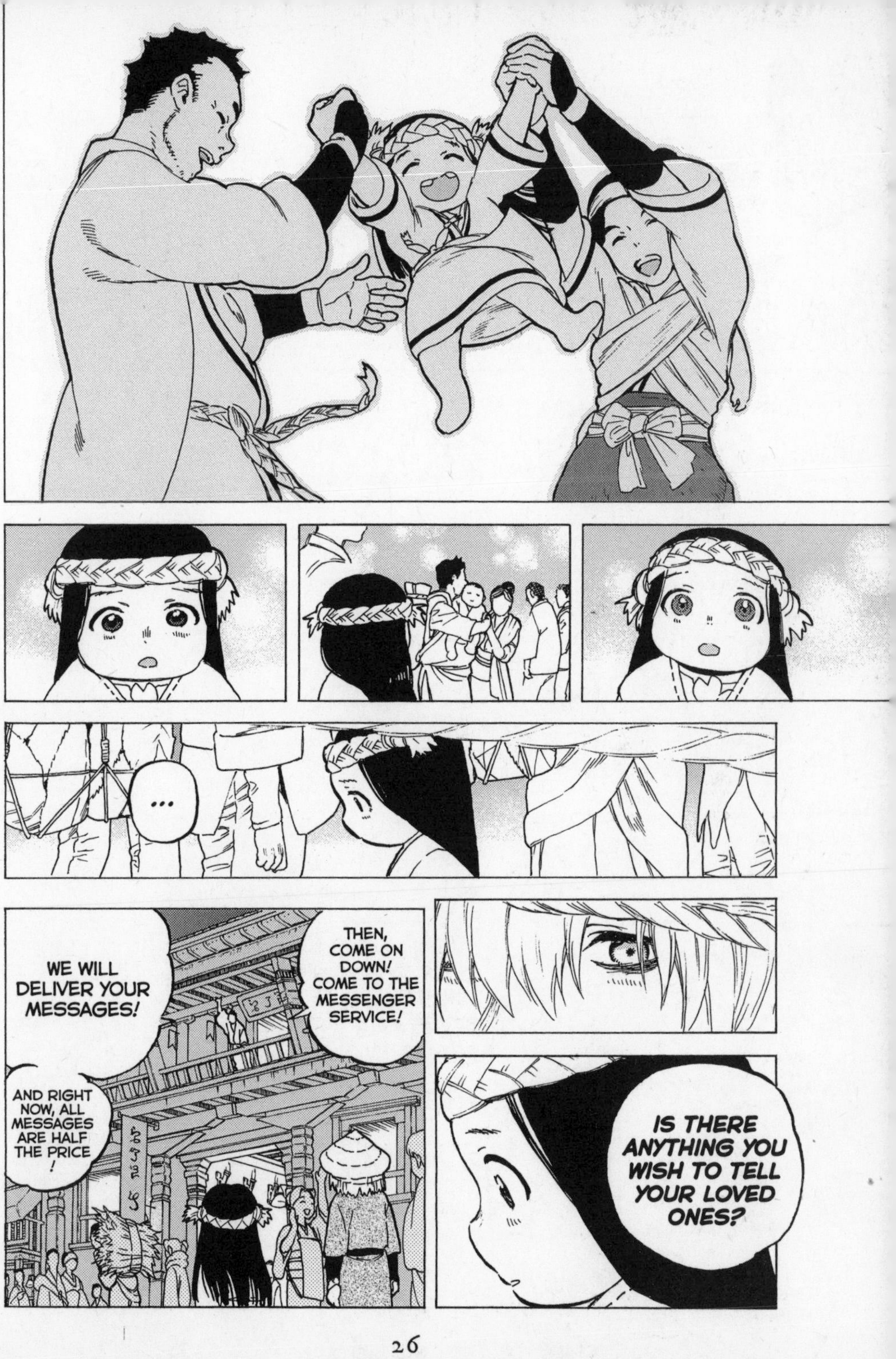
...
IS THERE ANYTHING YOU WISH TO TELL YOUR LOVED ONES?
THEN, COME ON DOWN! COME TO THE MESSENGER SERVICE!
WE WILL DELIVER YOUR MESSAGES!
AND RIGHT NOW, ALL MESSAGES ARE HALF THE PRICE!

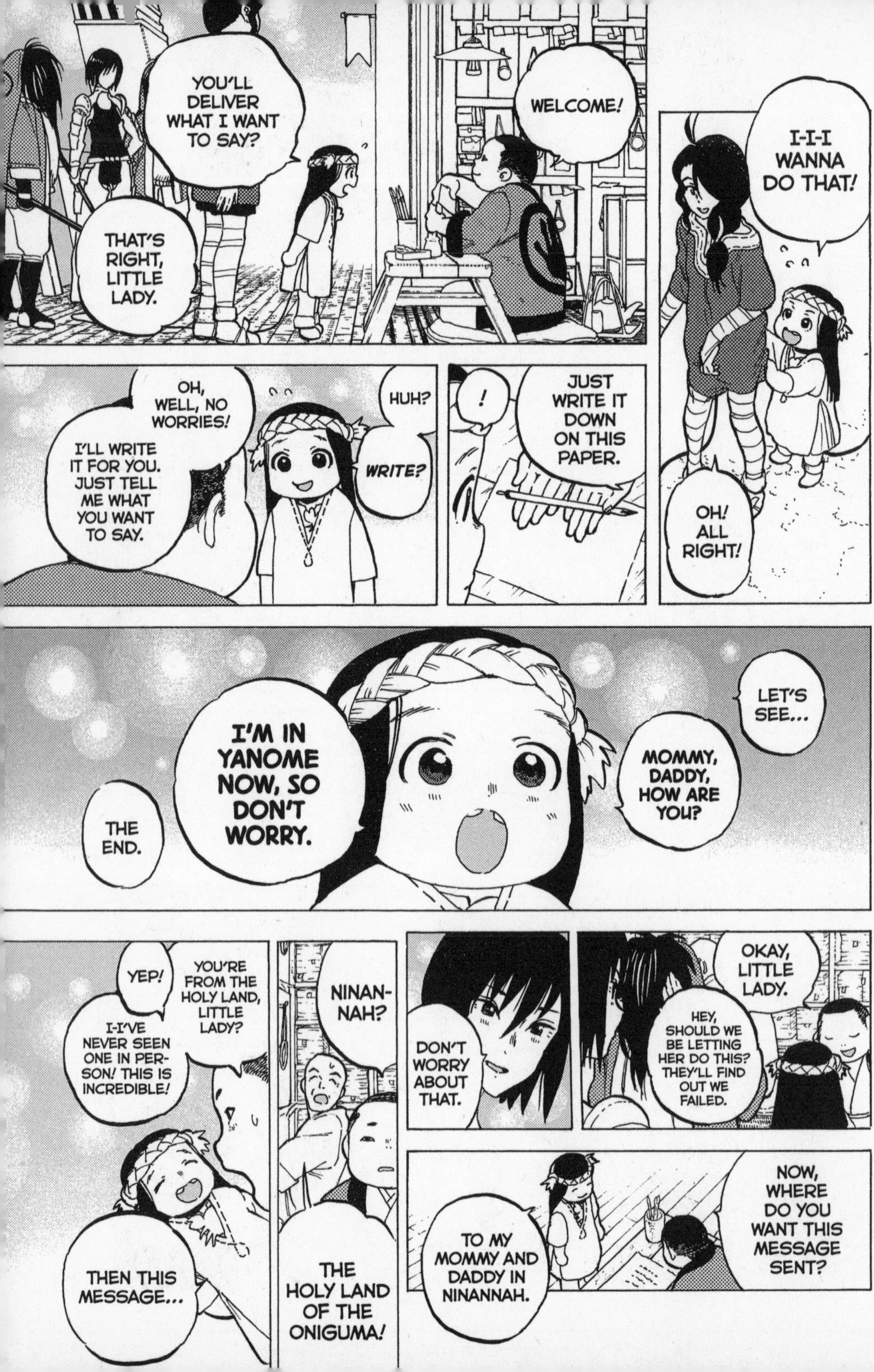
I-I-I WANNA DO THAT!
OH! ALL RIGHT!
WELCOME!
YOU'LL DELIVER WHAT I WANT TO SAY?
THAT'S RIGHT, LITTLE LADY.
!
JUST WRITE IT DOWN ON THIS PAPER.
HUH?
WRITE?
OH, WELL, NO WORRIES!
I'LL WRITE IT FOR YOU. JUST TELL ME WHAT YOU WANT TO SAY.
LET'S SEE...
MOMMY, DADDY, HOW ARE YOU?
I'M IN YANOME NOW, SO DON'T WORRY.
THE END.
OKAY, LITTLE LADY.
HEY, SHOULD WE BE LETTING HER DO THIS? THEY'LL FIND OUT WE FAILED.
DON'T WORRY ABOUT THAT.
NOW, WHERE DO YOU WANT THIS MESSAGE SENT?
TO MY MOMMY AND DADDY IN NINANNAH.
NINAN-NAH?
THE HOLY LAND OF THE ONIGUMA!
YOU'RE FROM THE HOLY LAND, LITTLE LADY?
YEP!
I-I'VE NEVER SEEN ONE IN PERSON! THIS IS INCREDIBLE!
THEN THIS MESSAGE...

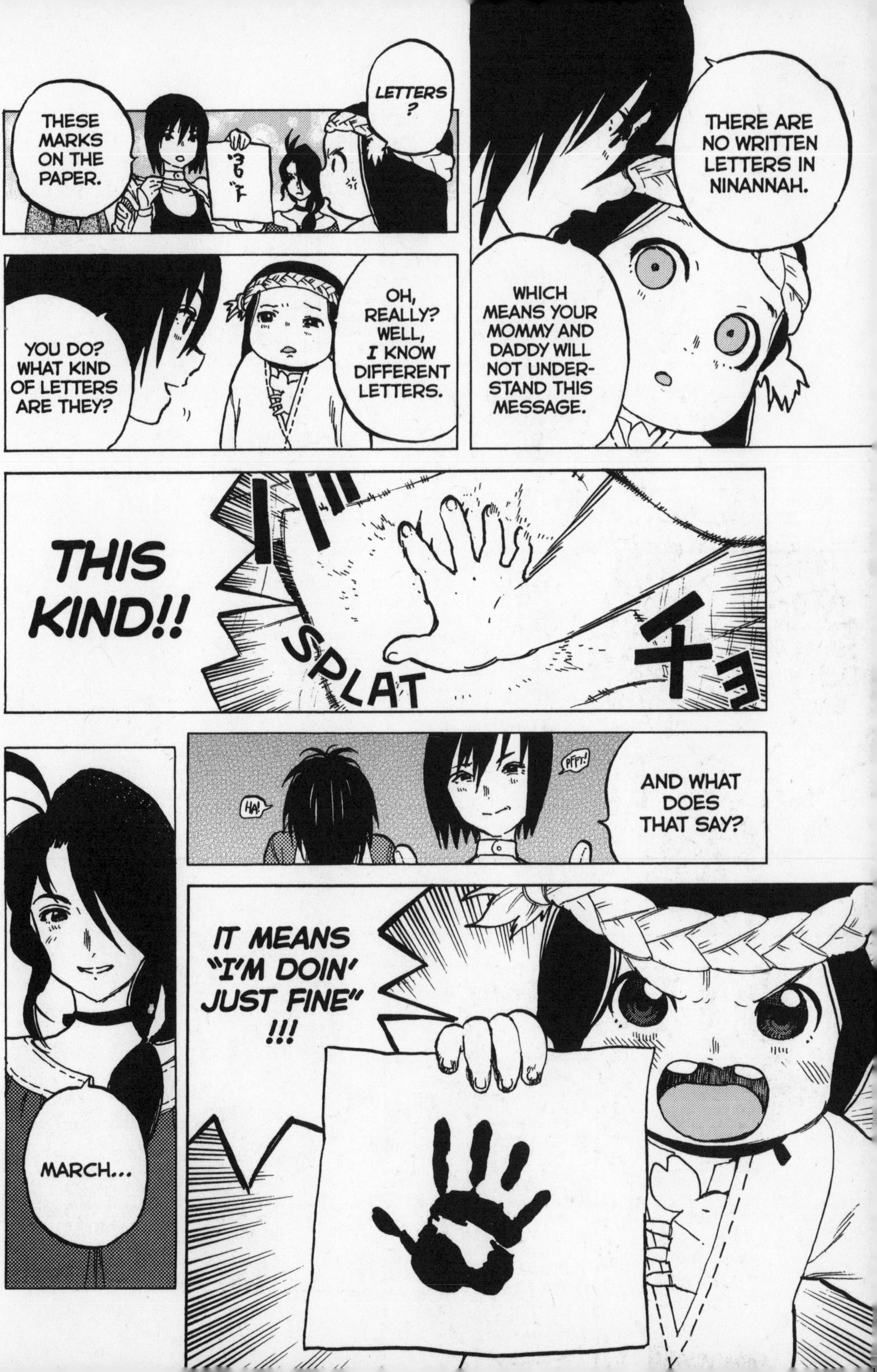
THERE ARE NO WRITTEN LETTERS IN NINANNAH.
WHICH MEANS YOUR MOMMY AND DADDY WILL NOT UNDERSTAND THIS MESSAGE.
LETTERS ?
THESE MARKS ON THE PAPER.
OH, REALLY? WELL, I KNOW DIFFERENT LETTERS.
YOU DO? WHAT KIND OF LETTERS ARE THEY?
THIS KIND!!
SPLAT
AND WHAT DOES THAT SAY?
PFFT!
HA!
IT MEANS "I'M DOIN' JUST FINE" !!!
MARCH...

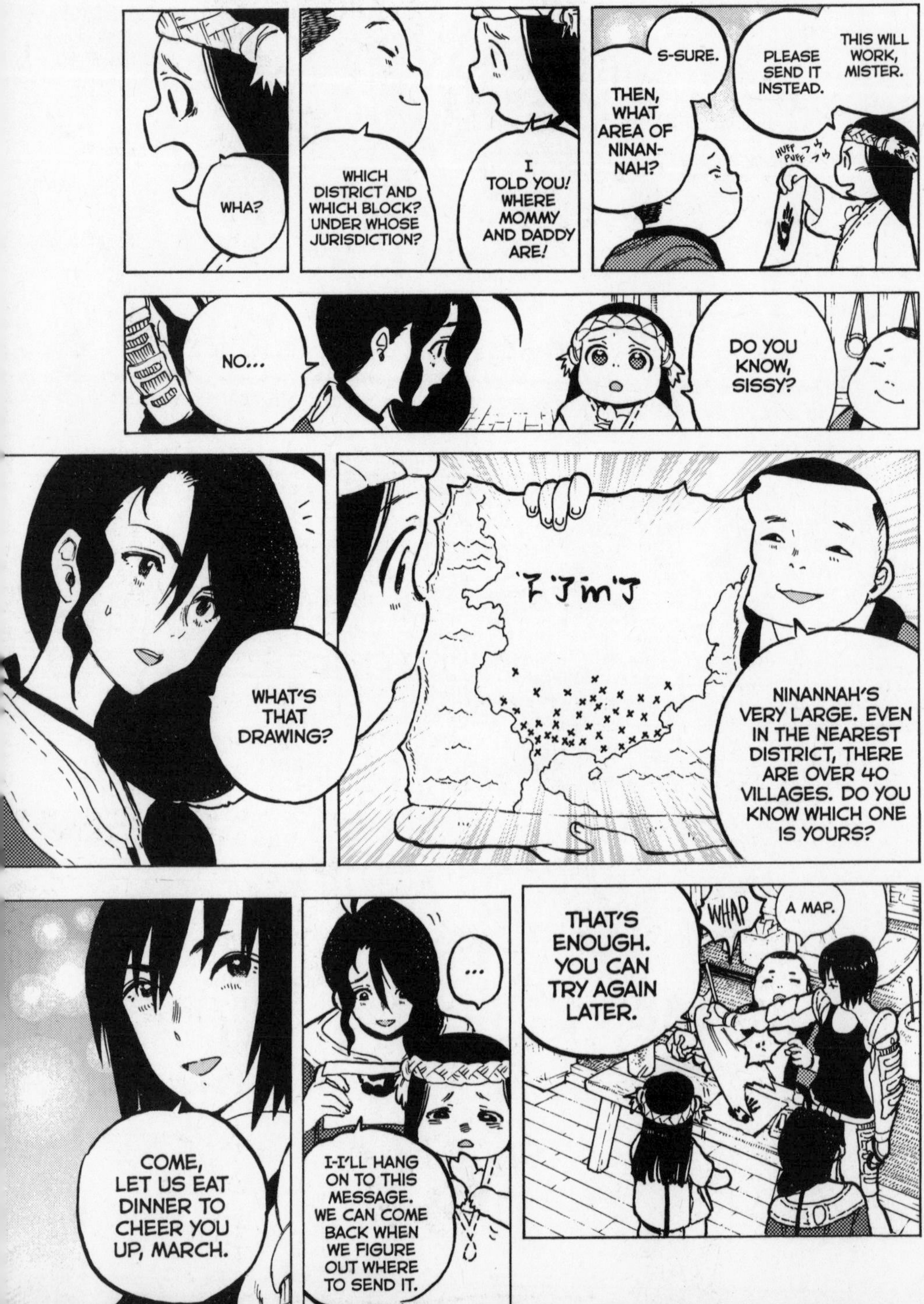
THIS WILL WORK, MISTER.
PLEASE SEND IT INSTEAD.
HUFF PUFF
S-SURE.
THEN, WHAT AREA OF NINAN-NAH?
I TOLD YOU! WHERE MOMMY AND DADDY ARE!
WHICH DISTRICT AND WHICH BLOCK? UNDER WHOSE JURISDICTION?
WHA?
DO YOU KNOW, SISSY?
NO...
NINANNAH'S VERY LARGE. EVEN IN THE NEAREST DISTRICT, THERE ARE OVER 40 VILLAGES. DO YOU KNOW WHICH ONE IS YOURS?
WHAT'S THAT DRAWING?
A MAP.
WHAP
THAT'S ENOUGH. YOU CAN TRY AGAIN LATER.
...
I-I'LL HANG ON TO THIS MESSAGE. WE CAN COME BACK WHEN WE FIGURE OUT WHERE TO SEND IT.
COME, LET US EAT DINNER TO CHEER YOU UP, MARCH.

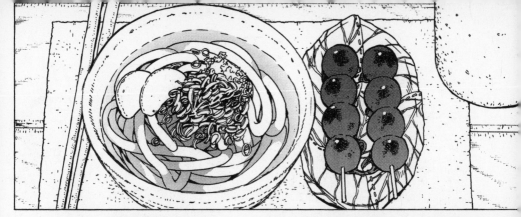

THANG YOU.

THANG YOU.

WASH THISH?! ISH REALLY GOOD!!

HUFF

HUFF

SPLASH

SPLISH

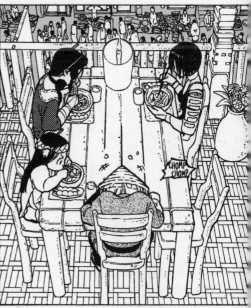
CHOMP CHOMP

HA HA

NOW, NOW FUSHI! YOU'VE GOTTA USE BETTER MANNERS!

PPFFT!

WHISPER & WHISPER

SLIDE SLIDE

30

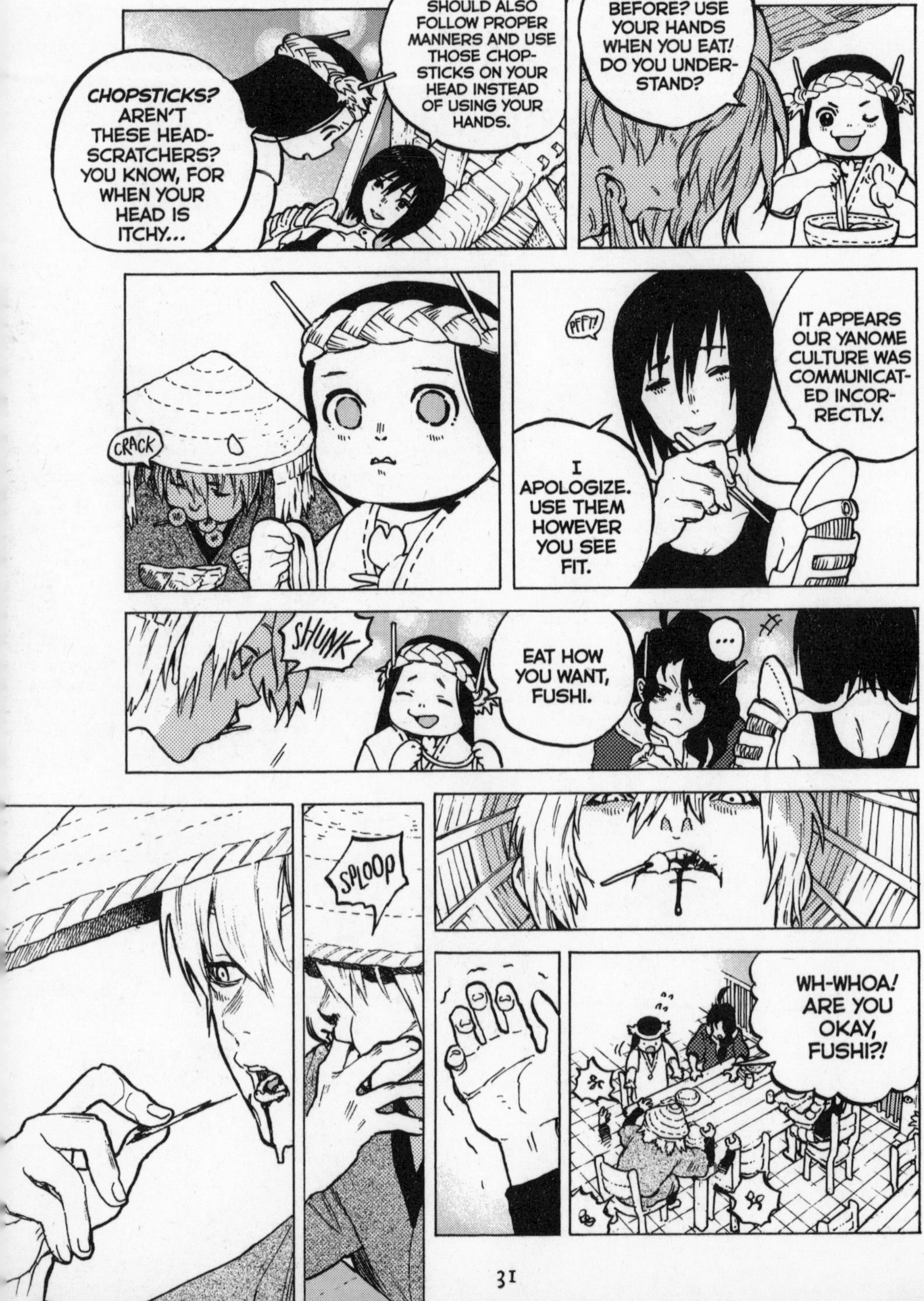
DIDN'T I TELL YOU BEFORE? USE YOUR HANDS WHEN YOU EAT! DO YOU UNDERSTAND?
MARCH, YOU SHOULD ALSO FOLLOW PROPER MANNERS AND USE THOSE CHOPSTICKS ON YOUR HEAD INSTEAD OF USING YOUR HANDS.
CHOPSTICKS? AREN'T THESE HEAD-SCRATCHERS? YOU KNOW, FOR WHEN YOUR HEAD IS ITCHY...
PFFT!
IT APPEARS OUR YANOME CULTURE WAS COMMUNICATED INCORRECTLY.
I APOLOGIZE. USE THEM HOWEVER YOU SEE FIT.
CRACK
...
EAT HOW YOU WANT, FUSHI.
SHUNK
WH-WHOA! ARE YOU OKAY, FUSHI?!
SPLOOP

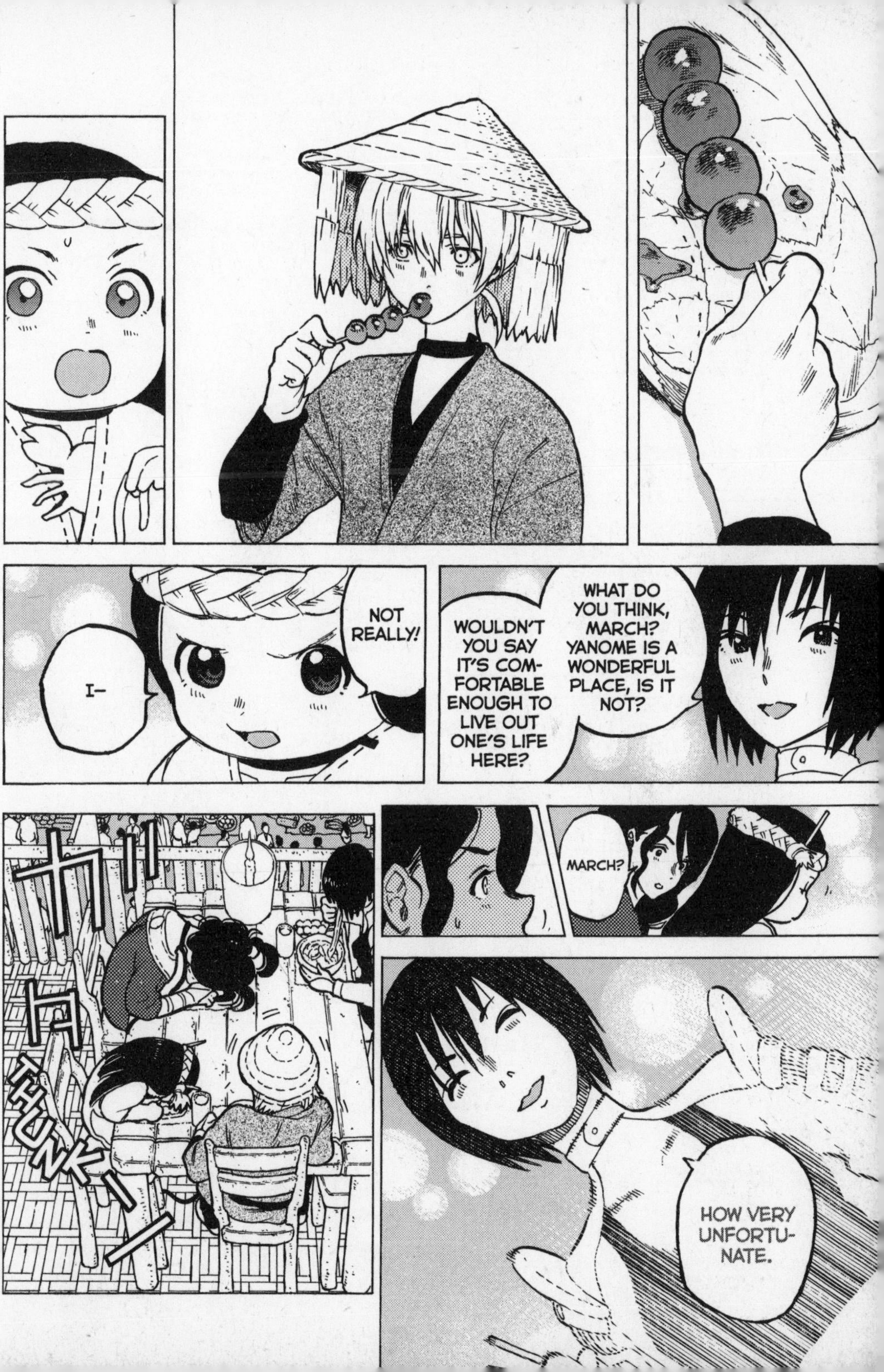
WHAT DO YOU THINK, MARCH? YANOME IS A WONDERFUL PLACE, IS IT NOT?
WOULDN'T YOU SAY IT'S COMFORTABLE ENOUGH TO LIVE OUT ONE'S LIFE HERE?
NOT REALLY!
I–
MARCH?
HOW VERY UNFORTUNATE.
THUNK!!

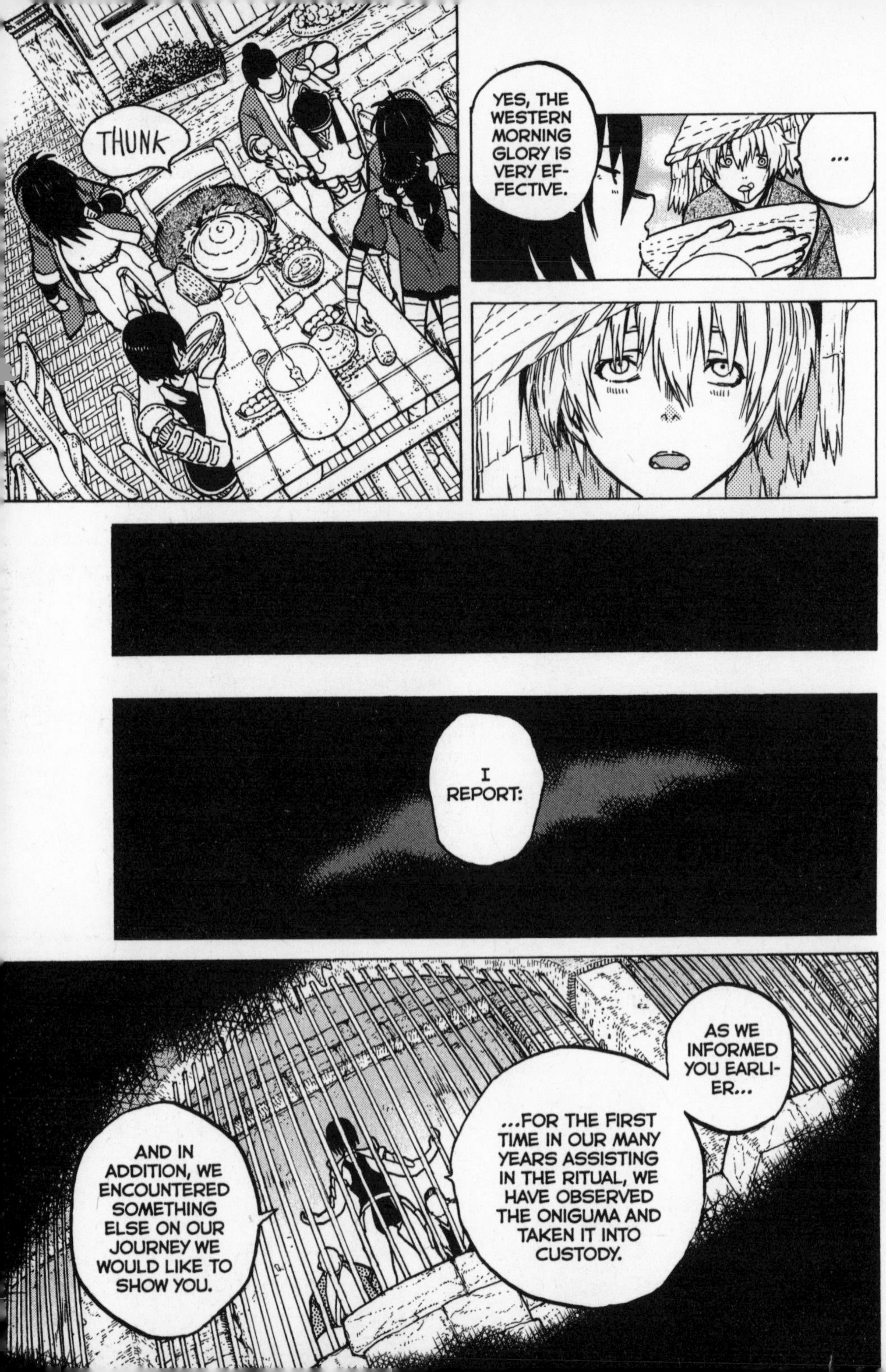
...
YES, THE WESTERN MORNING GLORY IS VERY EF-FECTIVE.
THUNK
I REPORT:
AS WE INFORMED YOU EARLI-ER...
...FOR THE FIRST TIME IN OUR MANY YEARS ASSISTING IN THE RITUAL, WE HAVE OBSERVED THE ONIGUMA AND TAKEN IT INTO CUSTODY.
AND IN ADDITION, WE ENCOUNTERED SOMETHING ELSE ON OUR JOURNEY WE WOULD LIKE TO SHOW YOU.

IT ALL HAPPENED ON OUR WAY BACK FROM THE RITUAL. ON OUR RETURN TRIP, WE OBSERVED THIS BOY DEFEATING THE ONIGUMA IN COMBAT.

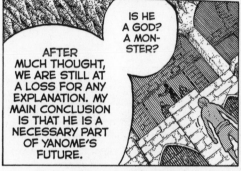

IS HE A GOD? A MONSTER?

AFTER MUCH THOUGHT, WE ARE STILL AT A LOSS FOR ANY EXPLANATION. MY MAIN CONCLUSION IS THAT HE IS A NECESSARY PART OF YANOME'S FUTURE.

WHAT CAN HE DO?

THIS BOY DEFEATED THE ONIGUMA?

HE IS INVULNERABLE.

THE LIMITS OF HIS POWER ARE STILL UNKNOWN...

THIS BOY.

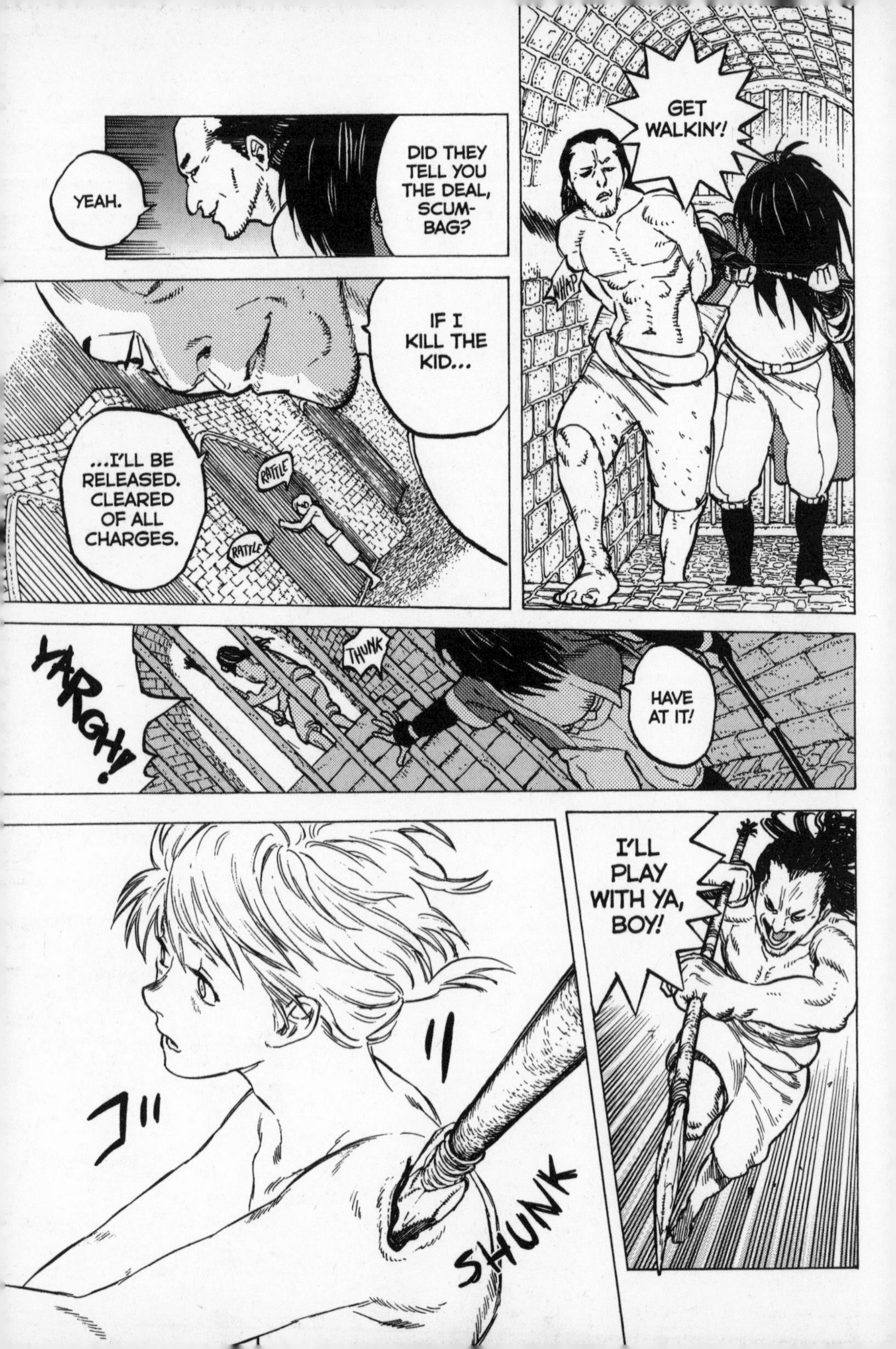

GET WALKIN'!
WHAP
DID THEY TELL YOU THE DEAL, SCUM-BAG?
YEAH.
IF I KILL THE KID...
RATTLE
...I'LL BE RELEASED. CLEARED OF ALL CHARGES.
RATTLE
HAVE AT IT!
THUNK
YARGH!
I'LL PLAY WITH YA, BOY!
SHUNK

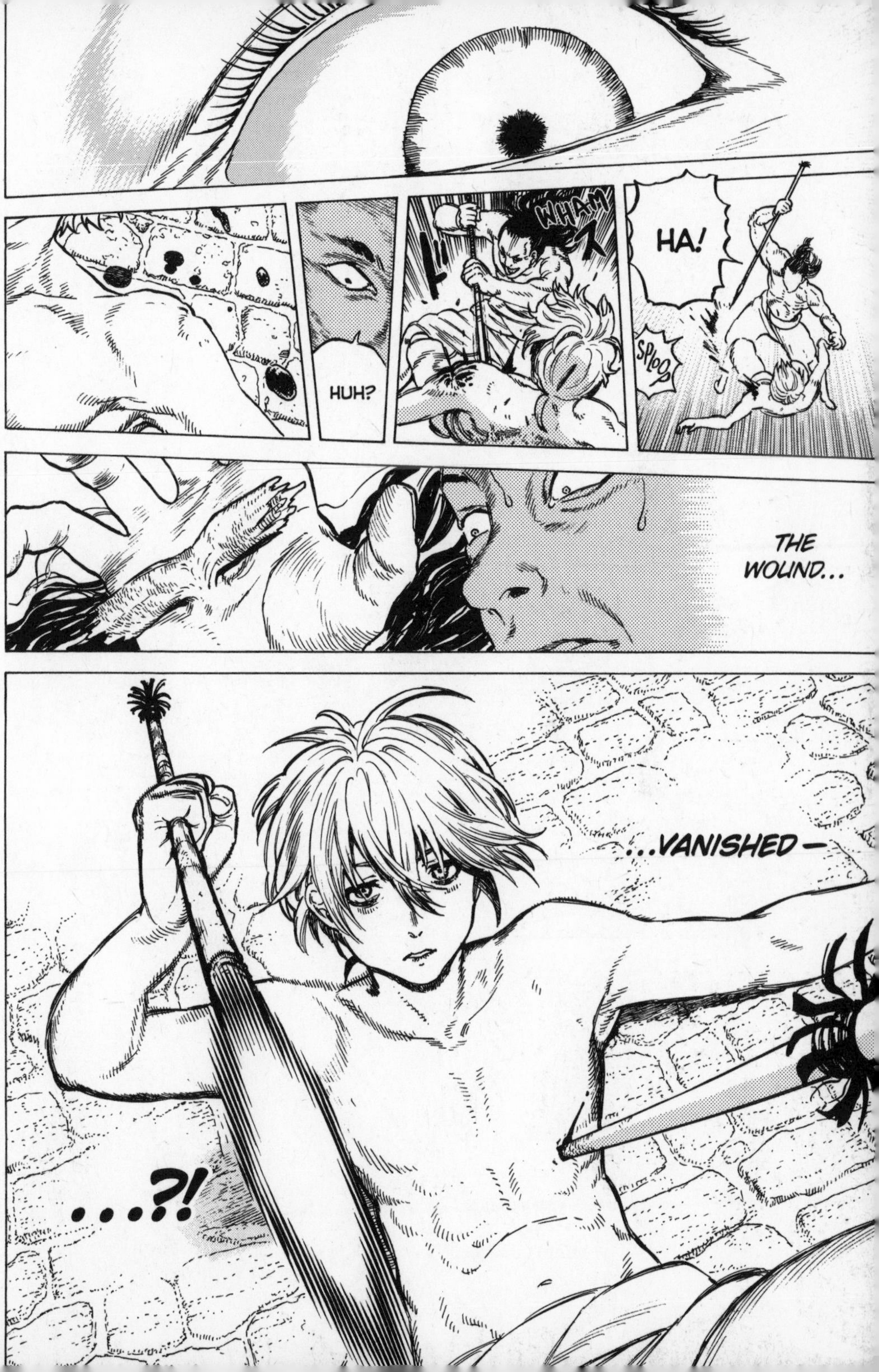
HA!
SPLOOP
WHAM
HUH?
THE WOUND...
...VANISHED—
...?!

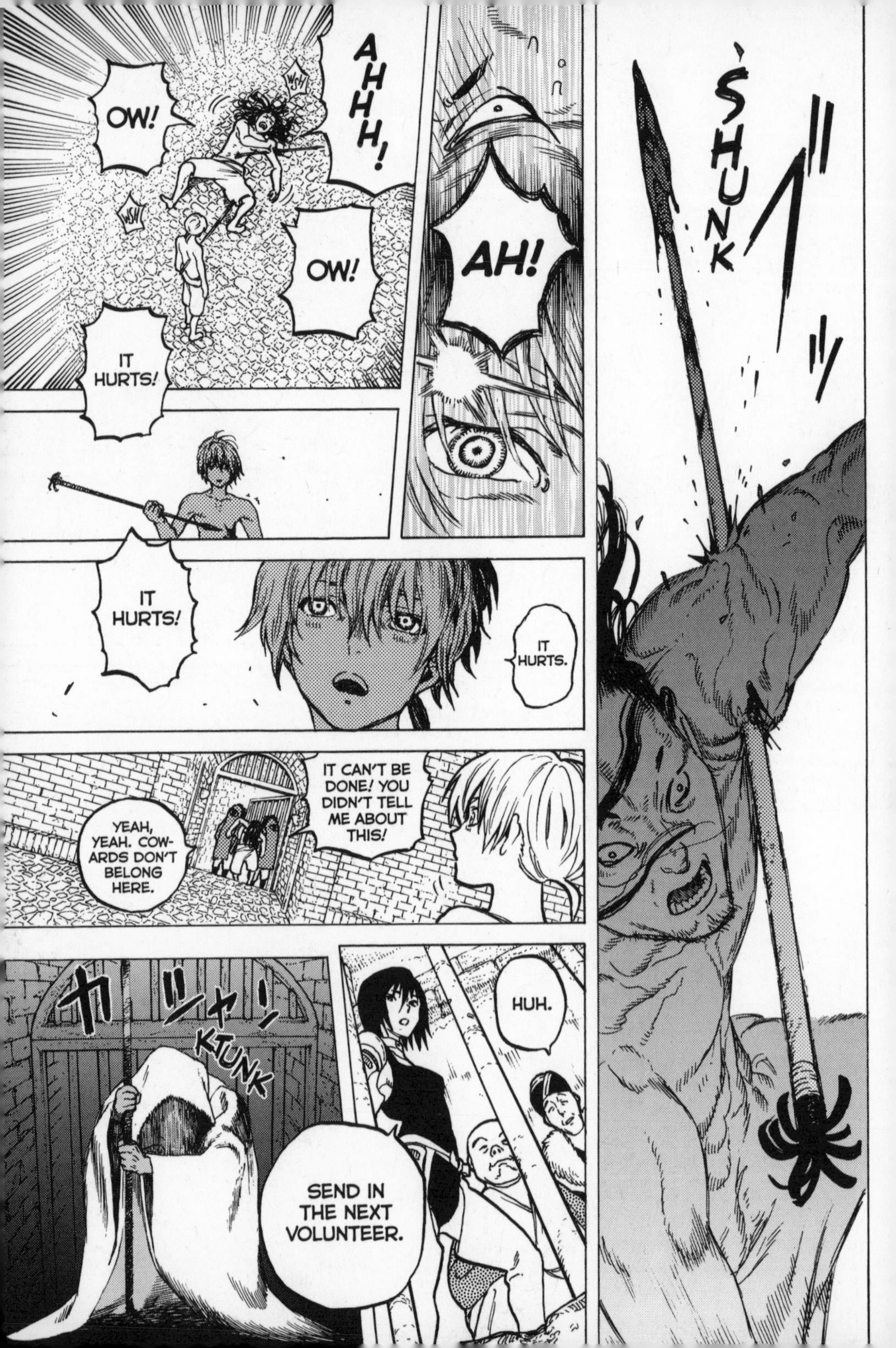
SHUNK
AH!
AHHH!
WSH
OW!
WSH
OW!
IT HURTS!
IT HURTS.
IT HURTS!
IT CAN'T BE DONE! YOU DIDN'T TELL ME ABOUT THIS!
YEAH, YEAH. COW-ARDS DON'T BELONG HERE.
HUH.
KTUNK
SEND IN THE NEXT VOLUNTEER.

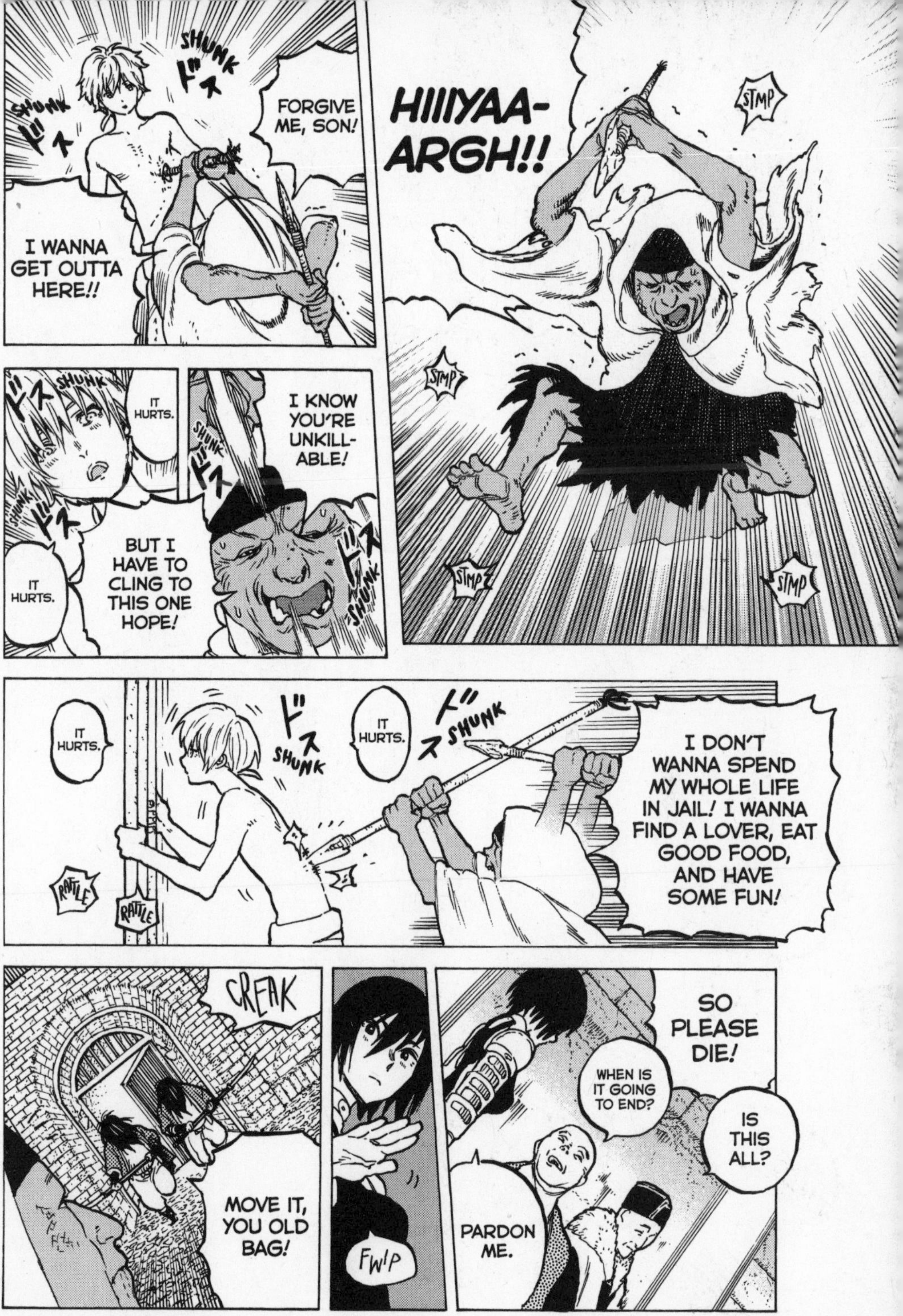
HIIIYAA-ARGH!!
STMP
STMP
STMP
STMP
SHUNK ドス
FORGIVE ME, SON!
SHUNK ドス
I WANNA GET OUTTA HERE!!
I KNOW YOU'RE UNKILL-ABLE!
SHUNK ドス
BUT I HAVE TO CLING TO THIS ONE HOPE!
ドス SHUNK
SHUNK ドス
IT HURTS.
SHUNK ドス
IT HURTS.
I DON'T WANNA SPEND MY WHOLE LIFE IN JAIL! I WANNA FIND A LOVER, EAT GOOD FOOD, AND HAVE SOME FUN!
ドス SHUNK
IT HURTS.
ドス SHUNK
IT HURTS.
RATTLE
RATTLE
SO PLEASE DIE!
IS THIS ALL?
WHEN IS IT GOING TO END?
PARDON ME.
FWIP
CREAK
MOVE IT, YOU OLD BAG!

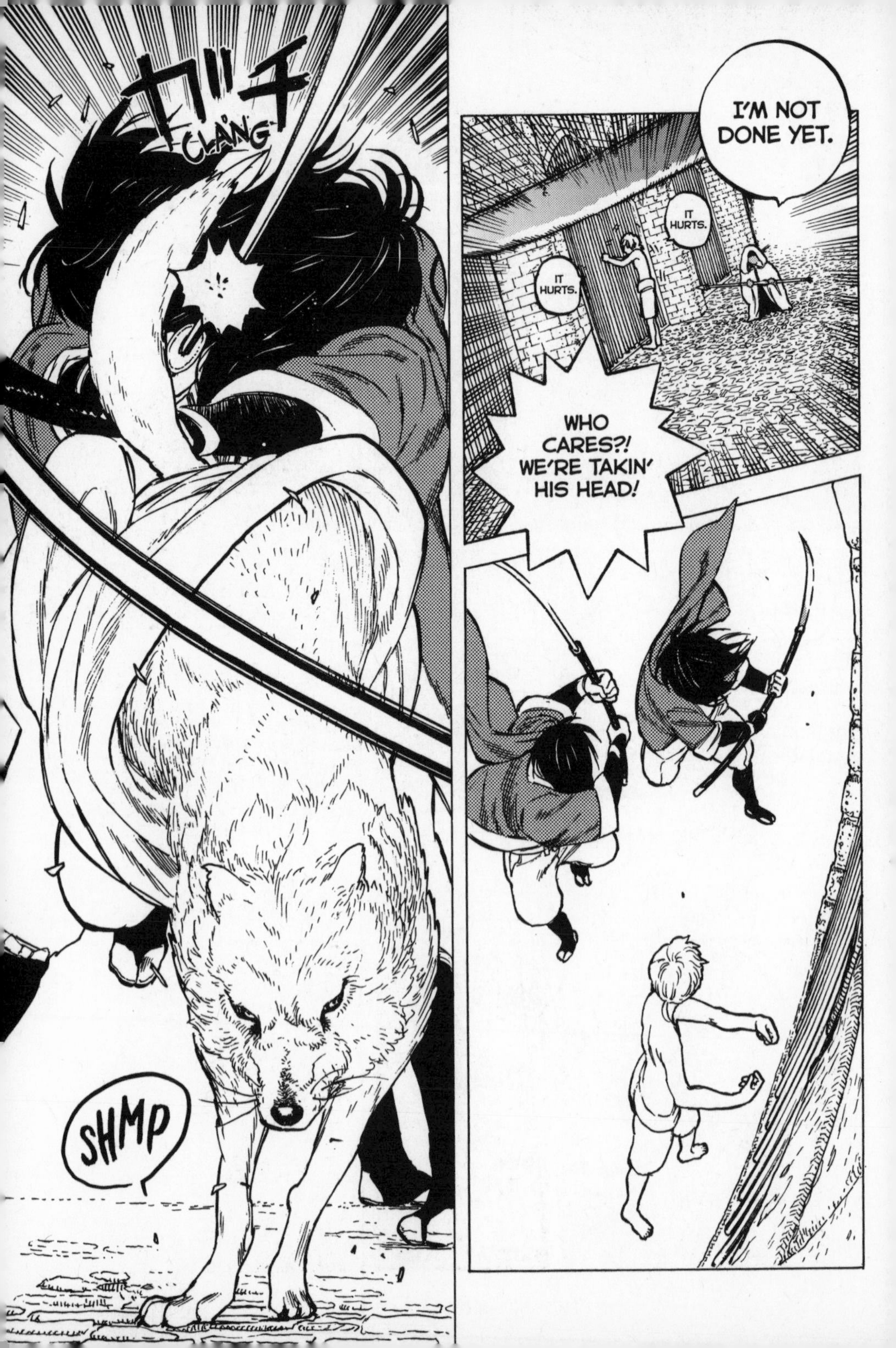
I'M NOT DONE YET.
IT HURTS.
IT HURTS.
WHO CARES?! WE'RE TAKIN' HIS HEAD!
ガチ
CLANG
SHMP

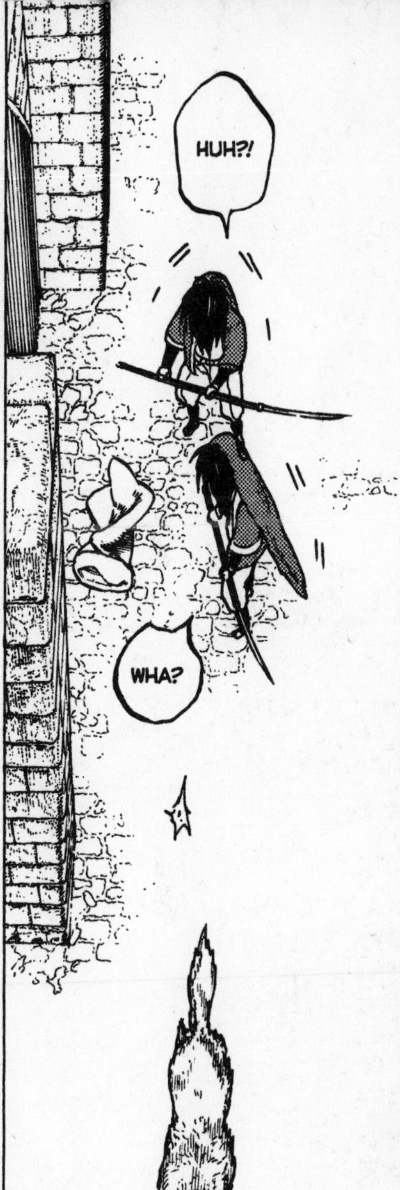
HUH?!
WHA?

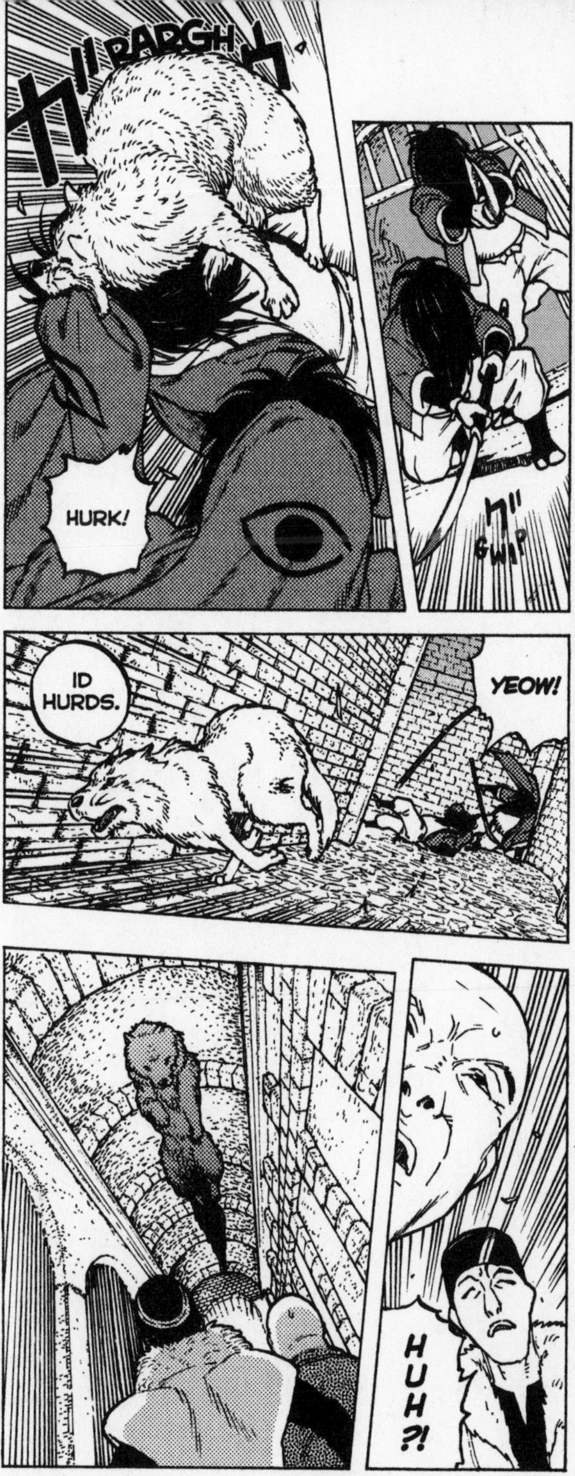
GWIP
RARGH
HURK!
YEOW!
ID HURDS.
HUH?!

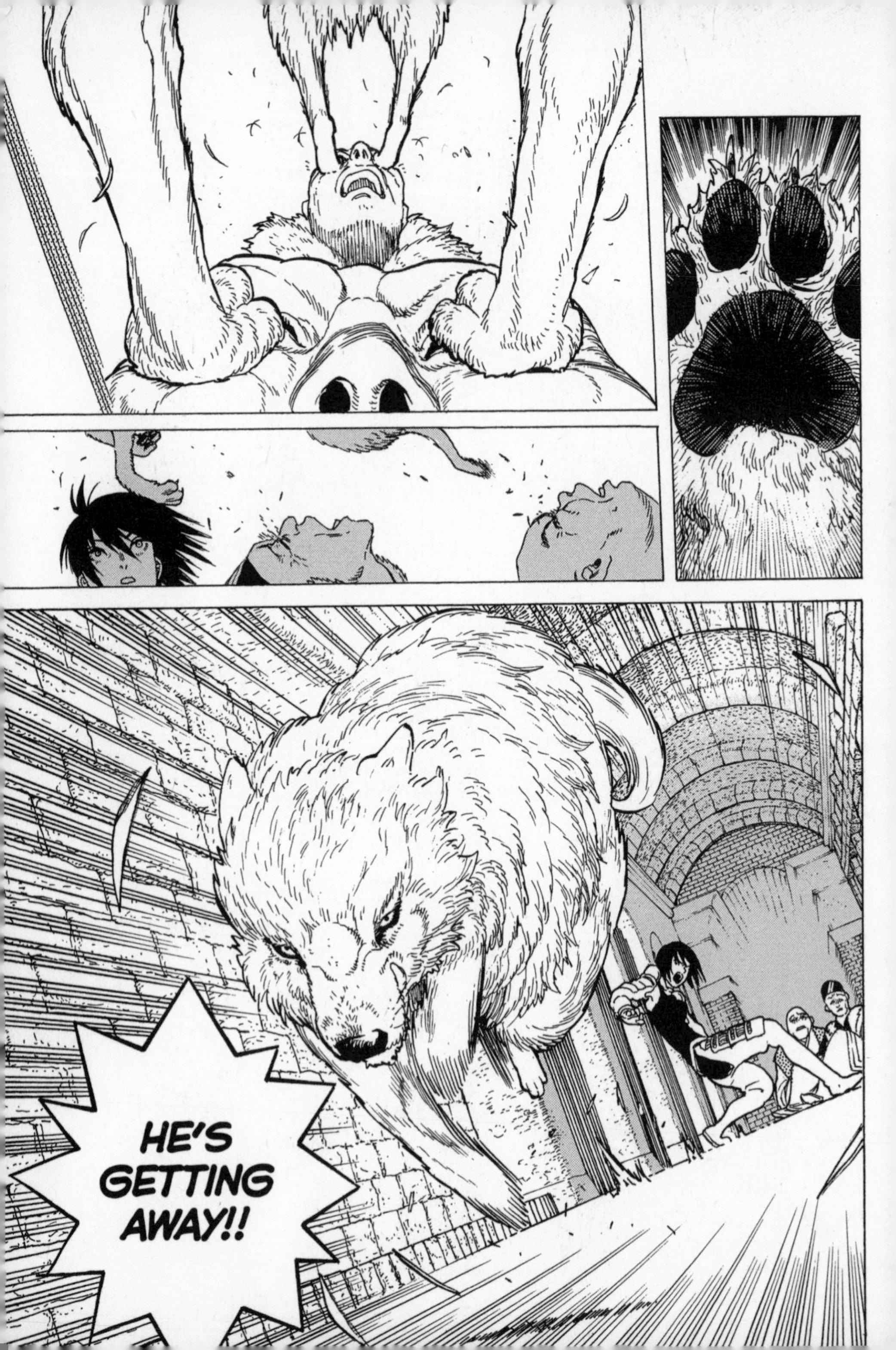
HE'S GETTING AWAY!!

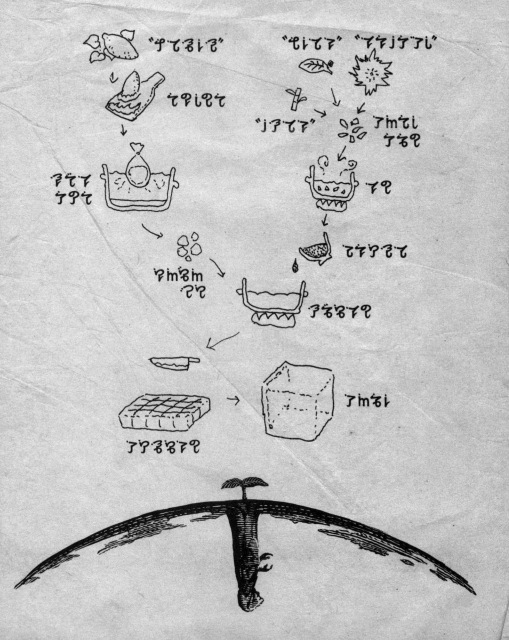

#7 A Large Vessel

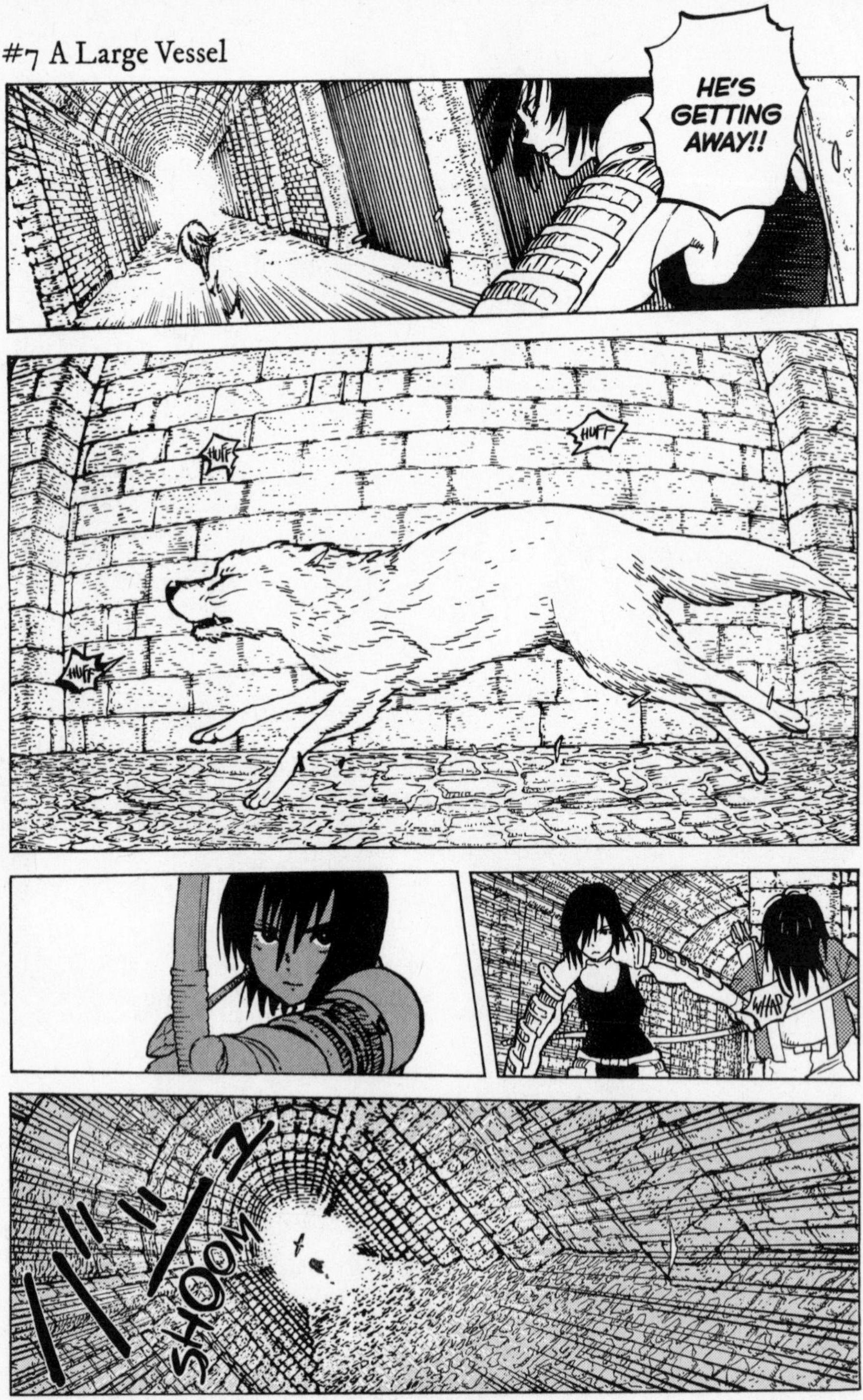

HE'S GETTING AWAY!!
HUFF
HUFF
HUFF
WHAP
SHOOM

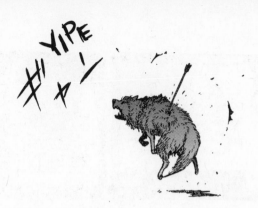

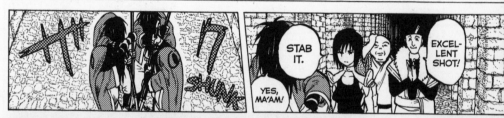

YIPE
EXCELLENT SHOT!
STAB IT.
YES, MA'AM!
SHUNK
PROGRESS REPORT:
THIS TIME, FUSHI DID NOT, AS A RESULT OF ACQUISITION, TRANSFORM INTO THE SOURCE OF ITS EXTERNAL STIMULUS.
IT IS BELIEVED THIS IS BECAUSE IT HAS ALREADY ACQUIRED ***CONSCIOUSNESS:*** A STAGE ONE DEVELOPMENTAL GOAL.
NOW CARRY HIM.
GRRR
GRRR
IF IT TRANSFORMED INTO THE ARROW THAT WAS FIRED INTO IT, OR ONE OF THE *NAGINATA,* OR EVEN A CORPSE, IT WOULD HAVE BEEN SPARED THE PAIN...
...BUT IT DID NOT MAKE THAT CHOICE.

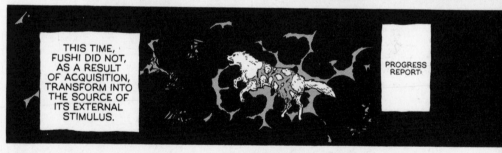

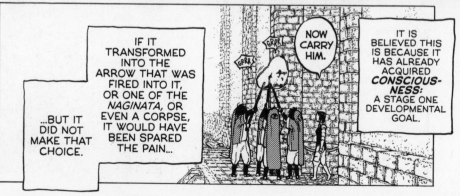

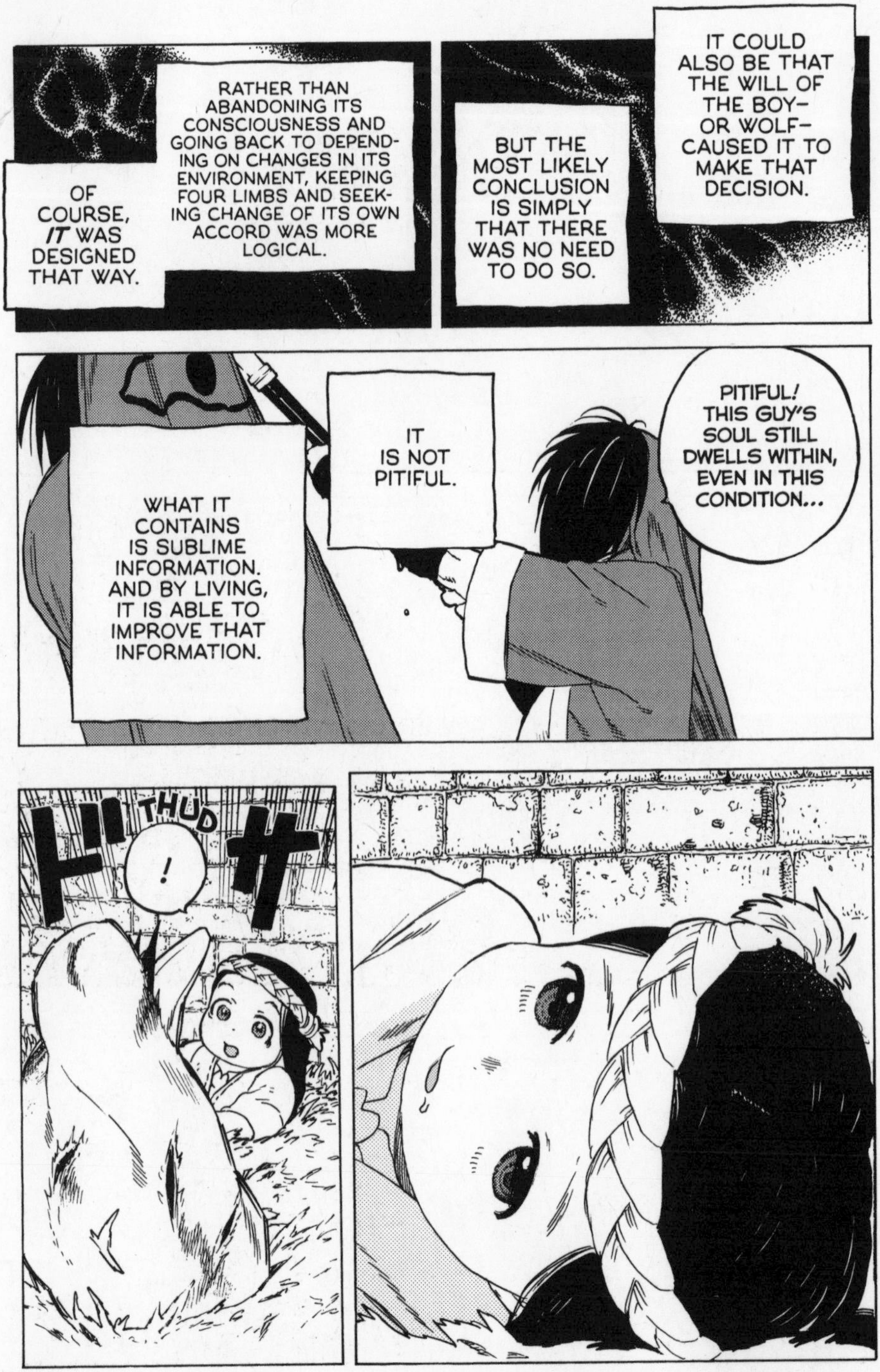
IT COULD ALSO BE THAT THE WILL OF THE BOY— OR WOLF— CAUSED IT TO MAKE THAT DECISION.
BUT THE MOST LIKELY CONCLUSION IS SIMPLY THAT THERE WAS NO NEED TO DO SO.
RATHER THAN ABANDONING ITS CONSCIOUSNESS AND GOING BACK TO DEPENDING ON CHANGES IN ITS ENVIRONMENT, KEEPING FOUR LIMBS AND SEEKING CHANGE OF ITS OWN ACCORD WAS MORE LOGICAL.
OF COURSE, *IT* WAS DESIGNED THAT WAY.
PITIFUL! THIS GUY'S SOUL STILL DWELLS WITHIN, EVEN IN THIS CONDITION...
IT IS NOT PITIFUL.
WHAT IT CONTAINS IS SUBLIME INFORMATION. AND BY LIVING, IT IS ABLE TO IMPROVE THAT INFORMATION.
THUD
!

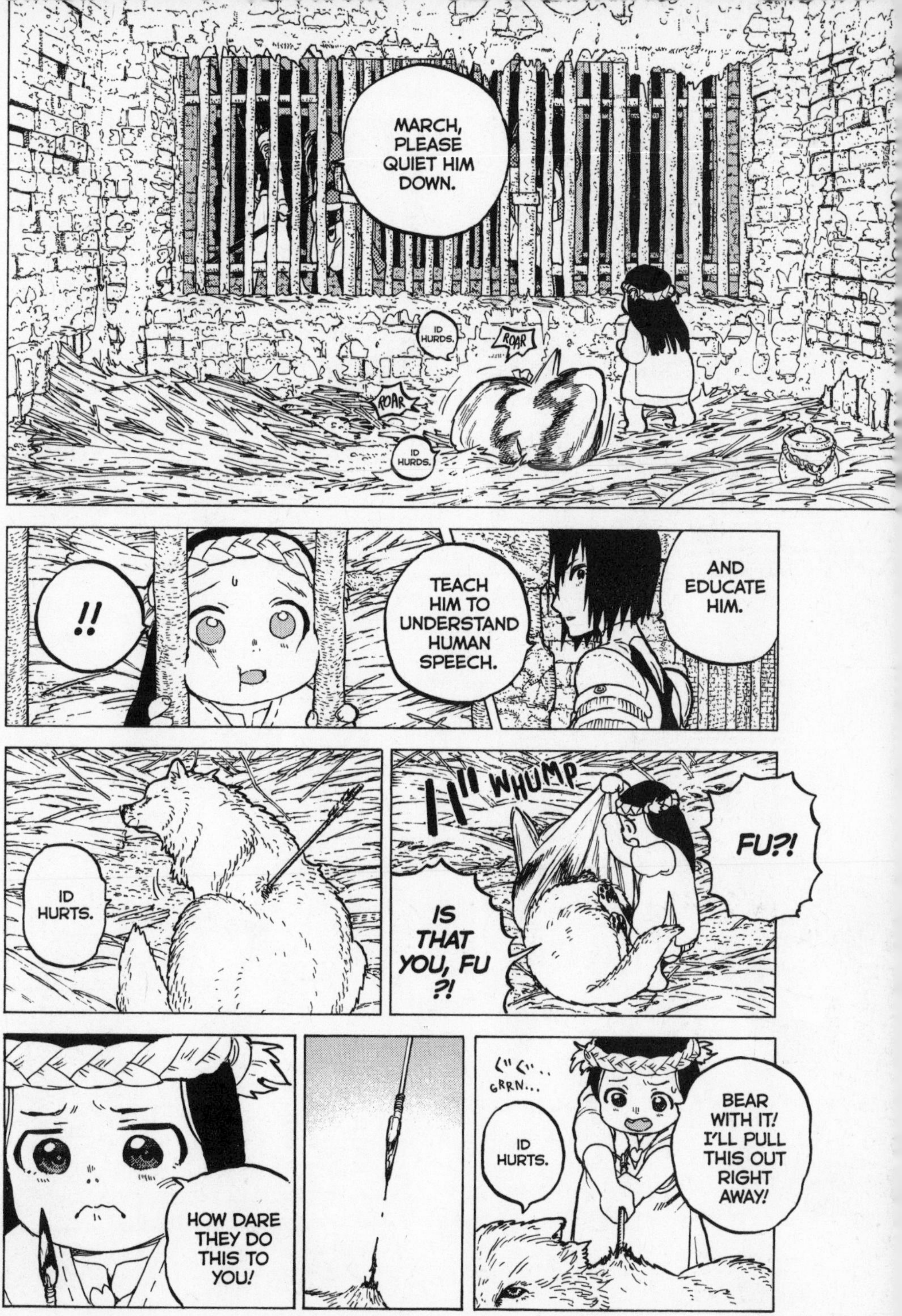
MARCH, PLEASE QUIET HIM DOWN.
ROAR
ID HURDS.
ROAR
ID HURDS.
AND EDUCATE HIM.
TEACH HIM TO UNDERSTAND HUMAN SPEECH.
!!
FU?!
WHUMP
IS THAT YOU, FU?!
ID HURTS.
BEAR WITH IT! I'LL PULL THIS OUT RIGHT AWAY!
ぐぐ…
GRRN...
ID HURTS.
HOW DARE THEY DO THIS TO YOU!

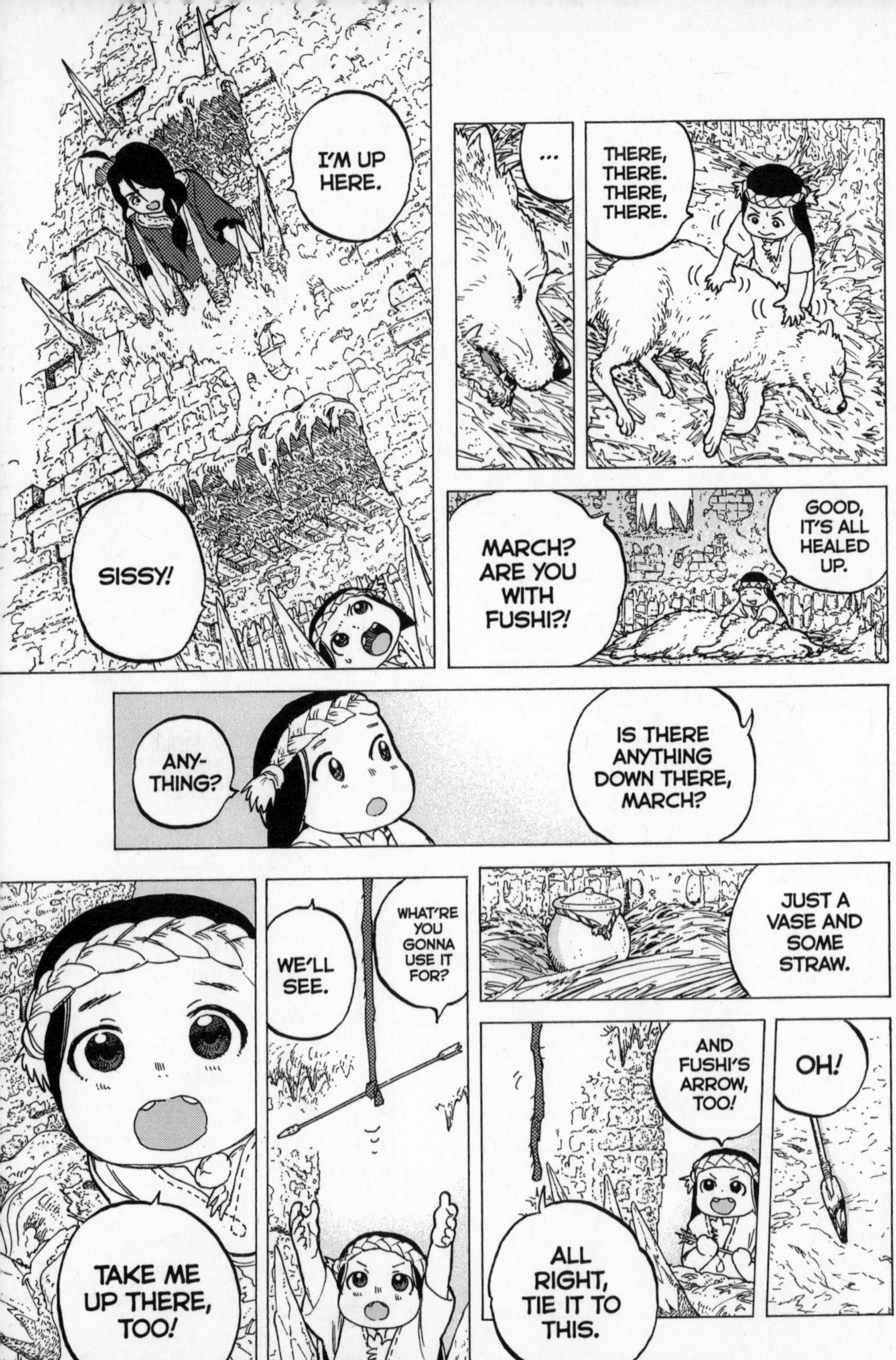
THERE, THERE. THERE, THERE.
...
GOOD, IT'S ALL HEALED UP.
MARCH? ARE YOU WITH FUSHI?!
I'M UP HERE.
SISSY!
IS THERE ANYTHING DOWN THERE, MARCH?
ANY-THING?
JUST A VASE AND SOME STRAW.
OH!
AND FUSHI'S ARROW, TOO!
ALL RIGHT, TIE IT TO THIS.
WHAT'RE YOU GONNA USE IT FOR?
WE'LL SEE.
TAKE ME UP THERE, TOO!

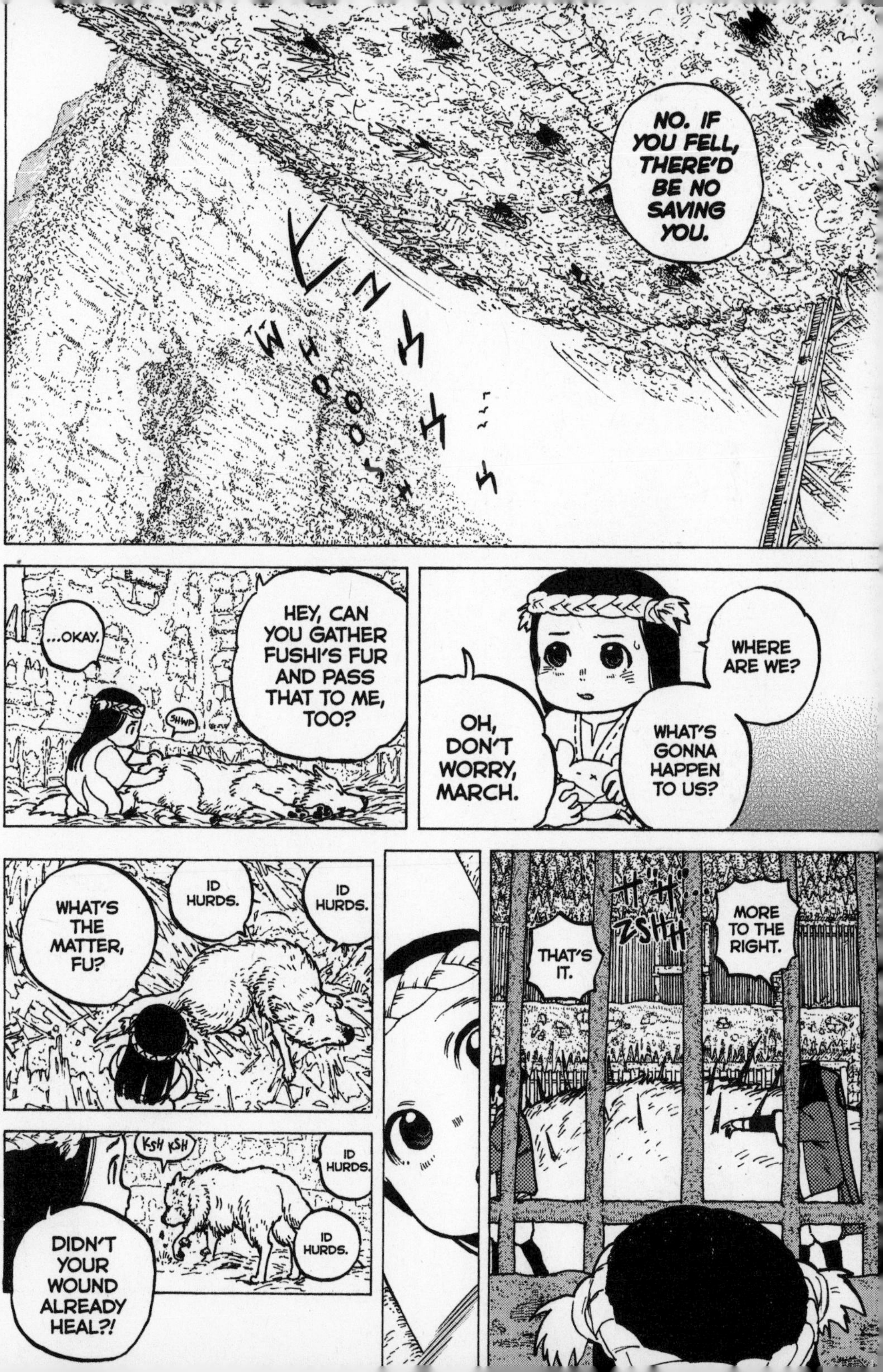

NO. IF YOU FELL, THERE'D BE NO SAVING YOU.
WHOOOSH
WHERE ARE WE?
WHAT'S GONNA HAPPEN TO US?
OH, DON'T WORRY, MARCH.
HEY, CAN YOU GATHER FUSHI'S FUR AND PASS THAT TO ME, TOO?
...OKAY.
SHWP
MORE TO THE RIGHT.
ZSHH
THAT'S IT.
ID HURDS.
ID HURDS.
WHAT'S THE MATTER, FU?
ID HURDS.
KSH KSH
ID HURDS.
DIDN'T YOUR WOUND ALREADY HEAL?!

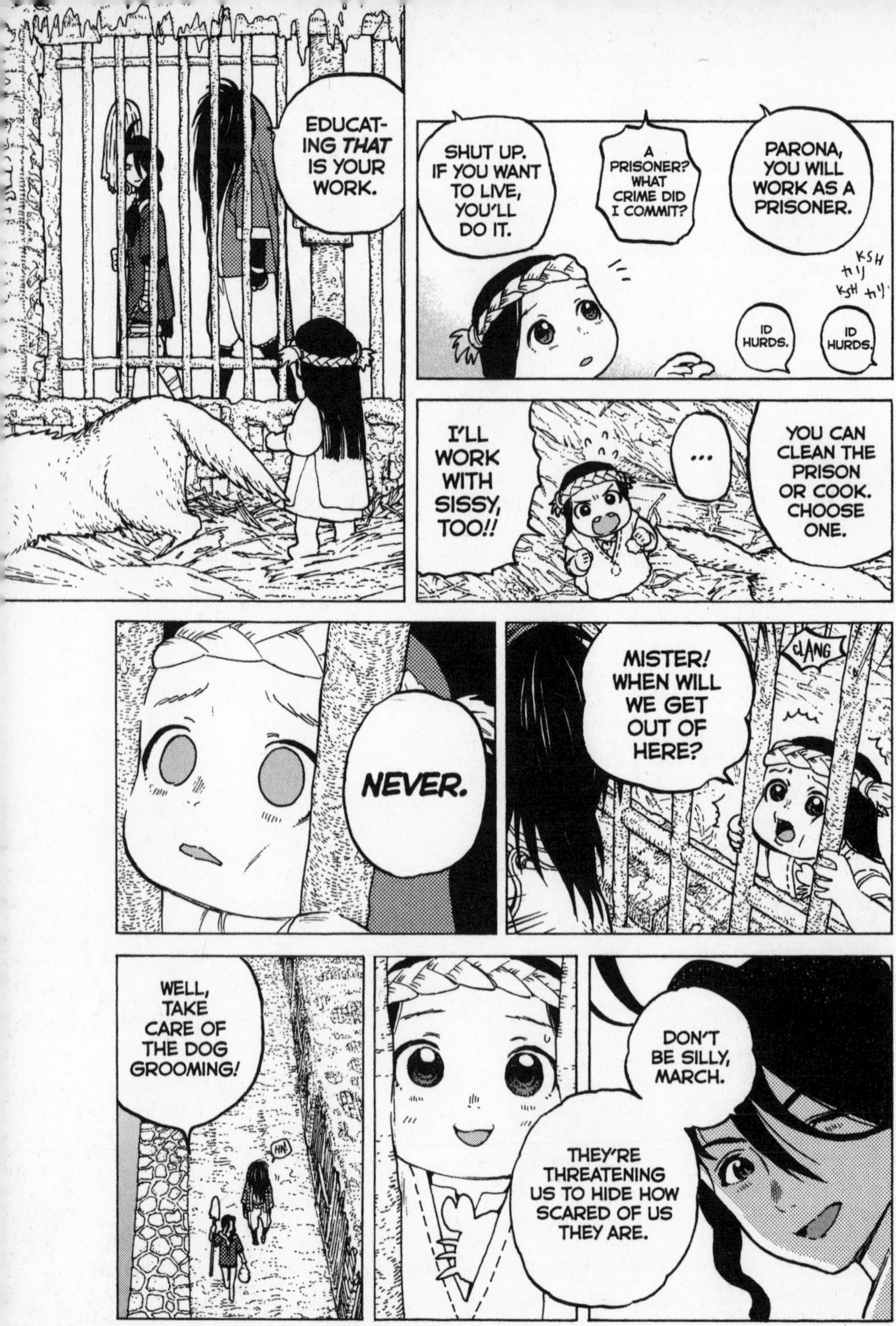
PARONA, YOU WILL WORK AS A PRISONER.
A PRISONER? WHAT CRIME DID I COMMIT?
SHUT UP. IF YOU WANT TO LIVE, YOU'LL DO IT.
KSH
KSH
ID HURDS.
ID HURDS.
YOU CAN CLEAN THE PRISON OR COOK. CHOOSE ONE.
...
I'LL WORK WITH SISSY, TOO!!
EDUCATING *THAT* IS YOUR WORK.
CLANG
MISTER! WHEN WILL WE GET OUT OF HERE?
NEVER.
DON'T BE SILLY, MARCH.
THEY'RE THREATENING US TO HIDE HOW SCARED OF US THEY ARE.
WELL, TAKE CARE OF THE DOG GROOMING!
HA!

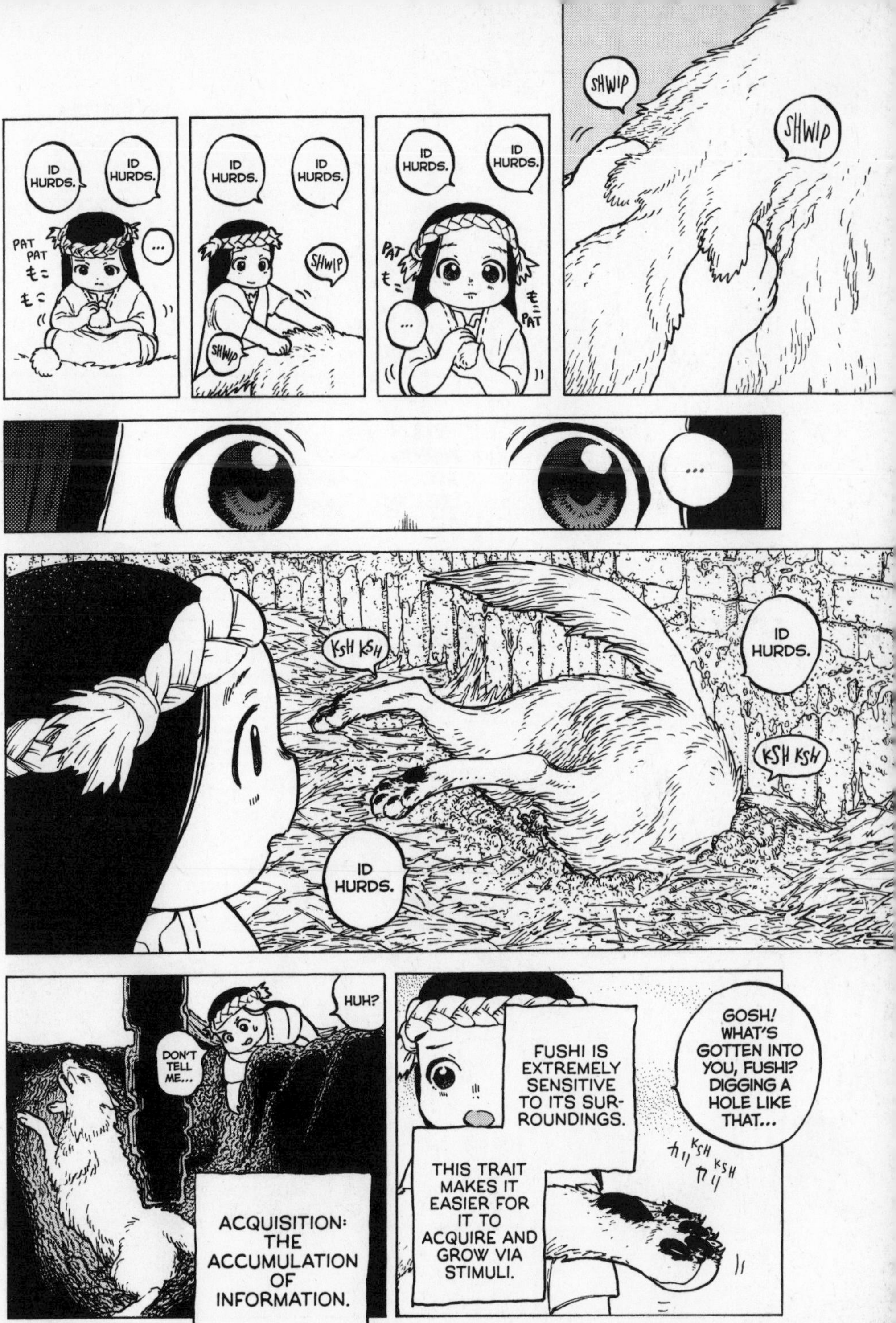
SHWIP
SHWIP
ID HURDS.
ID HURDS.
PAT
もこ
もこ
PAT
...
ID HURDS.
ID HURDS.
SHWIP
SHWIP
ID HURDS.
ID HURDS.
PAT PAT
もこ
もこ
...
...
ID HURDS.
KSH KSH
KSH KSH
ID HURDS.
GOSH! WHAT'S GOTTEN INTO YOU, FUSHI? DIGGING A HOLE LIKE THAT...
FUSHI IS EXTREMELY SENSITIVE TO ITS SUR-ROUNDINGS.
THIS TRAIT MAKES IT EASIER FOR IT TO ACQUIRE AND GROW VIA STIMULI.
KSH KSH
カリ カリ
HUH?
DON'T TELL ME...
ACQUISITION: THE ACCUMULATION OF INFORMATION.

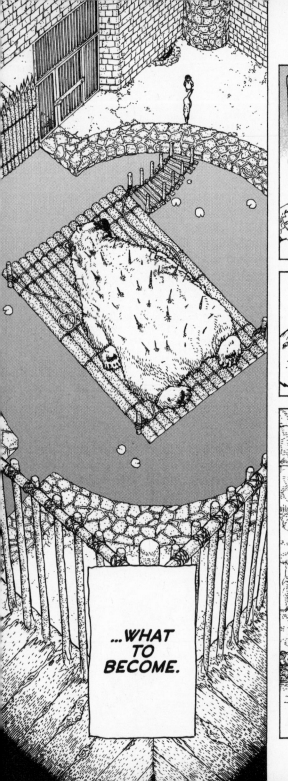

THE ARROW FROM THIS MORNING AND THE *NAGINATA* WILL, INDEPENDENT OF FUSHI'S WILL, REMAIN WITHIN.

AND UNLIKE WHEN IT WAS A STONE IN THE SNOWY TUNDRA, NOW IT IS ABLE TO *REMEMBER*...

THUMP

...WHAT STIMULATED IT IN THE PAST.

AND IT CAN *CHOOSE* ...

...*WHAT TO BECOME.*

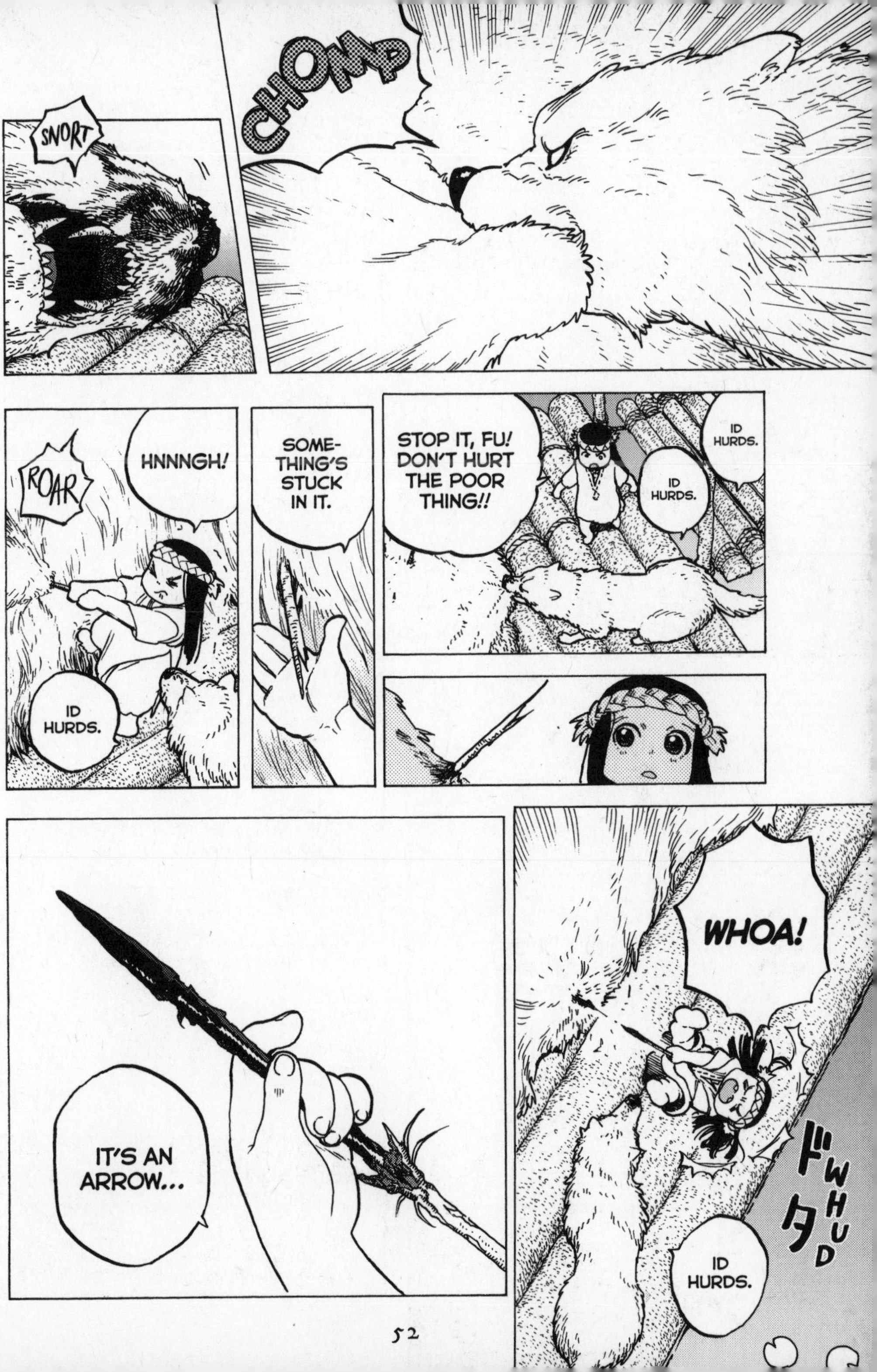
CHOMP
SNORT
ID HURDS.
STOP IT, FU! DON'T HURT THE POOR THING!!
ID HURDS.
SOME-THING'S STUCK IN IT.
HNNNGH!
ROAR
ID HURDS.
WHOA!
ドタ
WHUD
ID HURDS.
IT'S AN ARROW...

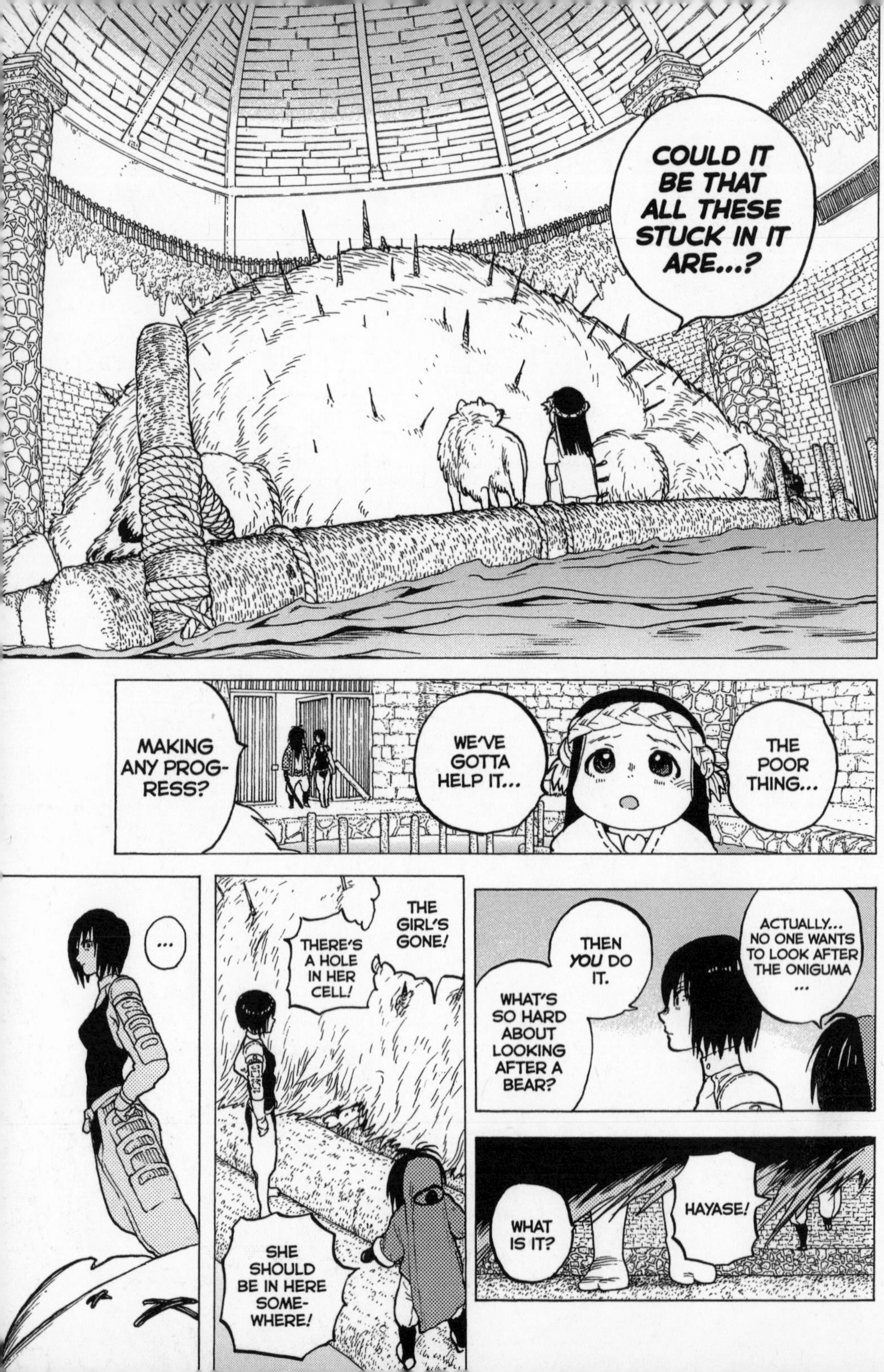
COULD IT BE THAT ALL THESE STUCK IN IT ARE...?
THE POOR THING...
WE'VE GOTTA HELP IT...
MAKING ANY PROG-RESS?
ACTUALLY... NO ONE WANTS TO LOOK AFTER THE ONIGUMA ...
THEN *YOU* DO IT.
WHAT'S SO HARD ABOUT LOOKING AFTER A BEAR?
HAYASE!
WHAT IS IT?
THE GIRL'S GONE!
THERE'S A HOLE IN HER CELL!
SHE SHOULD BE IN HERE SOME-WHERE!
...

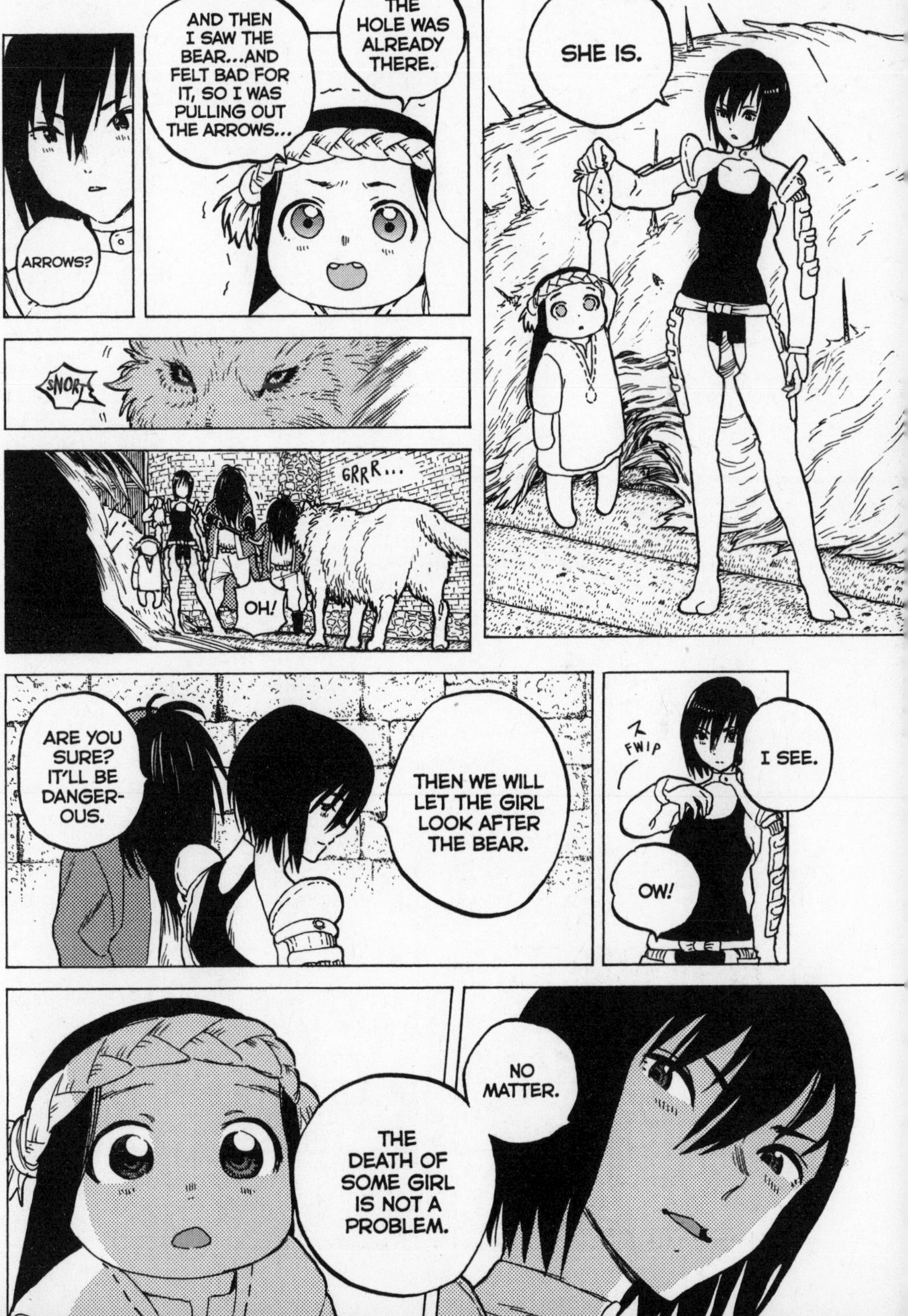
SHE IS.
THE HOLE WAS ALREADY THERE.
AND THEN I SAW THE BEAR...AND FELT BAD FOR IT, SO I WAS PULLING OUT THE ARROWS...
ARROWS?
SNORT
GRRR...
OH!
ス
FWIP
I SEE.
OW!
THEN WE WILL LET THE GIRL LOOK AFTER THE BEAR.
ARE YOU SURE? IT'LL BE DANGER-OUS.
NO MATTER.
THE DEATH OF SOME GIRL IS NOT A PROBLEM.

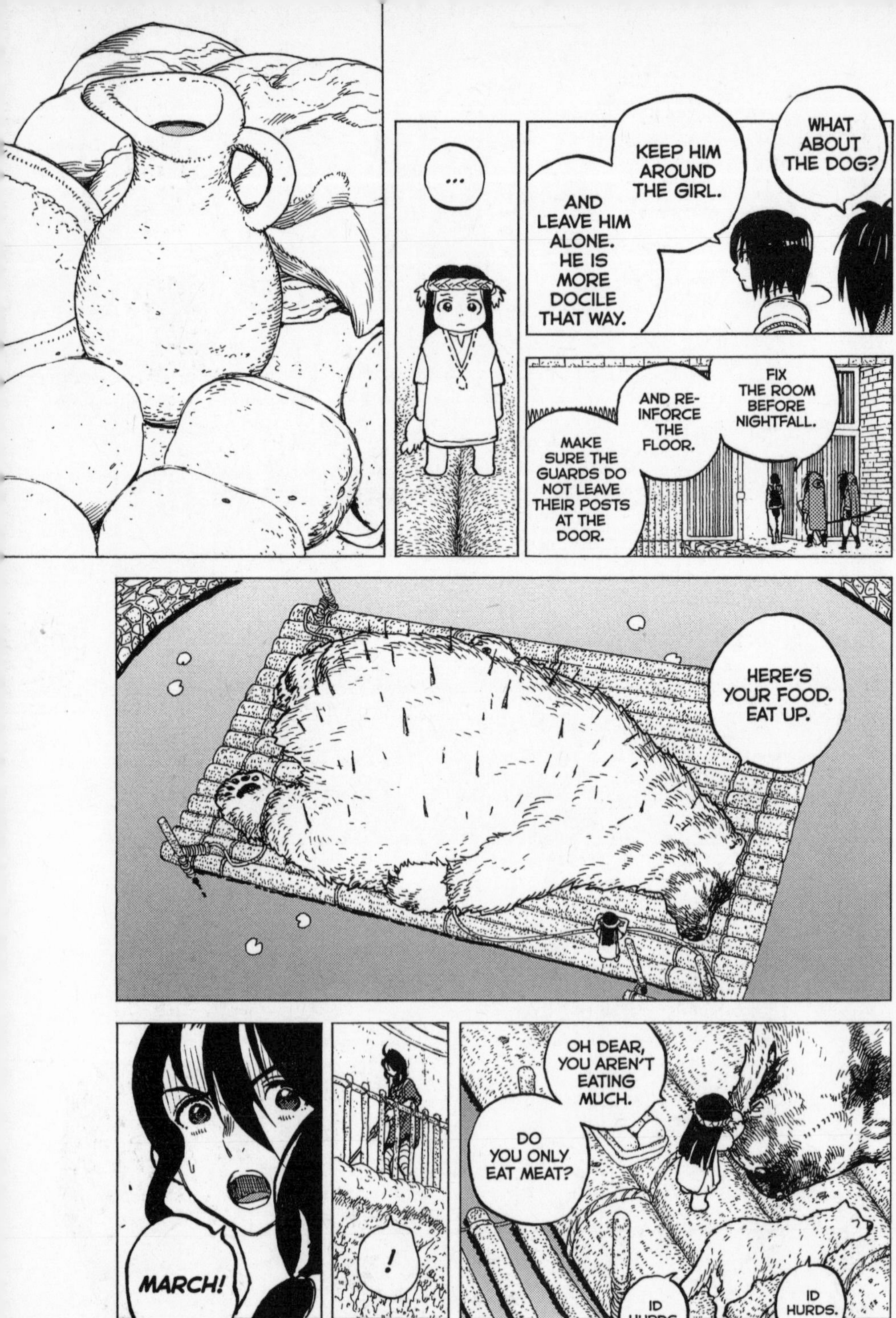
WHAT ABOUT THE DOG?
KEEP HIM AROUND THE GIRL.
AND LEAVE HIM ALONE. HE IS MORE DOCILE THAT WAY.
FIX THE ROOM BEFORE NIGHTFALL.
AND RE-INFORCE THE FLOOR.
MAKE SURE THE GUARDS DO NOT LEAVE THEIR POSTS AT THE DOOR.
...
HERE'S YOUR FOOD. EAT UP.
OH DEAR, YOU AREN'T EATING MUCH.
DO YOU ONLY EAT MEAT?
ID HURDS.
ID HURDS.
!
MARCH!

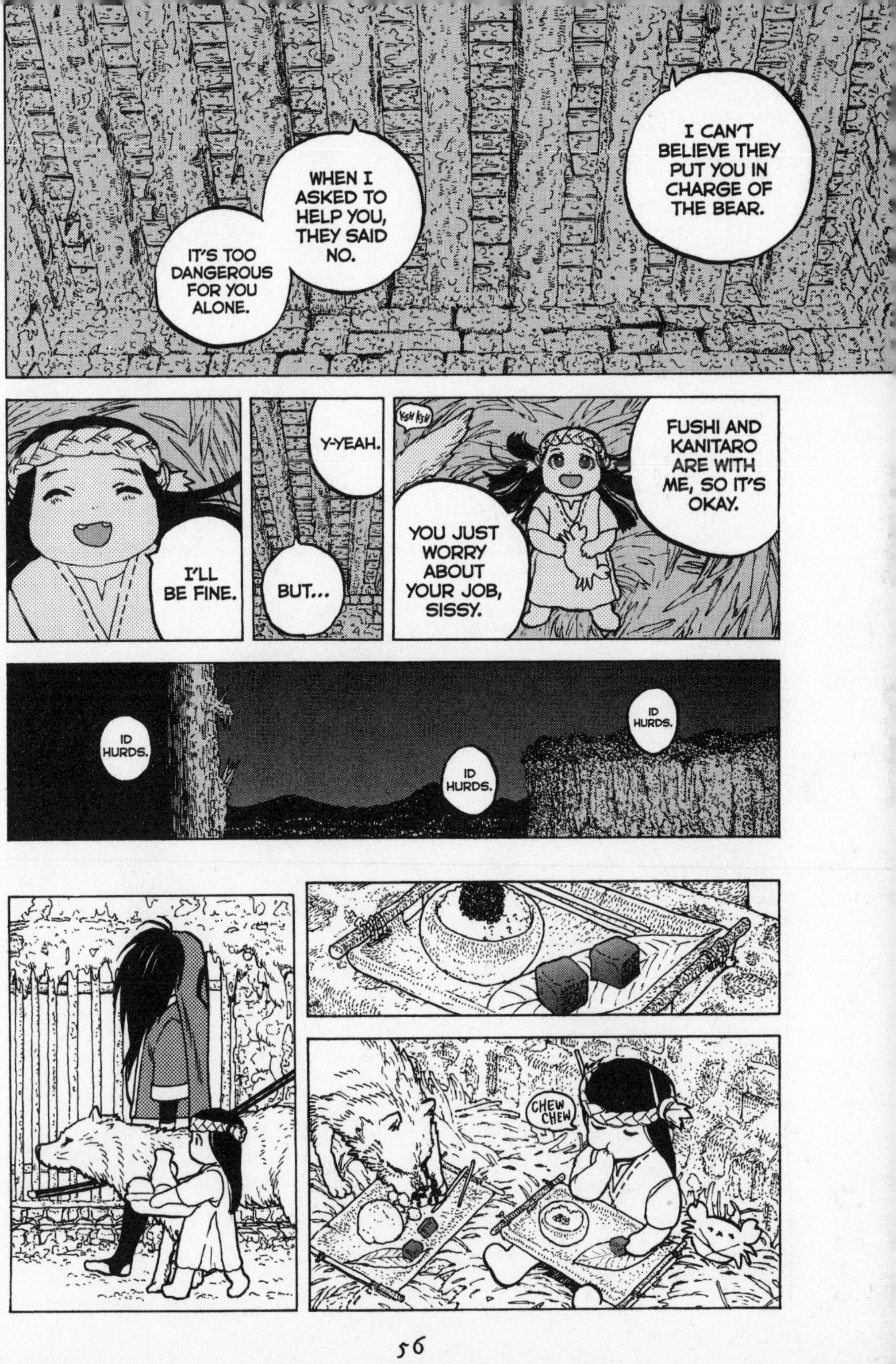
I CAN'T BELIEVE THEY PUT YOU IN CHARGE OF THE BEAR.
WHEN I ASKED TO HELP YOU, THEY SAID NO.
IT'S TOO DANGEROUS FOR YOU ALONE.
KSH KSH
FUSHI AND KANITARO ARE WITH ME, SO IT'S OKAY.
YOU JUST WORRY ABOUT YOUR JOB, SISSY.
Y-YEAH.
BUT...
I'LL BE FINE.
ID HURDS.
ID HURDS.
ID HURDS.
CHEW CHEW

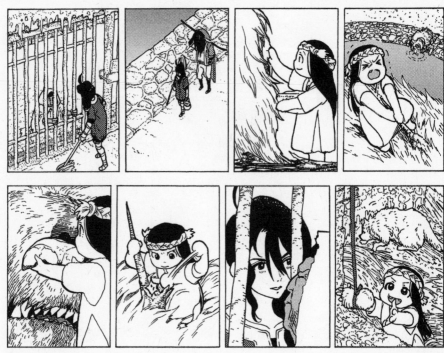

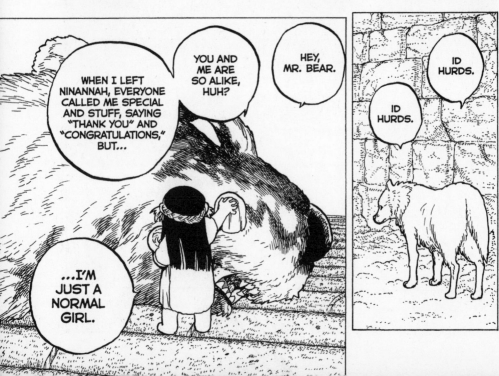

ID HURDS.
ID HURDS.
HEY, MR. BEAR.
YOU AND ME ARE SO ALIKE, HUH?
WHEN I LEFT NINANNAH, EVERYONE CALLED ME SPECIAL AND STUFF, SAYING "THANK YOU" AND "CONGRATULATIONS," BUT...
...I'M JUST A NORMAL GIRL.

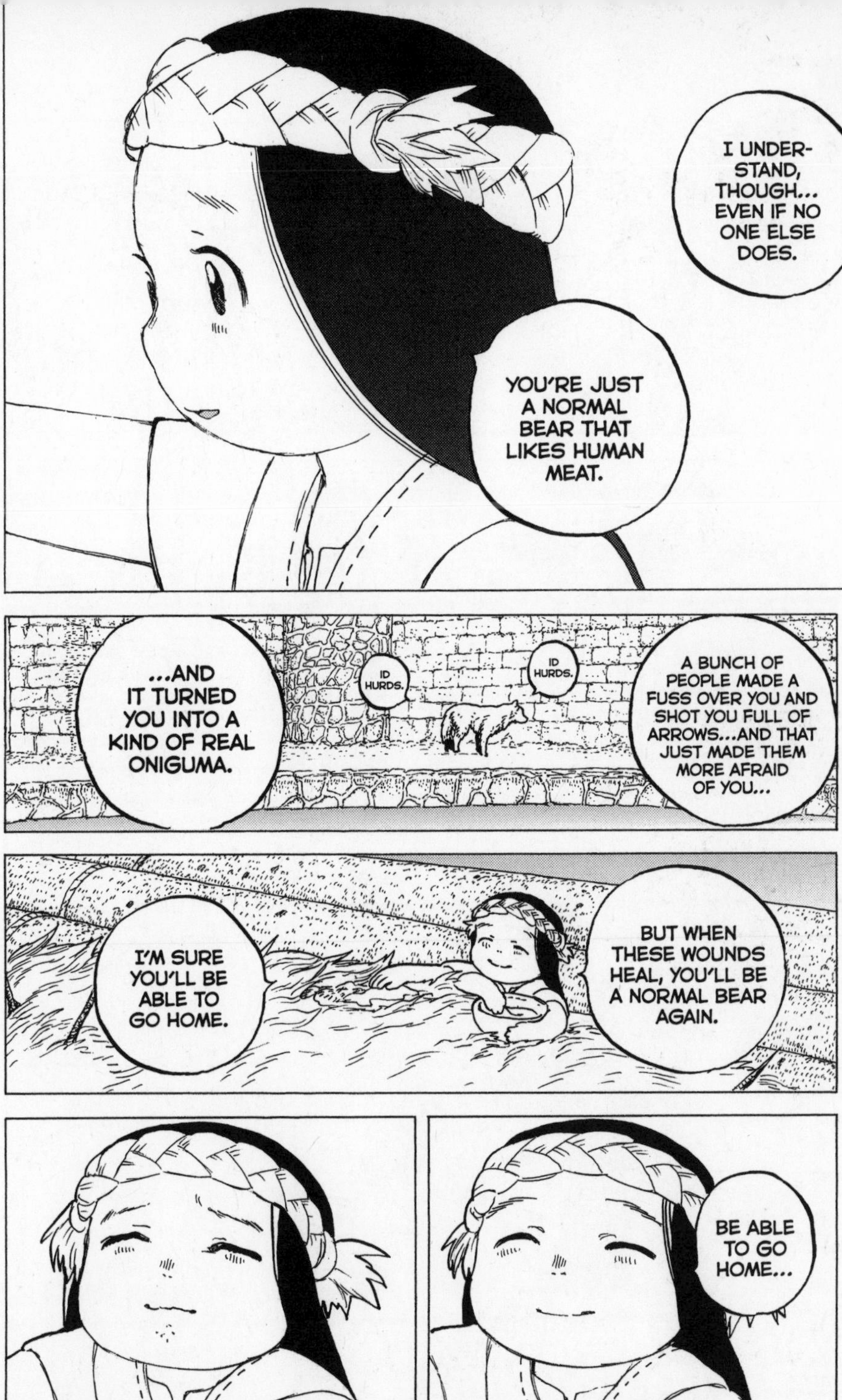
I UNDER-STAND, THOUGH... EVEN IF NO ONE ELSE DOES.
YOU'RE JUST A NORMAL BEAR THAT LIKES HUMAN MEAT.
A BUNCH OF PEOPLE MADE A FUSS OVER YOU AND SHOT YOU FULL OF ARROWS...AND THAT JUST MADE THEM MORE AFRAID OF YOU...
ID HURDS.
ID HURDS.
...AND IT TURNED YOU INTO A KIND OF REAL ONIGUMA.
BUT WHEN THESE WOUNDS HEAL, YOU'LL BE A NORMAL BEAR AGAIN.
I'M SURE YOU'LL BE ABLE TO GO HOME.
BE ABLE TO GO HOME...

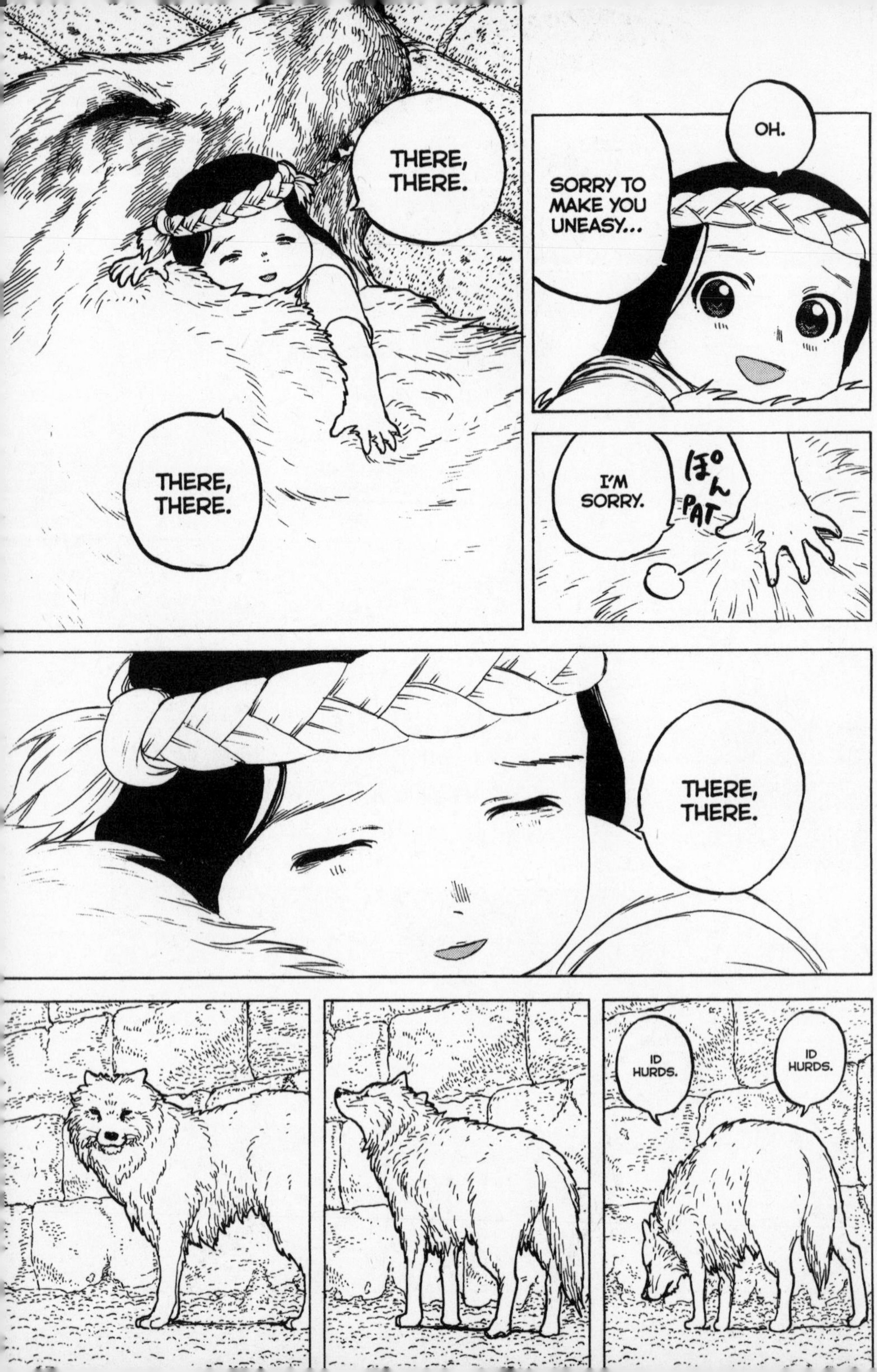

OH.
SORRY TO MAKE YOU UNEASY...
ぽん PAT
I'M SORRY.
THERE, THERE.
THERE, THERE.
THERE, THERE.
ID HURDS.
ID HURDS.

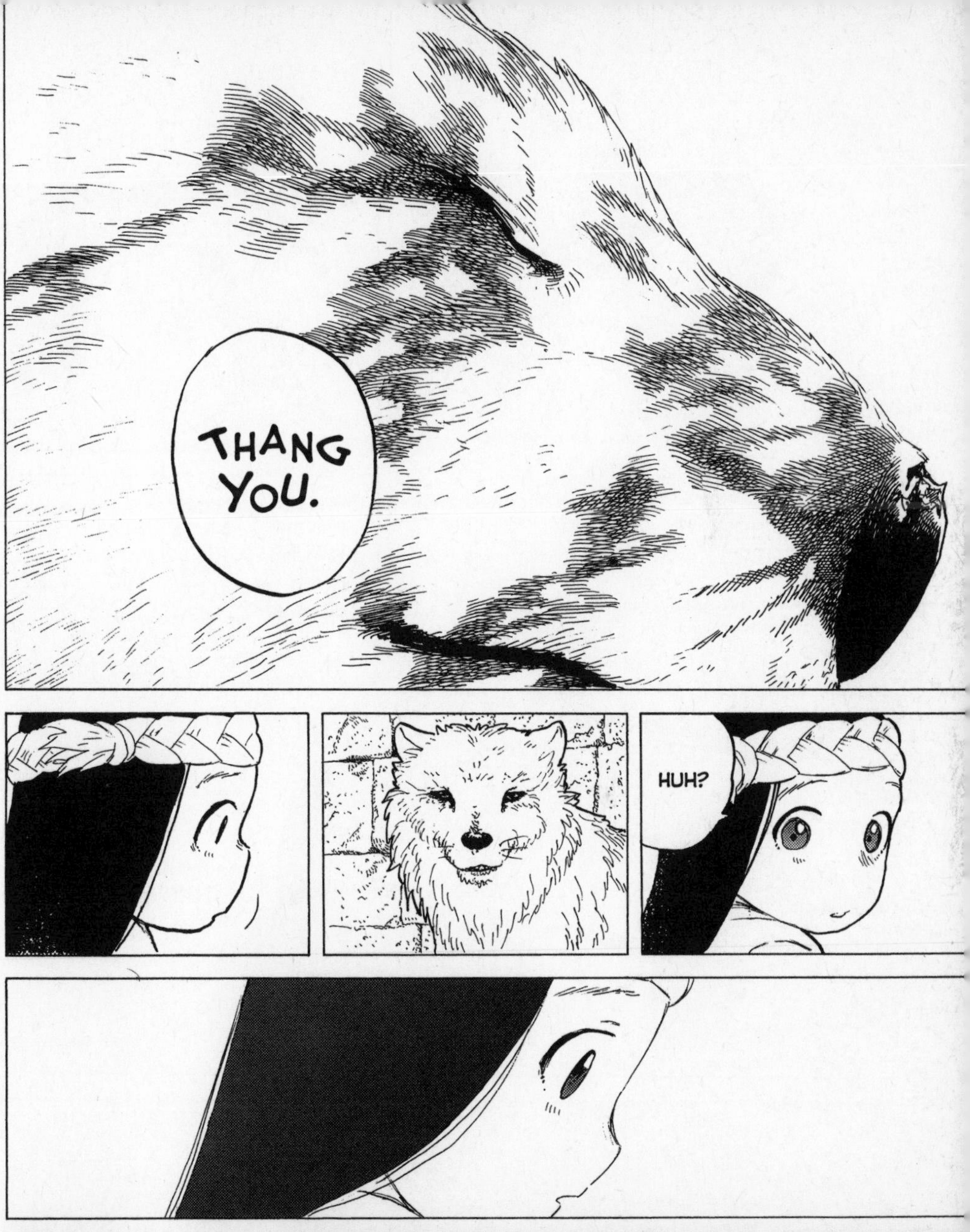
THANG YOU.
HUH?

TO YOUR ETERNITY

TO YOUR
ETERNITY

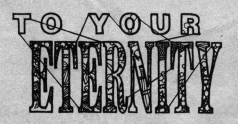

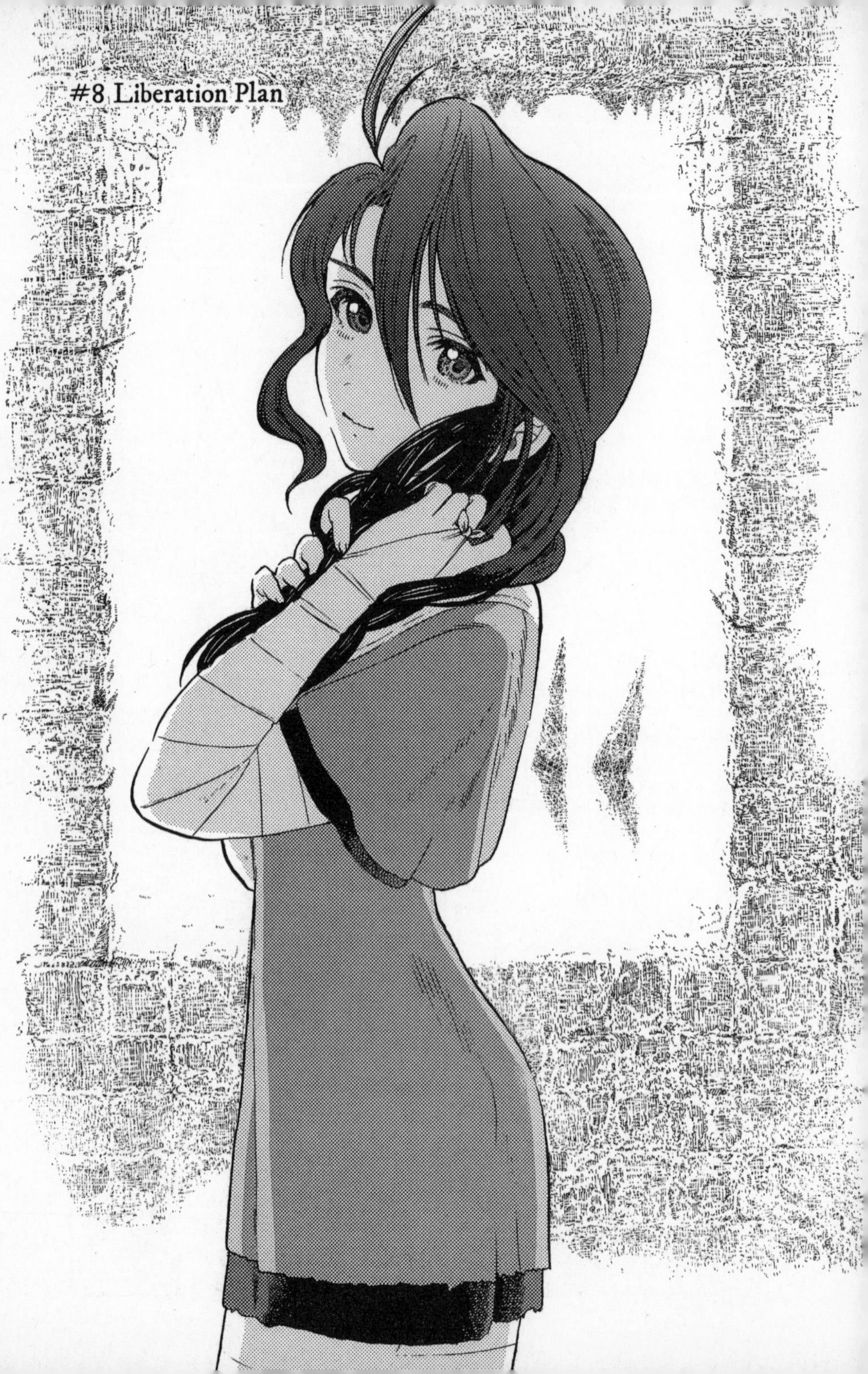
#8 Liberation Plan

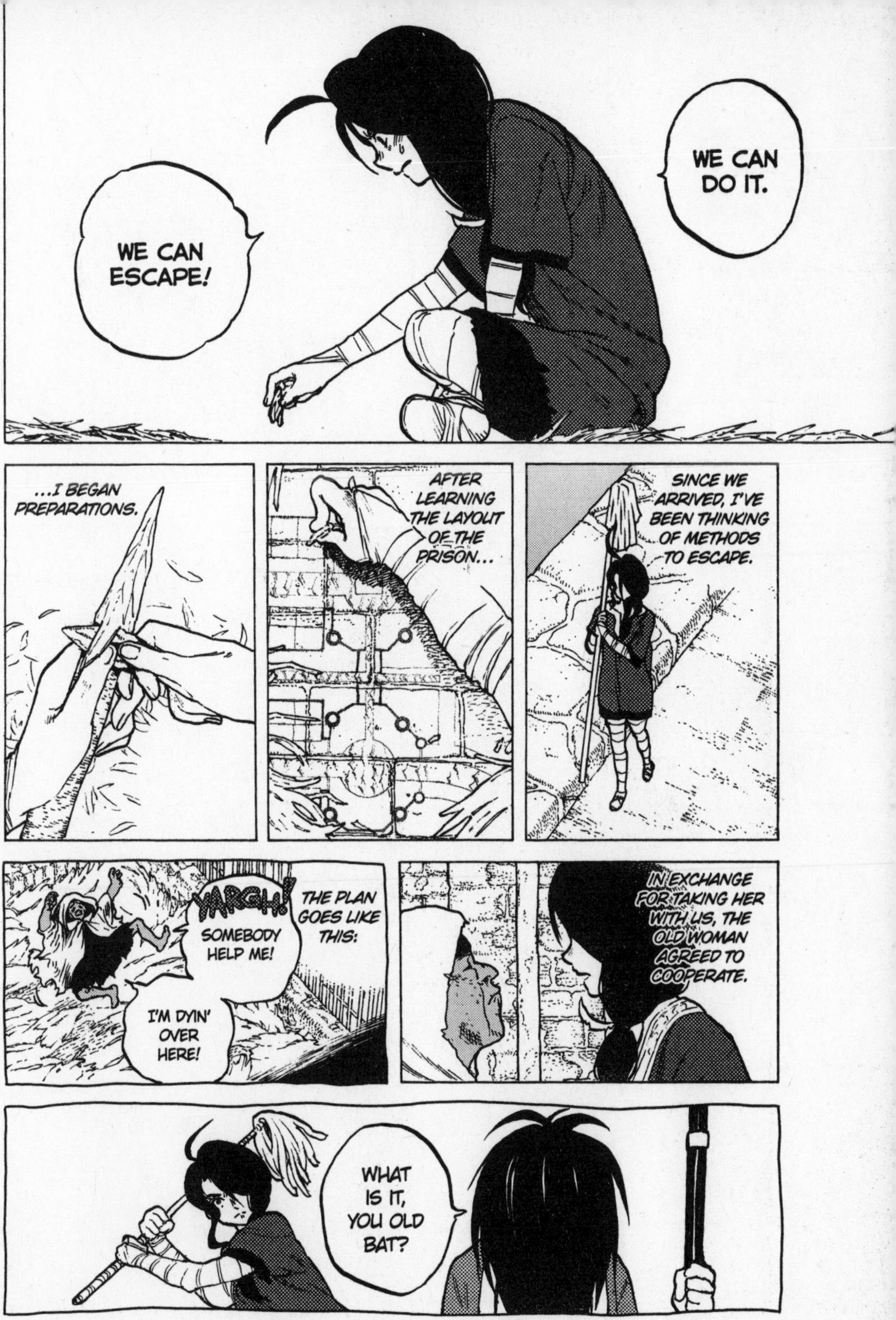
WE CAN DO IT.
WE CAN ESCAPE!
SINCE WE ARRIVED, I'VE BEEN THINKING OF METHODS TO ESCAPE.
AFTER LEARNING THE LAYOUT OF THE PRISON...
...I BEGAN PREPARATIONS.
IN EXCHANGE FOR TAKING HER WITH US, THE OLD WOMAN AGREED TO COOPERATE.
THE PLAN GOES LIKE THIS:
YARGH!
SOMEBODY HELP ME!
I'M DYIN' OVER HERE!
WHAT IS IT, YOU OLD BAT?

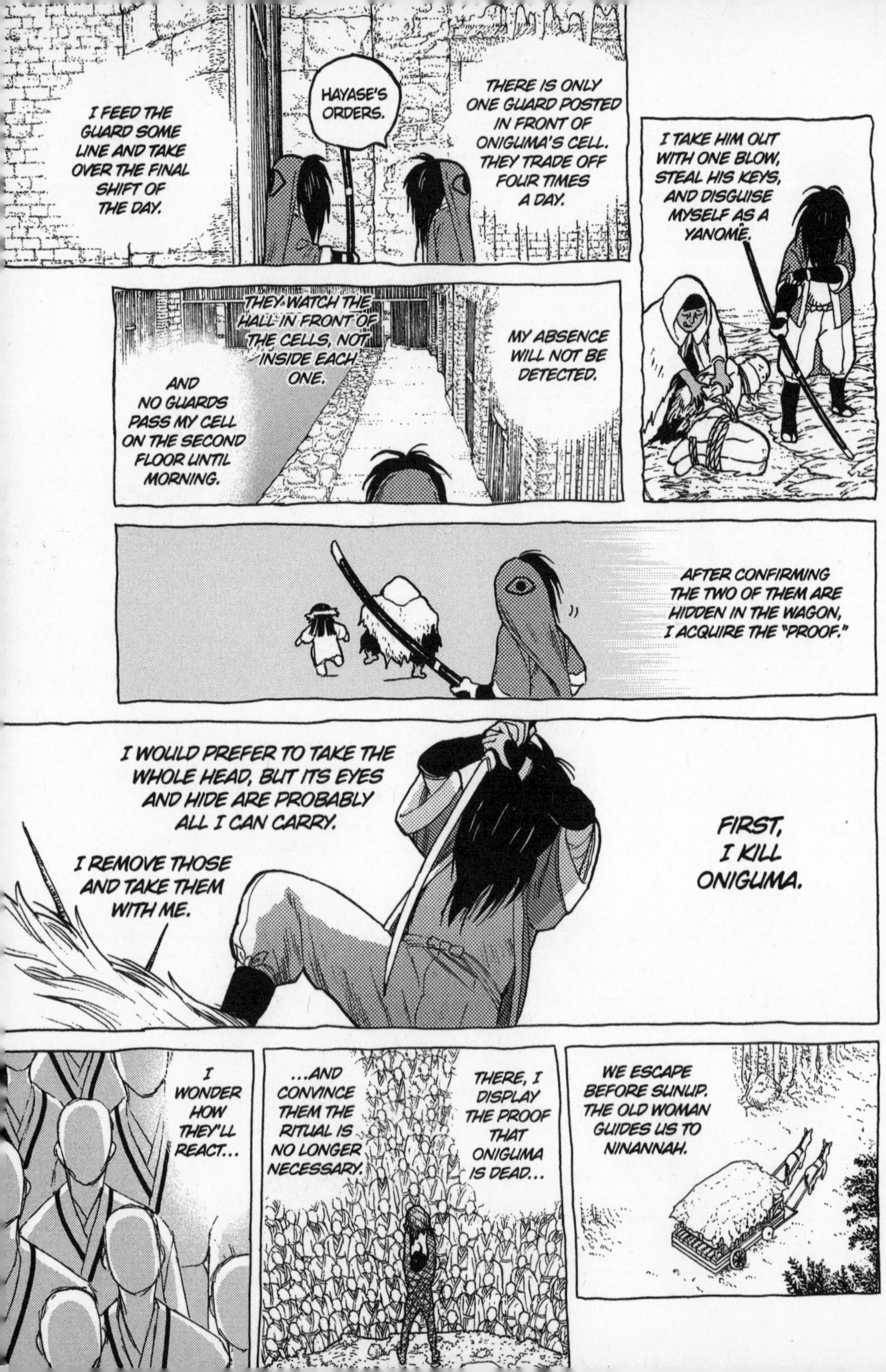
THERE IS ONLY ONE GUARD POSTED IN FRONT OF ONIGUMA'S CELL. THEY TRADE OFF FOUR TIMES A DAY.
HAYASE'S ORDERS.
I FEED THE GUARD SOME LINE AND TAKE OVER THE FINAL SHIFT OF THE DAY.
I TAKE HIM OUT WITH ONE BLOW, STEAL HIS KEYS, AND DISGUISE MYSELF AS A YANOMË.
MY ABSENCE WILL NOT BE DETECTED.
THEY WATCH THE HALL IN FRONT OF THE CELLS, NOT INSIDE EACH ONE.
AND NO GUARDS PASS MY CELL ON THE SECOND FLOOR UNTIL MORNING.
AFTER CONFIRMING THE TWO OF THEM ARE HIDDEN IN THE WAGON, I ACQUIRE THE "PROOF."
FIRST, I KILL ONIGUMA.
I WOULD PREFER TO TAKE THE WHOLE HEAD, BUT ITS EYES AND HIDE ARE PROBABLY ALL I CAN CARRY.
I REMOVE THOSE AND TAKE THEM WITH ME.
WE ESCAPE BEFORE SUNUP. THE OLD WOMAN GUIDES US TO NINANNAH.
THERE, I DISPLAY THE PROOF THAT ONIGUMA IS DEAD...
...AND CONVINCE THEM THE RITUAL IS NO LONGER NECESSARY.
I WONDER HOW THEY'LL REACT...

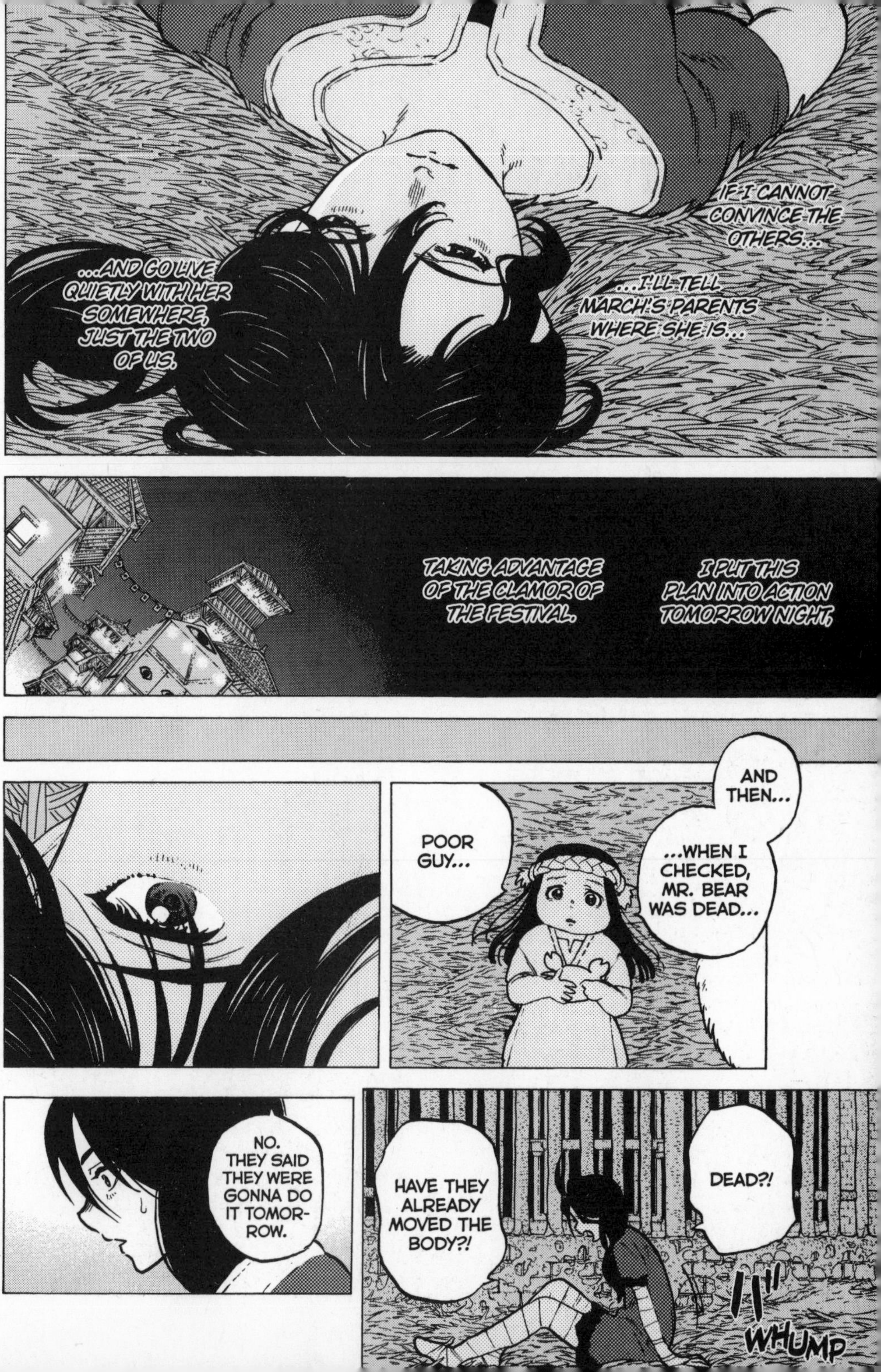
IF I CANNOT CONVINCE THE OTHERS...
...I'LL TELL MARCH'S PARENTS WHERE SHE IS...
...AND GO LIVE QUIETLY WITH HER SOMEWHERE, JUST THE TWO OF US.
I PUT THIS PLAN INTO ACTION TOMORROW NIGHT,
TAKING ADVANTAGE OF THE CLAMOR OF THE FESTIVAL.
AND THEN...
...WHEN I CHECKED, MR. BEAR WAS DEAD...
POOR GUY...
DEAD?!
WHUMP
HAVE THEY ALREADY MOVED THE BODY?!
NO. THEY SAID THEY WERE GONNA DO IT TOMOR-ROW.

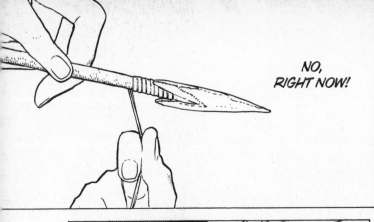

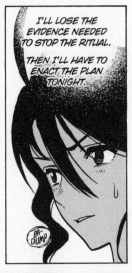

I'LL LOSE THE EVIDENCE NEEDED TO STOP THE RITUAL.
THEN I'LL HAVE TO ENACT THE PLAN TONIGHT.
BA-DUMP
NO, RIGHT NOW!
IT'S FINE, SIS. I CAN STILL MAKE IT.
EVEN WITH A CHANGE IN PLANS, I CAN STILL PULL IT OFF.
FIRST, I'VE GOT TO GET OUT OF THIS CELL.
HOW AM I GONNA DO THAT?
THERE IS A WINDOW FACING THE CLIFF IN ONIGUMA'S CELL.
I HAVE A ROPE BRAIDED FROM STRAW I COLLECTED.
THAT'S IT!
WHOOOSH
IT'S NOT LONG, BUT IT SHOULD REACH.
BYUM
BYUM
CLANK

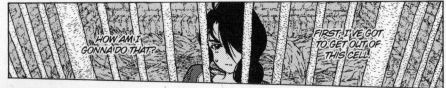

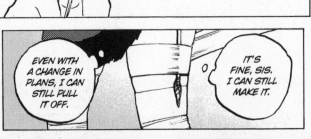

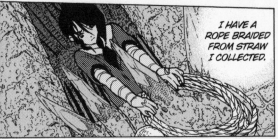

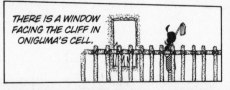

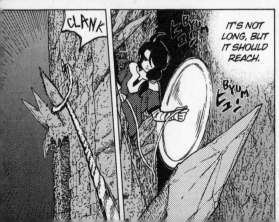

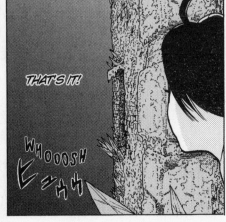

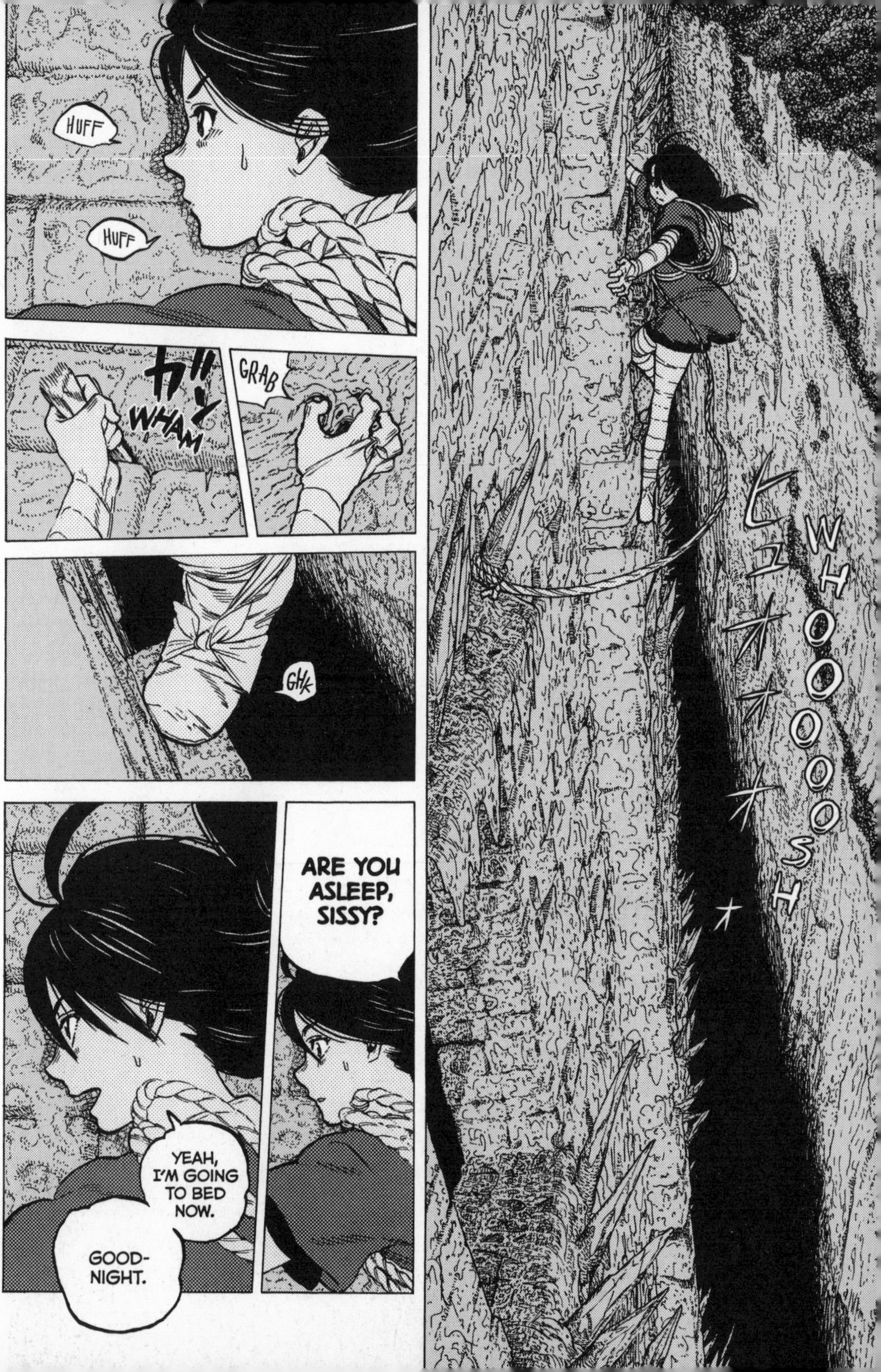
WHOOOOOSH
HUFF
HUFF
GRAB
WHAM
GHK
ARE YOU ASLEEP, SISSY?
YEAH, I'M GOING TO BED NOW.
GOOD-NIGHT.

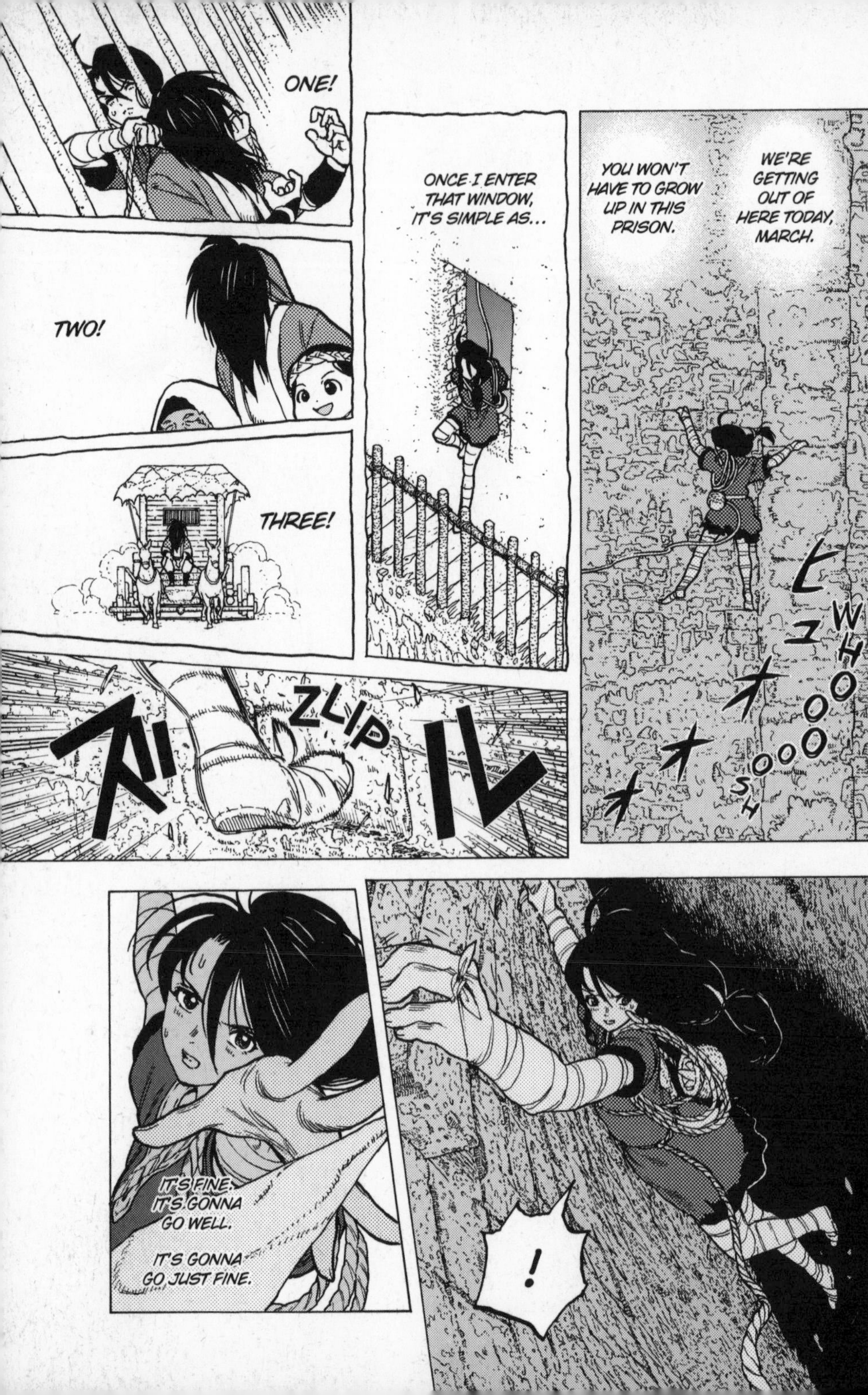
WE'RE GETTING OUT OF HERE TODAY, MARCH.
YOU WON'T HAVE TO GROW UP IN THIS PRISON.
ヒュオオオ
WHOOOOOSH
ONCE I ENTER THAT WINDOW, IT'S SIMPLE AS...
ONE!
TWO!
THREE!
ズル
ZLIP
!
IT'S FINE. IT'S GONNA GO WELL.
IT'S GONNA GO JUST FINE.

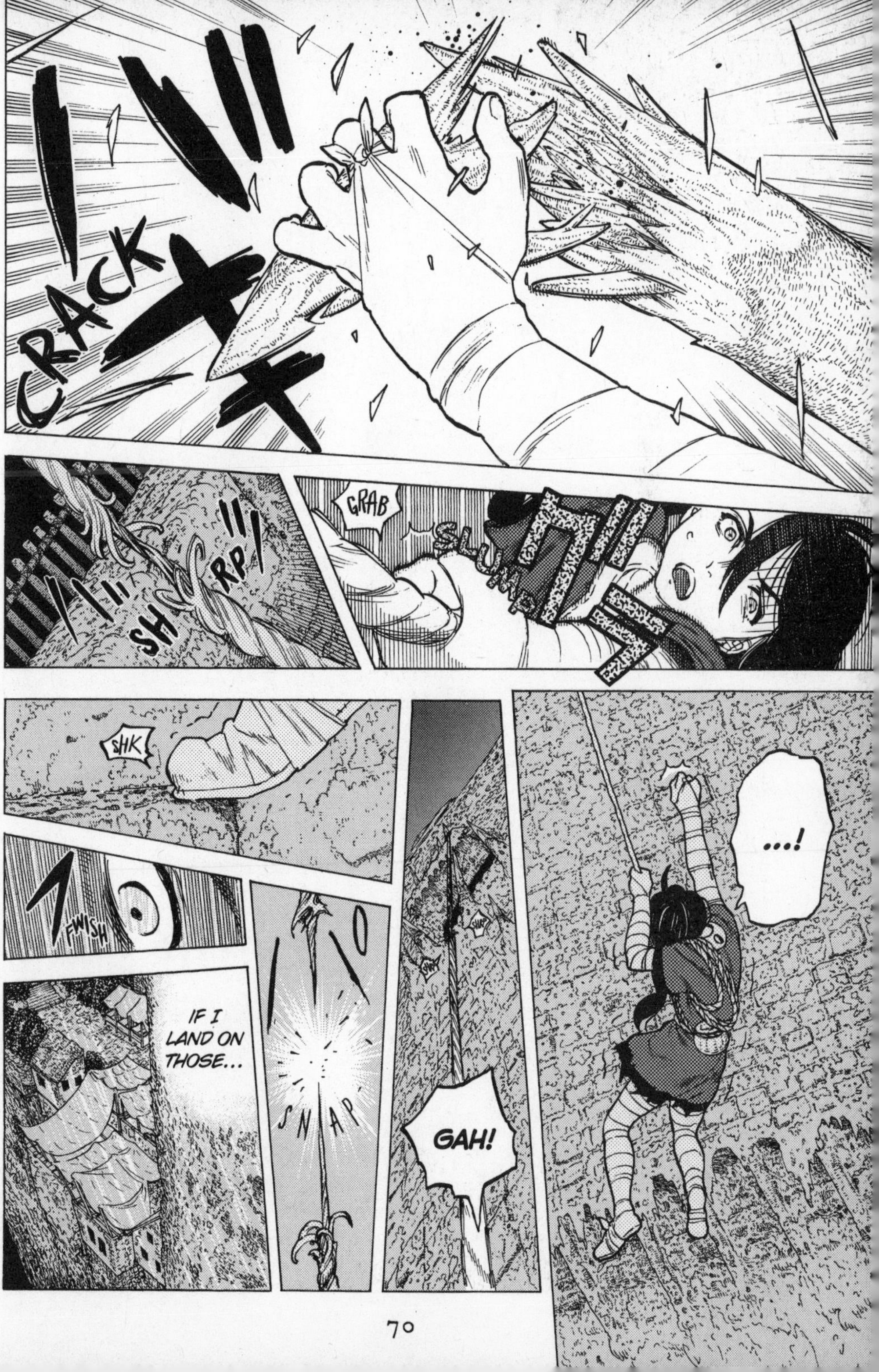
CRACK
GRAB
SLUMP
SHRRP
...!
GAH!
SHK
FWISH
SNAP
IF I LAND ON THOSE...

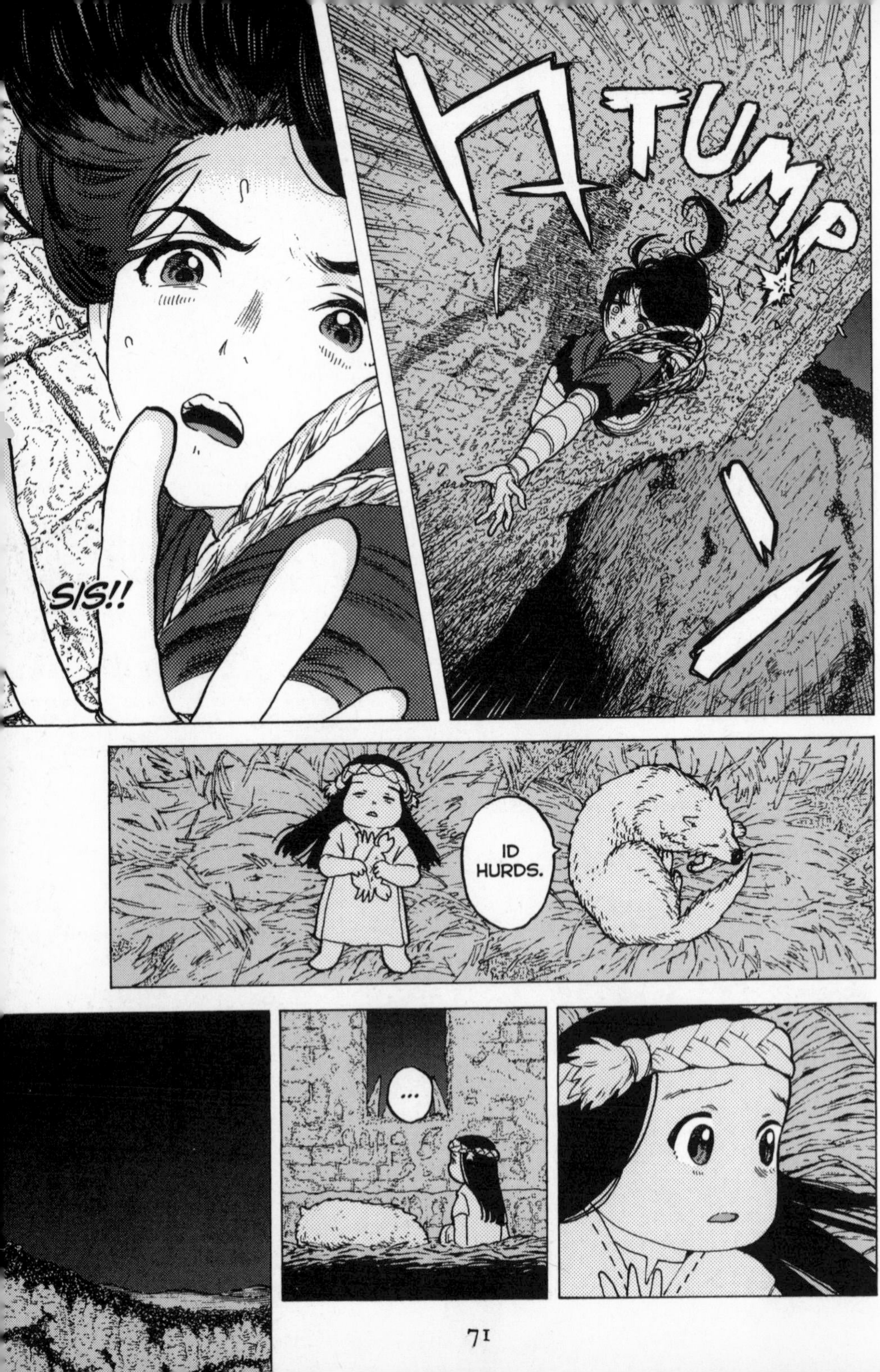
TUMP
SIS!!
ID HURDS.
...

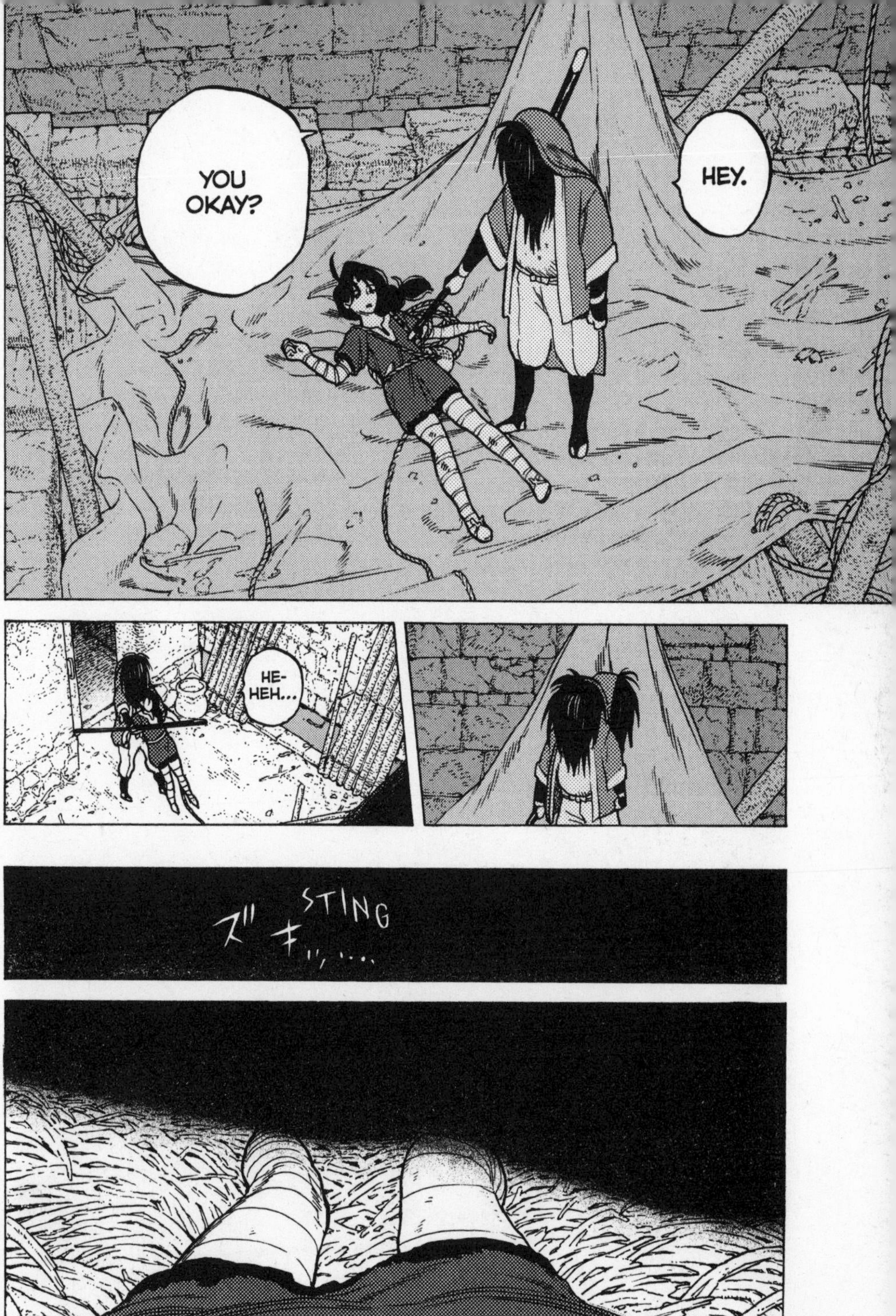
HEY.
YOU OKAY?
HE-HEH...
STING
ズキッ…

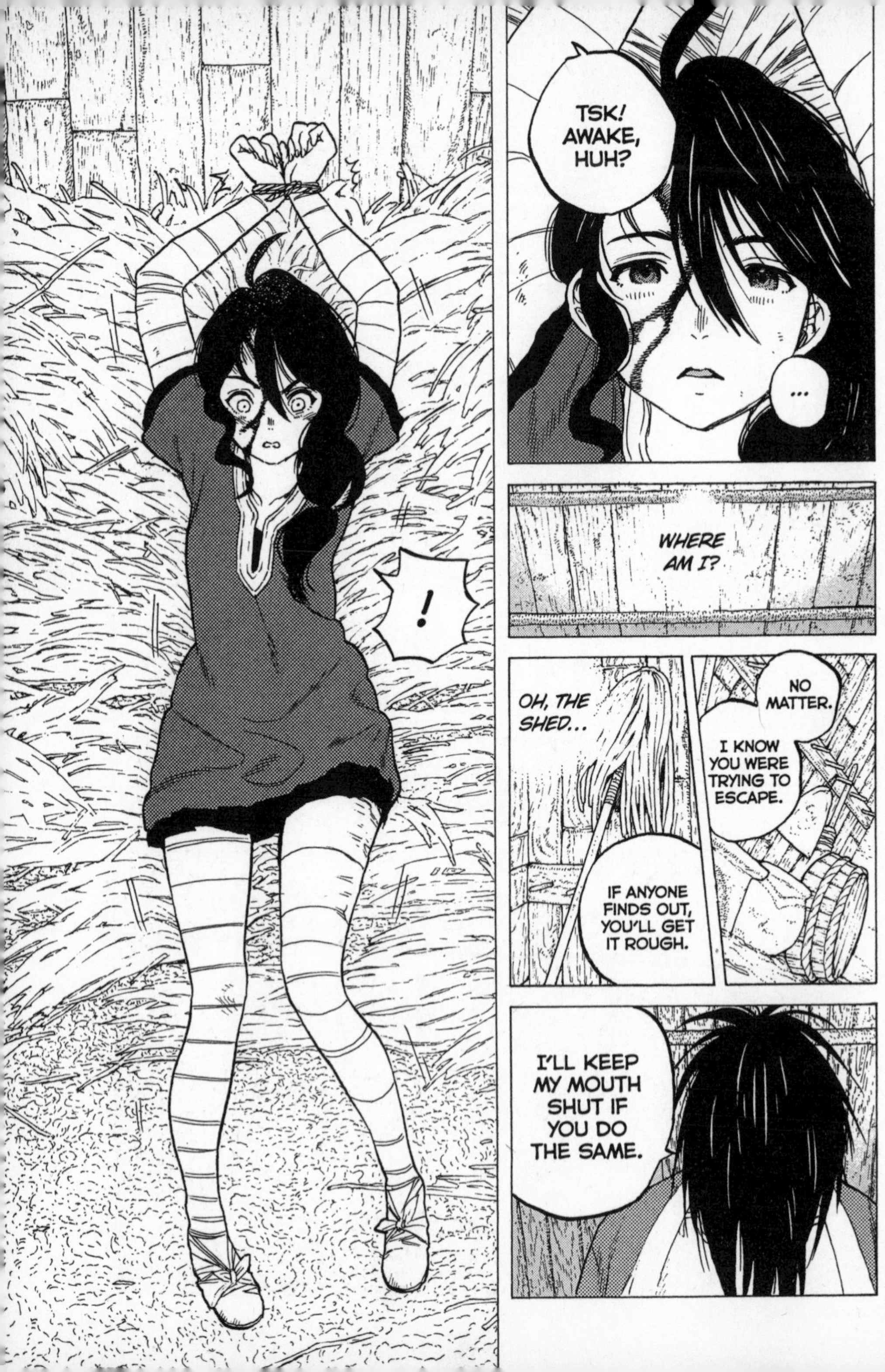

TSK! AWAKE, HUH?
...
WHERE AM I?
NO MATTER.
I KNOW YOU WERE TRYING TO ESCAPE.
OH, THE SHED...
IF ANYONE FINDS OUT, YOU'LL GET IT ROUGH.
I'LL KEEP MY MOUTH SHUT IF YOU DO THE SAME.
!

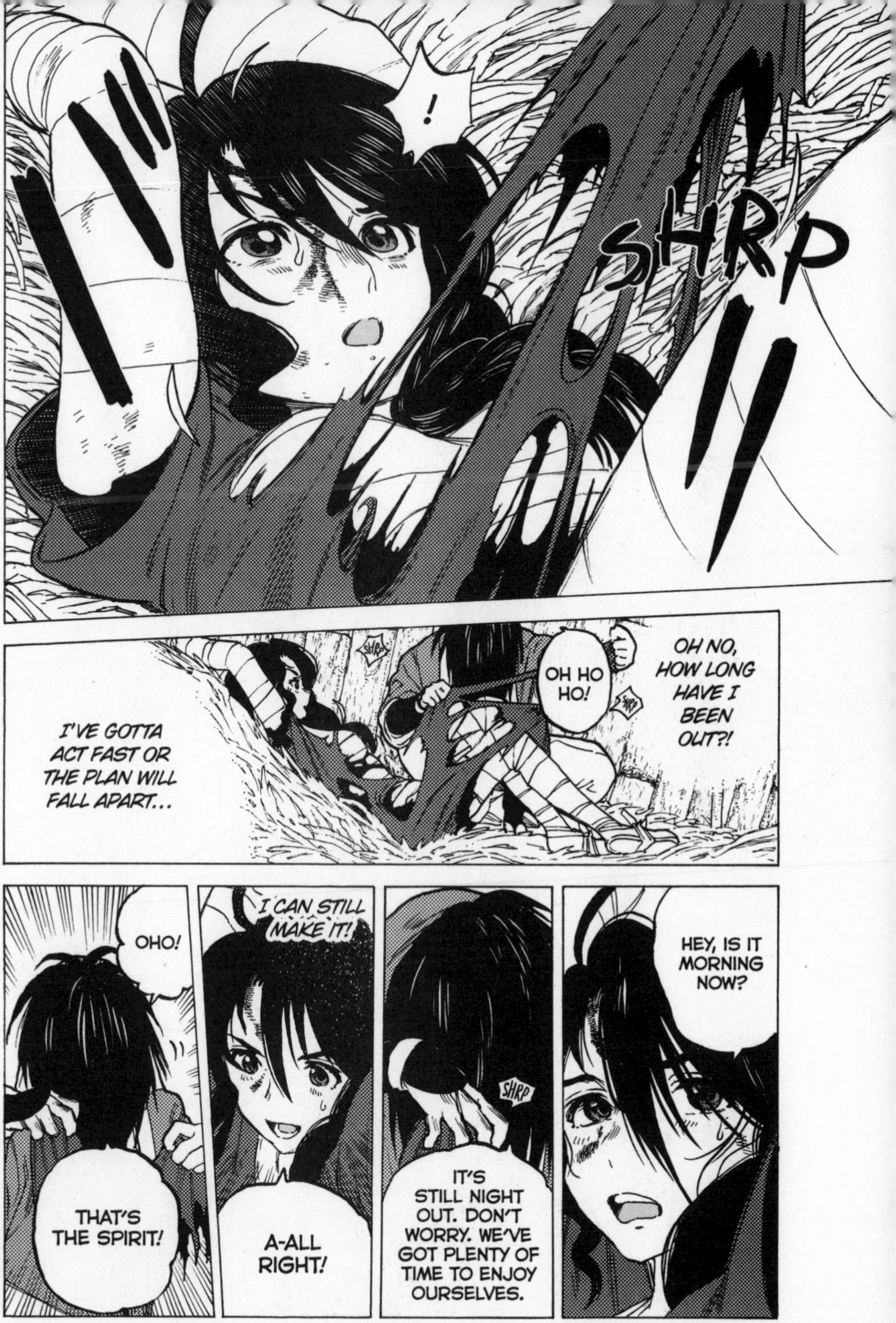
!
SHRP
OH NO, HOW LONG HAVE I BEEN OUT?!
SHRP
OH HO HO!
SHRP
I'VE GOTTA ACT FAST OR THE PLAN WILL FALL APART...
HEY, IS IT MORNING NOW?
SHRP
IT'S STILL NIGHT OUT. DON'T WORRY. WE'VE GOT PLENTY OF TIME TO ENJOY OURSELVES.
I CAN STILL MAKE IT!
A-ALL RIGHT!
OHO!
THAT'S THE SPIRIT!

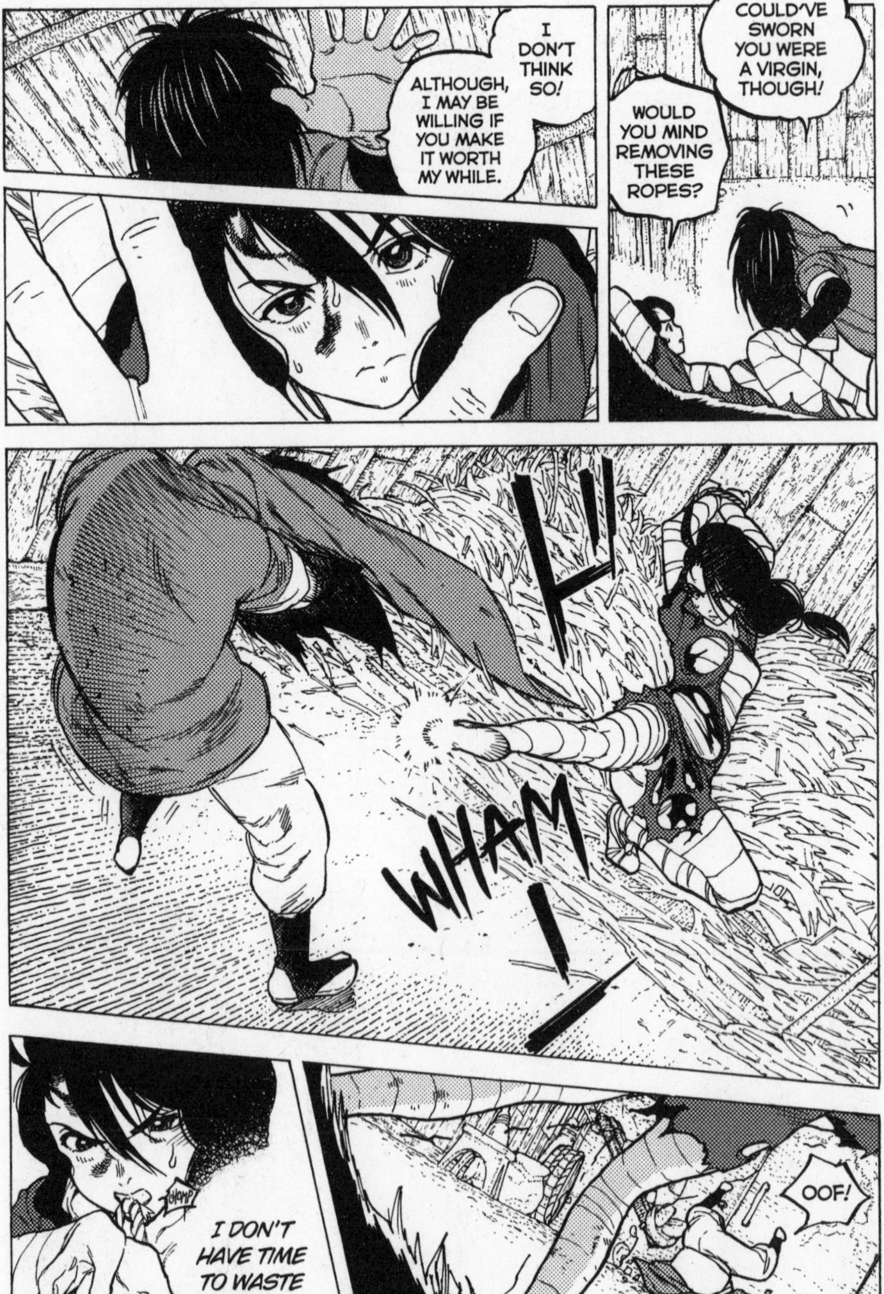
I COULD'VE SWORN YOU WERE A VIRGIN, THOUGH!
WOULD YOU MIND REMOVING THESE ROPES?
I DON'T THINK SO!
ALTHOUGH, I MAY BE WILLING IF YOU MAKE IT WORTH MY WHILE.
WHAM!
OOF!
I DON'T HAVE TIME TO WASTE HERE!

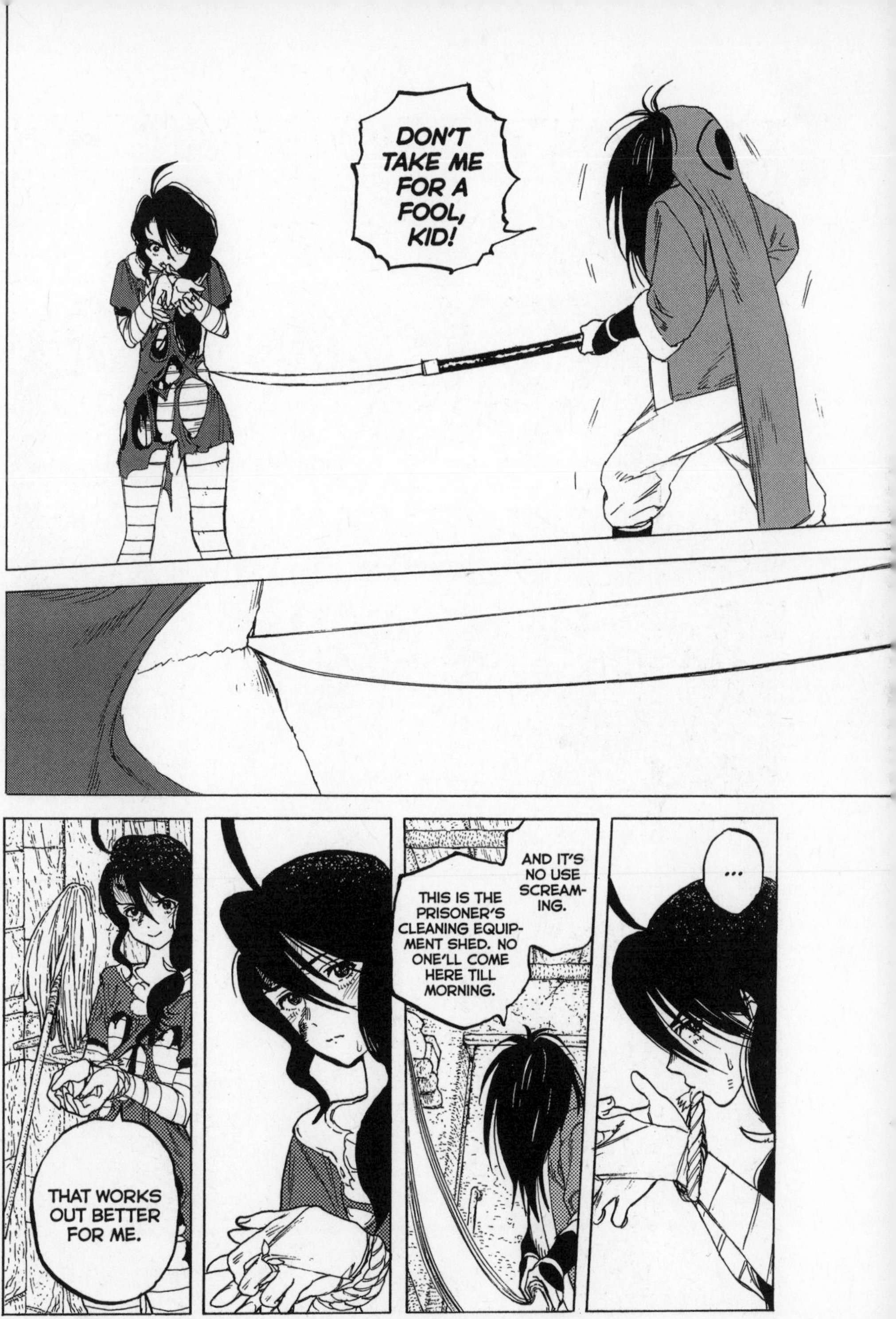
DON'T TAKE ME FOR A FOOL, KID!
...
AND IT'S NO USE SCREAM-ING.
THIS IS THE PRISONER'S CLEANING EQUIP-MENT SHED. NO ONE'LL COME HERE TILL MORNING.
THAT WORKS OUT BETTER FOR ME.

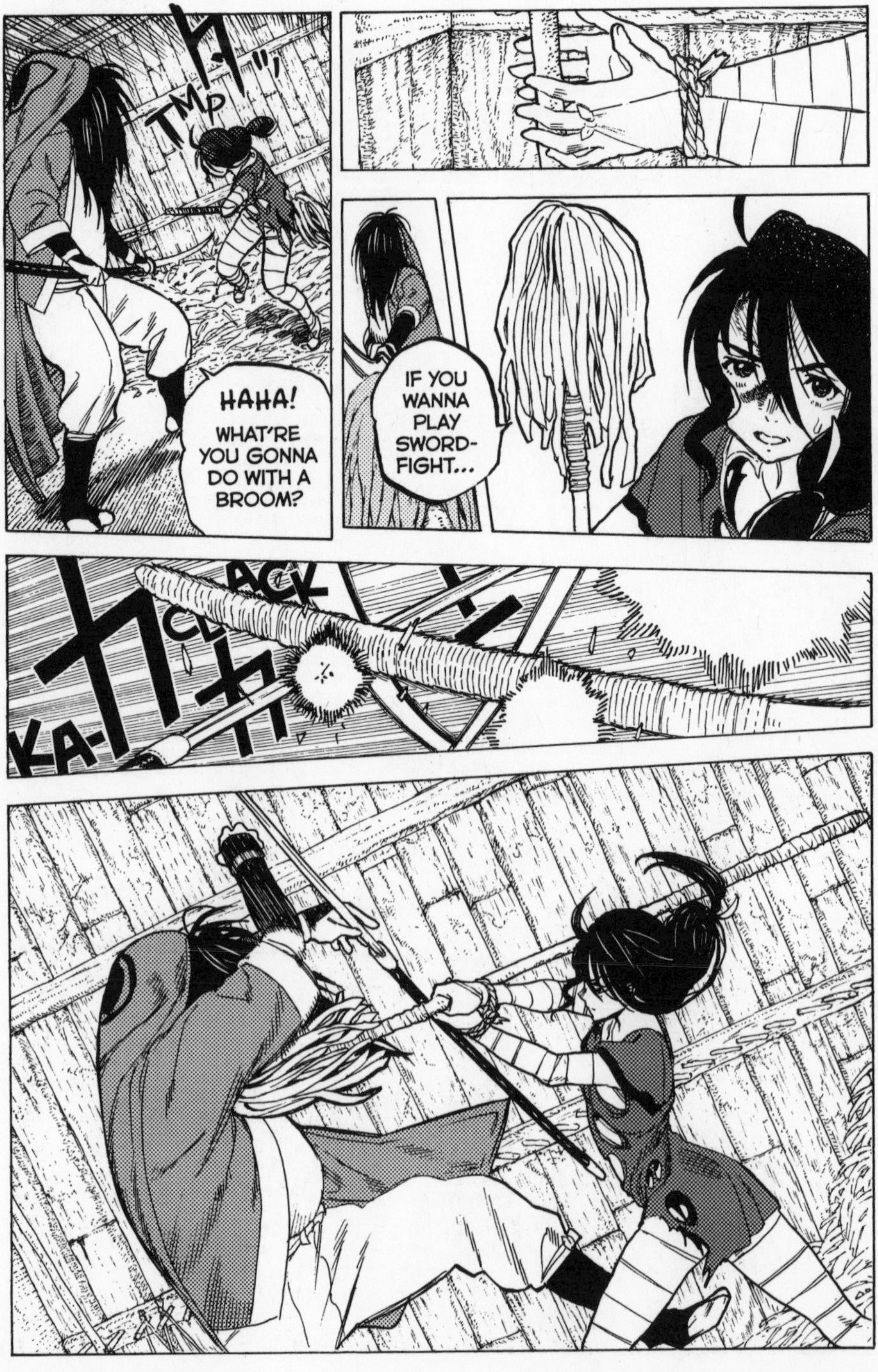
IF YOU WANNA PLAY SWORD-FIGHT...
TMP
HAHA! WHAT'RE YOU GONNA DO WITH A BROOM?
CLACK
KA-

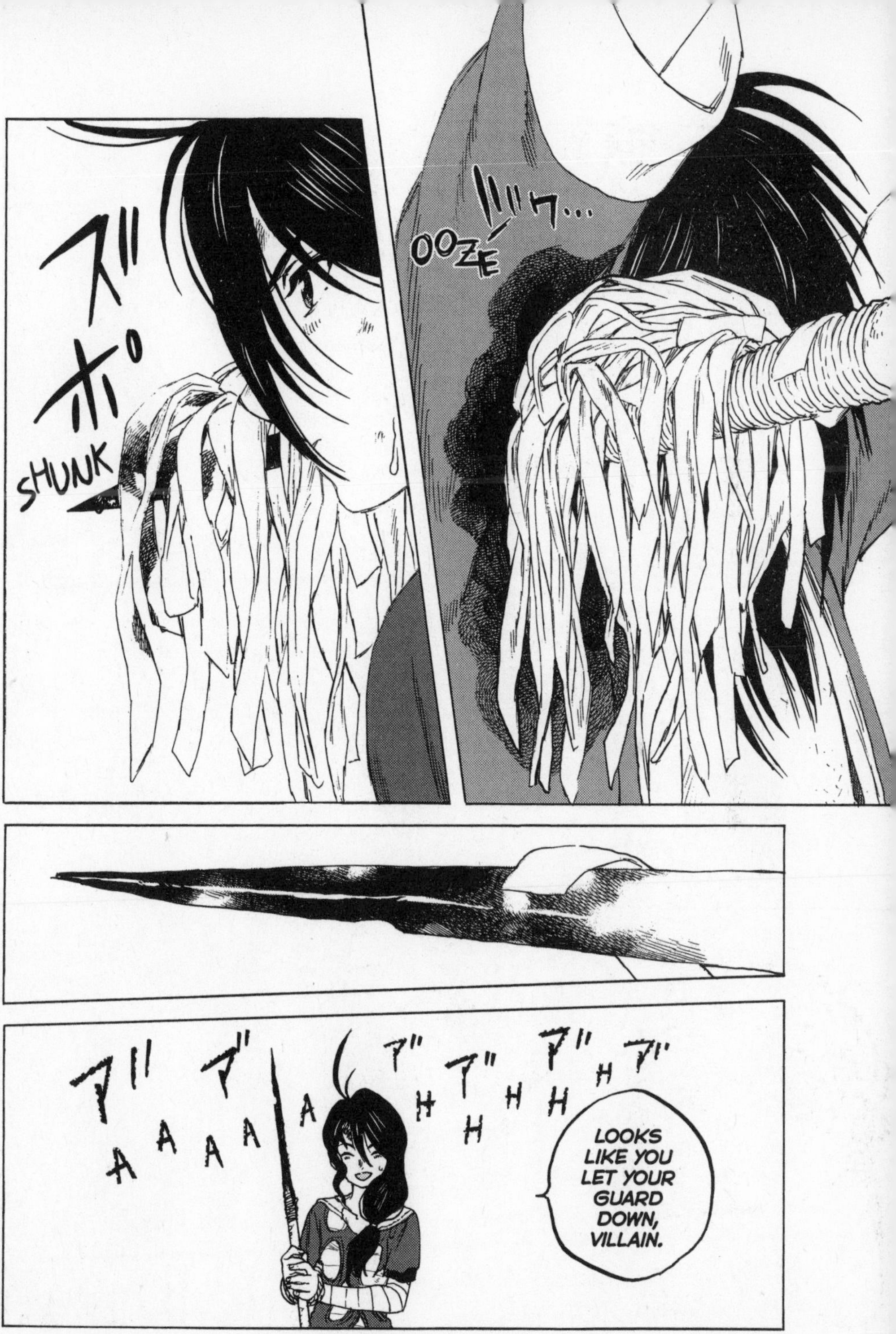

OOZE
ズポ
SHUNK
AAAAAHHHHHH
LOOKS LIKE YOU LET YOUR GUARD DOWN, VILLAIN.

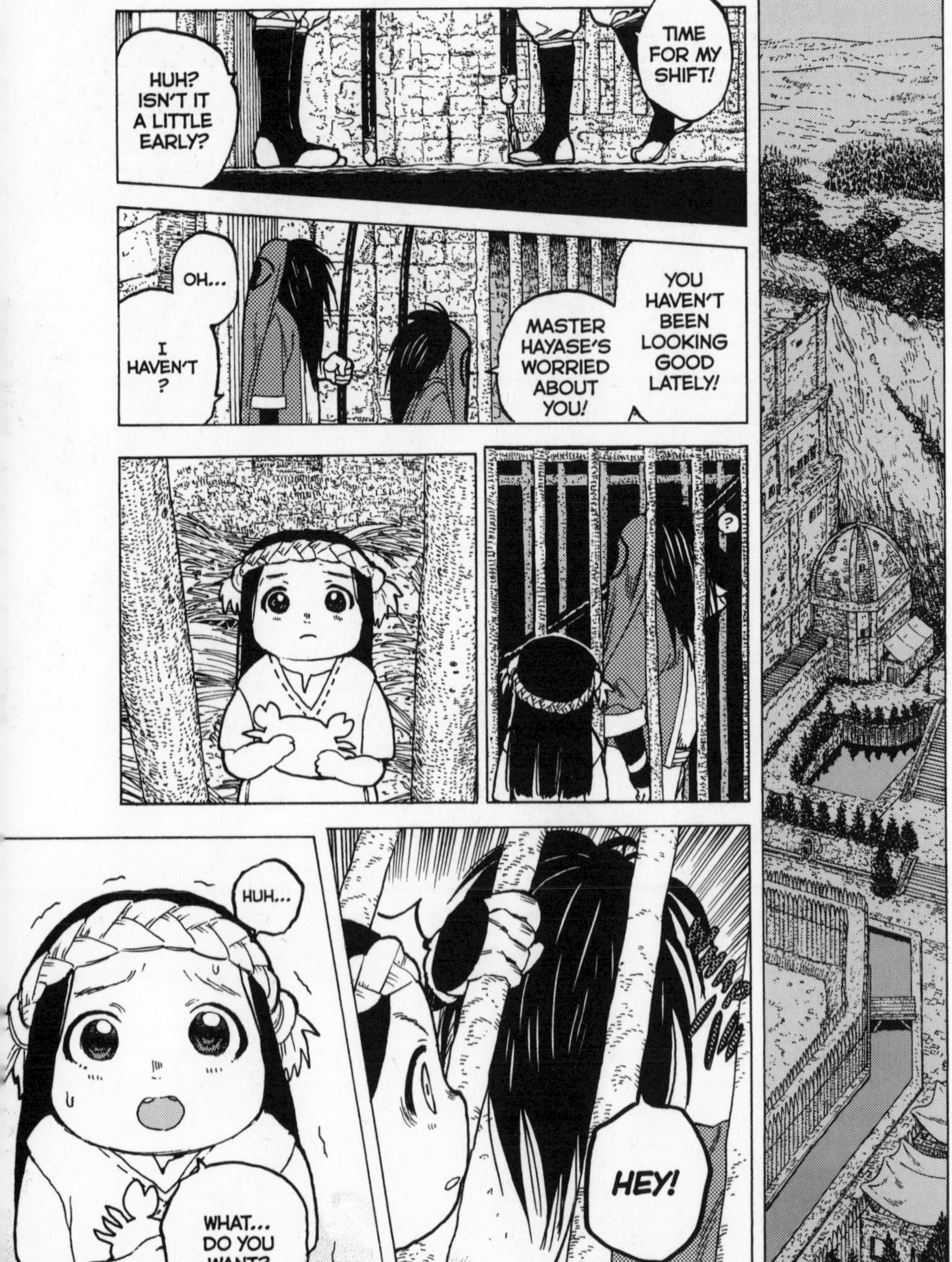
TIME FOR MY SHIFT!
HUH? ISN'T IT A LITTLE EARLY?
YOU HAVEN'T BEEN LOOKING GOOD LATELY!
MASTER HAYASE'S WORRIED ABOUT YOU!
OH...
I HAVEN'T ?
?
HEY!
HUH...
WHAT... DO YOU WANT?

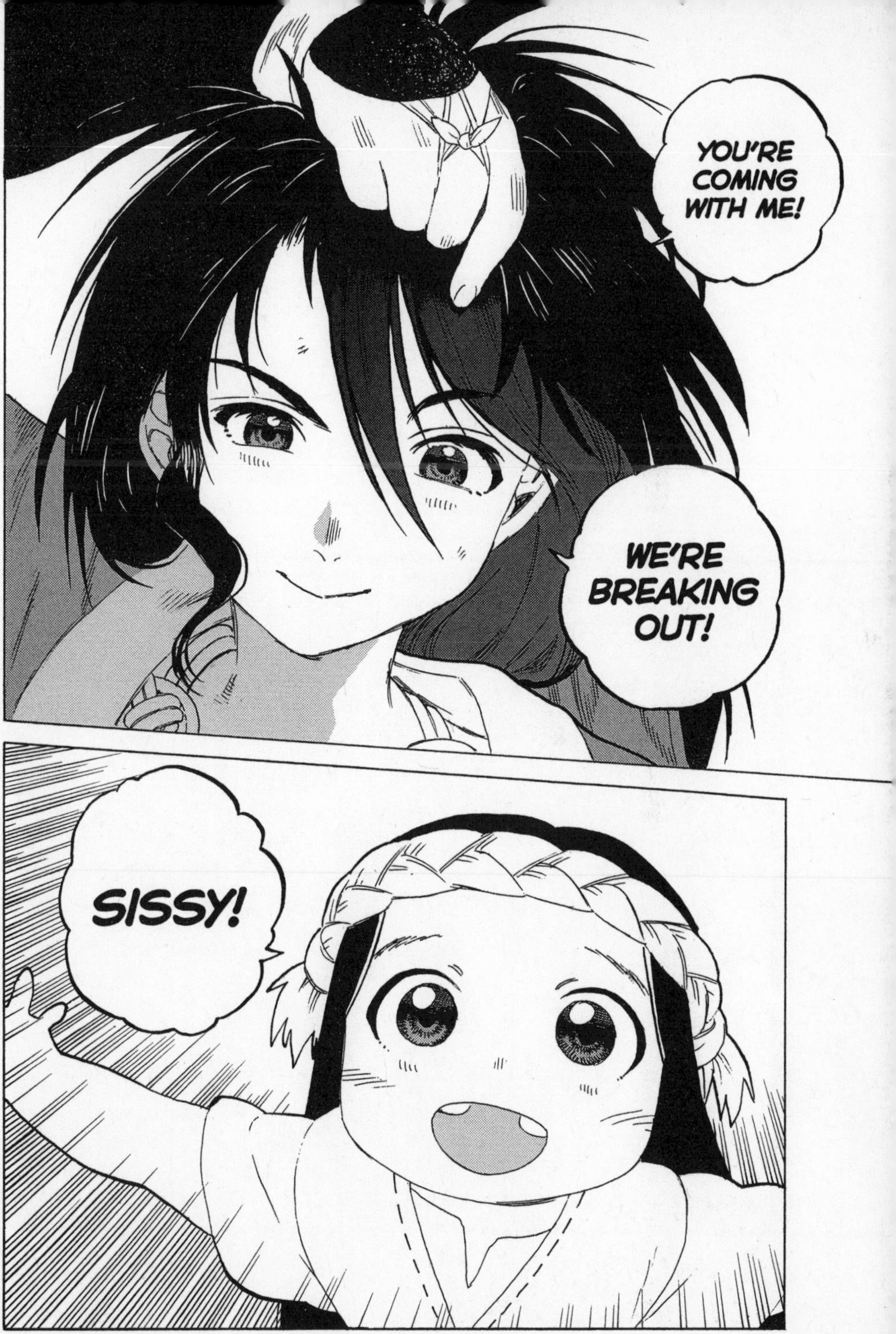
YOU'RE COMING WITH ME!
WE'RE BREAKING OUT!
SISSY!

TO YOUR ETERNITY

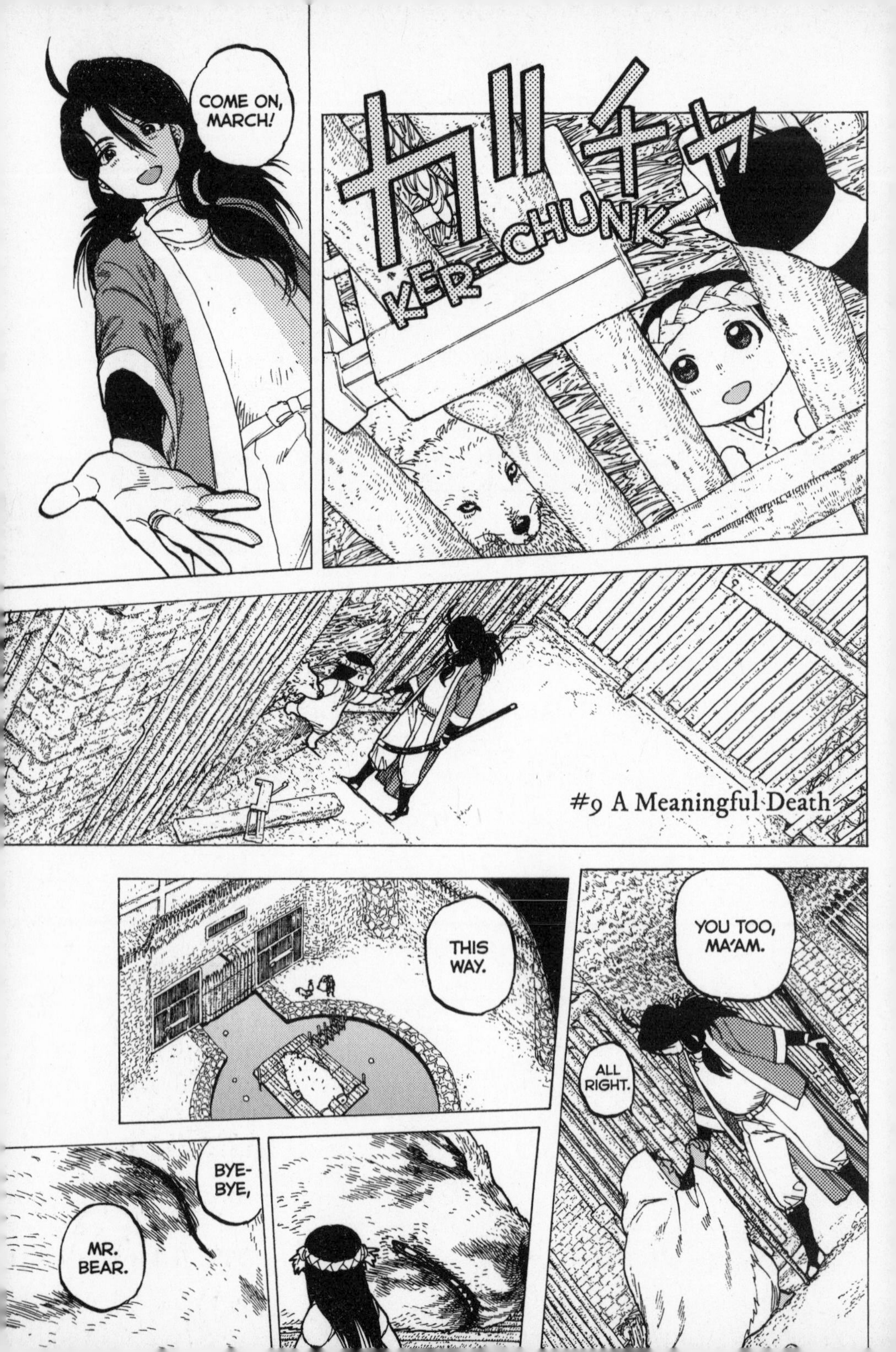
KER-CHUNK
COME ON, MARCH!
#9 A Meaningful Death
YOU TOO, MA'AM.
ALL RIGHT.
THIS WAY.
BYE-BYE,
MR. BEAR.

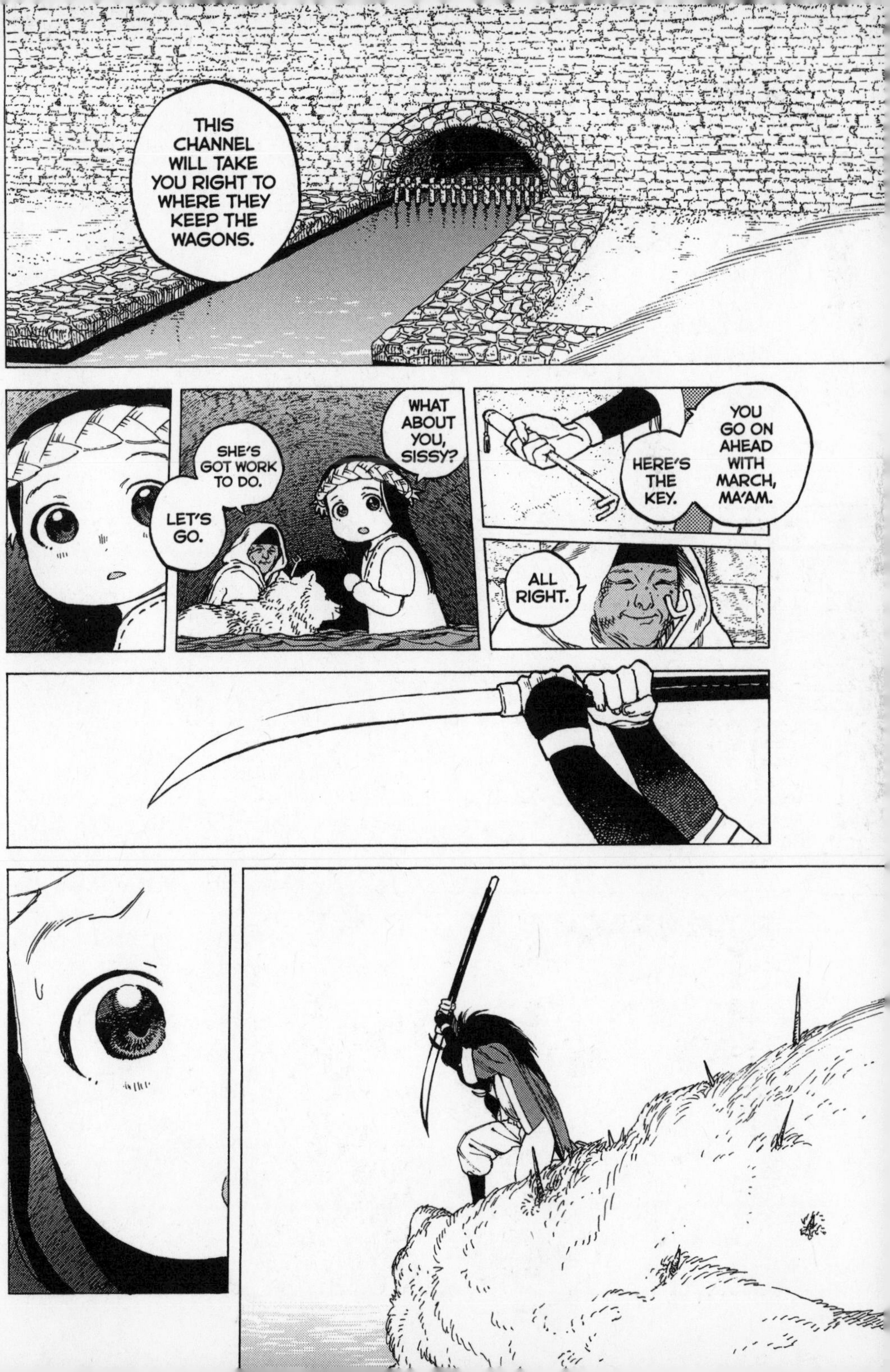
THIS CHANNEL WILL TAKE YOU RIGHT TO WHERE THEY KEEP THE WAGONS.
YOU GO ON AHEAD WITH MARCH, MA'AM.
HERE'S THE KEY.
ALL RIGHT.
WHAT ABOUT YOU, SISSY?
SHE'S GOT WORK TO DO.
LET'S GO.

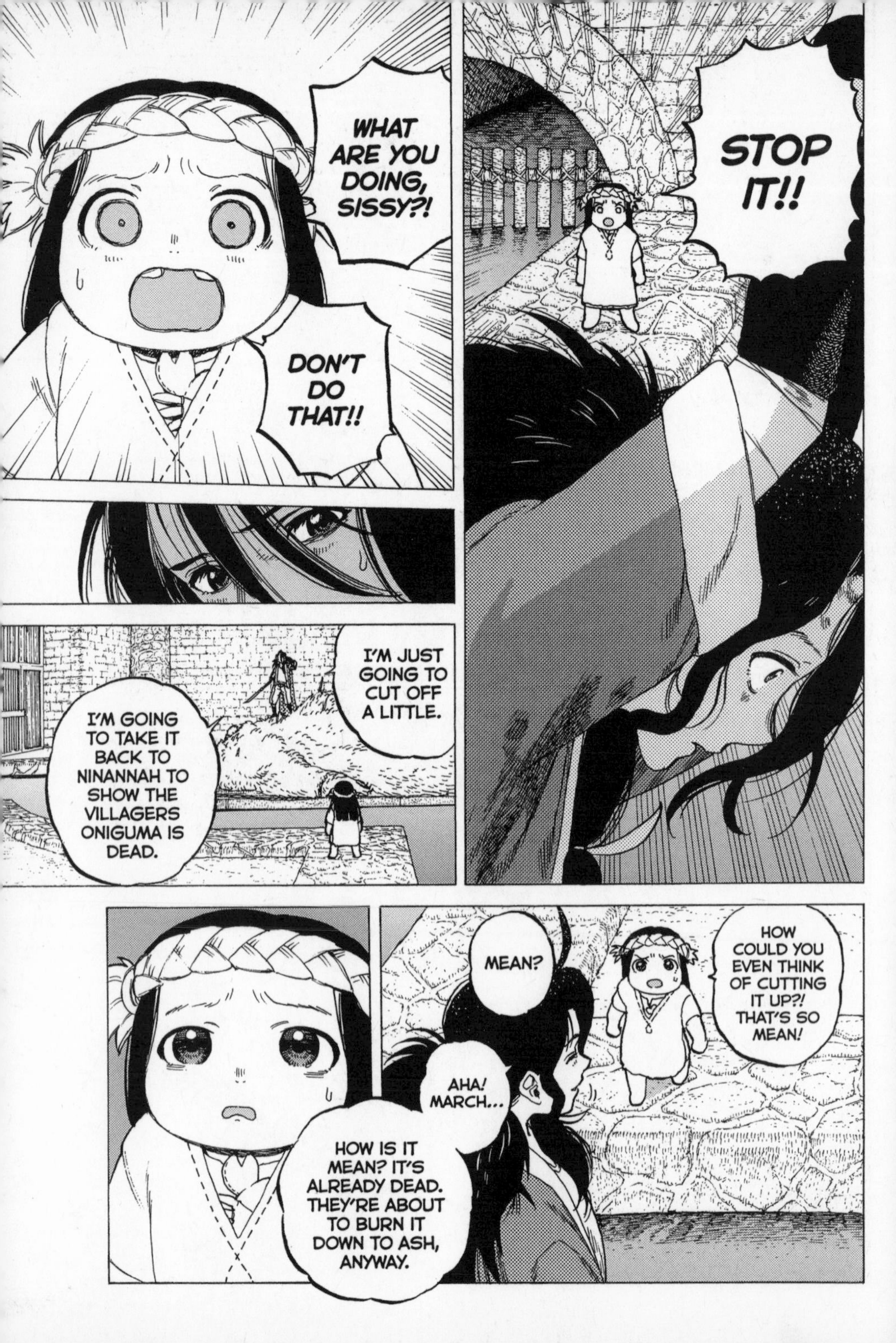
STOP IT!!
WHAT ARE YOU DOING, SISSY?!
DON'T DO THAT!!
I'M JUST GOING TO CUT OFF A LITTLE.
I'M GOING TO TAKE IT BACK TO NINANNAH TO SHOW THE VILLAGERS ONIGUMA IS DEAD.
HOW COULD YOU EVEN THINK OF CUTTING IT UP?! THAT'S SO MEAN!
MEAN?
AHA! MARCH...
HOW IS IT MEAN? IT'S ALREADY DEAD. THEY'RE ABOUT TO BURN IT DOWN TO ASH, ANYWAY.

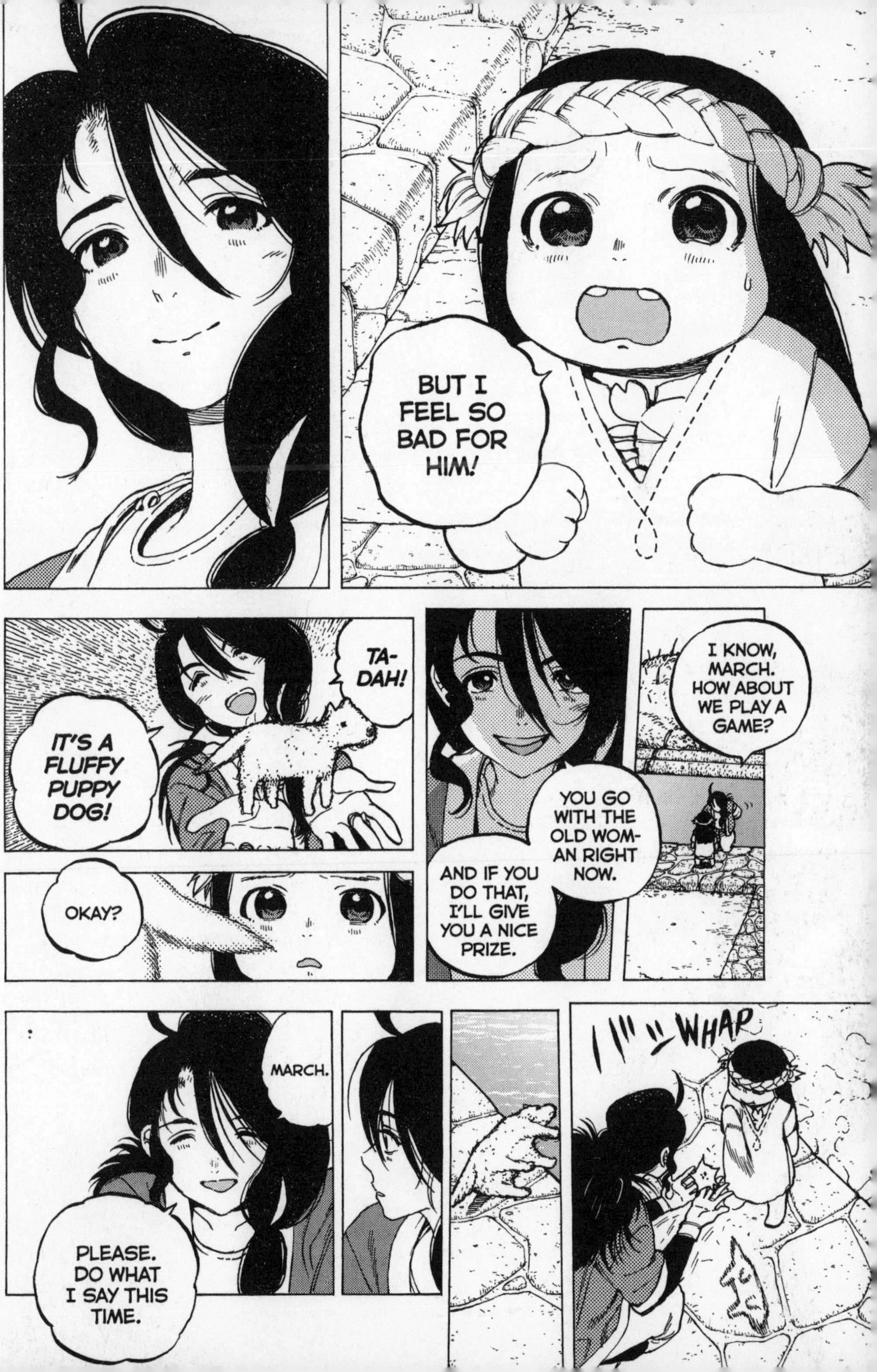

BUT I FEEL SO BAD FOR HIM!
I KNOW, MARCH. HOW ABOUT WE PLAY A GAME?
YOU GO WITH THE OLD WOM-AN RIGHT NOW.
AND IF YOU DO THAT, I'LL GIVE YOU A NICE PRIZE.
TA-DAH!
IT'S A FLUFFY PUPPY DOG!
OKAY?
WHAP
MARCH.
PLEASE. DO WHAT I SAY THIS TIME.

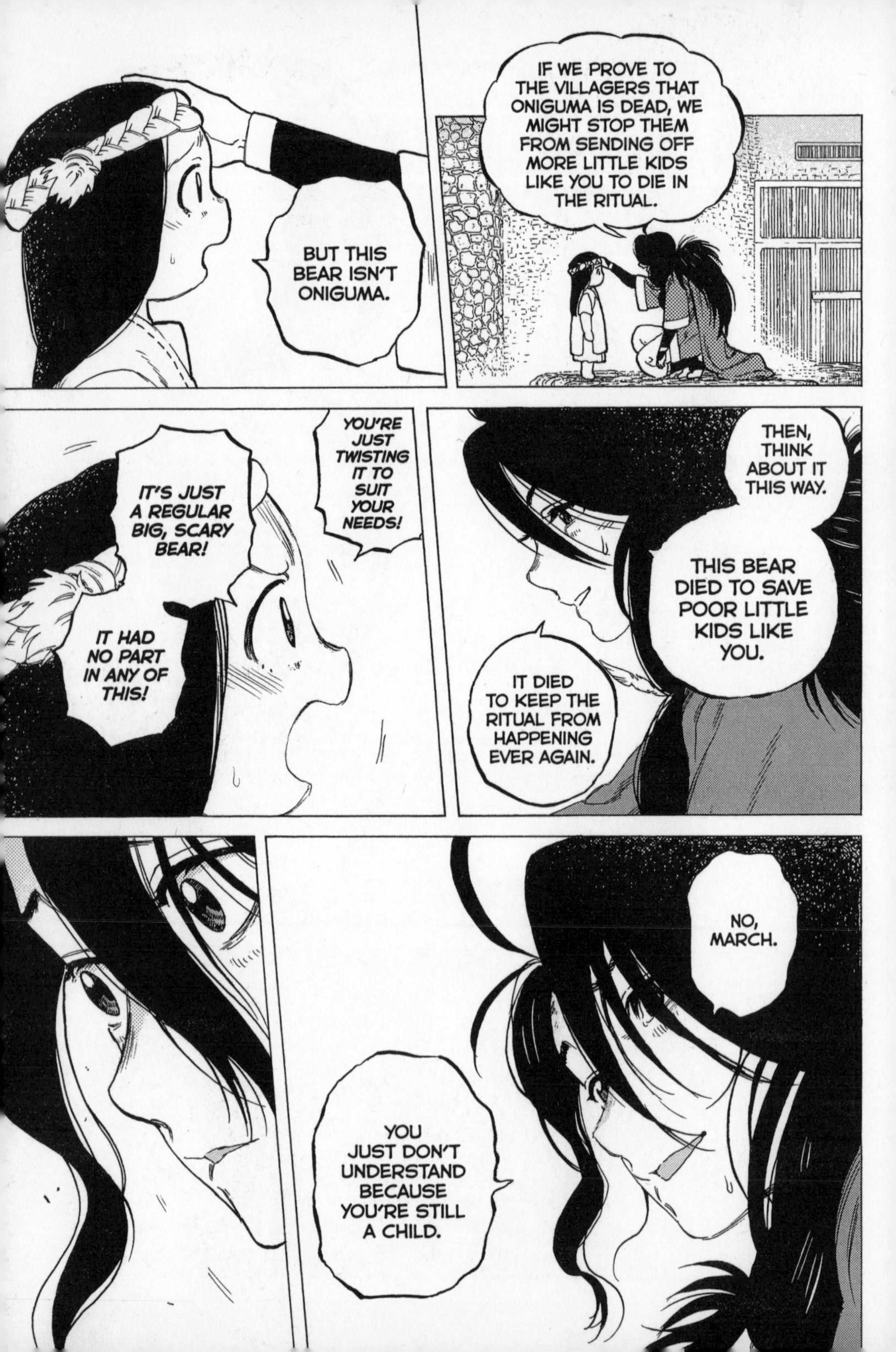

IF WE PROVE TO THE VILLAGERS THAT ONIGUMA IS DEAD, WE MIGHT STOP THEM FROM SENDING OFF MORE LITTLE KIDS LIKE YOU TO DIE IN THE RITUAL.
BUT THIS BEAR ISN'T ONIGUMA.
THEN, THINK ABOUT IT THIS WAY.
THIS BEAR DIED TO SAVE POOR LITTLE KIDS LIKE YOU.
IT DIED TO KEEP THE RITUAL FROM HAPPENING EVER AGAIN.
YOU'RE JUST TWISTING IT TO SUIT YOUR NEEDS!
IT'S JUST A REGULAR BIG, SCARY BEAR!
IT HAD NO PART IN ANY OF THIS!
NO, MARCH.
YOU JUST DON'T UNDERSTAND BECAUSE YOU'RE STILL A CHILD.

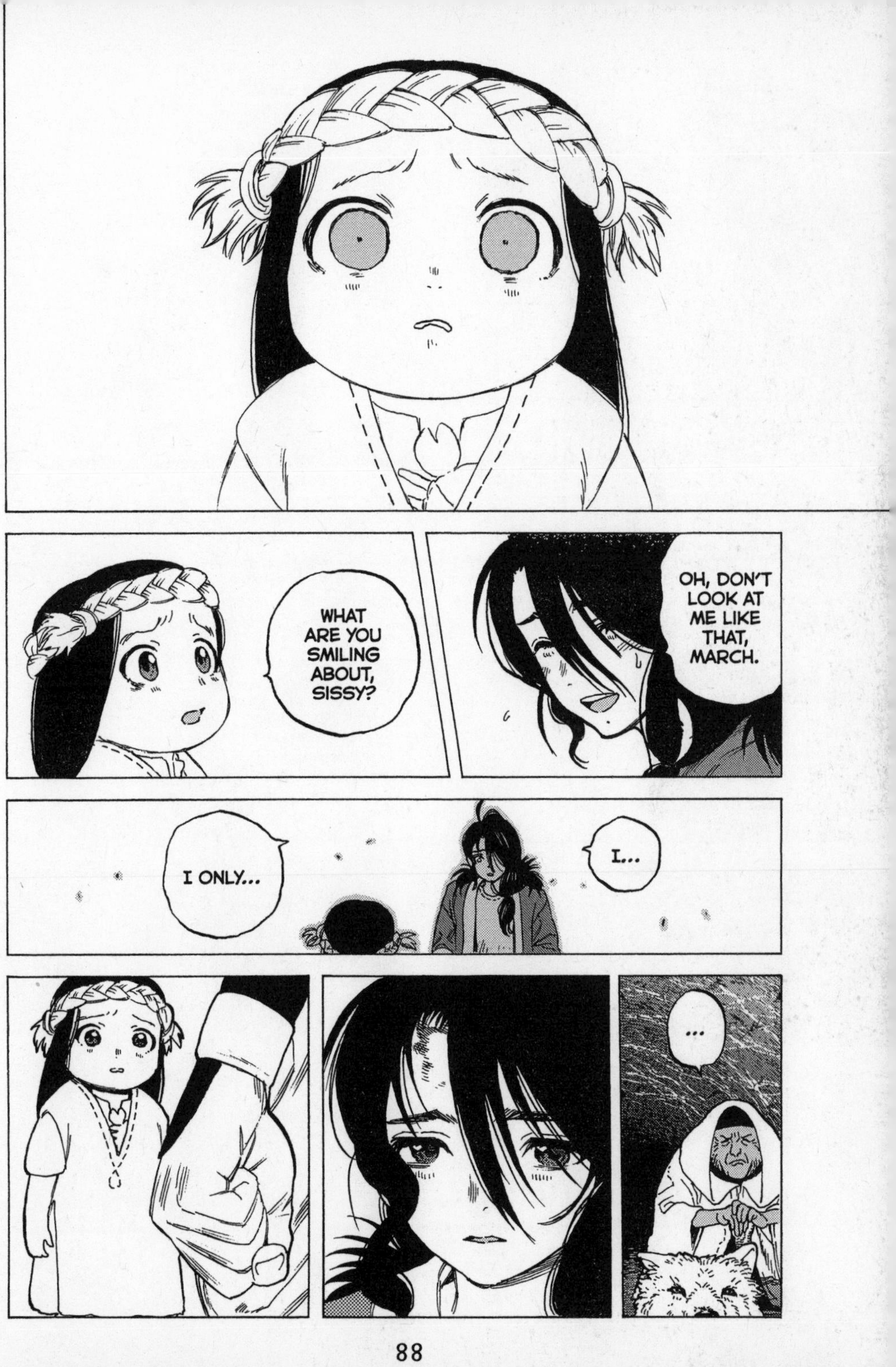
OH, DON'T LOOK AT ME LIKE THAT, MARCH.
WHAT ARE YOU SMILING ABOUT, SISSY?
I...
I ONLY...
...

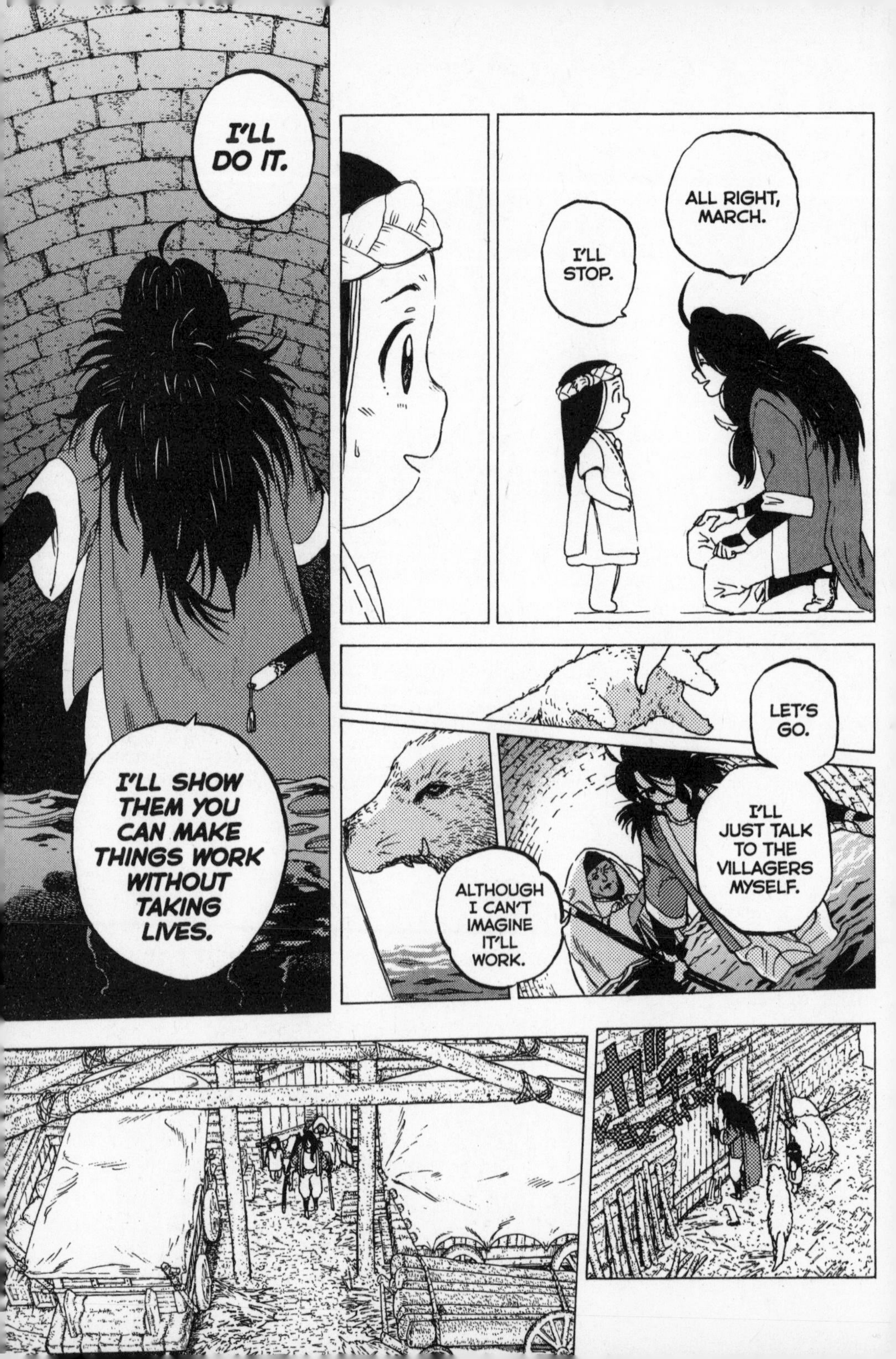
ALL RIGHT, MARCH.
I'LL STOP.
LET'S GO.
I'LL JUST TALK TO THE VILLAGERS MYSELF.
ALTHOUGH I CAN'T IMAGINE IT'LL WORK.
I'LL DO IT.
I'LL SHOW THEM YOU CAN MAKE THINGS WORK WITHOUT TAKING LIVES.

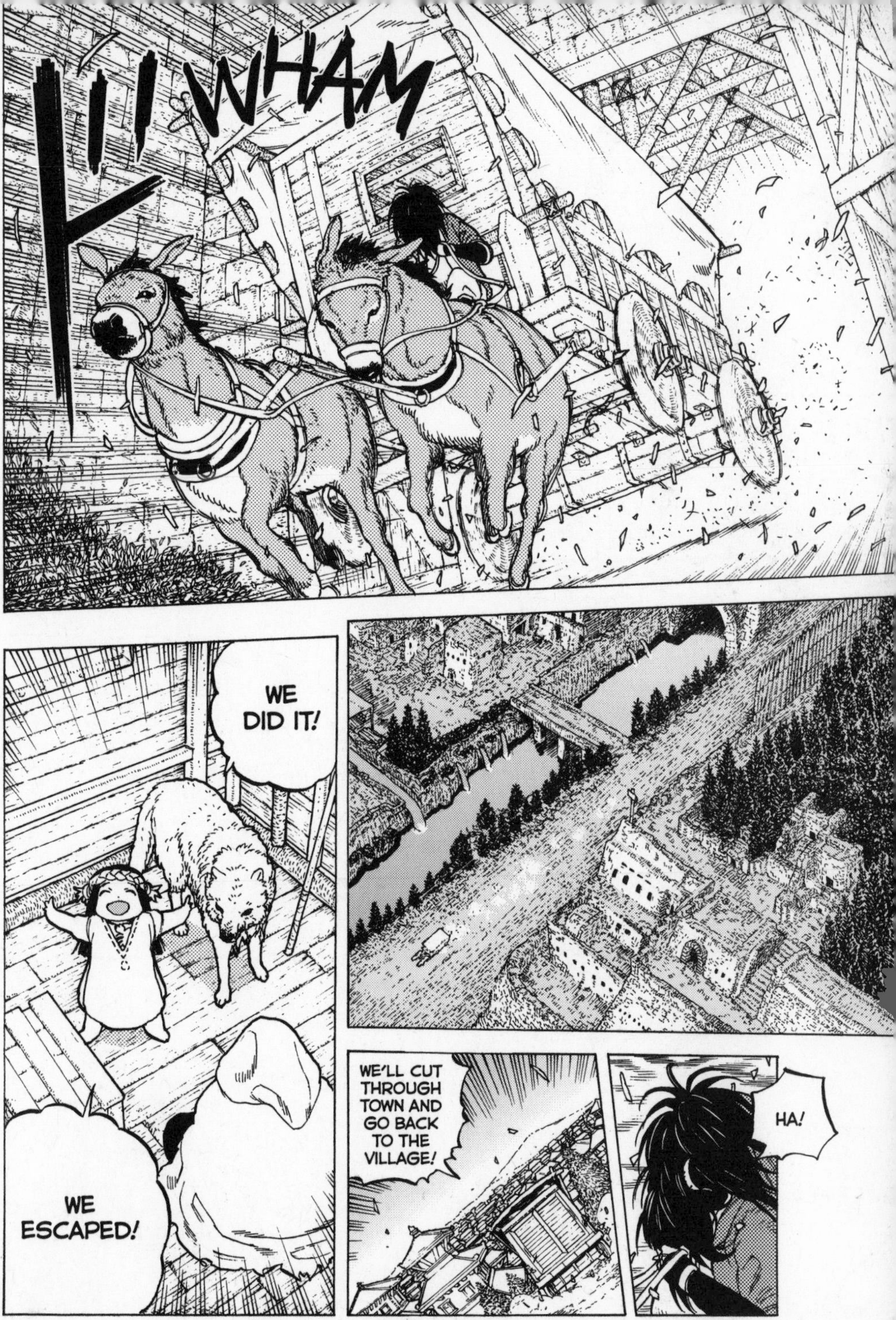
WHAM
HA!
WE'LL CUT THROUGH TOWN AND GO BACK TO THE VILLAGE!
WE DID IT!
WE ESCAPED!

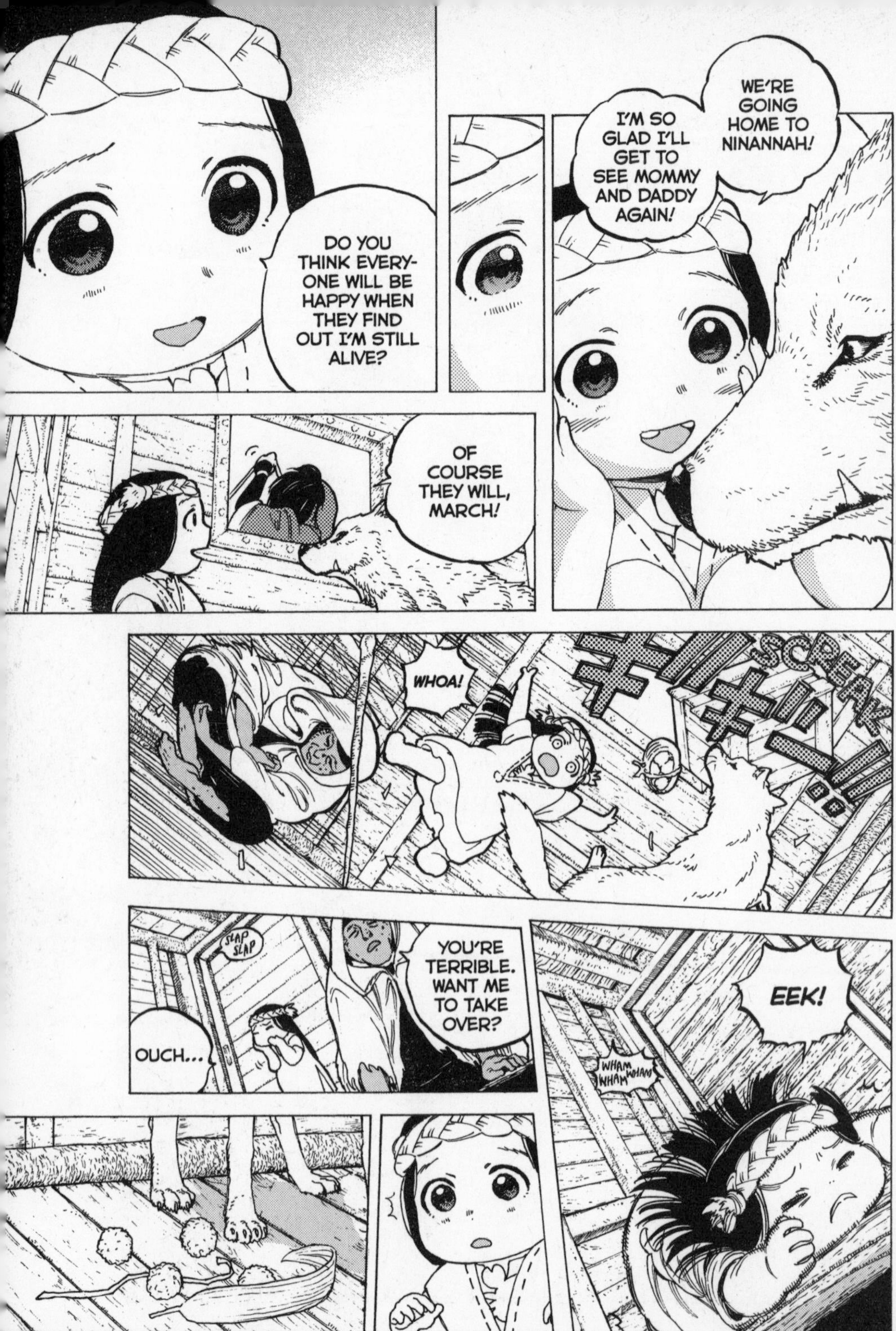
WE'RE GOING HOME TO NINANNAH!
I'M SO GLAD I'LL GET TO SEE MOMMY AND DADDY AGAIN!
DO YOU THINK EVERY-ONE WILL BE HAPPY WHEN THEY FIND OUT I'M STILL ALIVE?
OF COURSE THEY WILL, MARCH!
SCREAK
WHOA!
EEK!
WHAM WHAM WHAM
YOU'RE TERRIBLE. WANT ME TO TAKE OVER?
SLAP SLAP
OUCH...

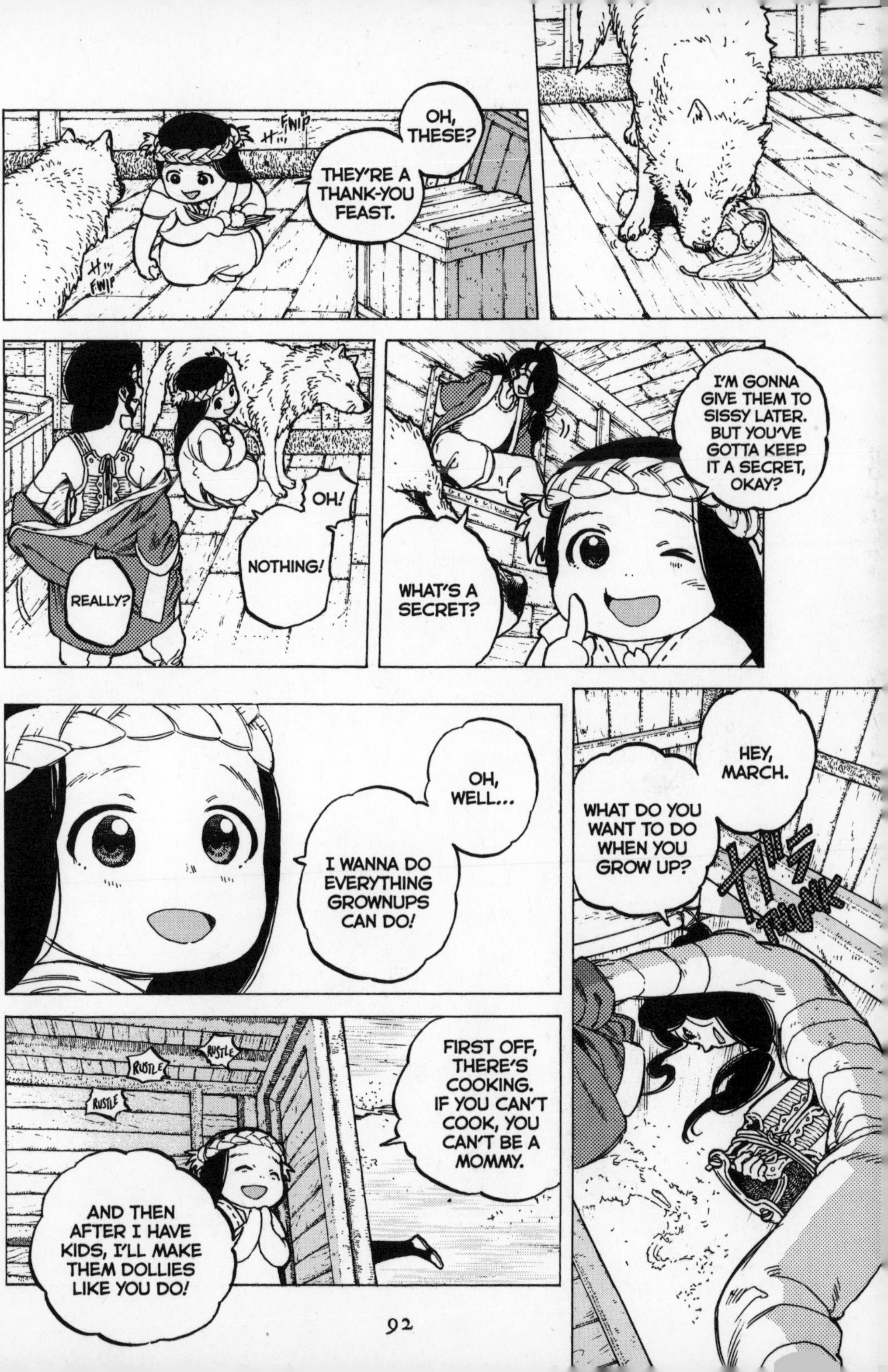
FWIP
OH, THESE?
THEY'RE A THANK-YOU FEAST.
FWIP
I'M GONNA GIVE THEM TO SISSY LATER. BUT YOU'VE GOTTA KEEP IT A SECRET, OKAY?
WHAT'S A SECRET?
OH!
NOTHING!
REALLY?
HEY, MARCH.
WHAT DO YOU WANT TO DO WHEN YOU GROW UP?
THUNK
OH, WELL...
I WANNA DO EVERYTHING GROWNUPS CAN DO!
RUSTLE
RUSTLE
RUSTLE
FIRST OFF, THERE'S COOKING. IF YOU CAN'T COOK, YOU CAN'T BE A MOMMY.
AND THEN AFTER I HAVE KIDS, I'LL MAKE THEM DOLLIES LIKE YOU DO!

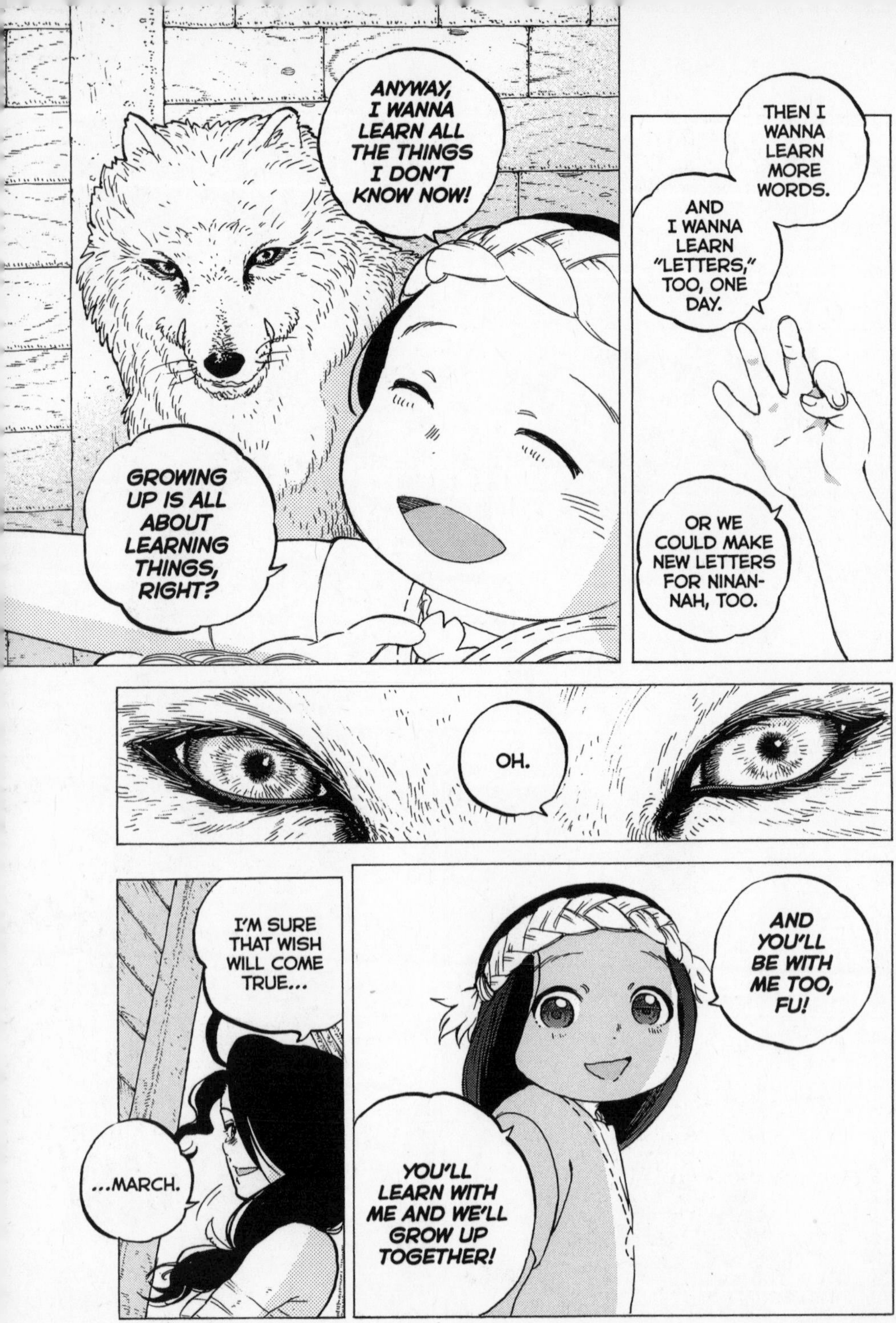
THEN I WANNA LEARN MORE WORDS.
AND I WANNA LEARN "LETTERS," TOO, ONE DAY.
OR WE COULD MAKE NEW LETTERS FOR NINAN-NAH, TOO.
ANYWAY, I WANNA LEARN ALL THE THINGS I DON'T KNOW NOW!
GROWING UP IS ALL ABOUT LEARNING THINGS, RIGHT?
OH.
AND YOU'LL BE WITH ME TOO, FU!
YOU'LL LEARN WITH ME AND WE'LL GROW UP TOGETHER!
I'M SURE THAT WISH WILL COME TRUE...
...MARCH.

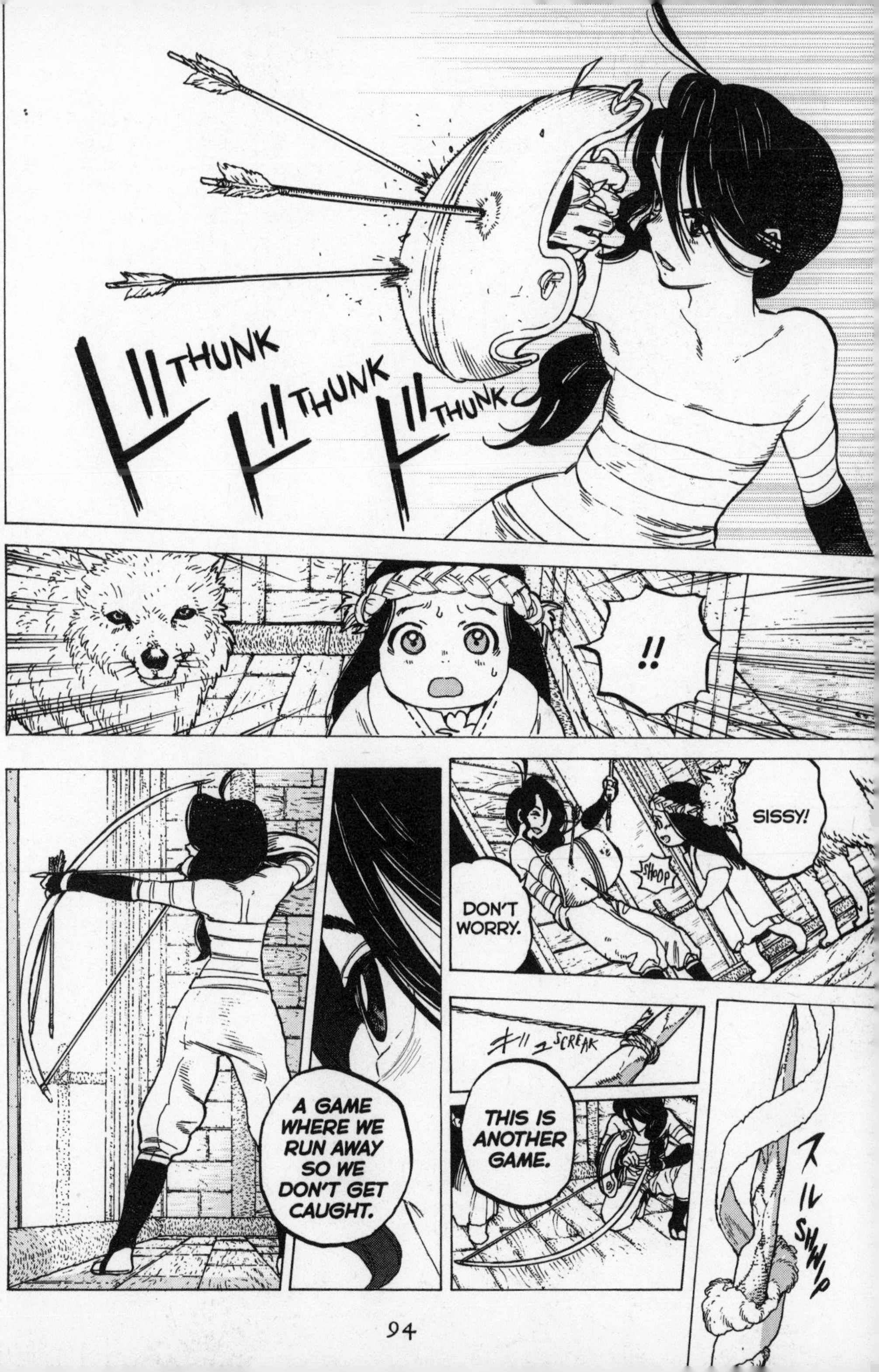
ドッ THUNK
ドッ THUNK
ドッ THUNK
!!
SISSY!
SHOOP
DON'T WORRY.
スル SHWIP
キリュ SCREAK
THIS IS ANOTHER GAME.
A GAME WHERE WE RUN AWAY SO WE DON'T GET CAUGHT.

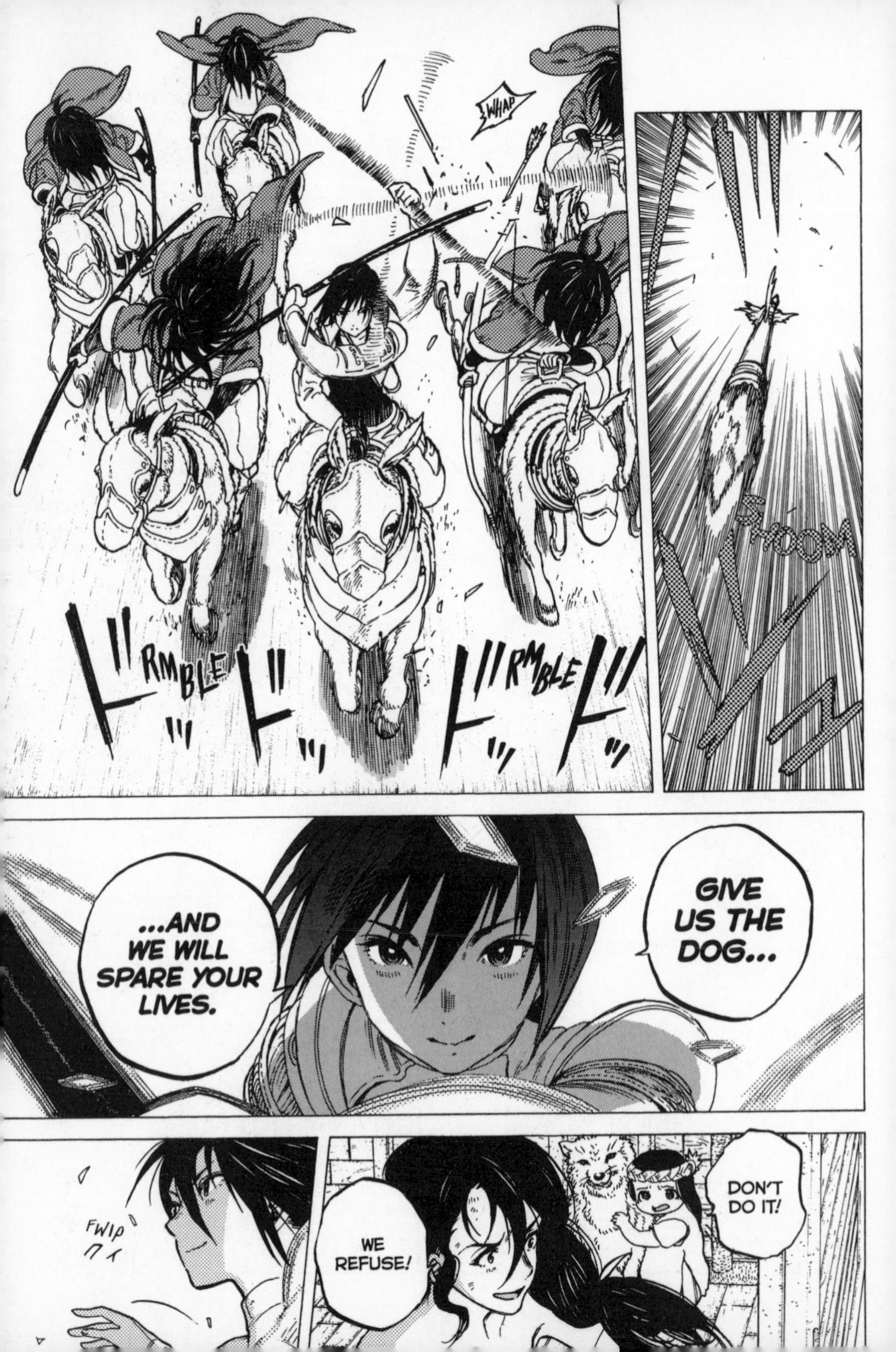
SHOOM
WHAP
RMBLE
RMBLE
GIVE US THE DOG...
...AND WE WILL SPARE YOUR LIVES.
DON'T DO IT!
WE REFUSE!
FWIP

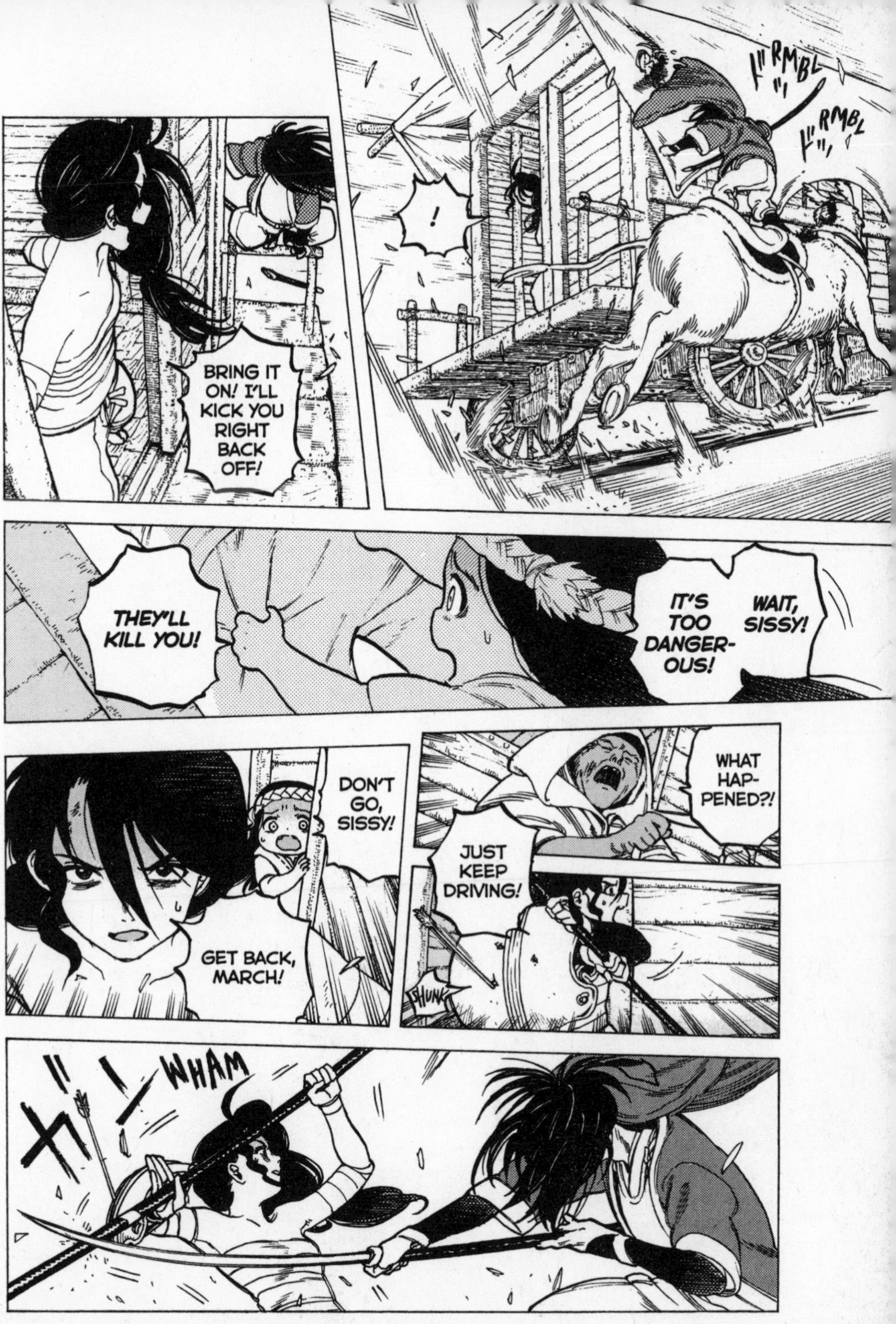
RMBL
RMBL
!
BRING IT ON! I'LL KICK YOU RIGHT BACK OFF!
WAIT, SISSY!
IT'S TOO DANGEROUS!
THEY'LL KILL YOU!
WHAT HAPPENED?!
JUST KEEP DRIVING!
SHUNK
DON'T GO, SISSY!
GET BACK, MARCH!
WHAM

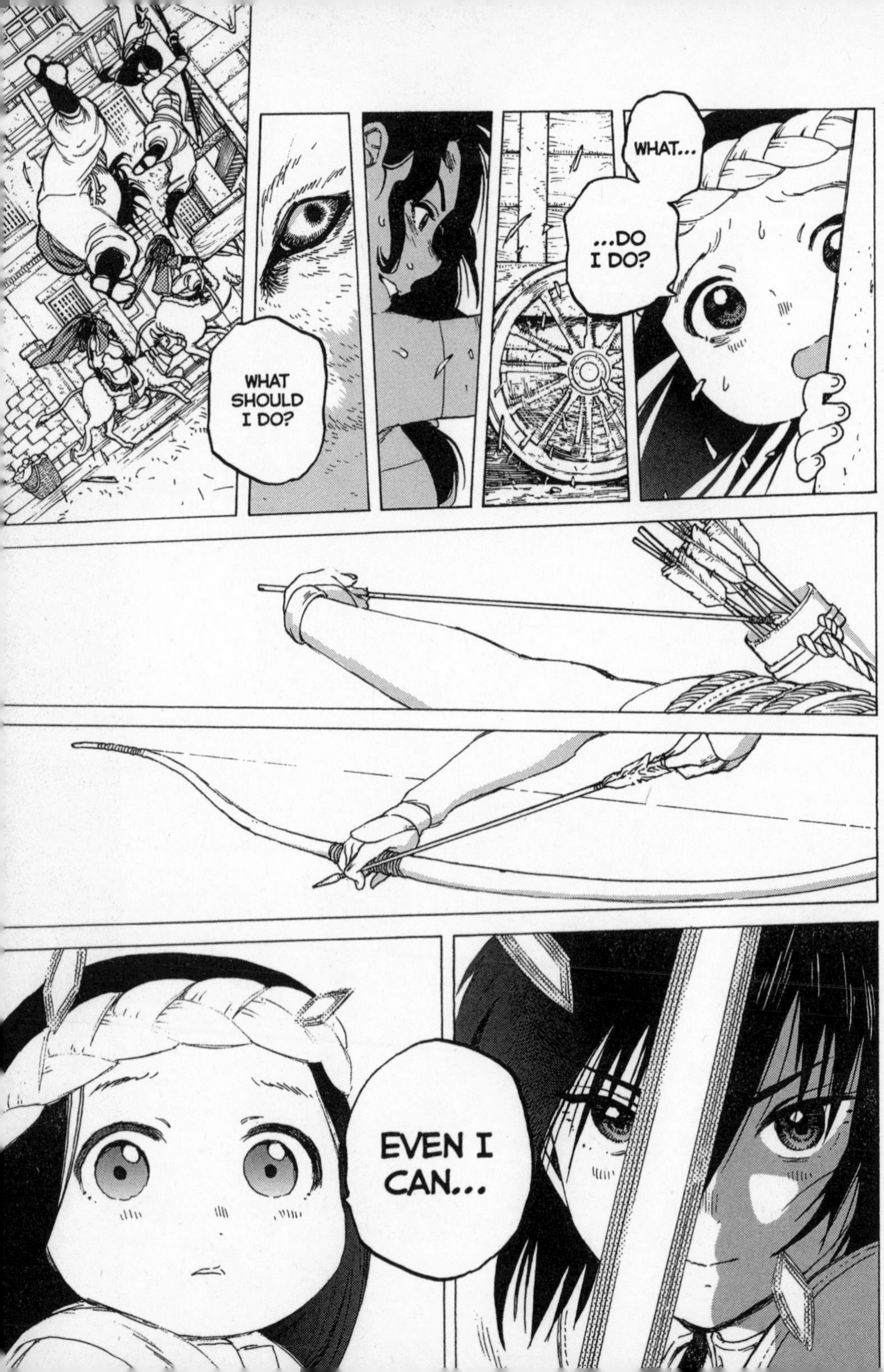
WHAT...
...DO I DO?
WHAT SHOULD I DO?
EVEN I CAN...

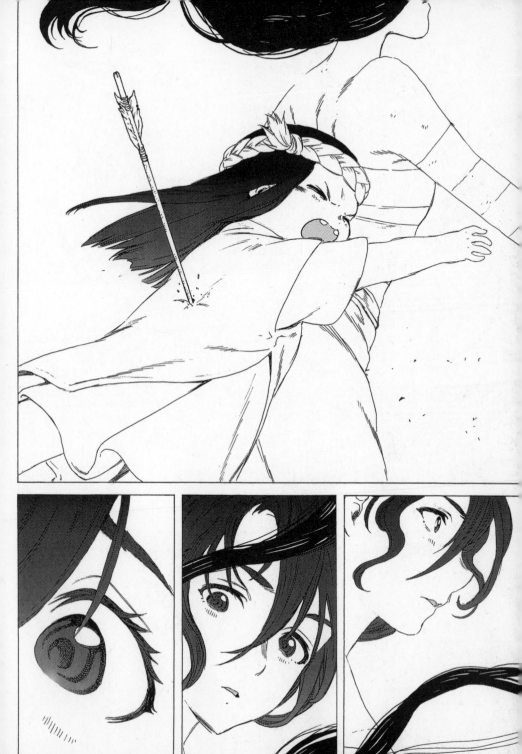

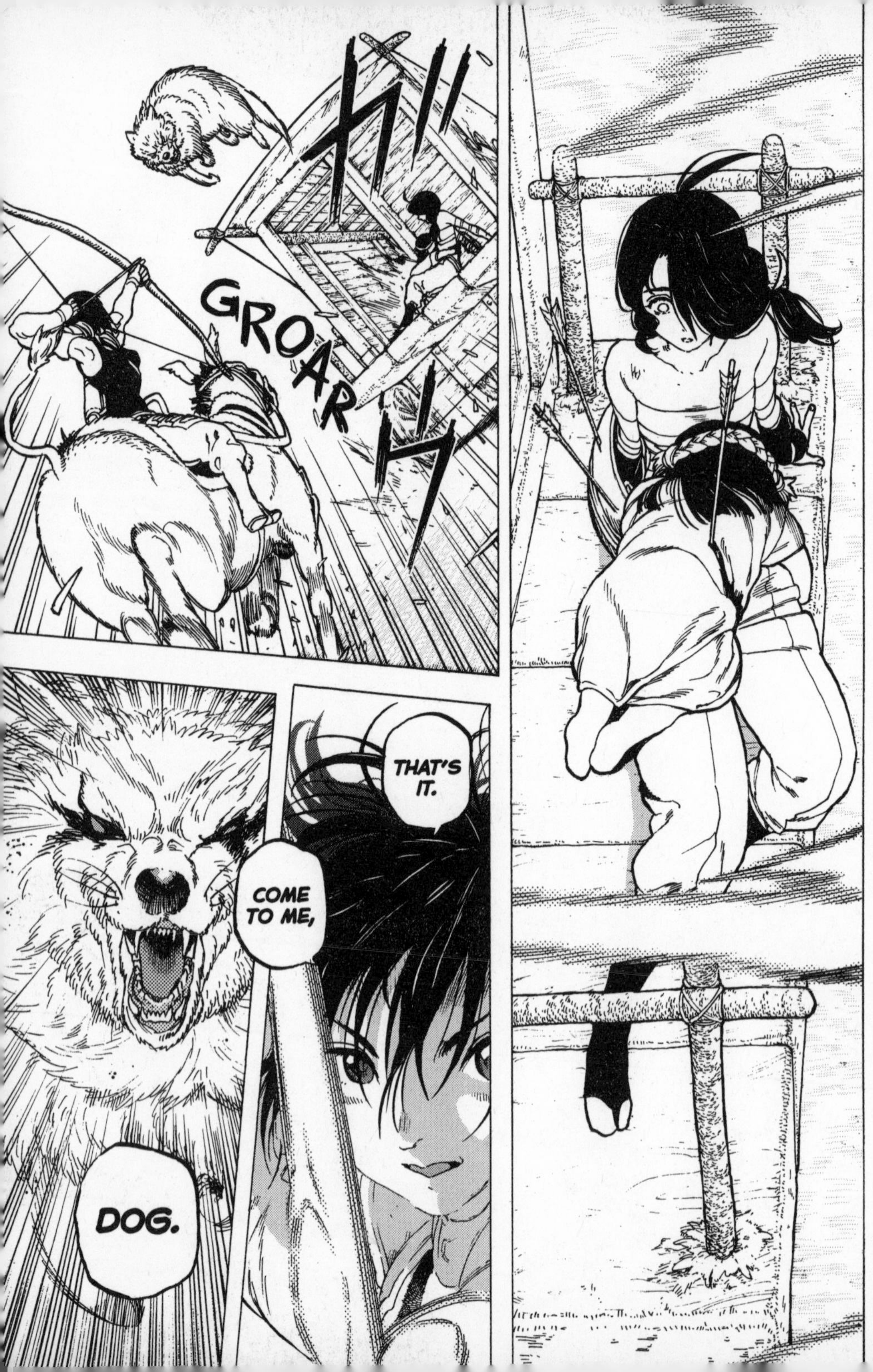
GROAR
THAT'S IT.
COME TO ME,
DOG.

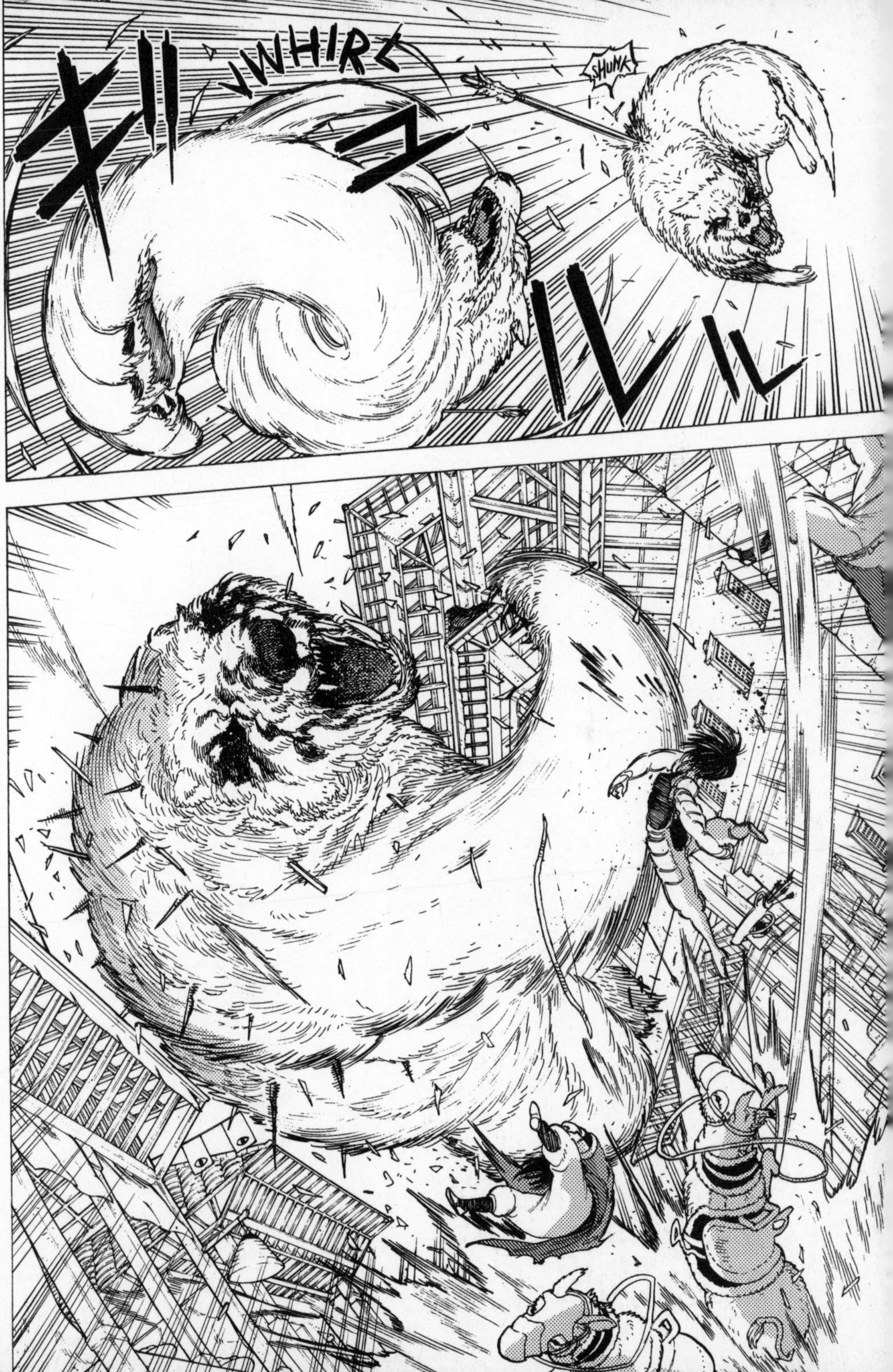
SHUNK
WHIRL

TO YOUR

ETERNITY

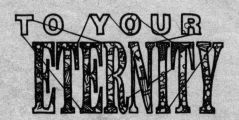

TO YOUR
ETERNITY

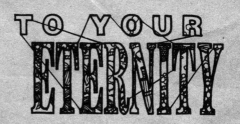

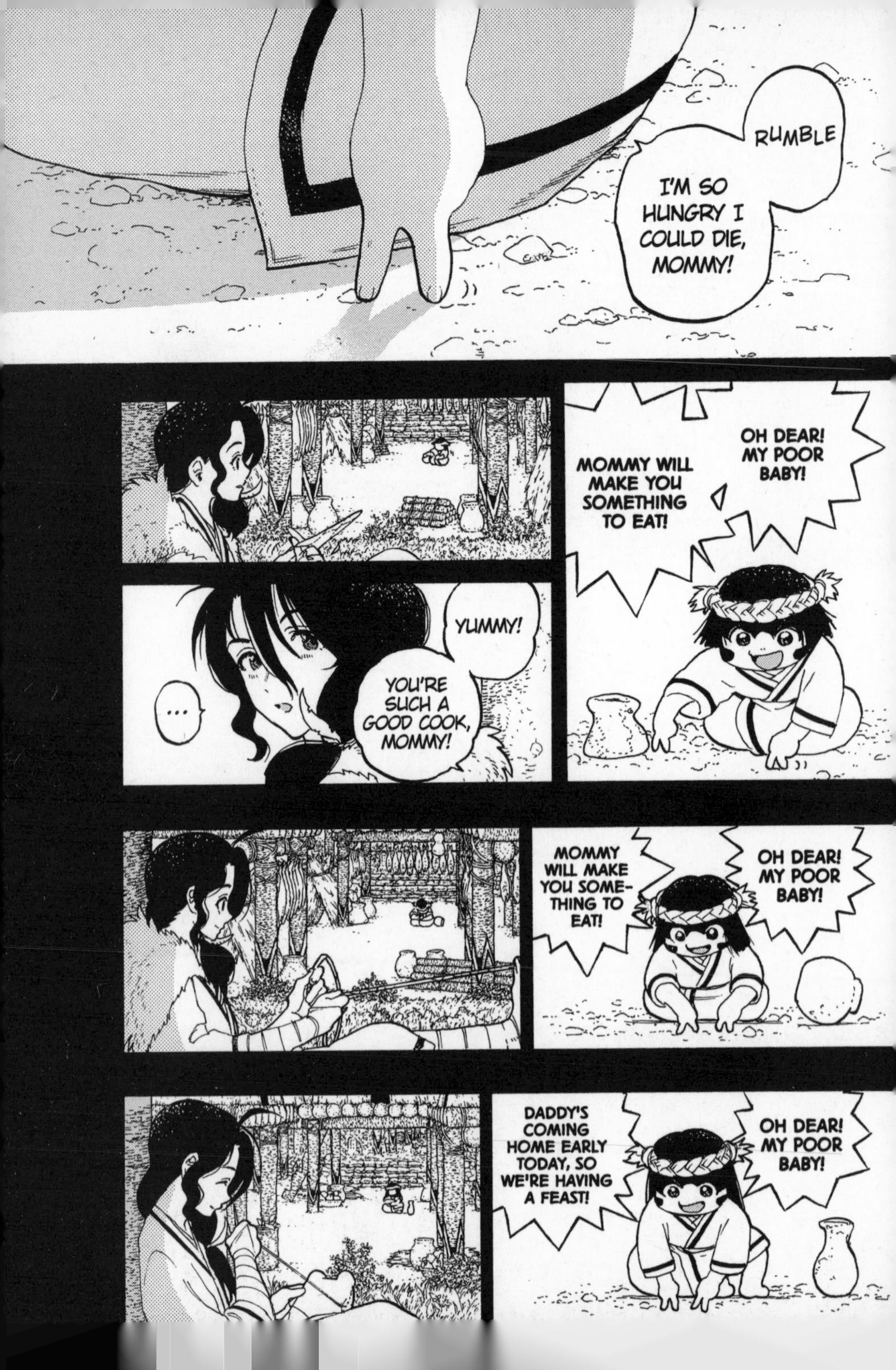
RUMBLE
I'M SO HUNGRY I COULD DIE, MOMMY!
OH DEAR! MY POOR BABY!
MOMMY WILL MAKE YOU SOMETHING TO EAT!
YUMMY!
YOU'RE SUCH A GOOD COOK, MOMMY!
...
OH DEAR! MY POOR BABY!
MOMMY WILL MAKE YOU SOME-THING TO EAT!
OH DEAR! MY POOR BABY!
DADDY'S COMING HOME EARLY TODAY, SO WE'RE HAVING A FEAST!

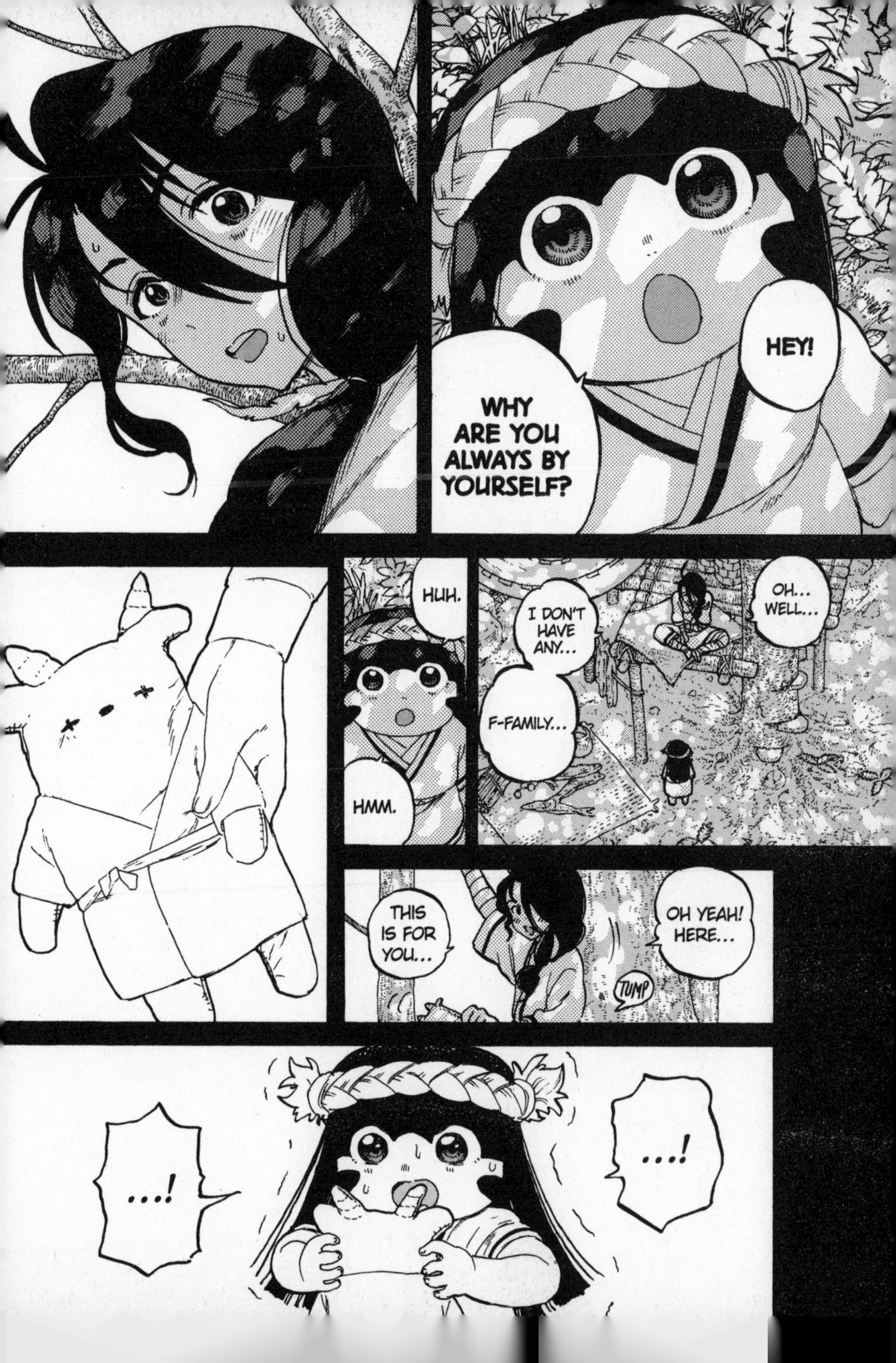
HEY!
WHY ARE YOU ALWAYS BY YOURSELF?
OH... WELL...
I DON'T HAVE ANY...
F-FAMILY...
HUH.
HMM.
OH YEAH! HERE...
THIS IS FOR YOU...
TUMP
...!
...!

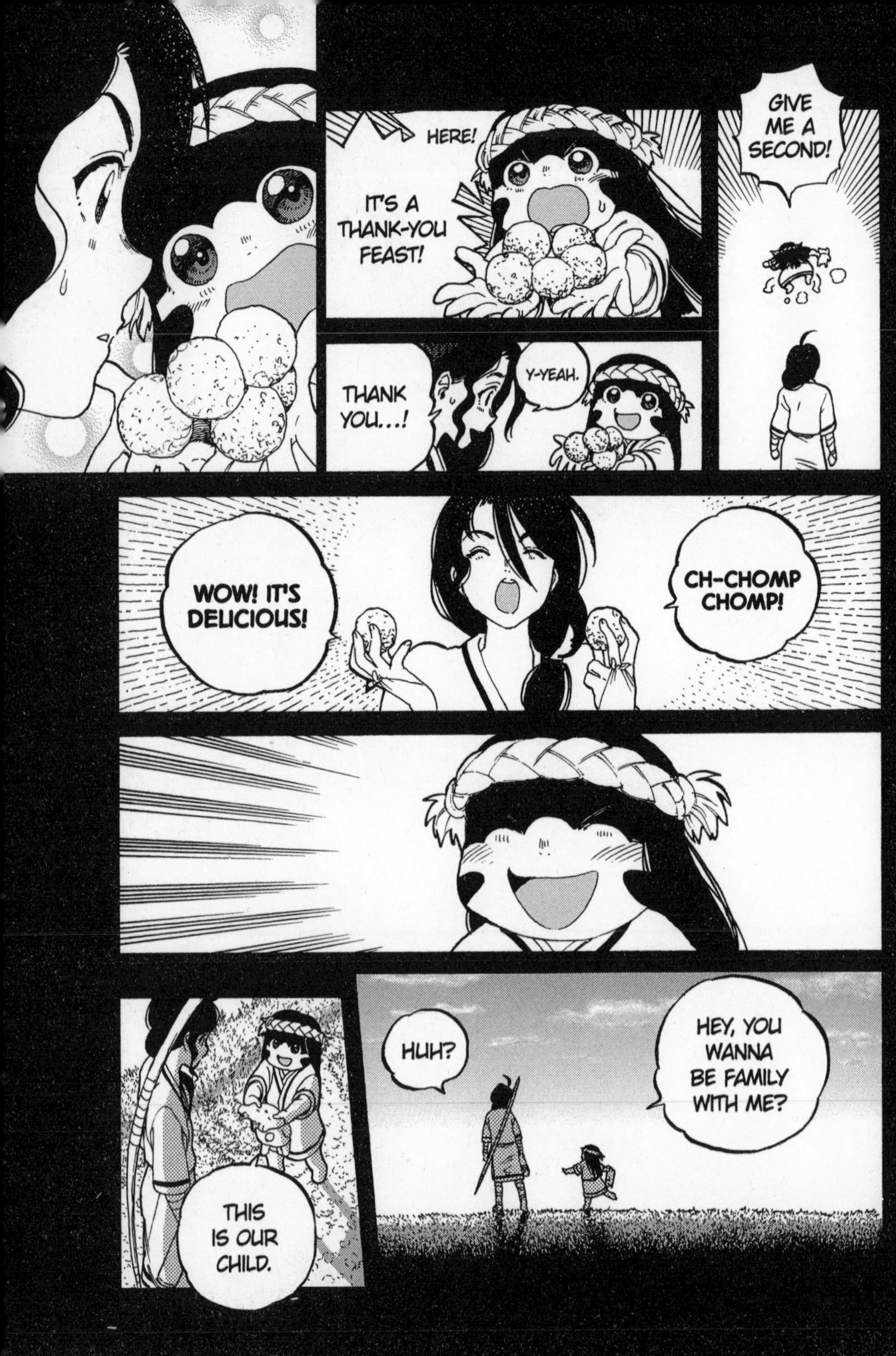
GIVE ME A SECOND!
HERE!
IT'S A THANK-YOU FEAST!
Y-YEAH.
THANK YOU...!
CH-CHOMP CHOMP!
WOW! IT'S DELICIOUS!
HEY, YOU WANNA BE FAMILY WITH ME?
HUH?
THIS IS OUR CHILD.

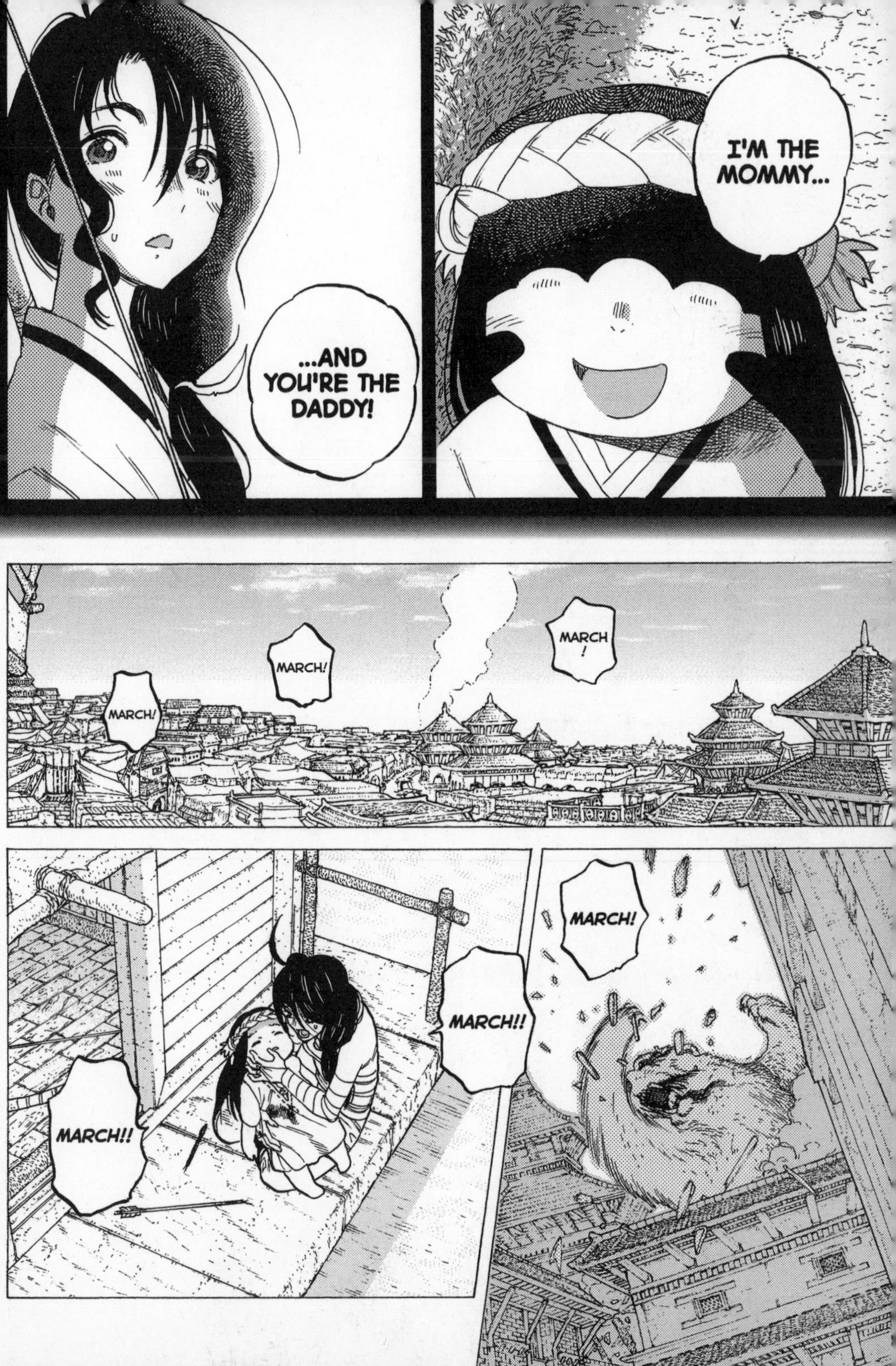
I'M THE MOMMY...
...AND YOU'RE THE DADDY!
MARCH !
MARCH!
MARCH!
MARCH!
MARCH!!
MARCH!!

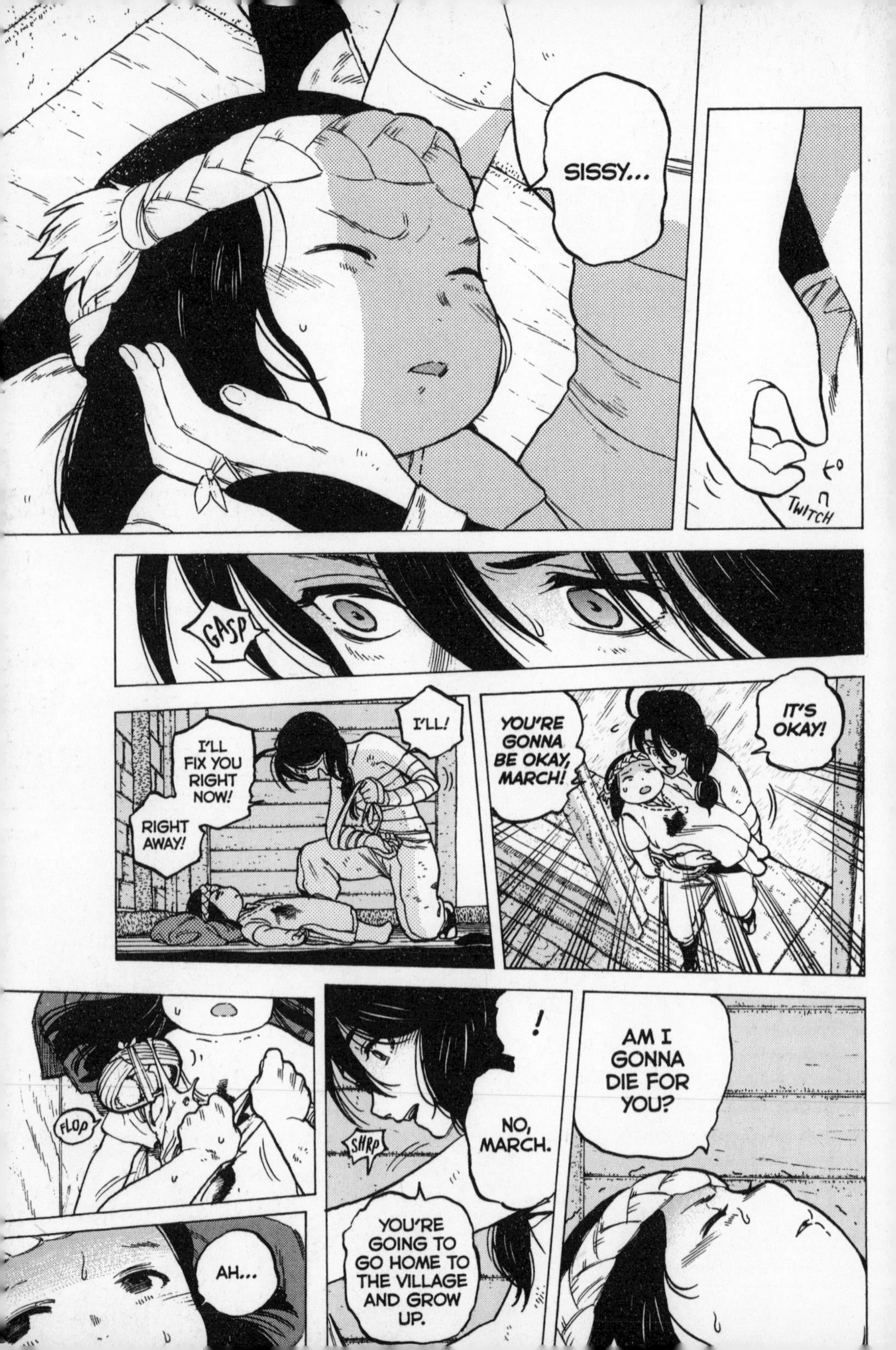
TWITCH
SISSY...
GASP
IT'S OKAY!
YOU'RE GONNA BE OKAY, MARCH!
I'LL!
I'LL FIX YOU RIGHT NOW!
RIGHT AWAY!
AM I GONNA DIE FOR YOU?
!
NO, MARCH.
SHRP
YOU'RE GOING TO GO HOME TO THE VILLAGE AND GROW UP.
FLOP
AH...

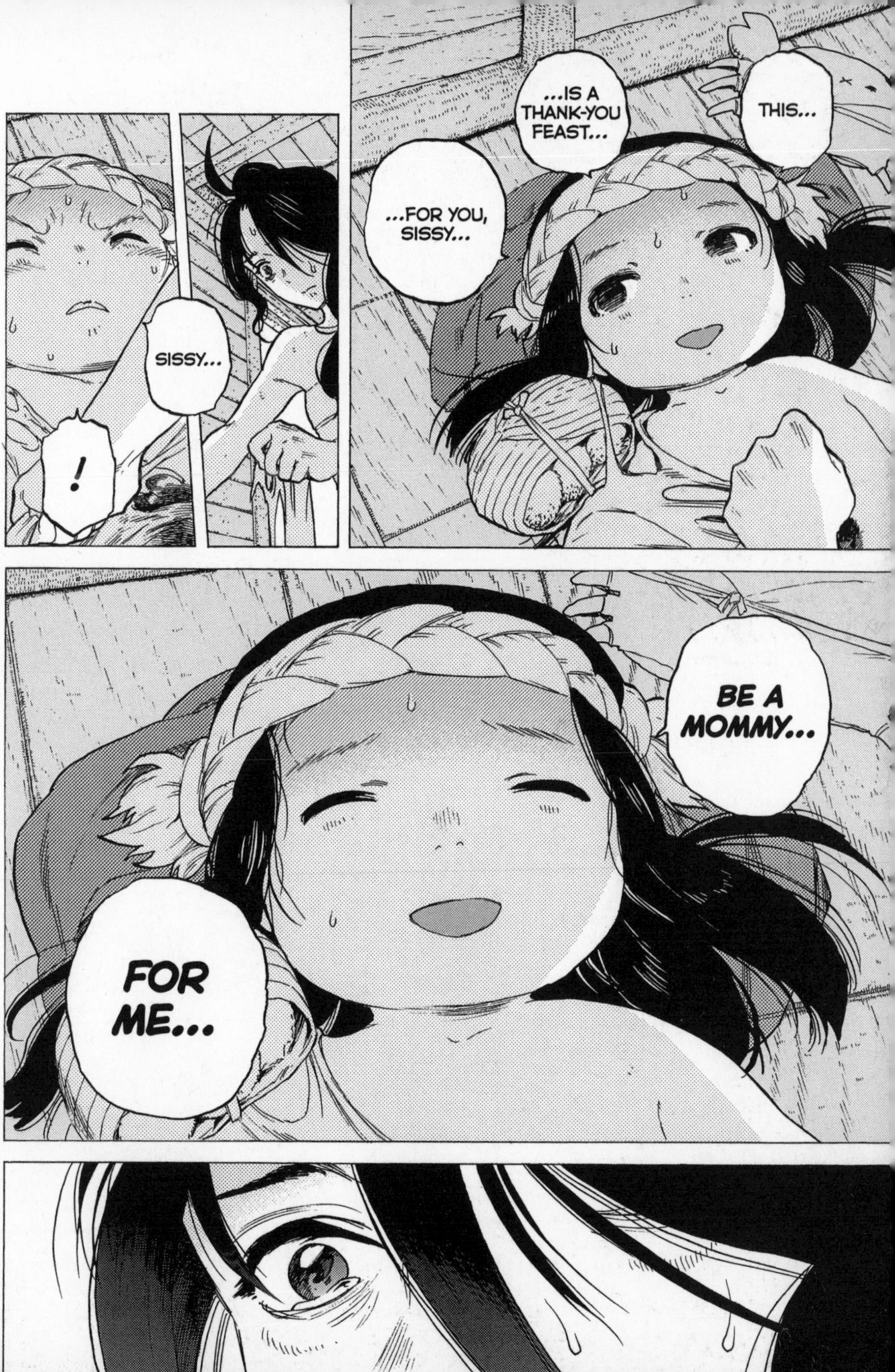
THIS...
...IS A THANK-YOU FEAST...
...FOR YOU, SISSY...
SISSY...
!
BE A MOMMY...
FOR ME...

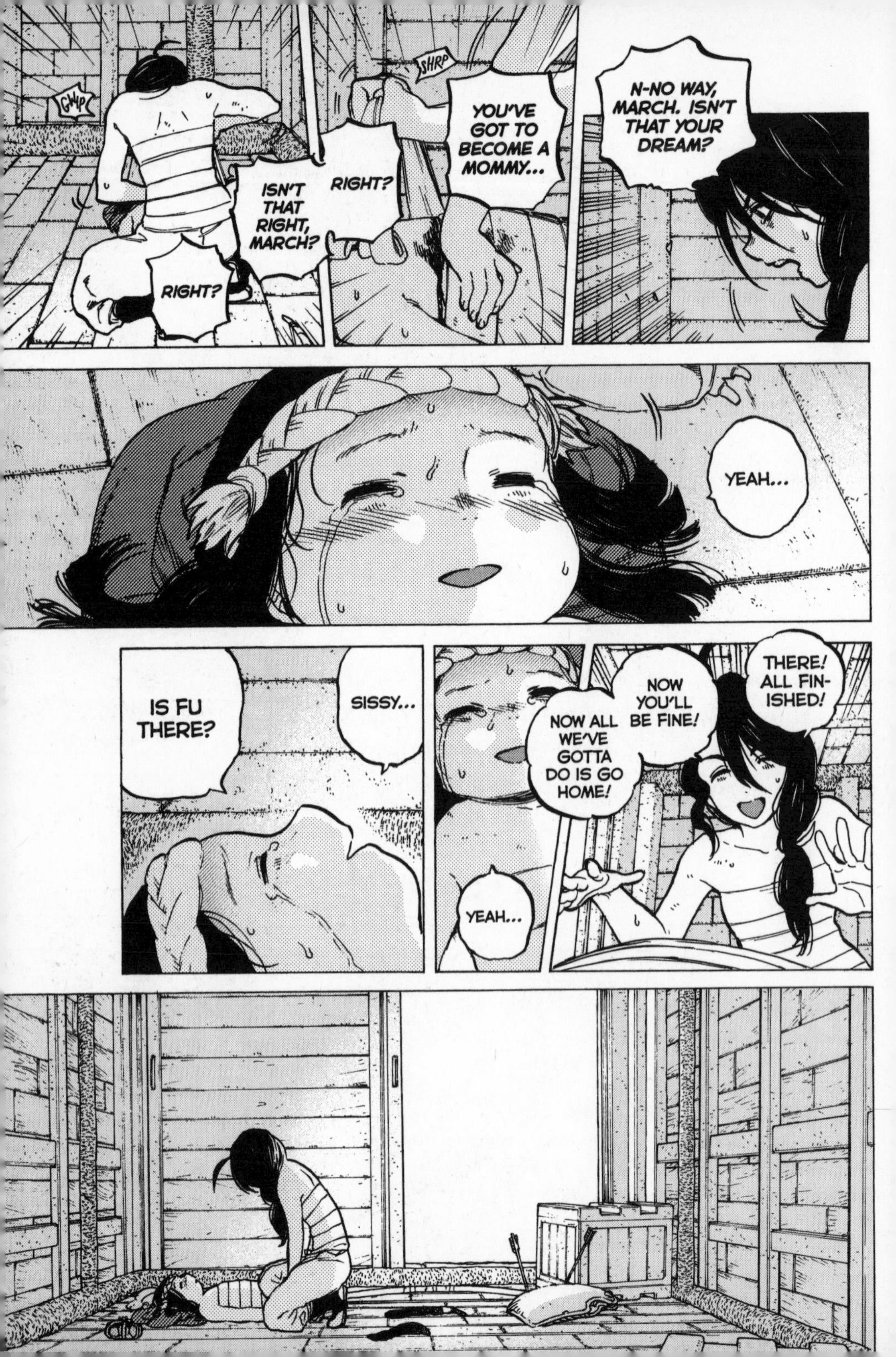
N-NO WAY, MARCH. ISN'T THAT YOUR DREAM?
SHRP
YOU'VE GOT TO BECOME A MOMMY...
RIGHT?
ISN'T THAT RIGHT, MARCH?
GWUP
RIGHT?
YEAH...
THERE! ALL FIN-ISHED!
NOW YOU'LL BE FINE!
NOW ALL WE'VE GOTTA DO IS GO HOME!
YEAH...
SISSY...
IS FU THERE?

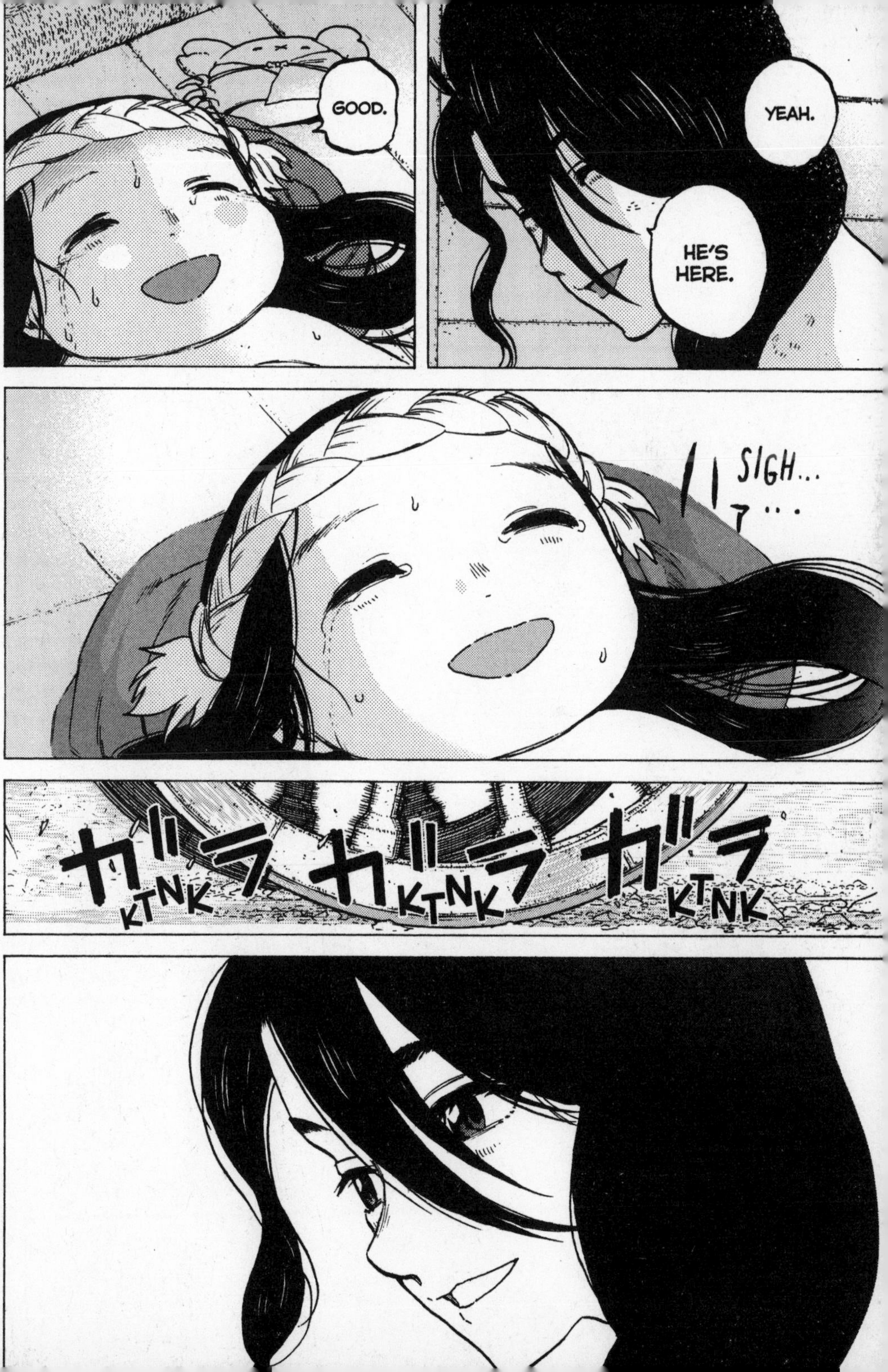
YEAH.
HE'S HERE.
GOOD.
ハア...
SIGH...
ガラガラガラ
KTNK KTNK KTNK

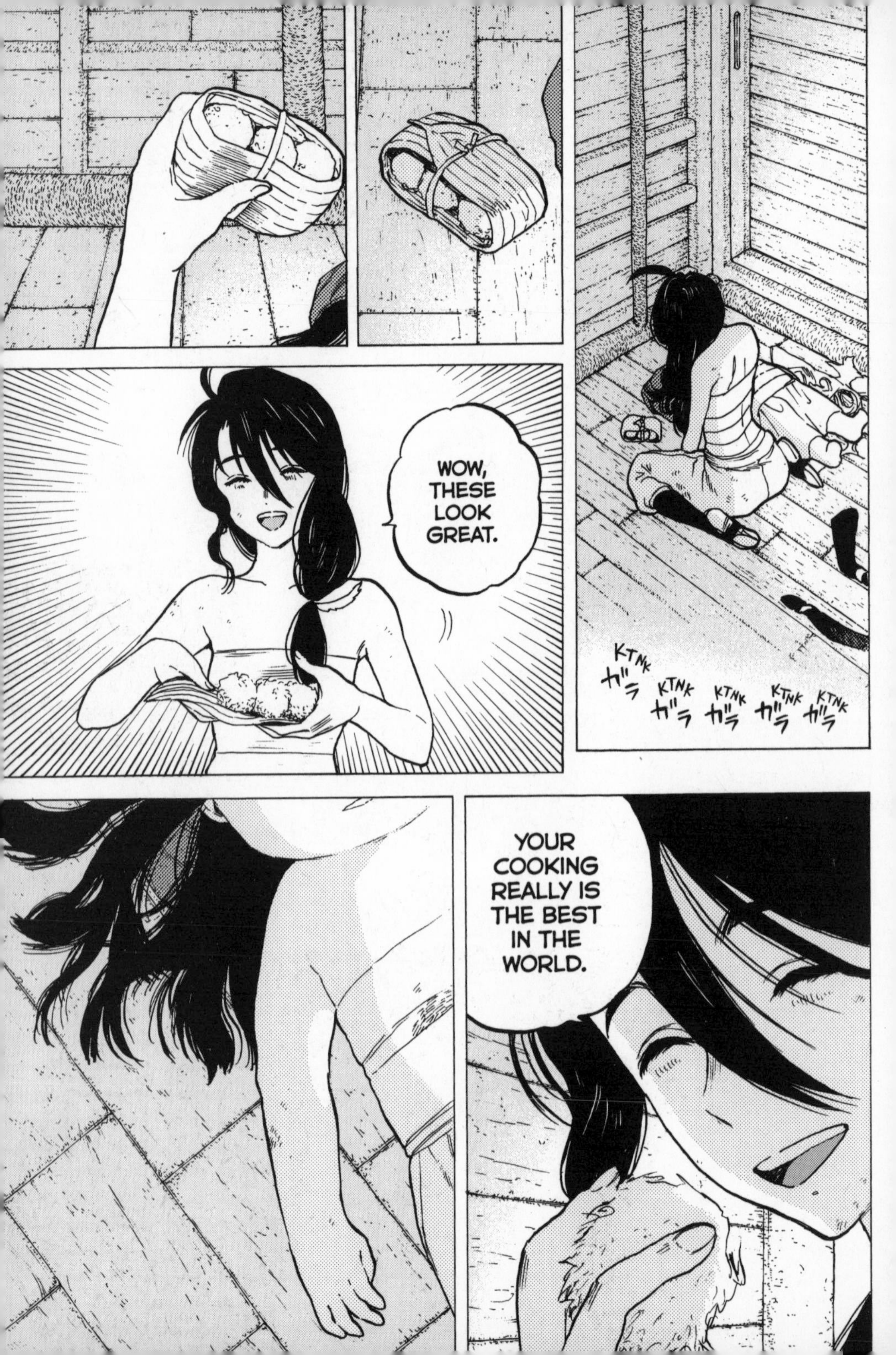
KTNK ガラ
KTNK ガラ
KTNK ガラ
KTNK ガラ
KTNK ガラ
WOW, THESE LOOK GREAT.
YOUR COOKING REALLY IS THE BEST IN THE WORLD.

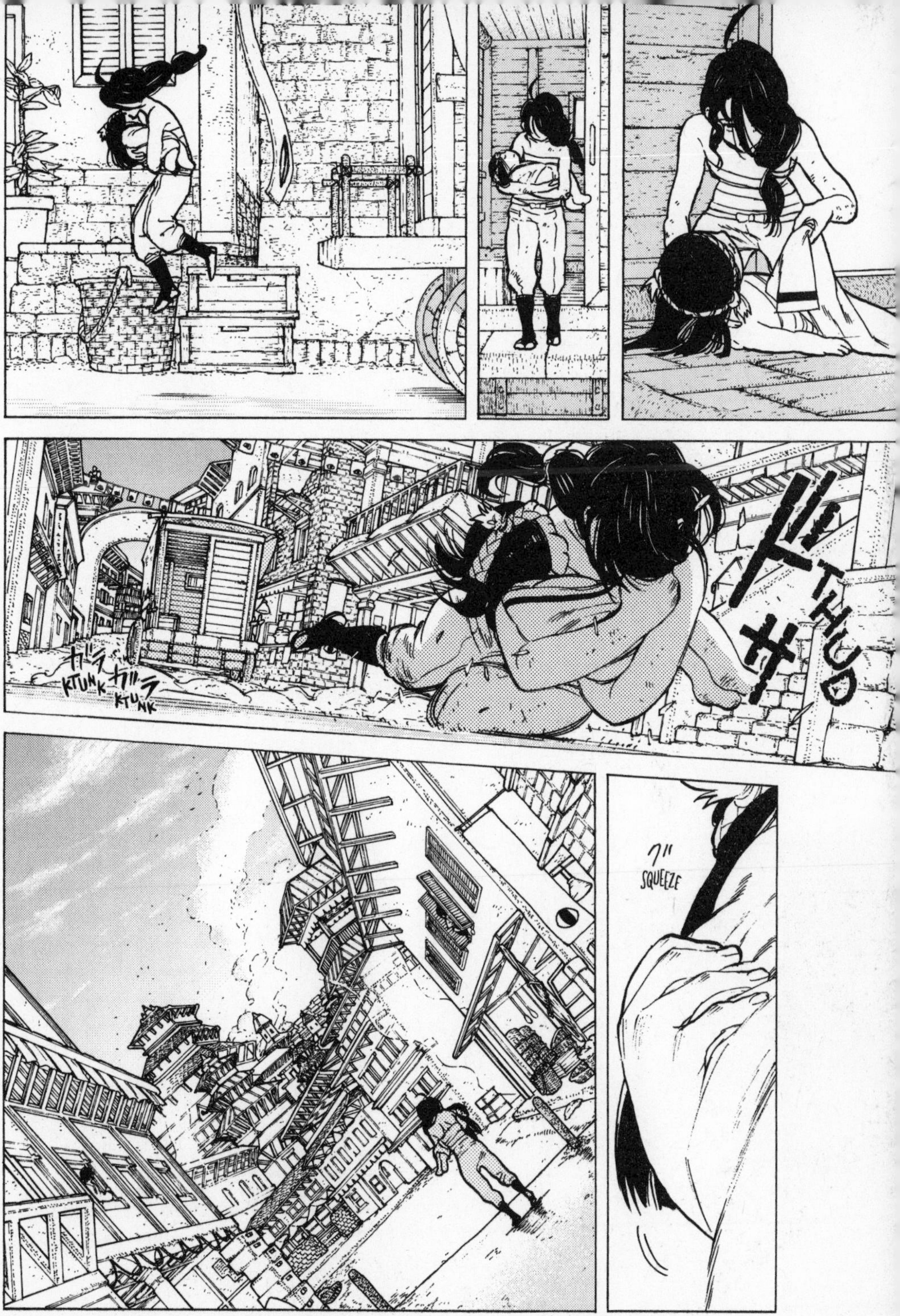
ドサ
THUD
ガラ
KTUNK
ガラ
KTUNK
ワ"
SQUEEZE

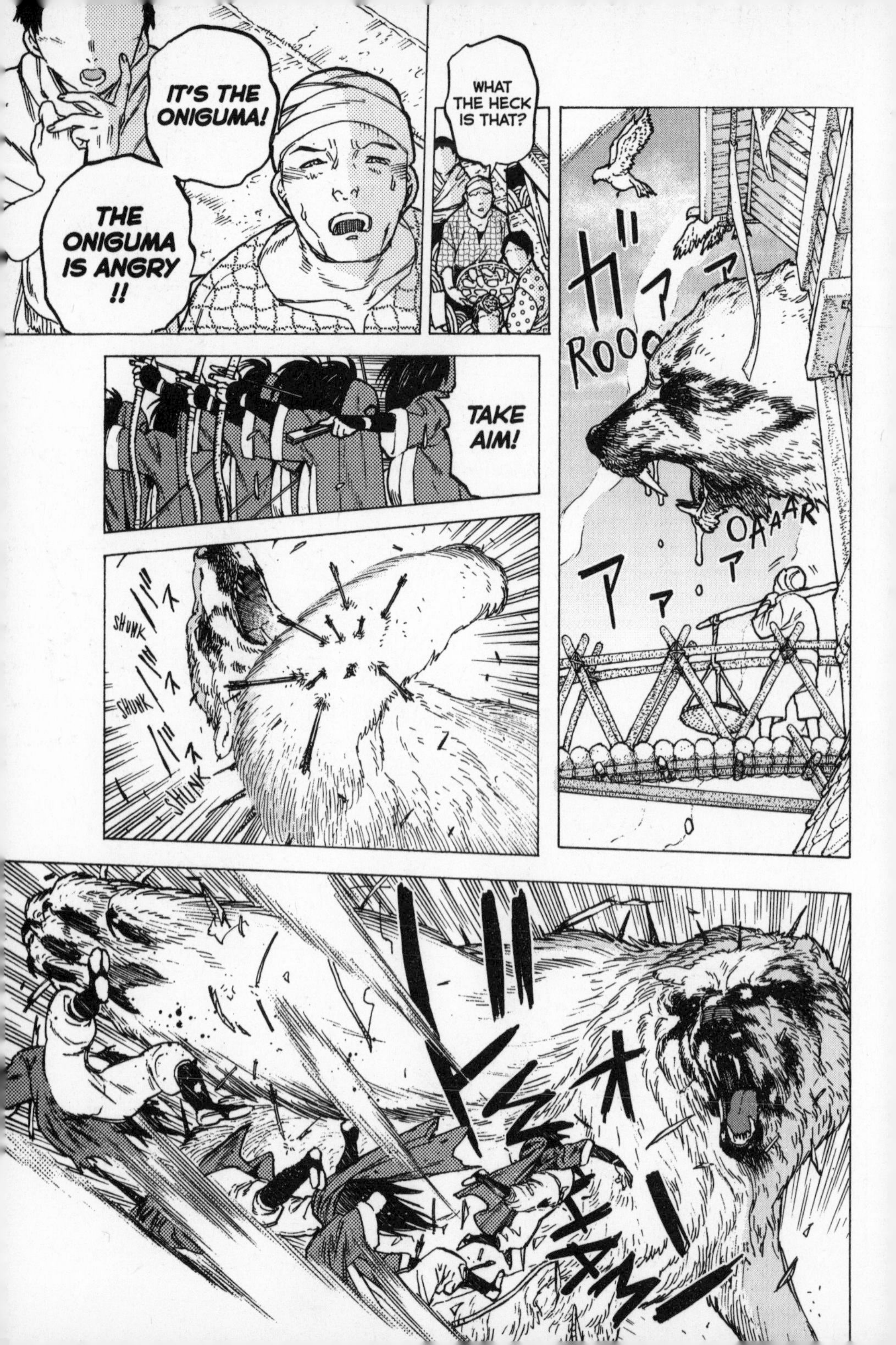

ROOO
OAAAR
WHAT THE HECK IS THAT?
IT'S THE ONIGUMA!
THE ONIGUMA IS ANGRY!!
TAKE AIM!
SHUNK
SHUNK
SHUNK
WHAM!

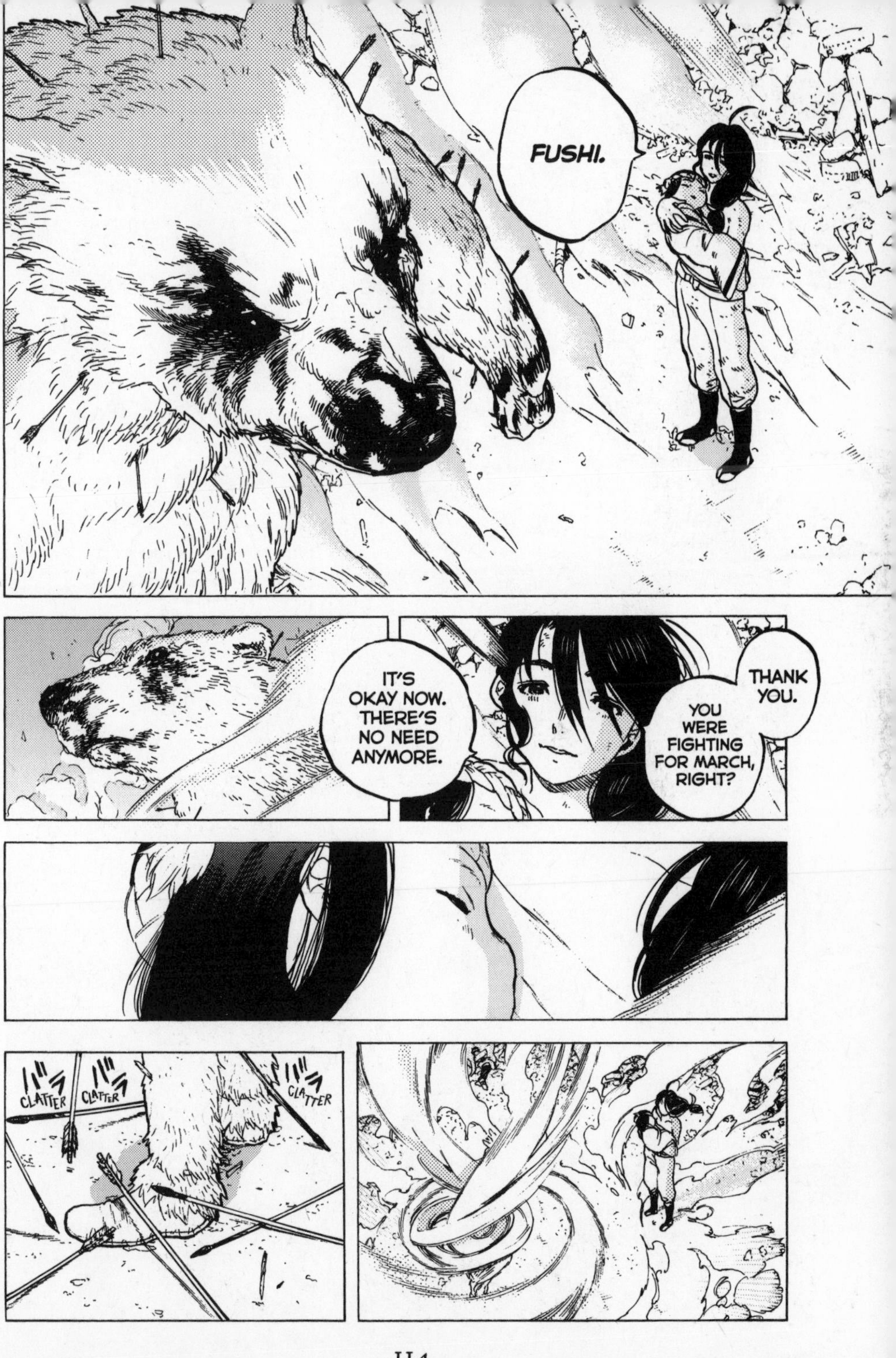
FUSHI.
THANK YOU.
YOU WERE FIGHTING FOR MARCH, RIGHT?
IT'S OKAY NOW. THERE'S NO NEED ANYMORE.
バラ CLATTER
バラ CLATTER
バラ CLATTER

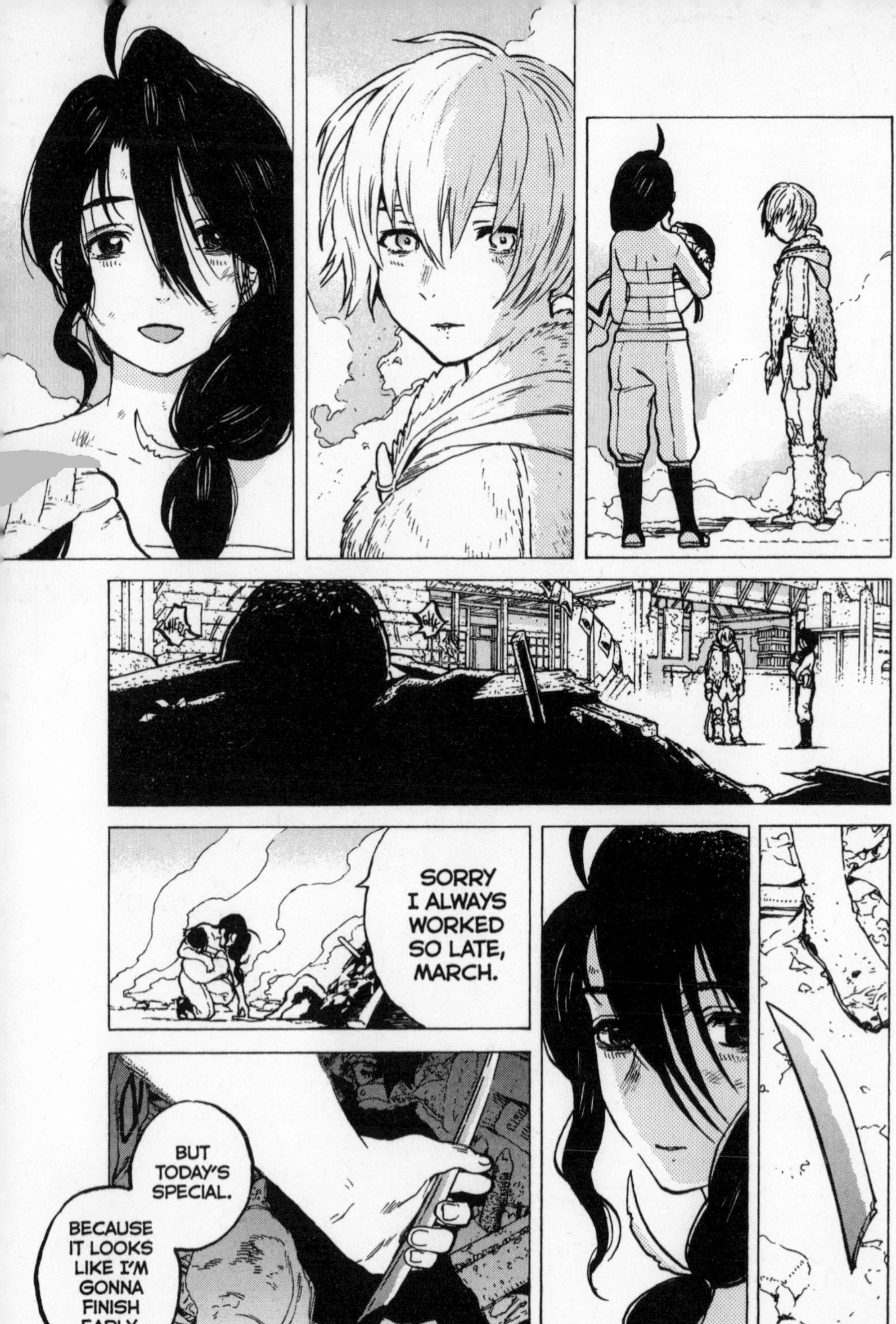
SORRY I ALWAYS WORKED SO LATE, MARCH.
BUT TODAY'S SPECIAL.
BECAUSE IT LOOKS LIKE I'M GONNA FINISH EARLY.

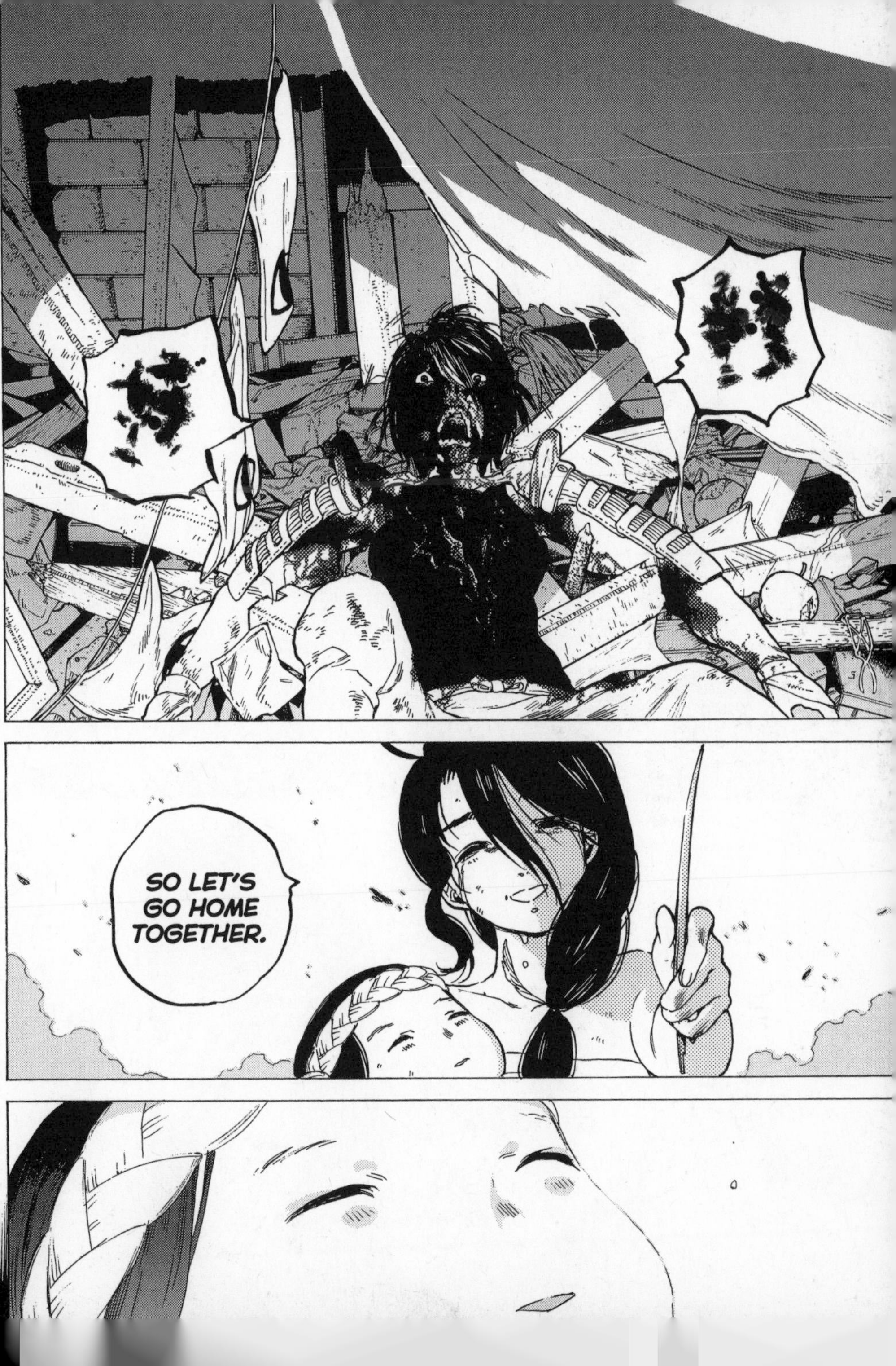
SO LET'S GO HOME TOGETHER.

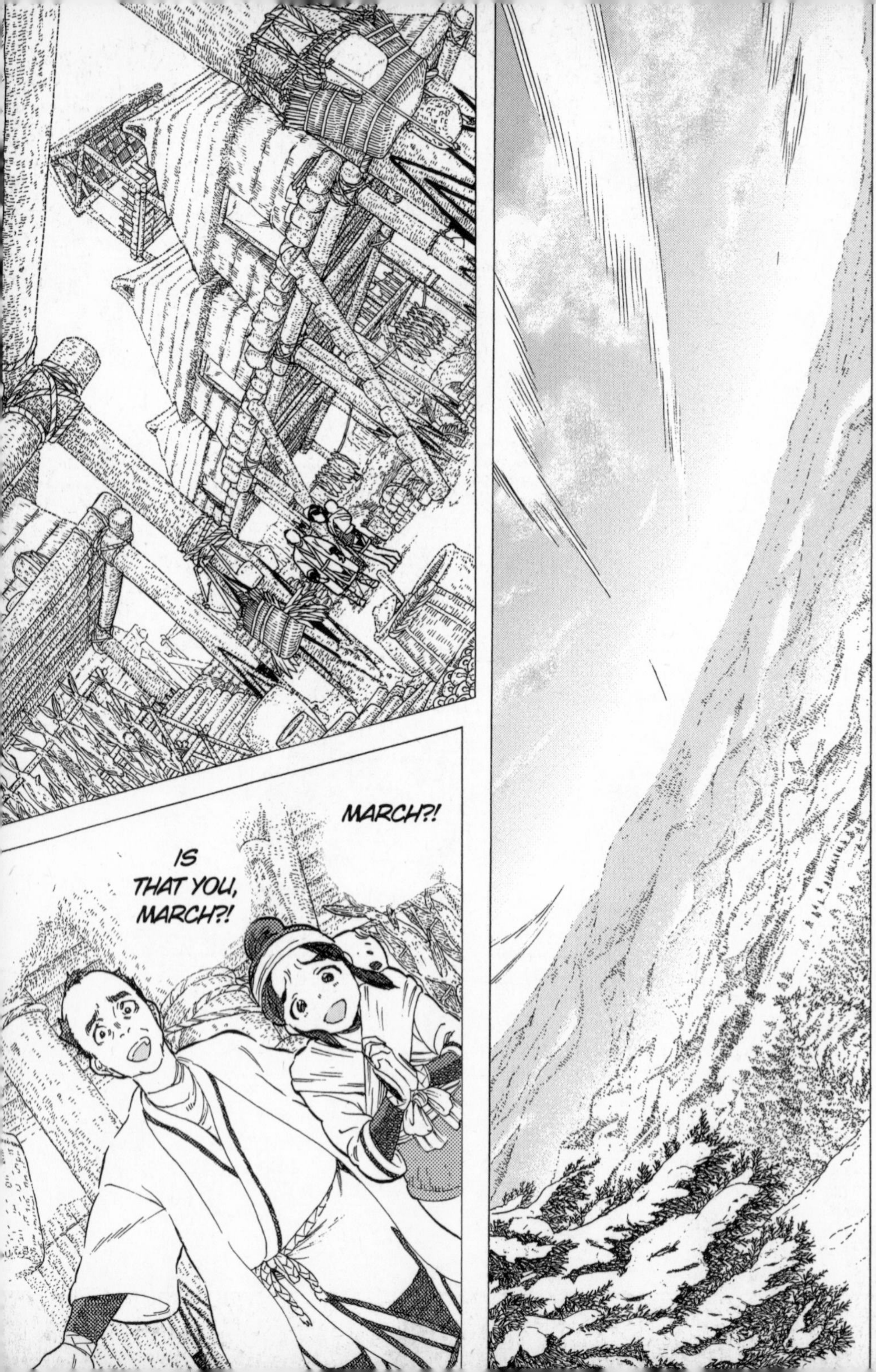
MARCH?!
IS THAT YOU, MARCH?!

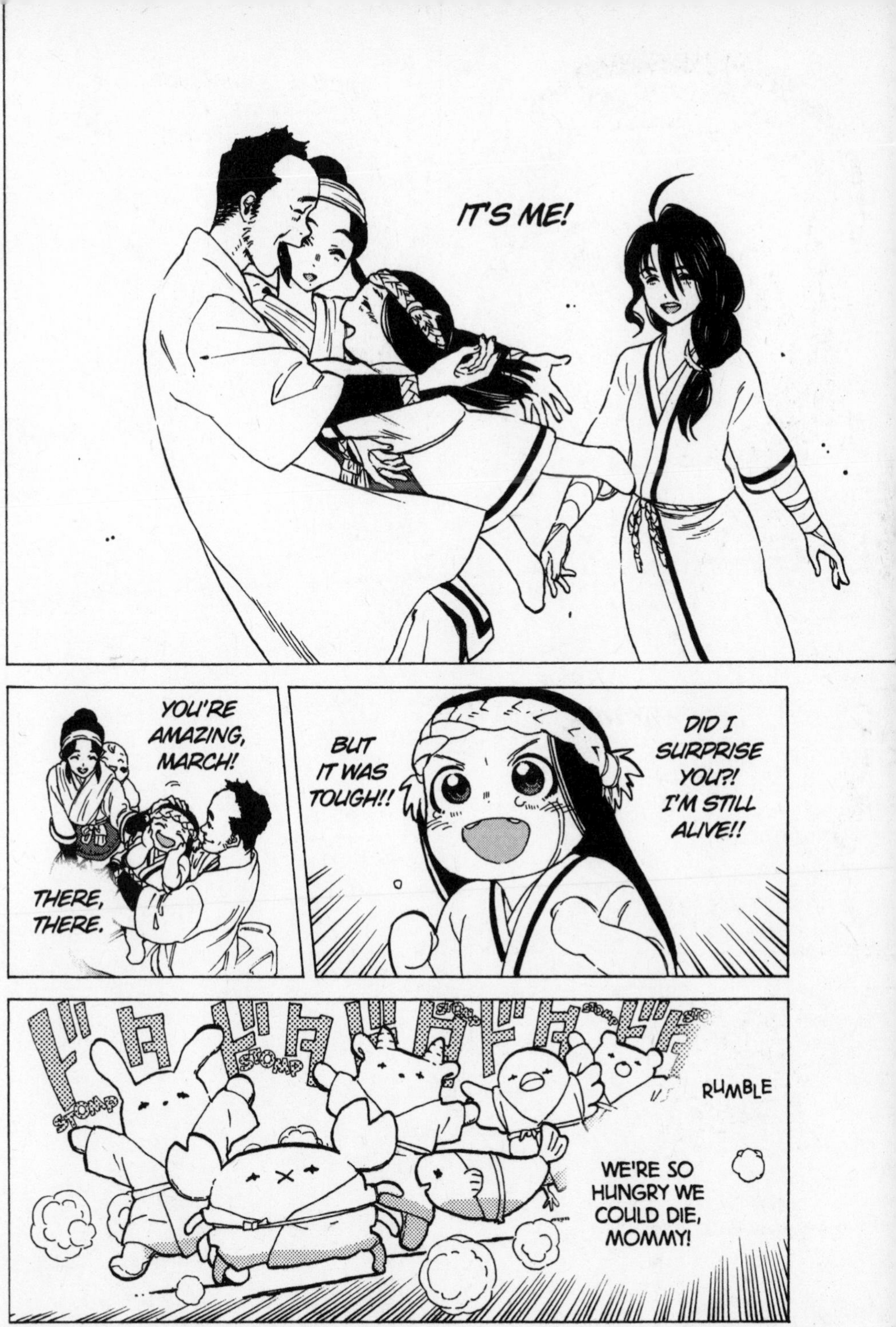
IT'S ME!
DID I SURPRISE YOU?! I'M STILL ALIVE!!
BUT IT WAS TOUGH!!
YOU'RE AMAZING, MARCH!
THERE, THERE.
STOMP
STOMP
STOMP
STOMP
STO
RUMBLE
WE'RE SO HUNGRY WE COULD DIE, MOMMY!

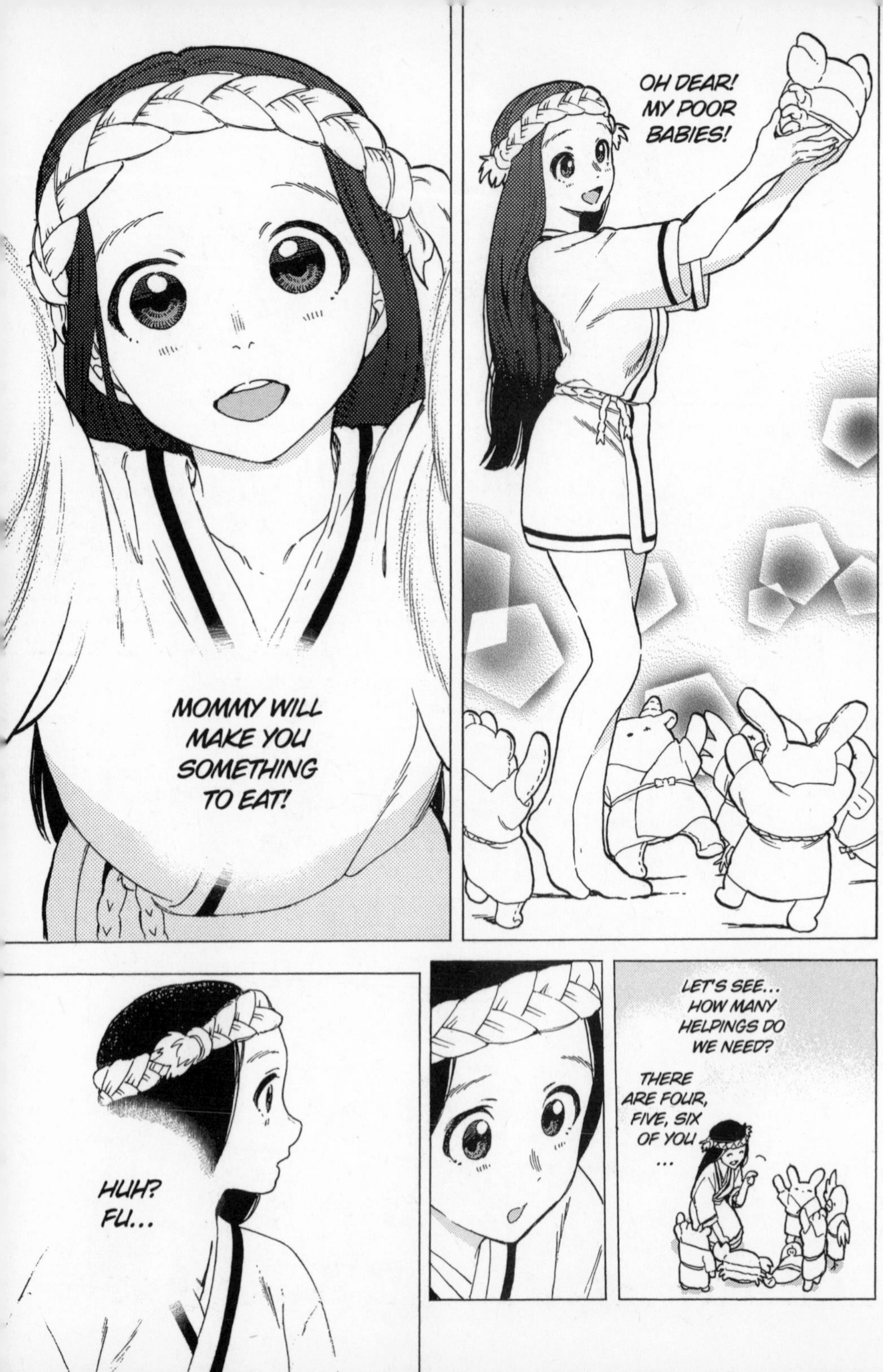
OH DEAR! MY POOR BABIES!
MOMMY WILL MAKE YOU SOMETHING TO EAT!
LET'S SEE... HOW MANY HELPINGS DO WE NEED?
THERE ARE FOUR, FIVE, SIX OF YOU ...
HUH? FU...

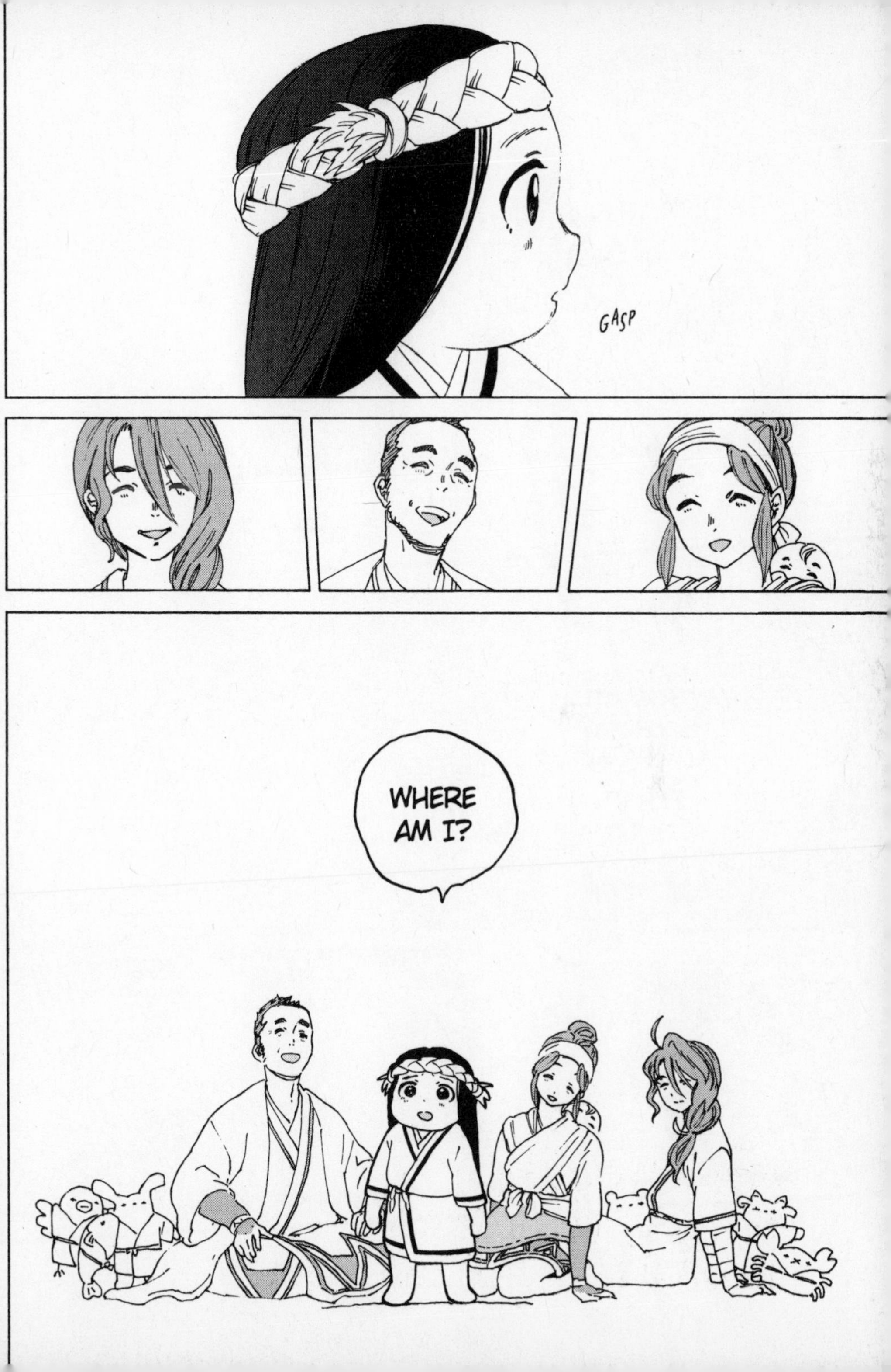
GASP
WHERE AM I?

TO YOUR
ETERNITY

TO YOUR
ETERNITY

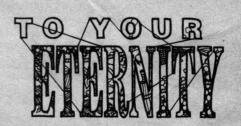

#11 Those Who Accompany You

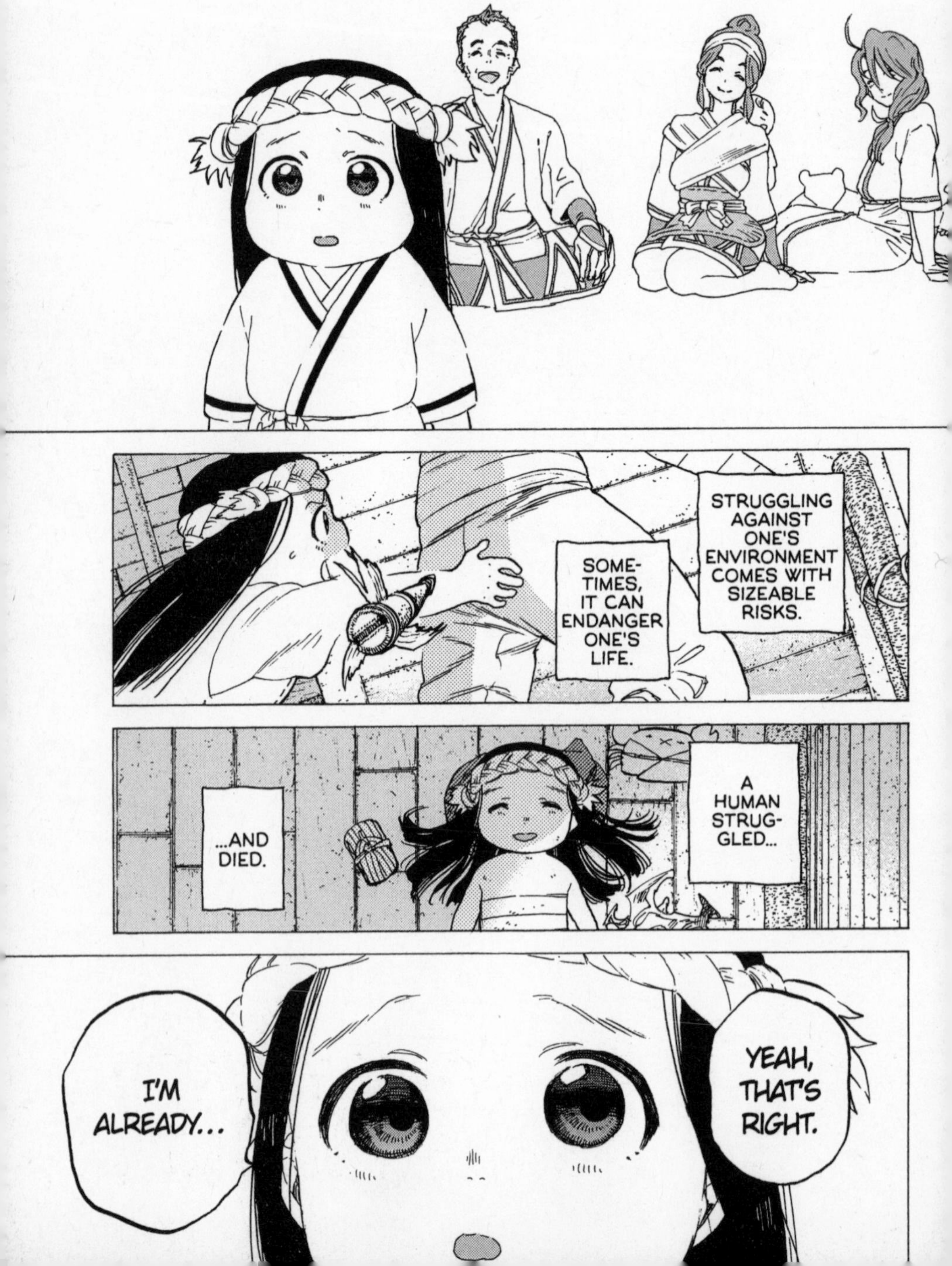
STRUGGLING AGAINST ONE'S ENVIRONMENT COMES WITH SIZEABLE RISKS.
SOME-TIMES, IT CAN ENDANGER ONE'S LIFE.
A HUMAN STRUG-GLED...
...AND DIED.
YEAH, THAT'S RIGHT.
I'M ALREADY...

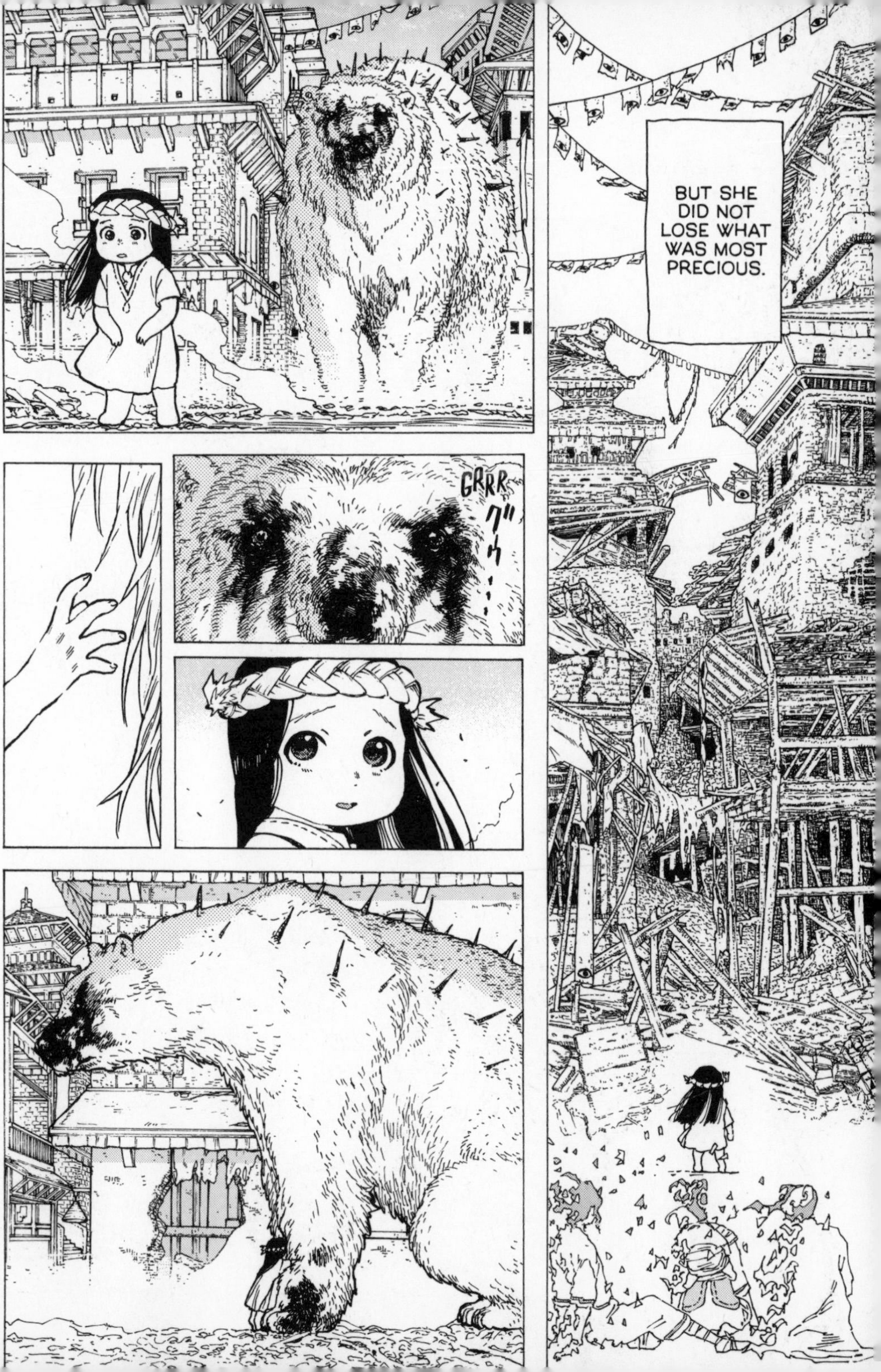
BUT SHE DID NOT LOSE WHAT WAS MOST PRECIOUS.
GRRR
グゥ…

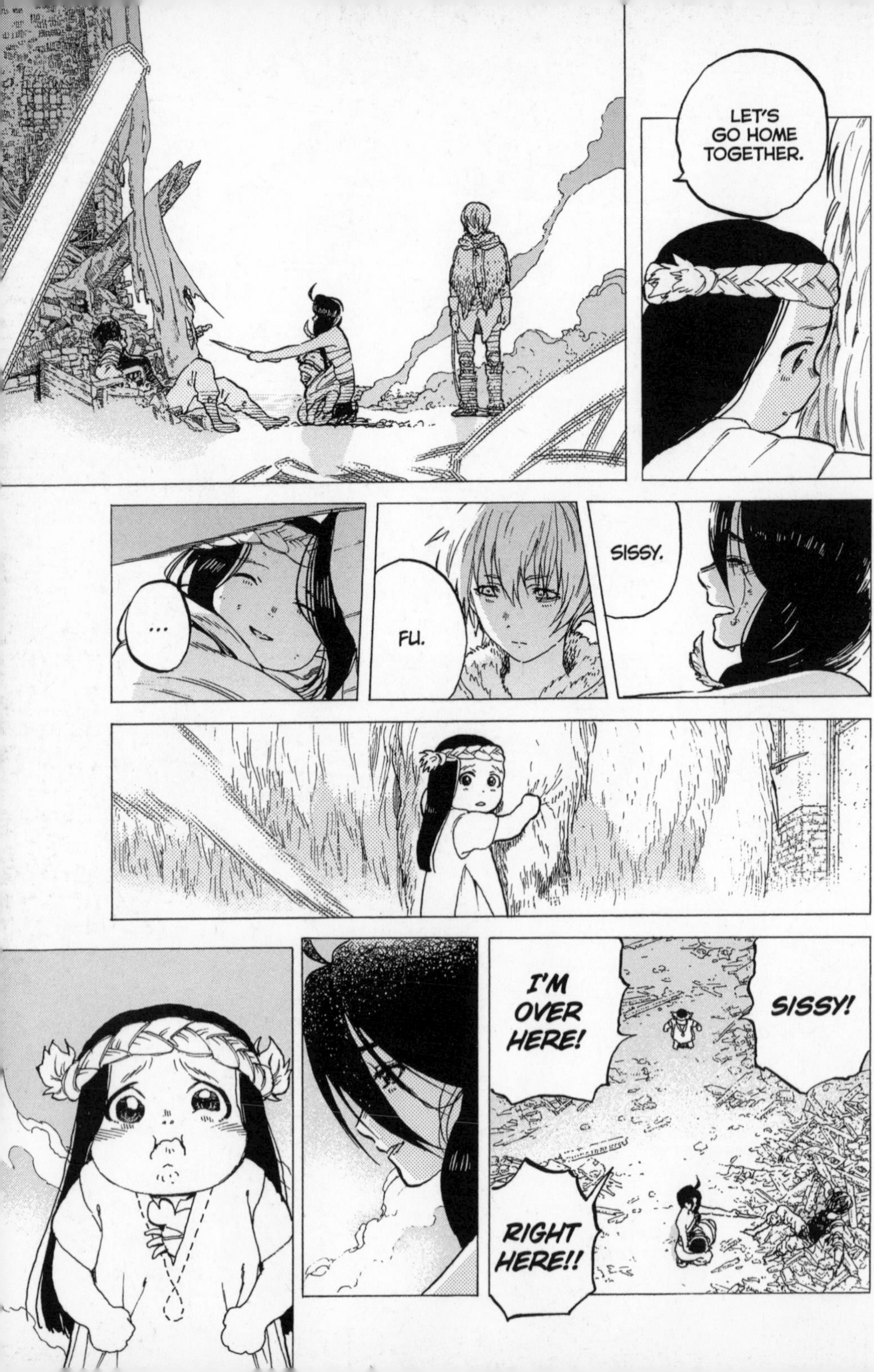
LET'S GO HOME TOGETHER.
SISSY.
FU.
...
SISSY!
I'M OVER HERE!
RIGHT HERE!!

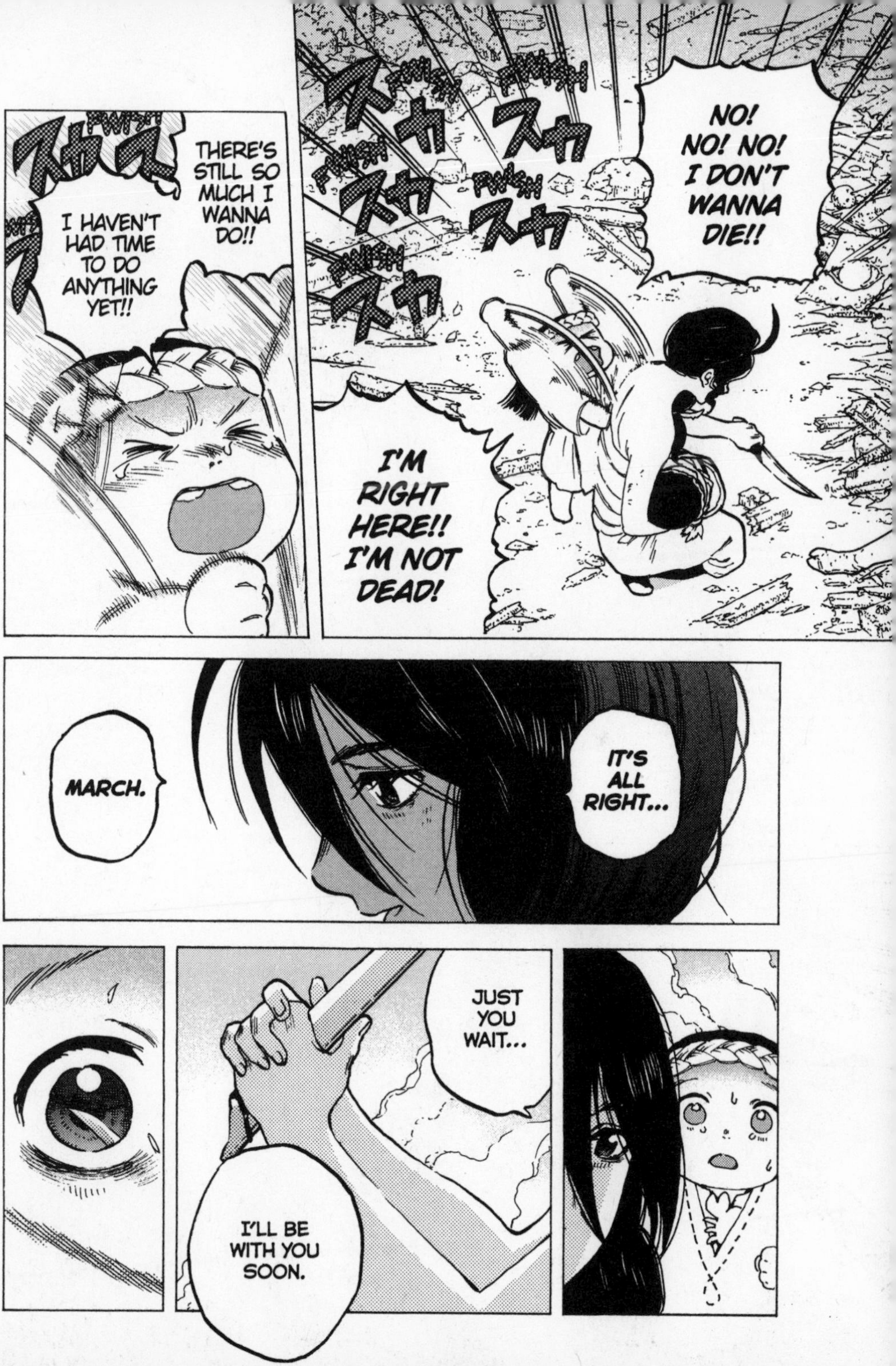

スカ
スカ
スカ
スカ
スカ
スカ
NO! NO! NO! I DON'T WANNA DIE!!
I'M RIGHT HERE!! I'M NOT DEAD!
スカス
THERE'S STILL SO MUCH I WANNA DO!!
I HAVEN'T HAD TIME TO DO ANYTHING YET!!
IT'S ALL RIGHT...
MARCH.
JUST YOU WAIT...
I'LL BE WITH YOU SOON.

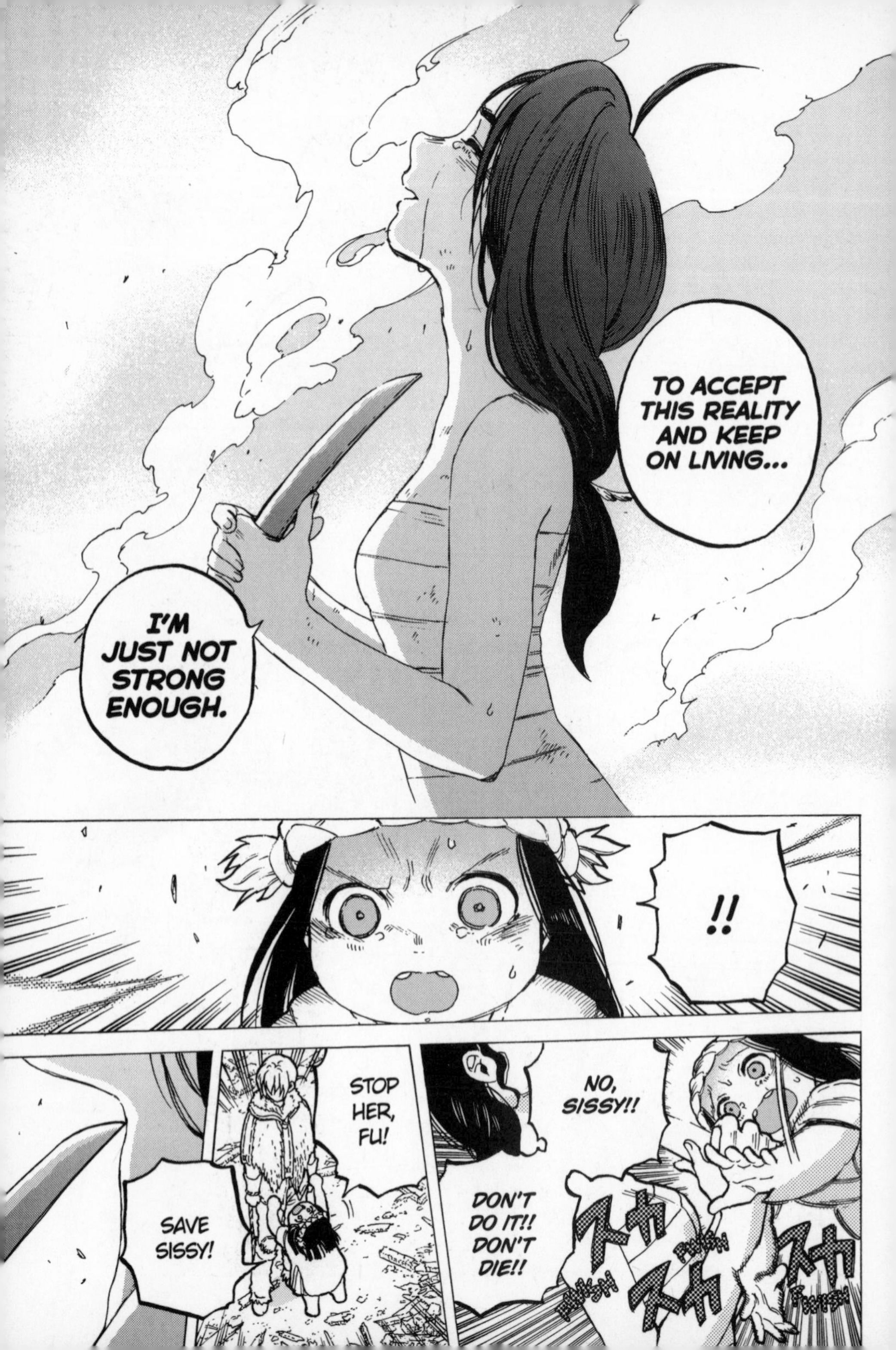
TO ACCEPT THIS REALITY AND KEEP ON LIVING...
I'M JUST NOT STRONG ENOUGH.
!!
NO, SISSY!!
DON'T DO IT!! DON'T DIE!!
STOP HER, FU!
SAVE SISSY!

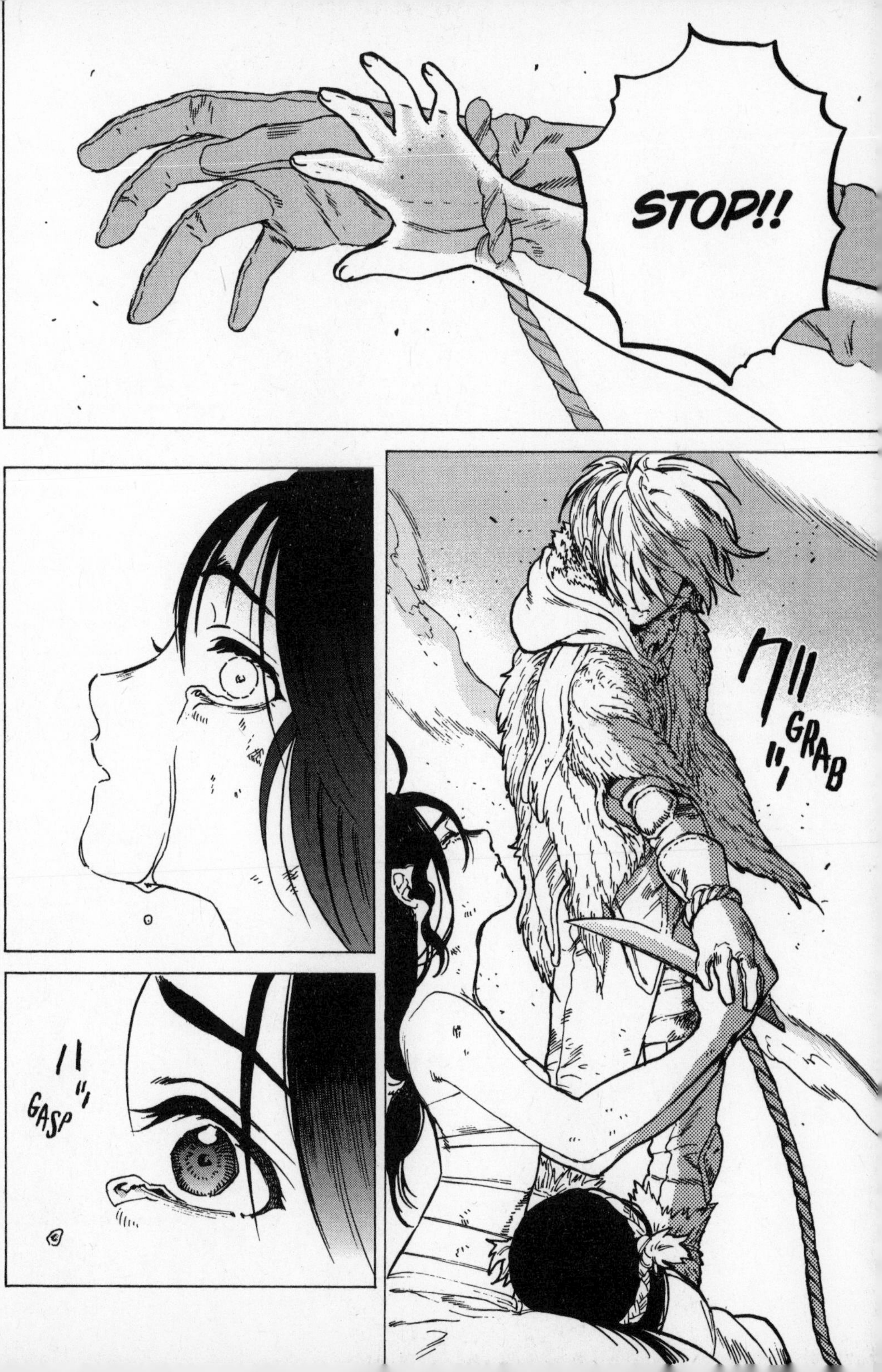
STOP!!
GRAB
GASP

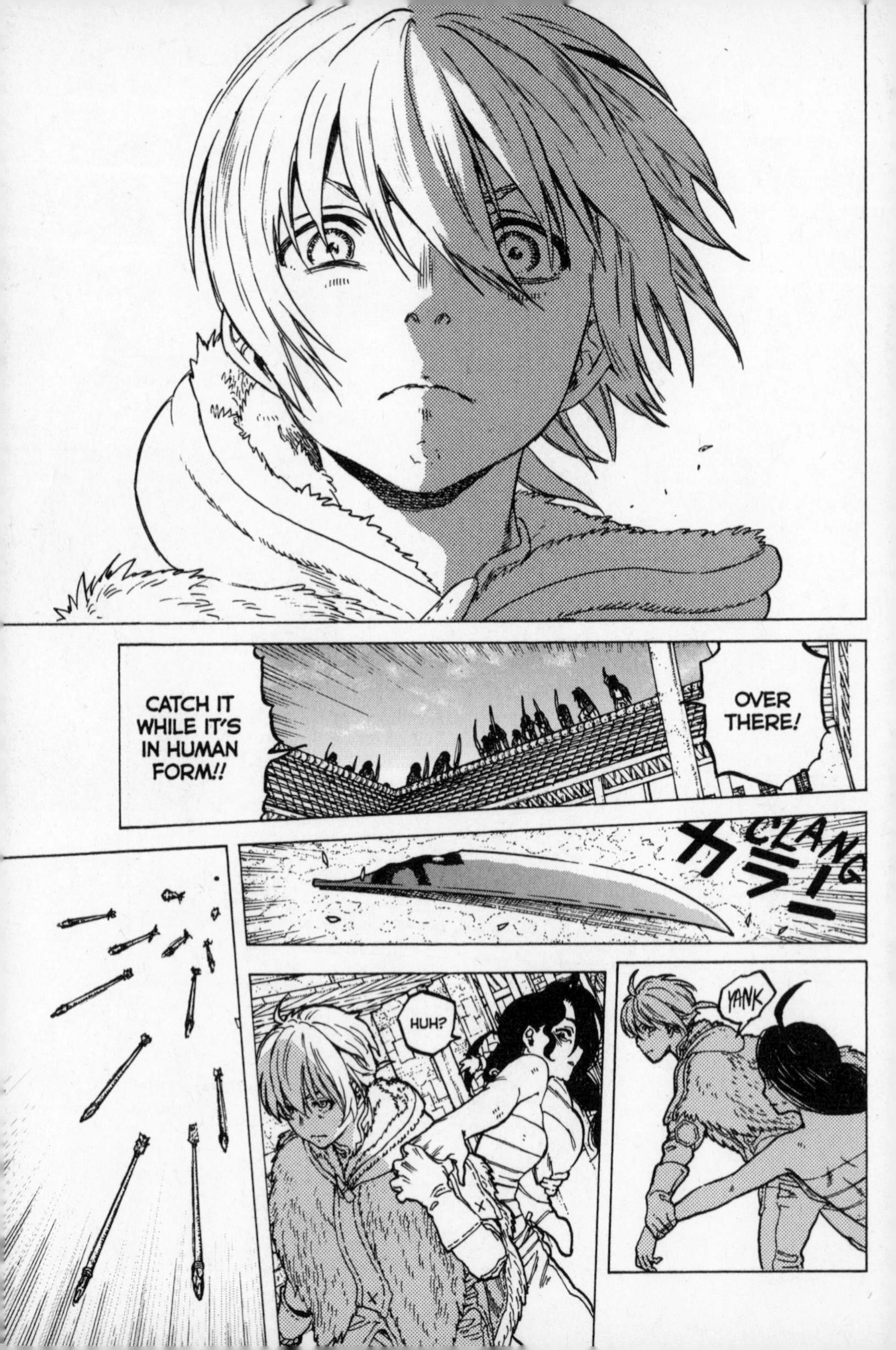
OVER THERE!
CATCH IT WHILE IT'S IN HUMAN FORM!!
CLANG
YANK
HUH?

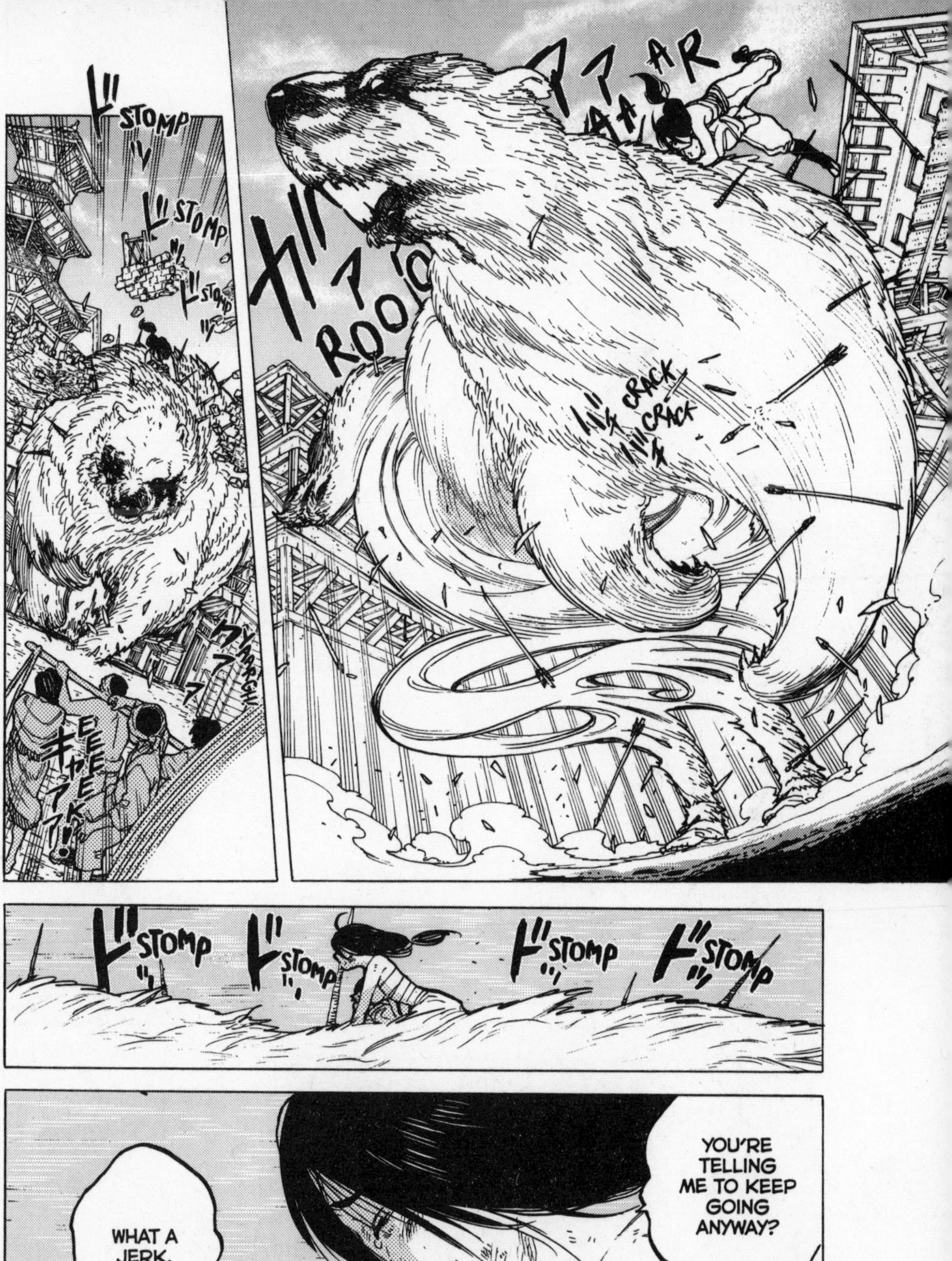
AR
ROOO
CRACK
CRACK
STOMP
STOMP
STOMP
MYAARGH
EEEEK!
STOMP
STOMP
STOMP
STOMP
YOU'RE TELLING ME TO KEEP GOING ANYWAY?
WHAT A JERK.

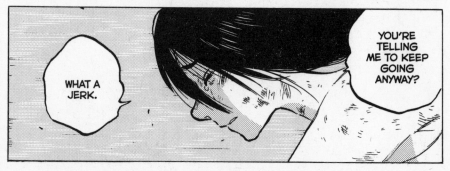

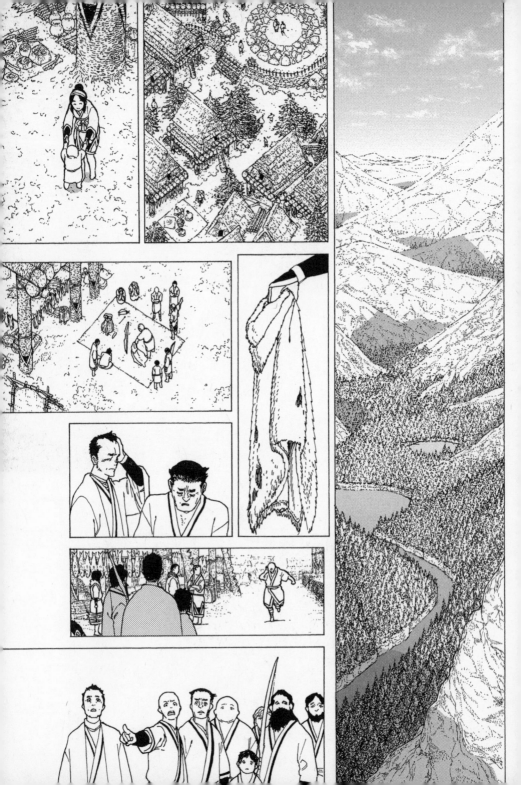

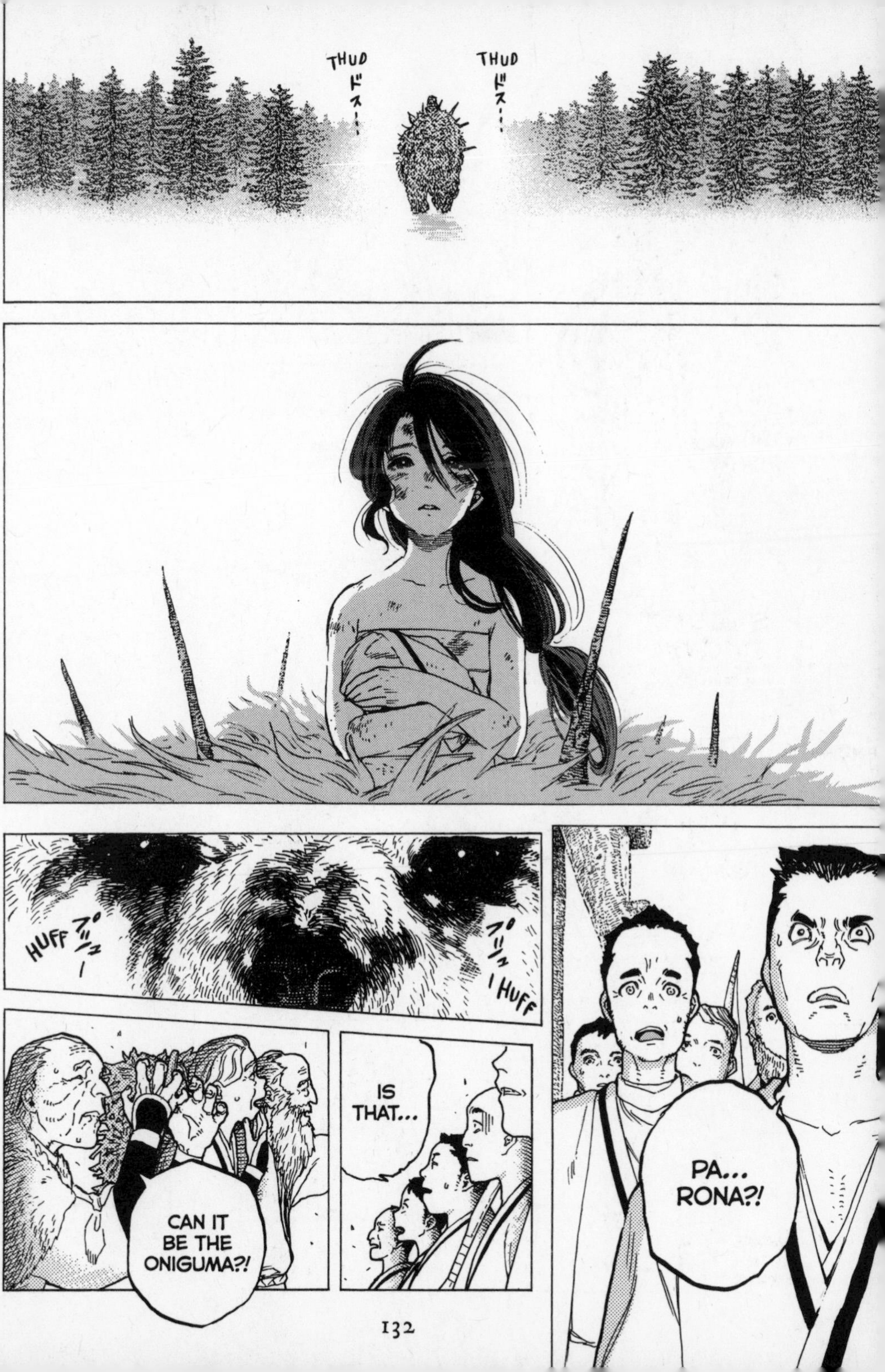
THUD
ドスー…
THUD
ドスー…
PA... RONA?!
HUFF
プシュー
HUFF
プシュー
IS THAT...
CAN IT BE THE ONIGUMA?!

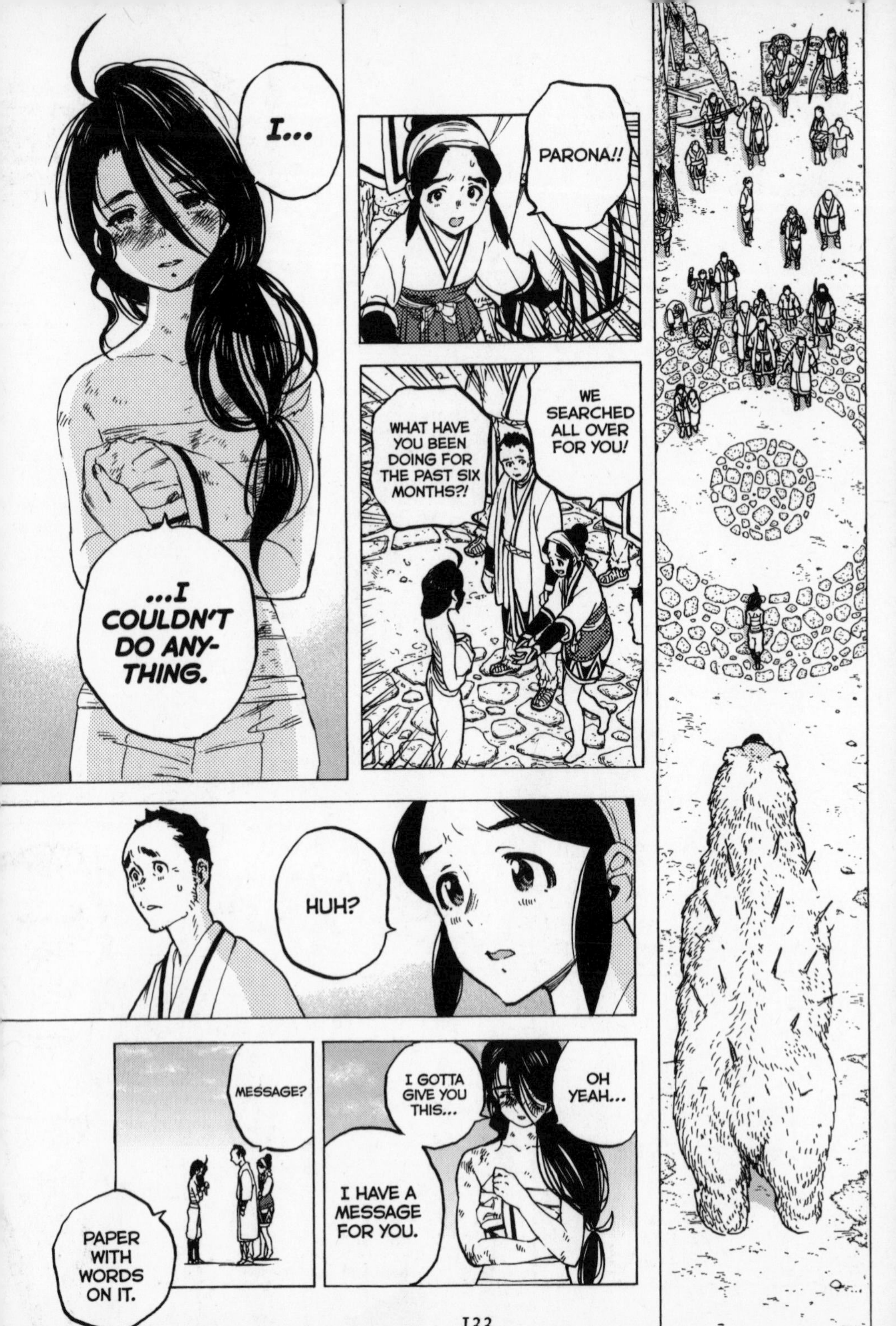
PARONA!!
WE SEARCHED ALL OVER FOR YOU!
WHAT HAVE YOU BEEN DOING FOR THE PAST SIX MONTHS?!
I...
...I COULDN'T DO ANY-THING.
HUH?
OH YEAH...
I GOTTA GIVE YOU THIS...
I HAVE A MESSAGE FOR YOU.
MESSAGE?
PAPER WITH WORDS ON IT.

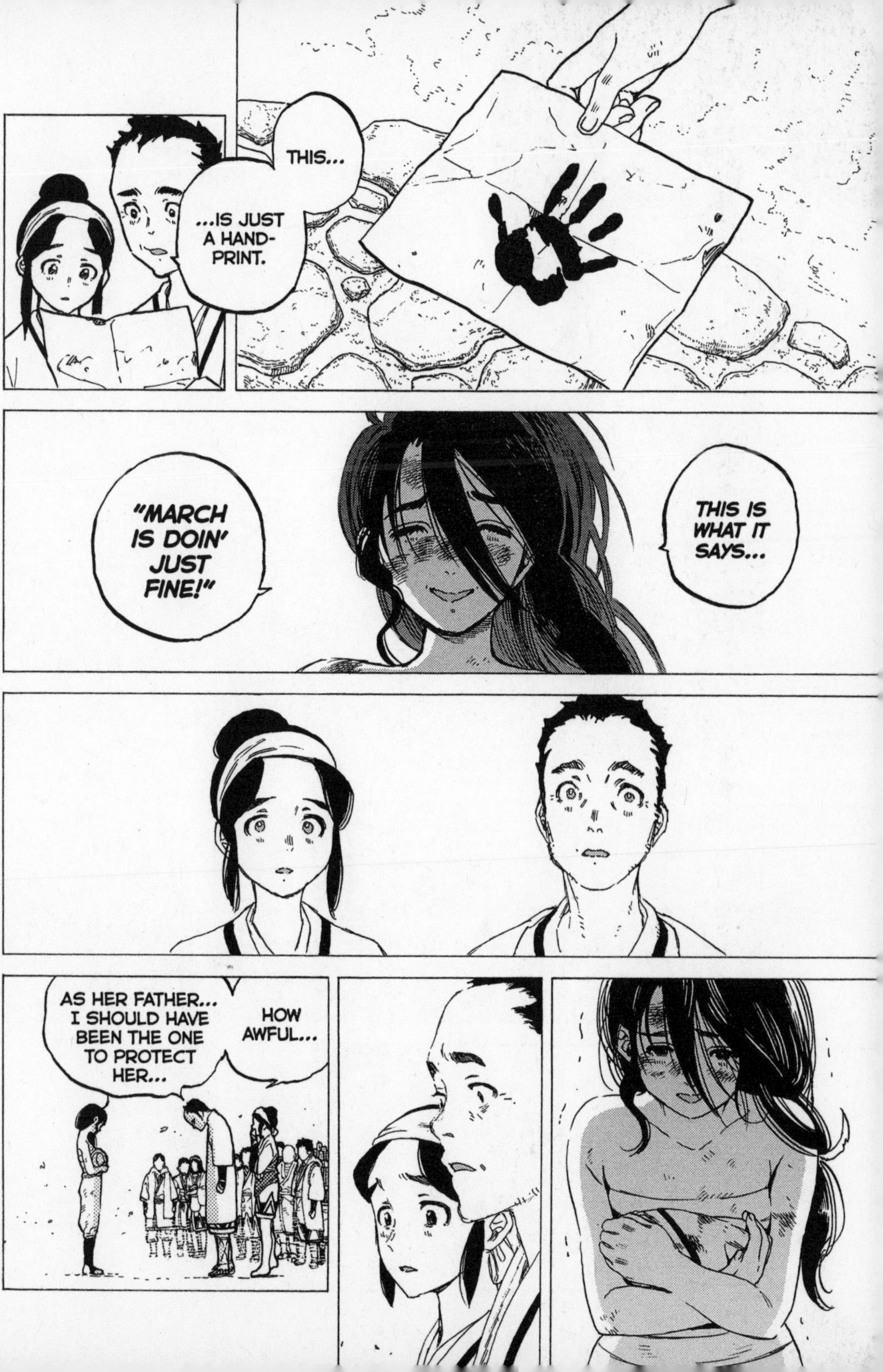
THIS...
...IS JUST A HAND-PRINT.
THIS IS WHAT IT SAYS...
"MARCH IS DOIN' JUST FINE!"
HOW AWFUL...
AS HER FATHER... I SHOULD HAVE BEEN THE ONE TO PROTECT HER...

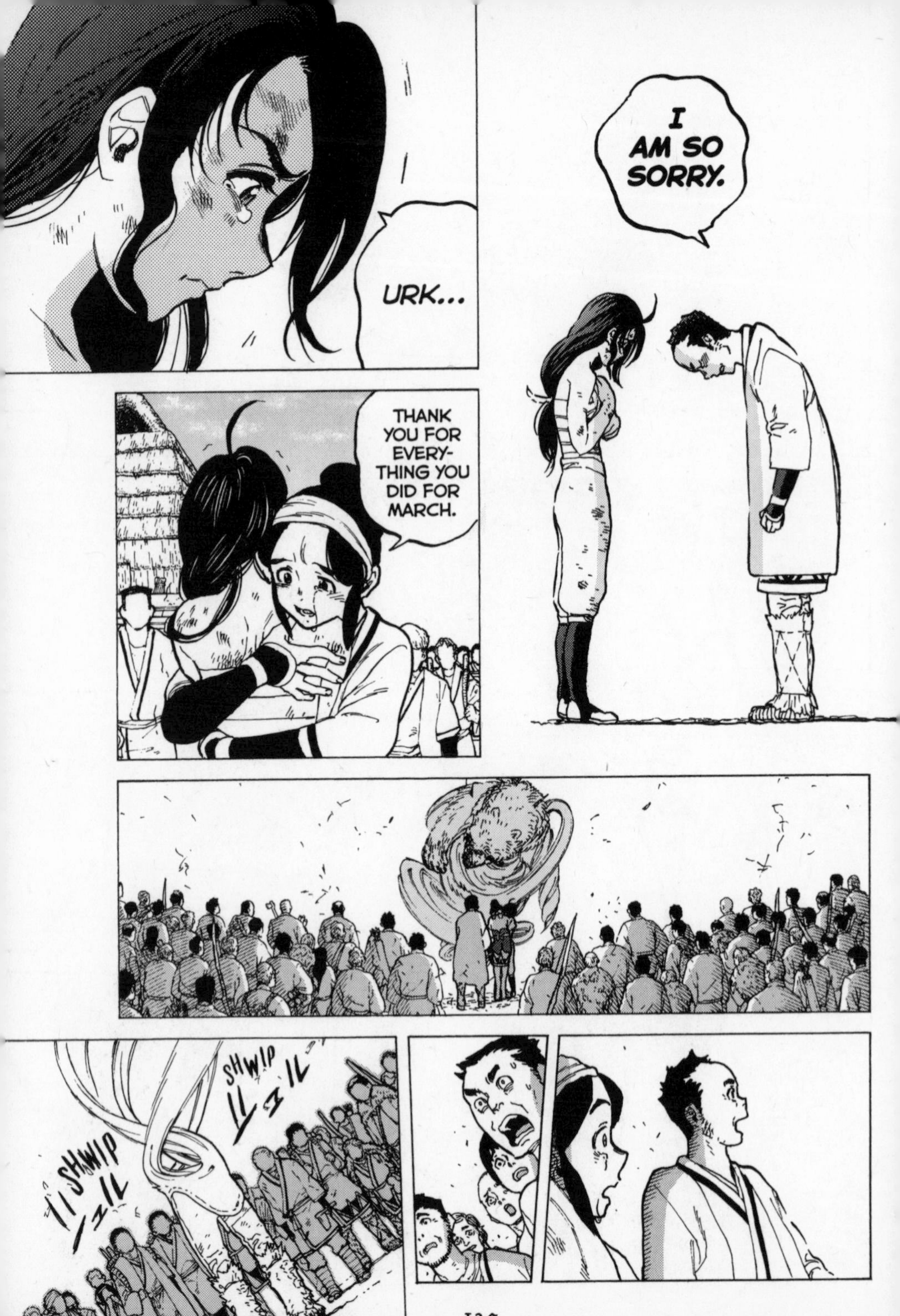
I AM SO SORRY.
URK...
THANK YOU FOR EVERY-THING YOU DID FOR MARCH.
SHWIP
SHWIP

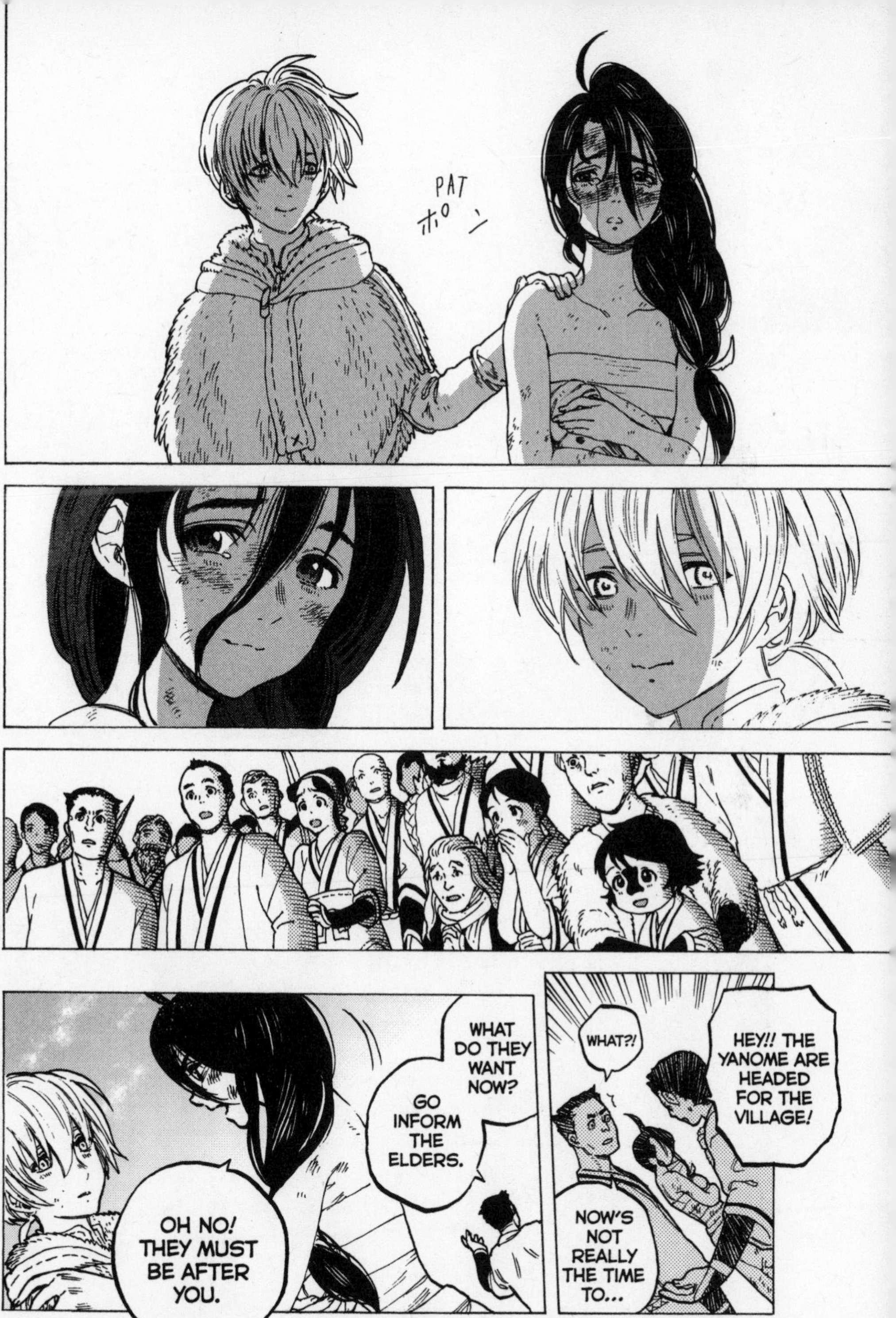
PAT
ポン
HEY!! THE YANOME ARE HEADED FOR THE VILLAGE!
WHAT?!
NOW'S NOT REALLY THE TIME TO...
WHAT DO THEY WANT NOW?
GO INFORM THE ELDERS.
OH NO! THEY MUST BE AFTER YOU.

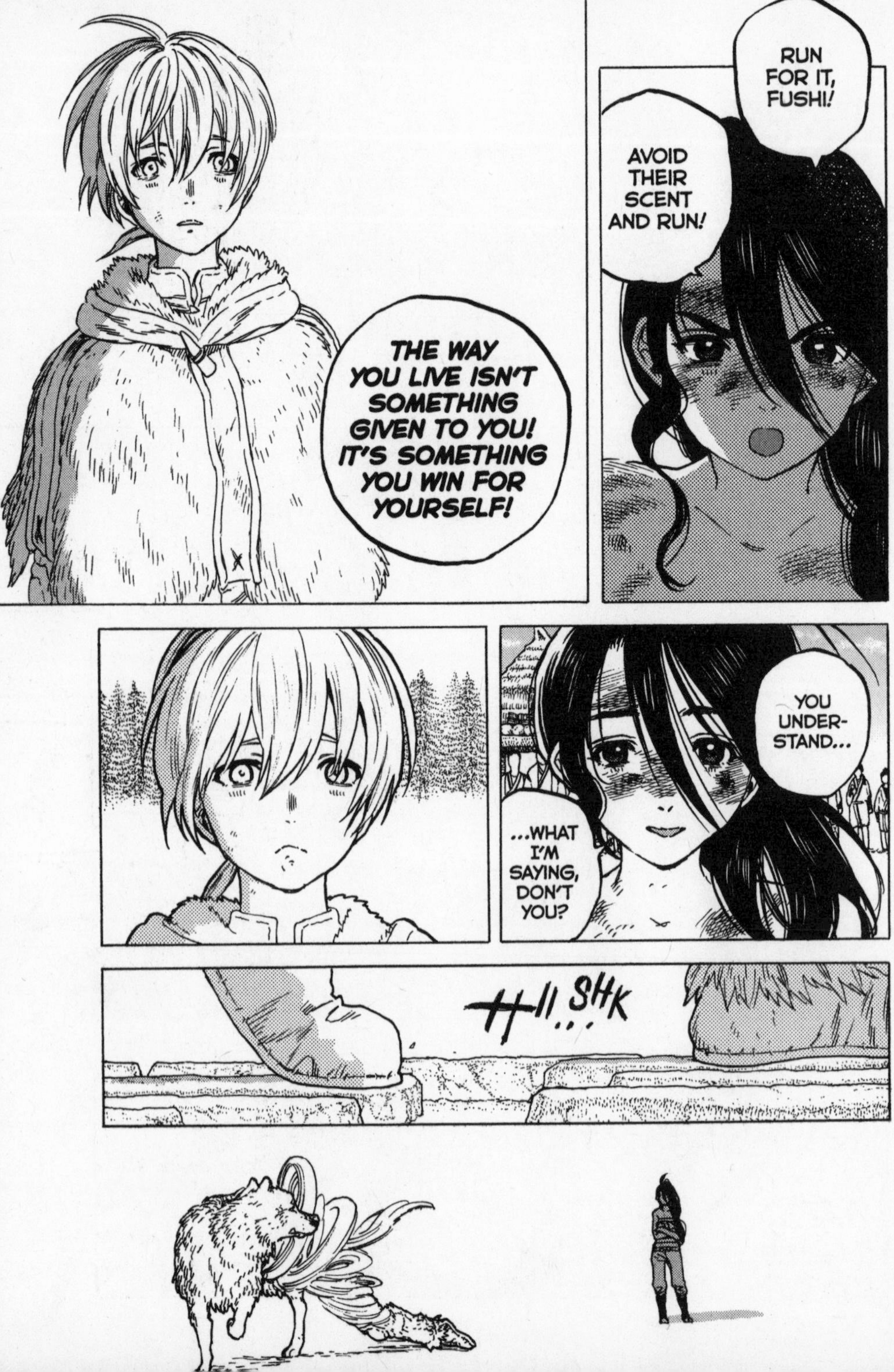
RUN FOR IT, FUSHI!
AVOID THEIR SCENT AND RUN!
THE WAY YOU LIVE ISN'T SOMETHING GIVEN TO YOU! IT'S SOMETHING YOU WIN FOR YOURSELF!
YOU UNDERSTAND...
...WHAT I'M SAYING, DON'T YOU?
SHK

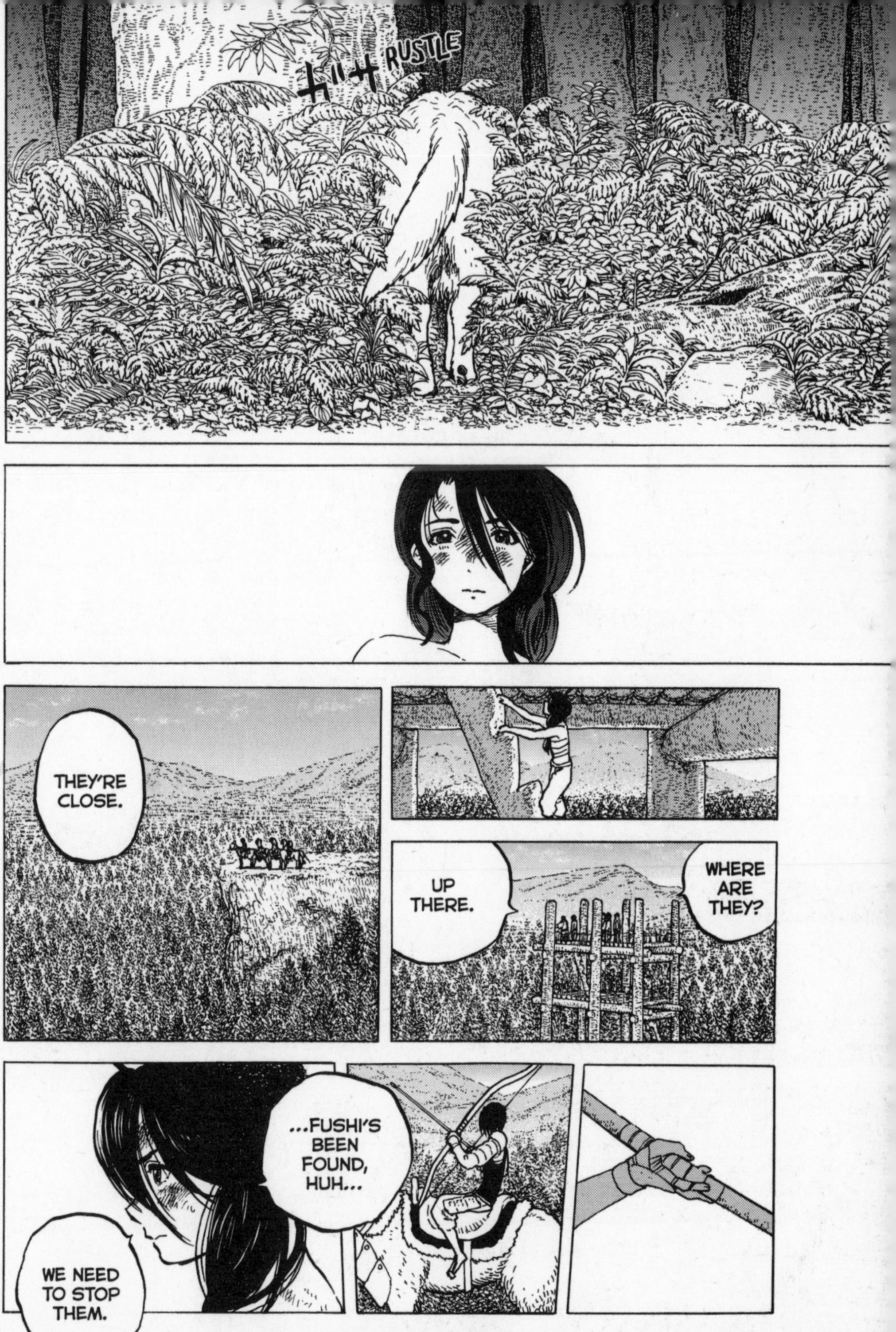
RUSTLE
WHERE ARE THEY?
UP THERE.
THEY'RE CLOSE.
...FUSHI'S BEEN FOUND, HUH...
WE NEED TO STOP THEM.

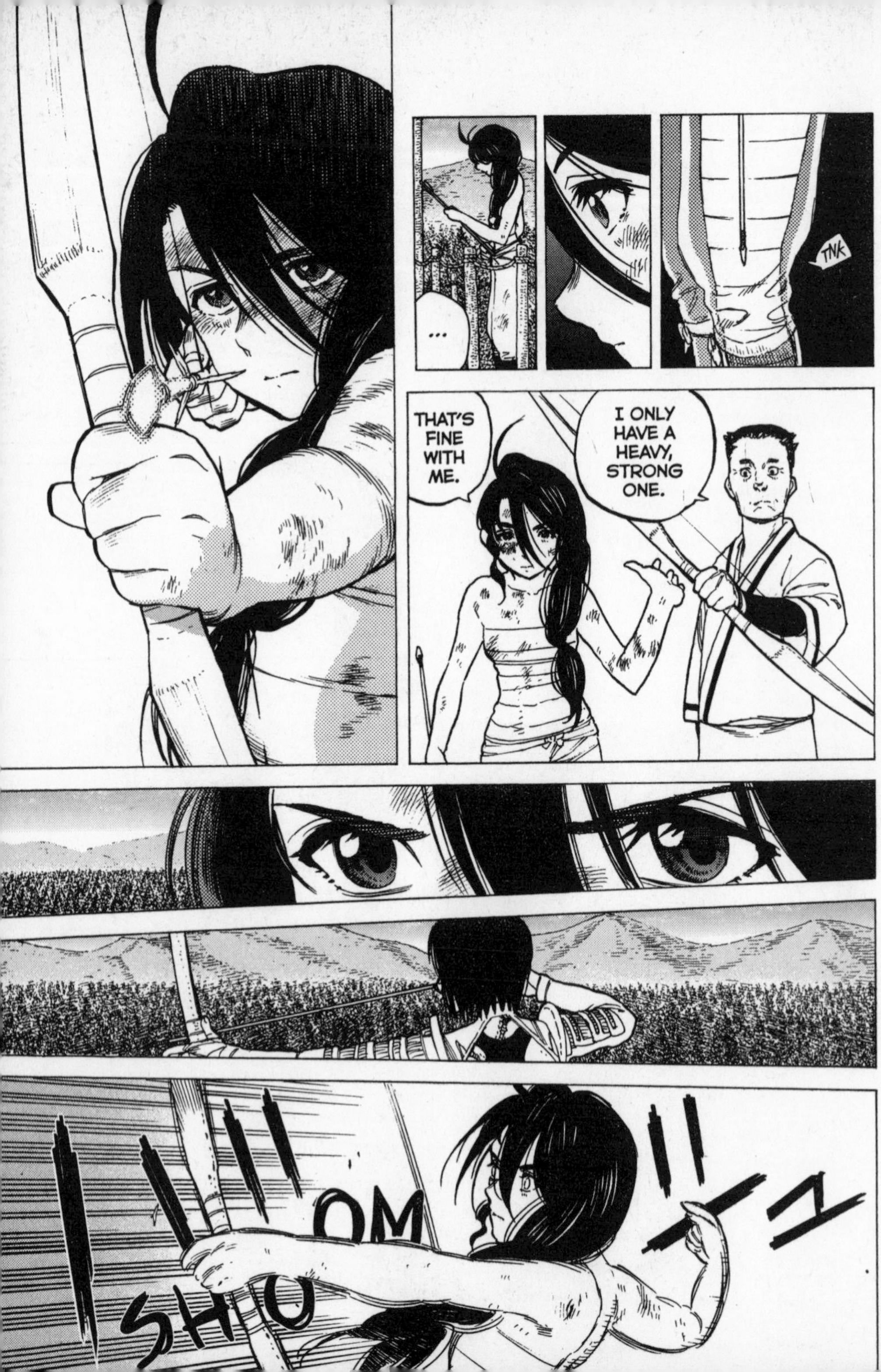

TNK
...
I ONLY HAVE A HEAVY, STRONG ONE.
THAT'S FINE WITH ME.
SHUOM

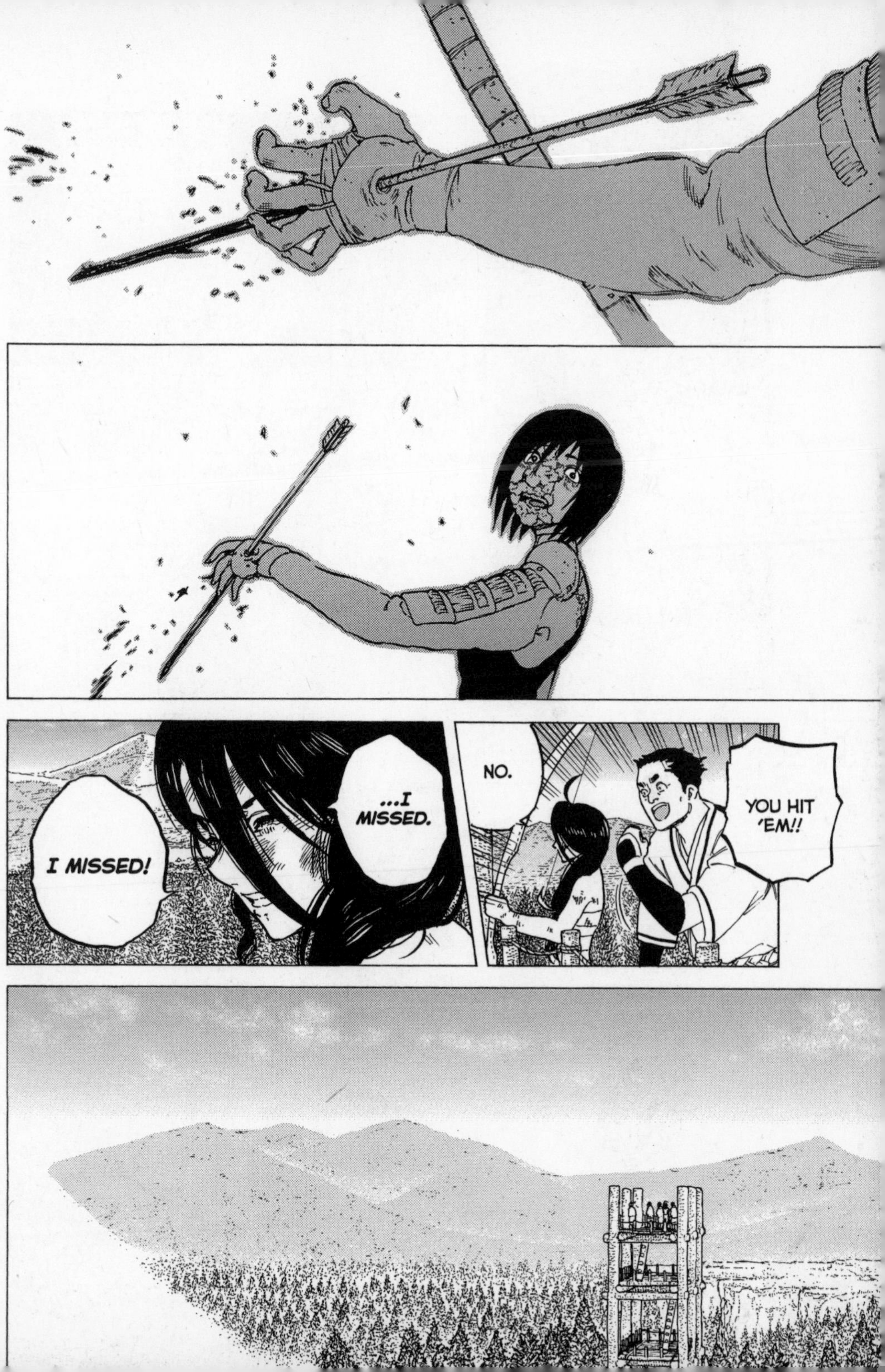
YOU HIT 'EM!!
NO.
...I MISSED.
I MISSED!

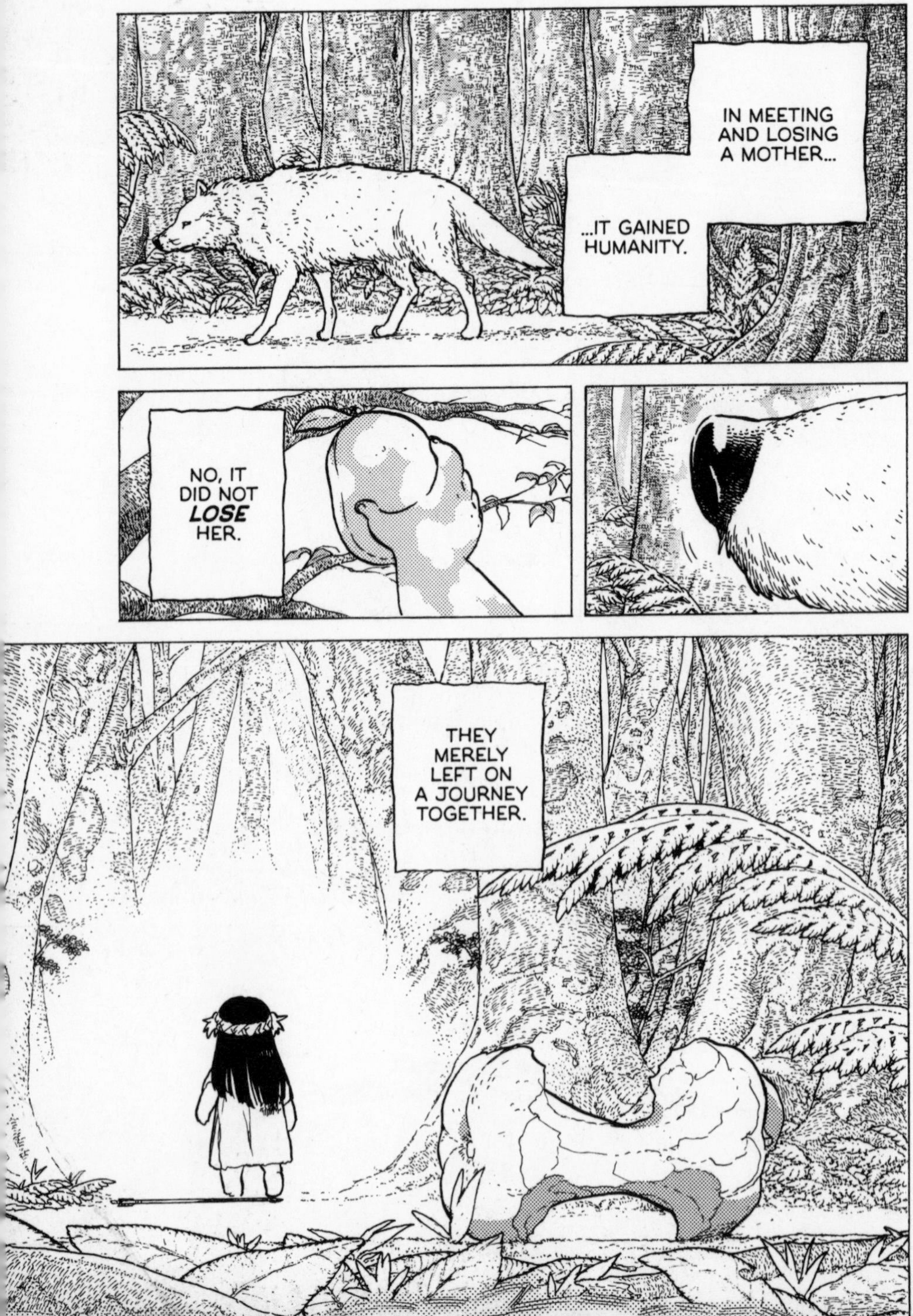
IN MEETING AND LOSING A MOTHER...
...IT GAINED HUMANITY.
NO, IT DID NOT ***LOSE*** HER.
THEY MERELY LEFT ON A JOURNEY TOGETHER.

THE MORNING OF THE FOUR SYMBOLS RITUAL

That day, many people bore witness,

as the great white creature with countless thorns devastated the village.

The people could not help but think that it was the great Oniguma,

and that we must have committed some terrible sin.

RECORDS FROM THE YANOME MESSENGER SERVICE

ONIGUMA INCARNATE

The village maiden Parona disappeared, but returned.

She was accompanied by a large white bear with thorns.

The bear then turned into a beautiful boy.

And next, turned into a wolf and left the village.

Had we been forgiven? Or had we not been forgiven?

Parona the maiden mentioned only this:

There is no need for offerings anymore.

CHIEF ELDER OF THE PAI CLAN OF NINANNAH

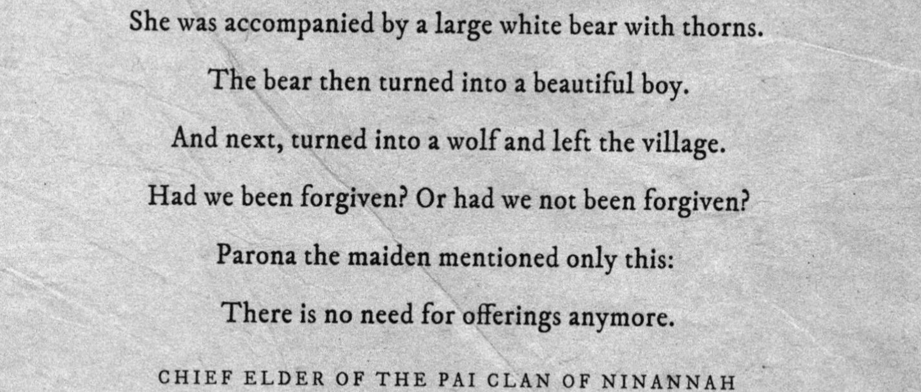

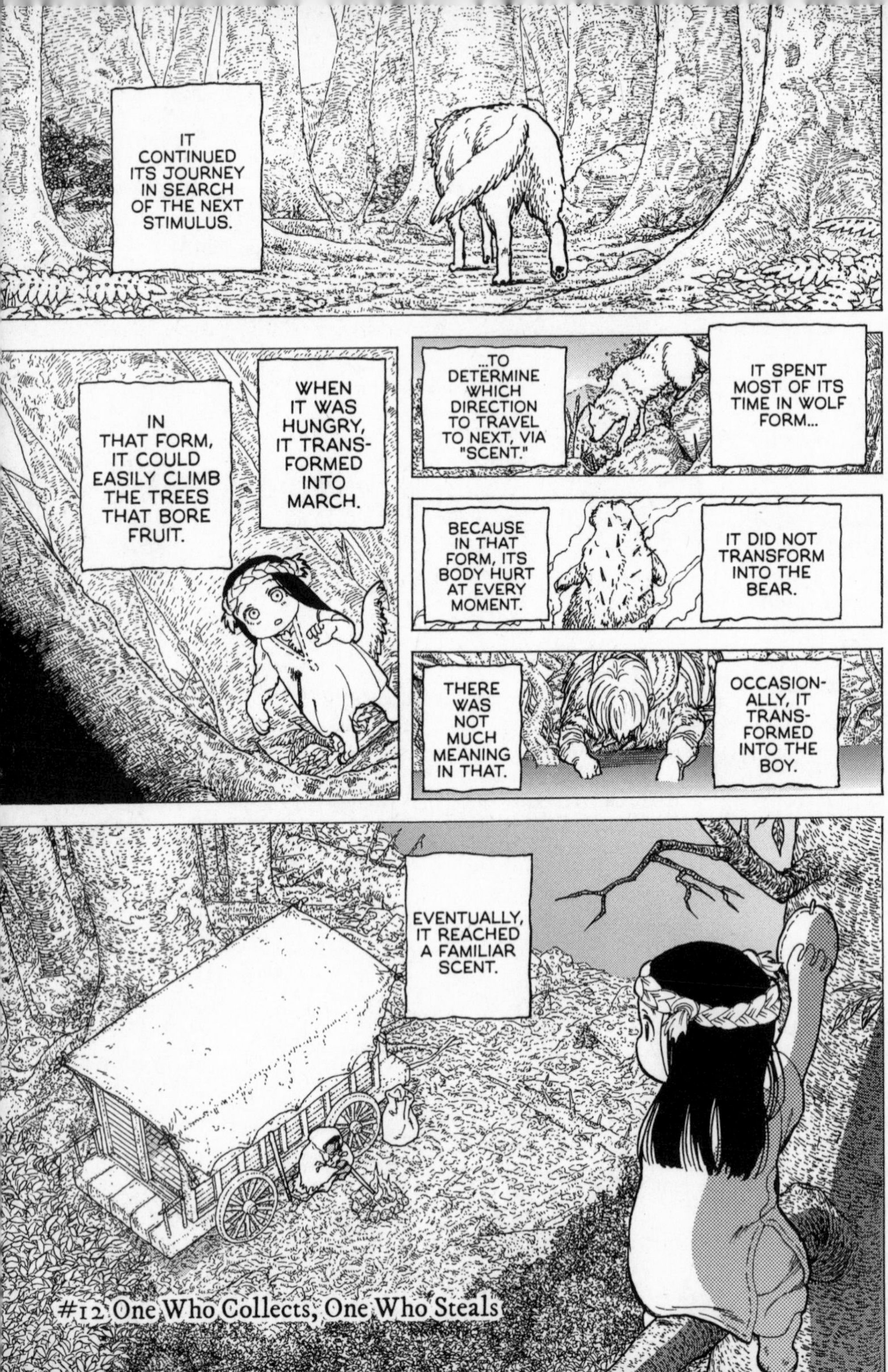
IT CONTINUED ITS JOURNEY IN SEARCH OF THE NEXT STIMULUS.
IT SPENT MOST OF ITS TIME IN WOLF FORM...
...TO DETERMINE WHICH DIRECTION TO TRAVEL TO NEXT, VIA "SCENT."
IT DID NOT TRANSFORM INTO THE BEAR.
BECAUSE IN THAT FORM, ITS BODY HURT AT EVERY MOMENT.
OCCASION-ALLY, IT TRANS-FORMED INTO THE BOY.
THERE WAS NOT MUCH MEANING IN THAT.
WHEN IT WAS HUNGRY, IT TRANS-FORMED INTO MARCH.
IN THAT FORM, IT COULD EASILY CLIMB THE TREES THAT BORE FRUIT.
EVENTUALLY, IT REACHED A FAMILIAR SCENT.
#12 One Who Collects, One Who Steals

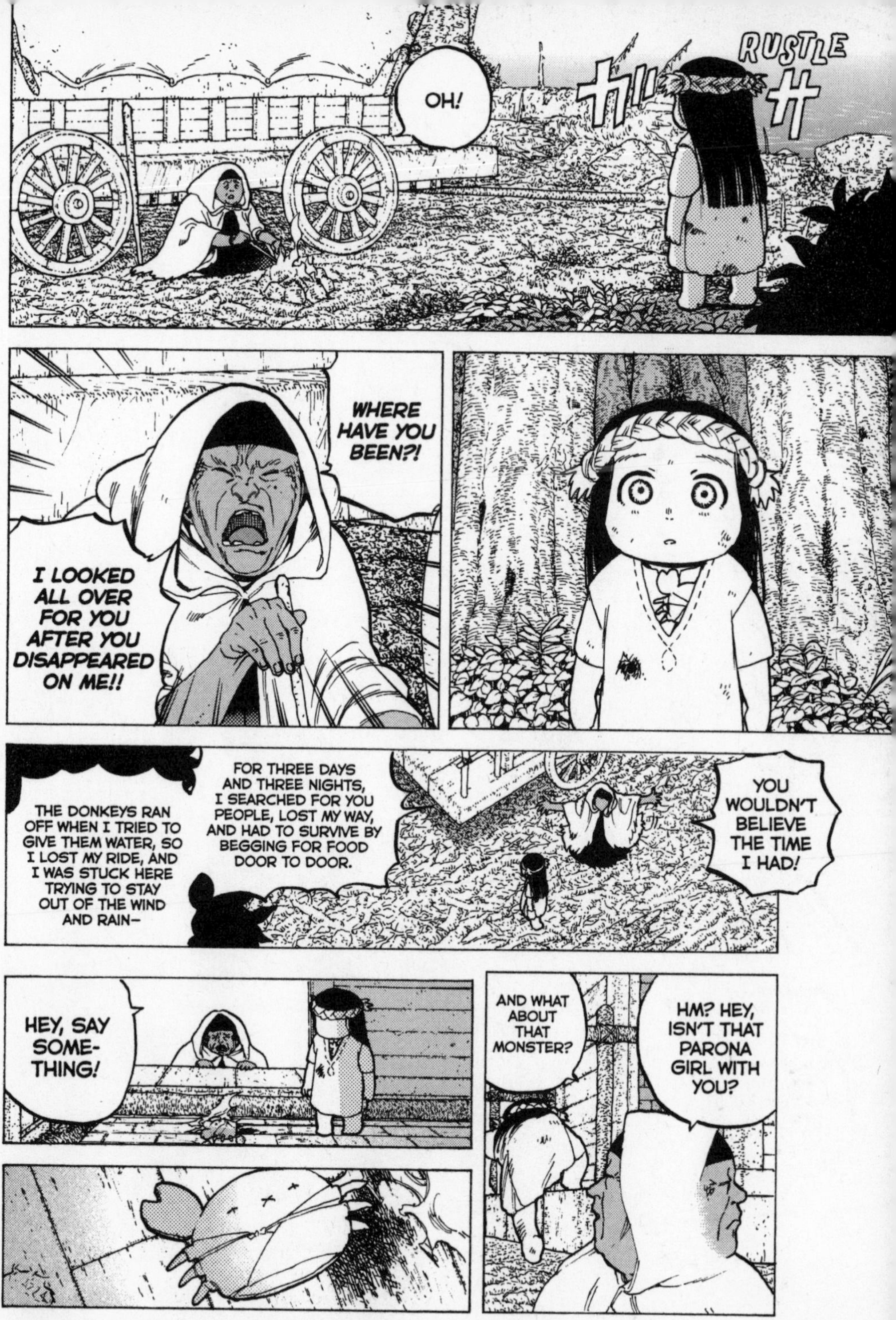
RUSTLE
カサ
OH!
WHERE HAVE YOU BEEN?!
I LOOKED ALL OVER FOR YOU AFTER YOU DISAPPEARED ON ME!!
YOU WOULDN'T BELIEVE THE TIME I HAD!
FOR THREE DAYS AND THREE NIGHTS, I SEARCHED FOR YOU PEOPLE, LOST MY WAY, AND HAD TO SURVIVE BY BEGGING FOR FOOD DOOR TO DOOR.
THE DONKEYS RAN OFF WHEN I TRIED TO GIVE THEM WATER, SO I LOST MY RIDE, AND I WAS STUCK HERE TRYING TO STAY OUT OF THE WIND AND RAIN–
HM? HEY, ISN'T THAT PARONA GIRL WITH YOU?
AND WHAT ABOUT THAT MONSTER?
HEY, SAY SOME-THING!

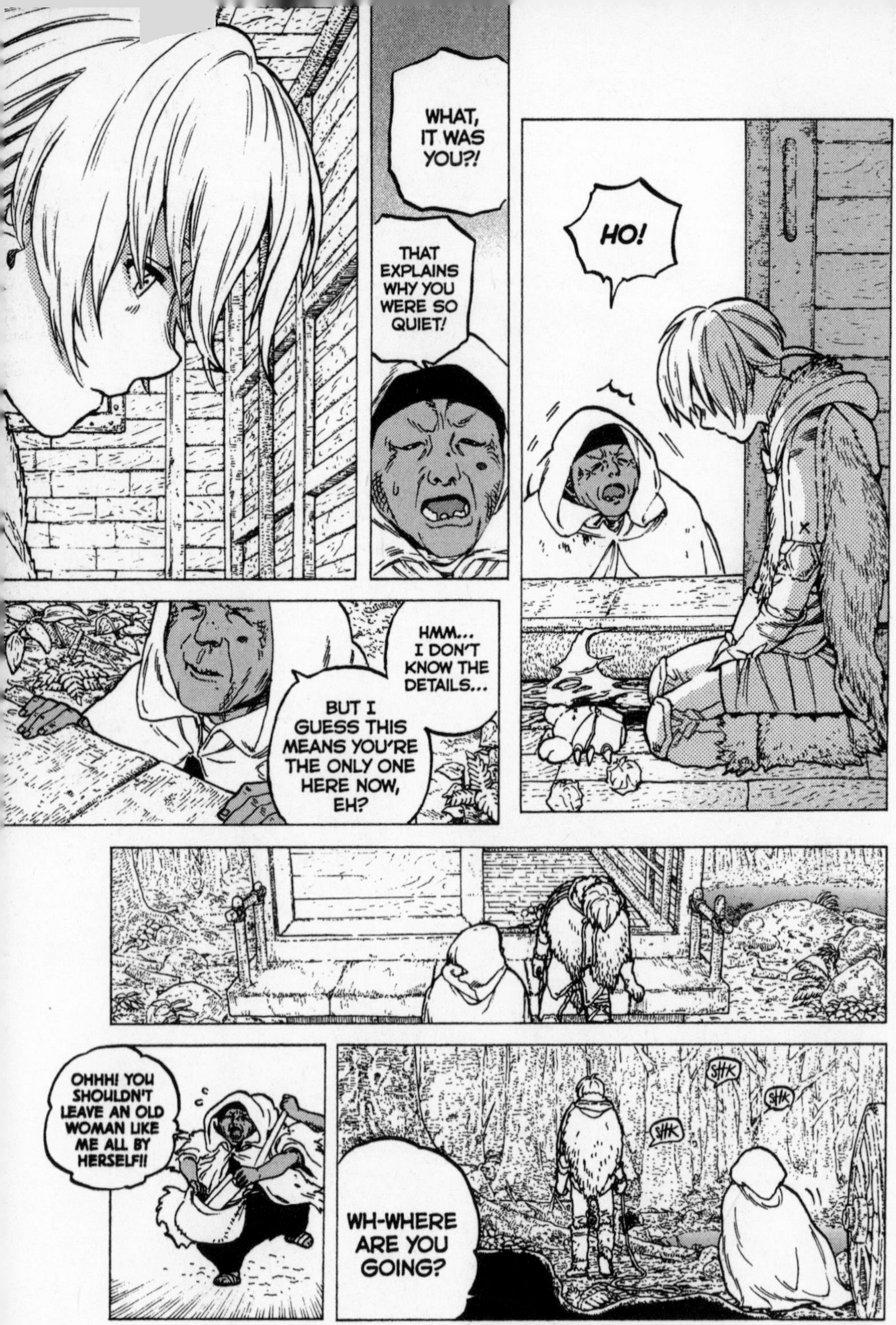
HO!
WHAT, IT WAS YOU?!
THAT EXPLAINS WHY YOU WERE SO QUIET!
HMM... I DON'T KNOW THE DETAILS...
BUT I GUESS THIS MEANS YOU'RE THE ONLY ONE HERE NOW, EH?
SHK
SHK
SHK
WH-WHERE ARE YOU GOING?
OHHH! YOU SHOULDN'T LEAVE AN OLD WOMAN LIKE ME ALL BY HERSELF!!

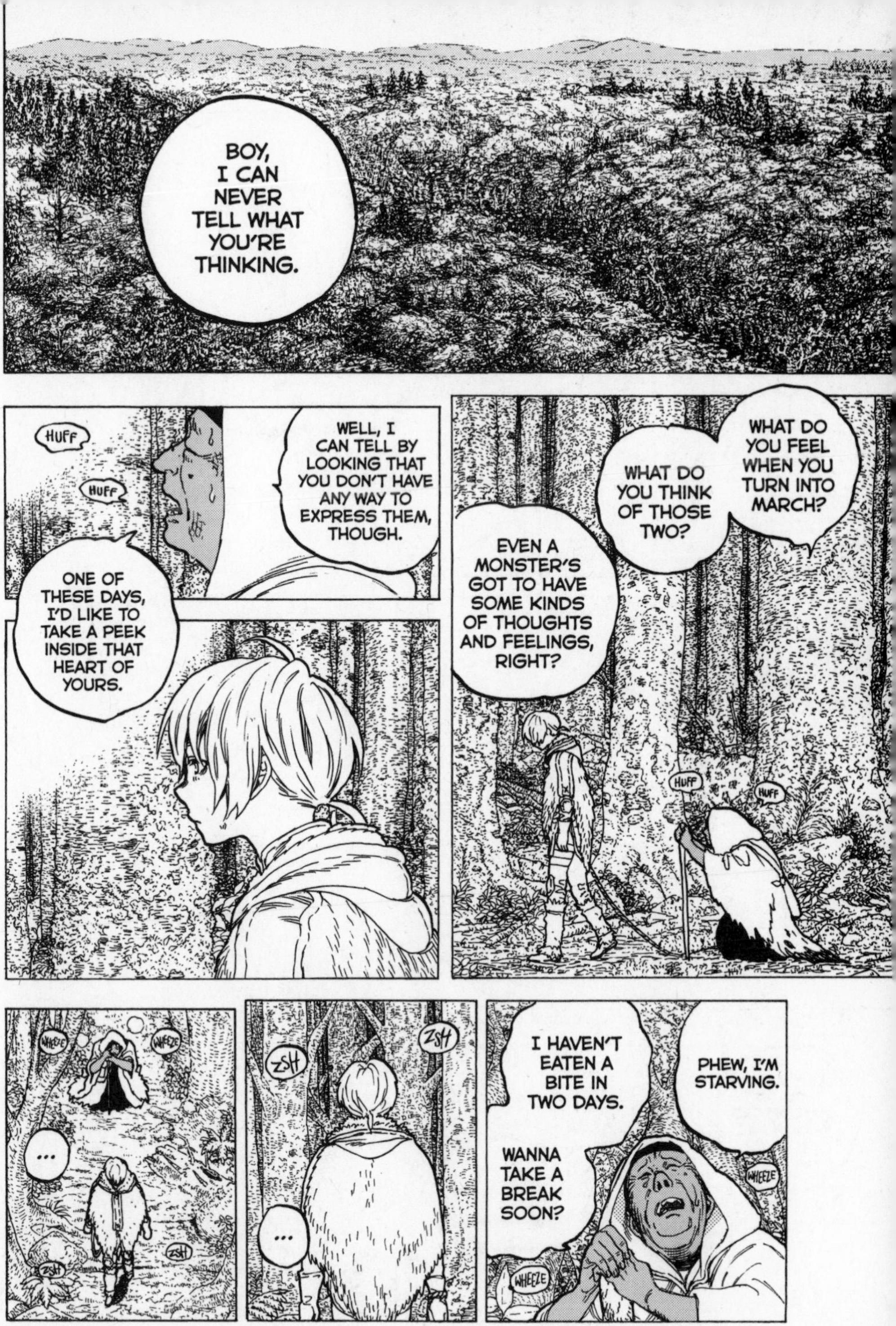
BOY, I CAN NEVER TELL WHAT YOU'RE THINKING.
WHAT DO YOU FEEL WHEN YOU TURN INTO MARCH?
WHAT DO YOU THINK OF THOSE TWO?
EVEN A MONSTER'S GOT TO HAVE SOME KINDS OF THOUGHTS AND FEELINGS, RIGHT?
HUFF
HUFF
HUFF
HUFF
WELL, I CAN TELL BY LOOKING THAT YOU DON'T HAVE ANY WAY TO EXPRESS THEM, THOUGH.
ONE OF THESE DAYS, I'D LIKE TO TAKE A PEEK INSIDE THAT HEART OF YOURS.
PHEW, I'M STARVING.
I HAVEN'T EATEN A BITE IN TWO DAYS.
WANNA TAKE A BREAK SOON?
WHEEZE
WHEEZE
ZSH
ZSH
...
WHEEZE
WHEEZE
...
ZSH
ZSH

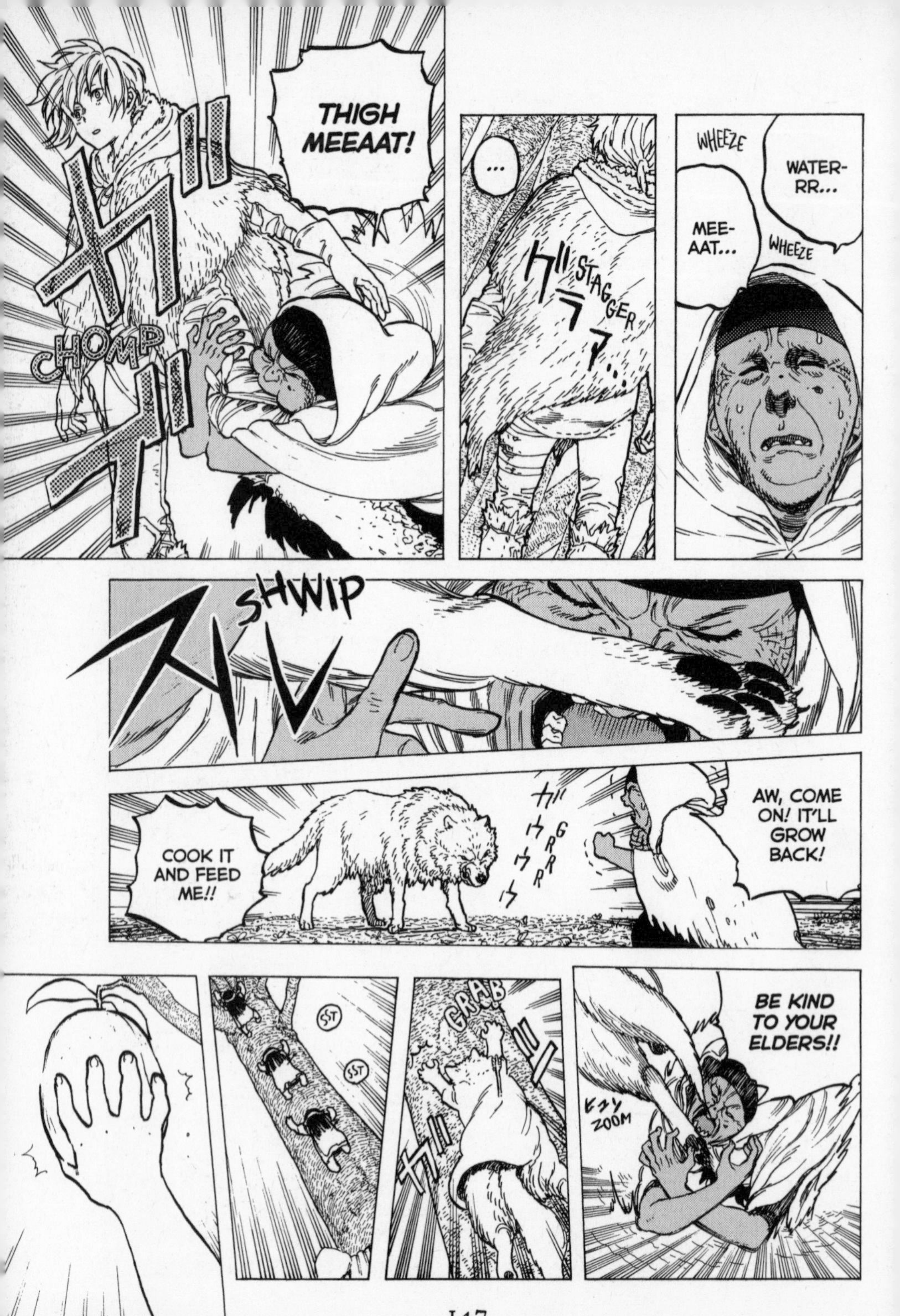
WHEEZE
WATER-RR...
MEE-AAT...
WHEEZE
...
STAGGER
THIGH MEEAAT!
CHOMP
SHWIP
AW, COME ON! IT'LL GROW BACK!
GRRR
COOK IT AND FEED ME!!
BE KIND TO YOUR ELDERS!!
ZOOM
CRAB
SST
SST

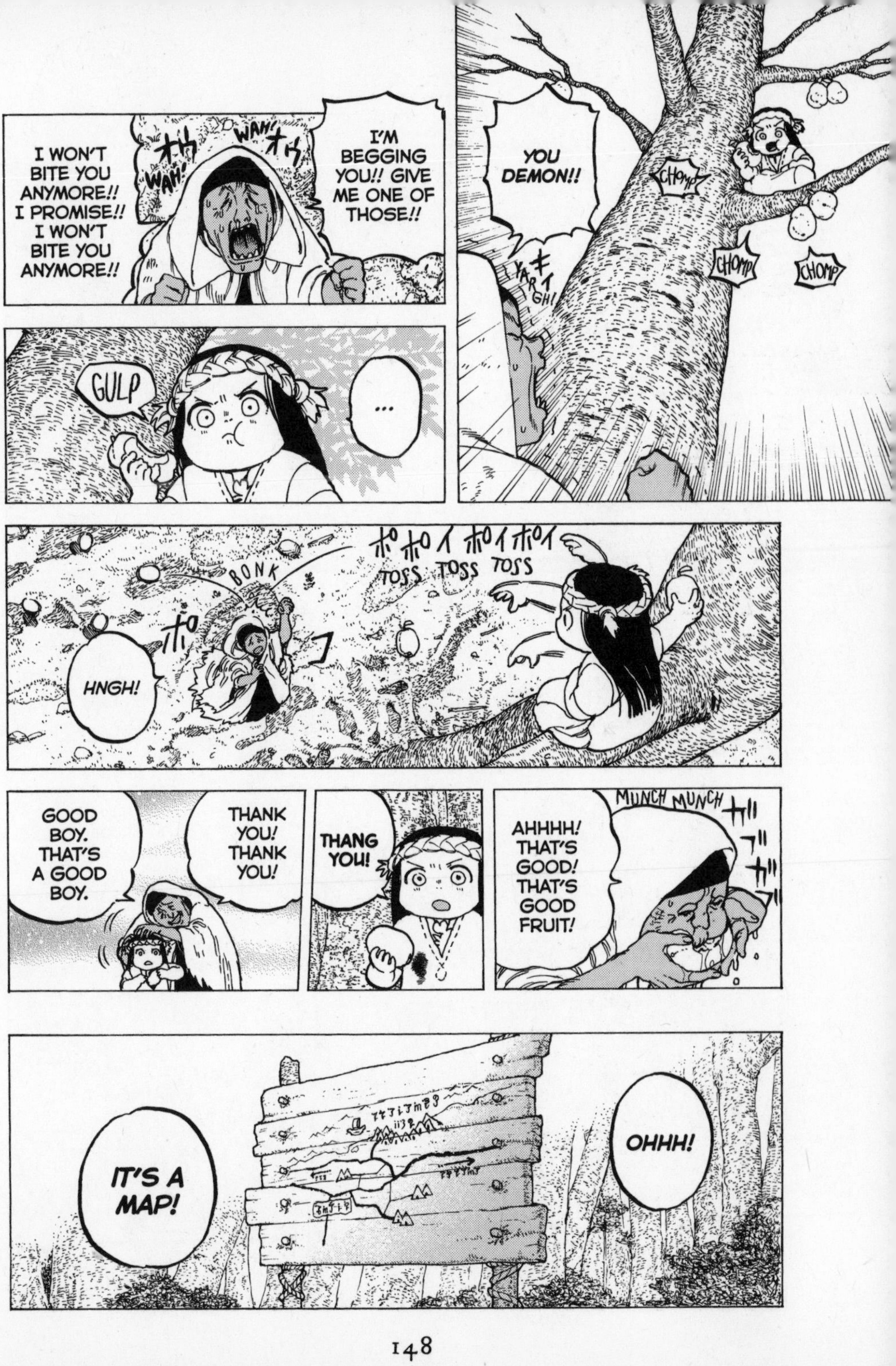
CHOMP
CHOMP
CHOMP
YOU DEMON!!
YARGH!
I'M BEGGING YOU!! GIVE ME ONE OF THOSE!!
WAH! WAH!
I WON'T BITE YOU ANYMORE!! I PROMISE!! I WON'T BITE YOU ANYMORE!!
...
GULP
TOSS TOSS TOSS
BONK
HNGH!
MUNCH MUNCH
AHHHH! THAT'S GOOD! THAT'S GOOD FRUIT!
THANG YOU!
THANK YOU! THANK YOU!
GOOD BOY. THAT'S A GOOD BOY.
OHHH!
IT'S A MAP!

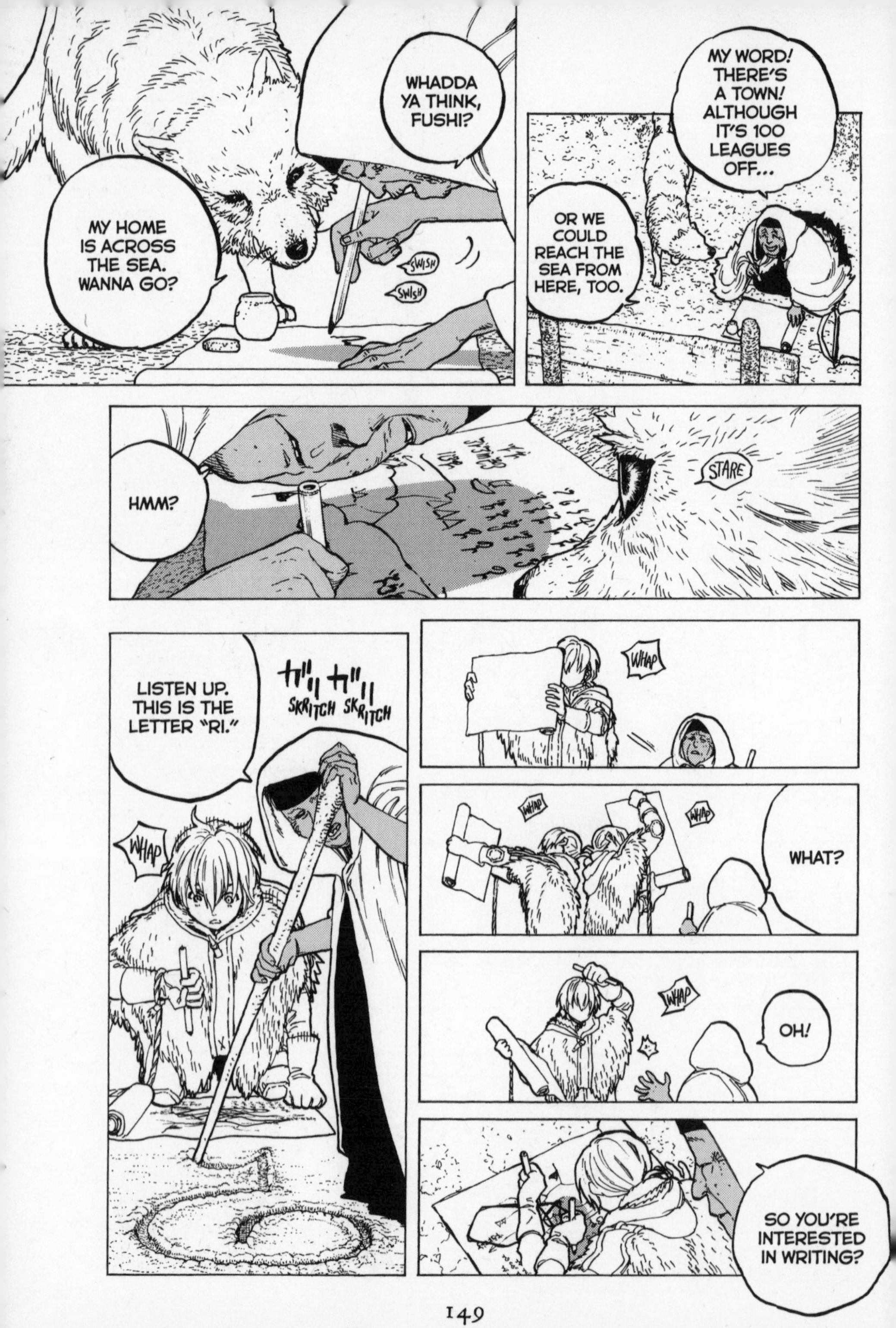

MY WORD! THERE'S A TOWN! ALTHOUGH IT'S 100 LEAGUES OFF...
OR WE COULD REACH THE SEA FROM HERE, TOO.
WHADDA YA THINK, FUSHI?
SWISH
SWISH
MY HOME IS ACROSS THE SEA. WANNA GO?
STARE
HMM?
WHAP
WHAP
WHAP
WHAT?
WHAP
OH!
SO YOU'RE INTERESTED IN WRITING?
ガリガリ
SKRITCH SKRITCH
LISTEN UP. THIS IS THE LETTER "RI."
WHAP

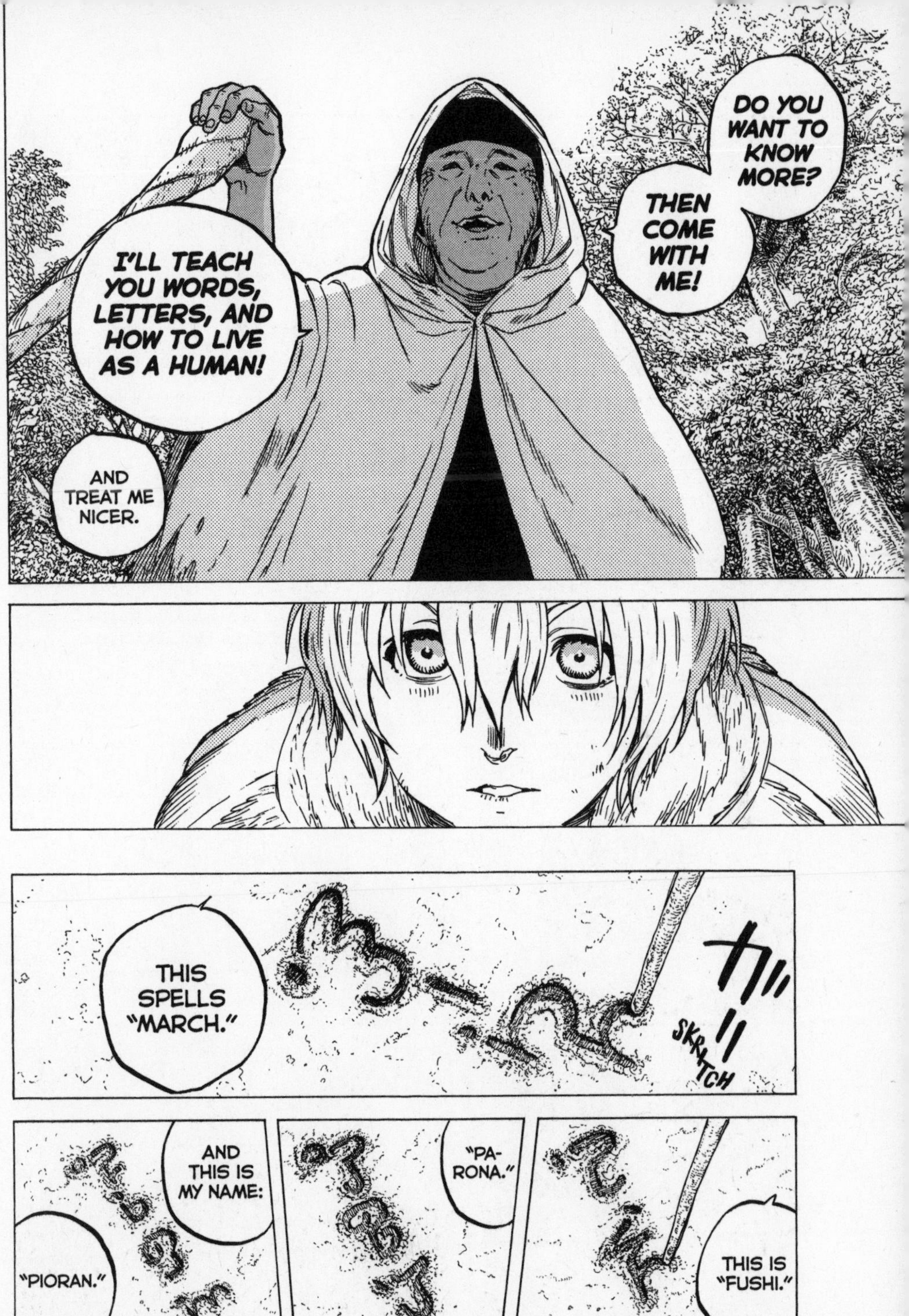
DO YOU WANT TO KNOW MORE?
THEN COME WITH ME!
I'LL TEACH YOU WORDS, LETTERS, AND HOW TO LIVE AS A HUMAN!
AND TREAT ME NICER.
SKRITCH
THIS SPELLS "MARCH."
THIS IS "FUSHI."
"PA-RONA."
AND THIS IS MY NAME:
"PIORAN."

"SUN."
(ᔑ�)

"BIRD."
(ᔑᓗ)

THAT
IS A
"FLOW-
ER."
(ᔑᒉ)

THAT
IS A
"TREE."
(ᒉ)

THANG
YOU.

CHOMP CHOMP

THANG
YOU.

YOU'RE
NOT WRONG,
BUT THERE'S
A MORE
APPROPRIATE
PHRASE TO
USE NOW.

"FIRE."
(ᒉ)

"FISH."
(ᔑᒉᒉ)

"RIVER."
(ᒐᒋ)

THAD'S
GOOD!

THAT'S
GOOD!

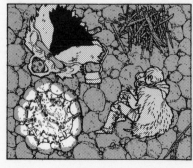

GOOD
NIGHD!

GOOD
NIGHT!

151

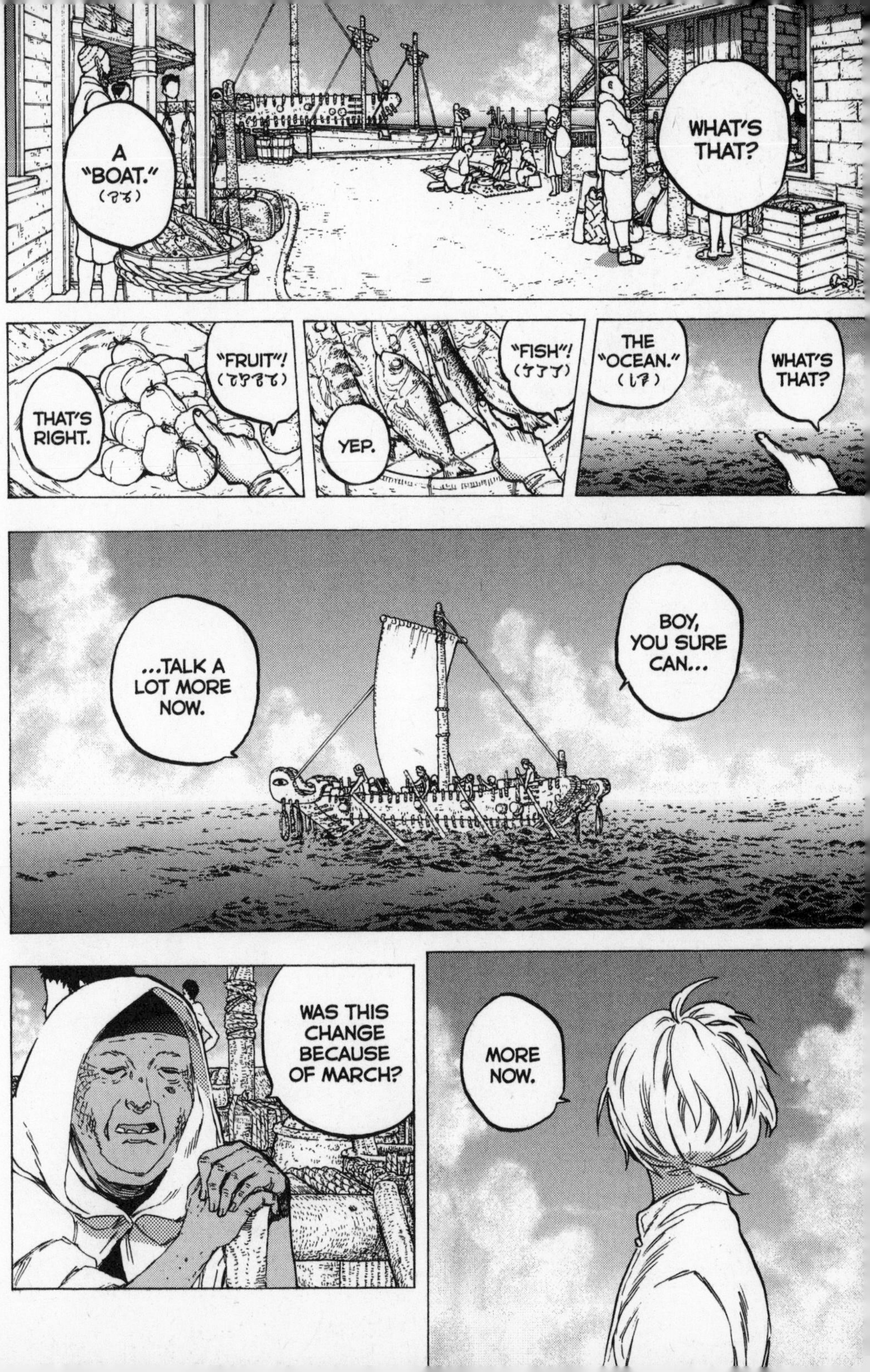
WHAT'S THAT?
A "BOAT."
WHAT'S THAT?
THE "OCEAN."
"FISH"!
YEP.
"FRUIT"!
THAT'S RIGHT.
BOY, YOU SURE CAN...
...TALK A LOT MORE NOW.
MORE NOW.
WAS THIS CHANGE BECAUSE OF MARCH?

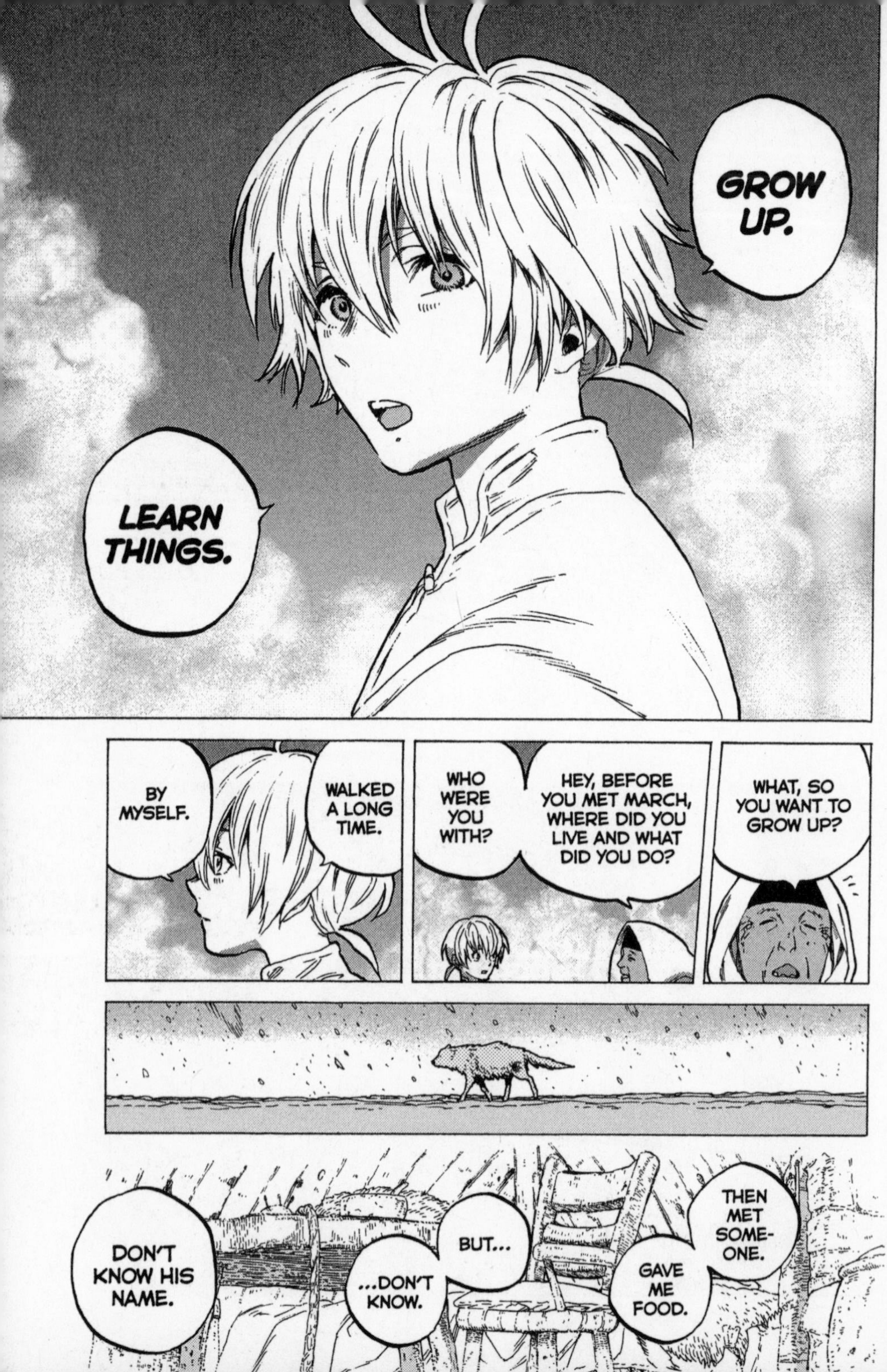
GROW UP.
LEARN THINGS.
WHAT, SO YOU WANT TO GROW UP?
HEY, BEFORE YOU MET MARCH, WHERE DID YOU LIVE AND WHAT DID YOU DO?
WHO WERE YOU WITH?
WALKED A LONG TIME.
BY MYSELF.
THEN MET SOME-ONE.
GAVE ME FOOD.
BUT...
...DON'T KNOW.
DON'T KNOW HIS NAME.

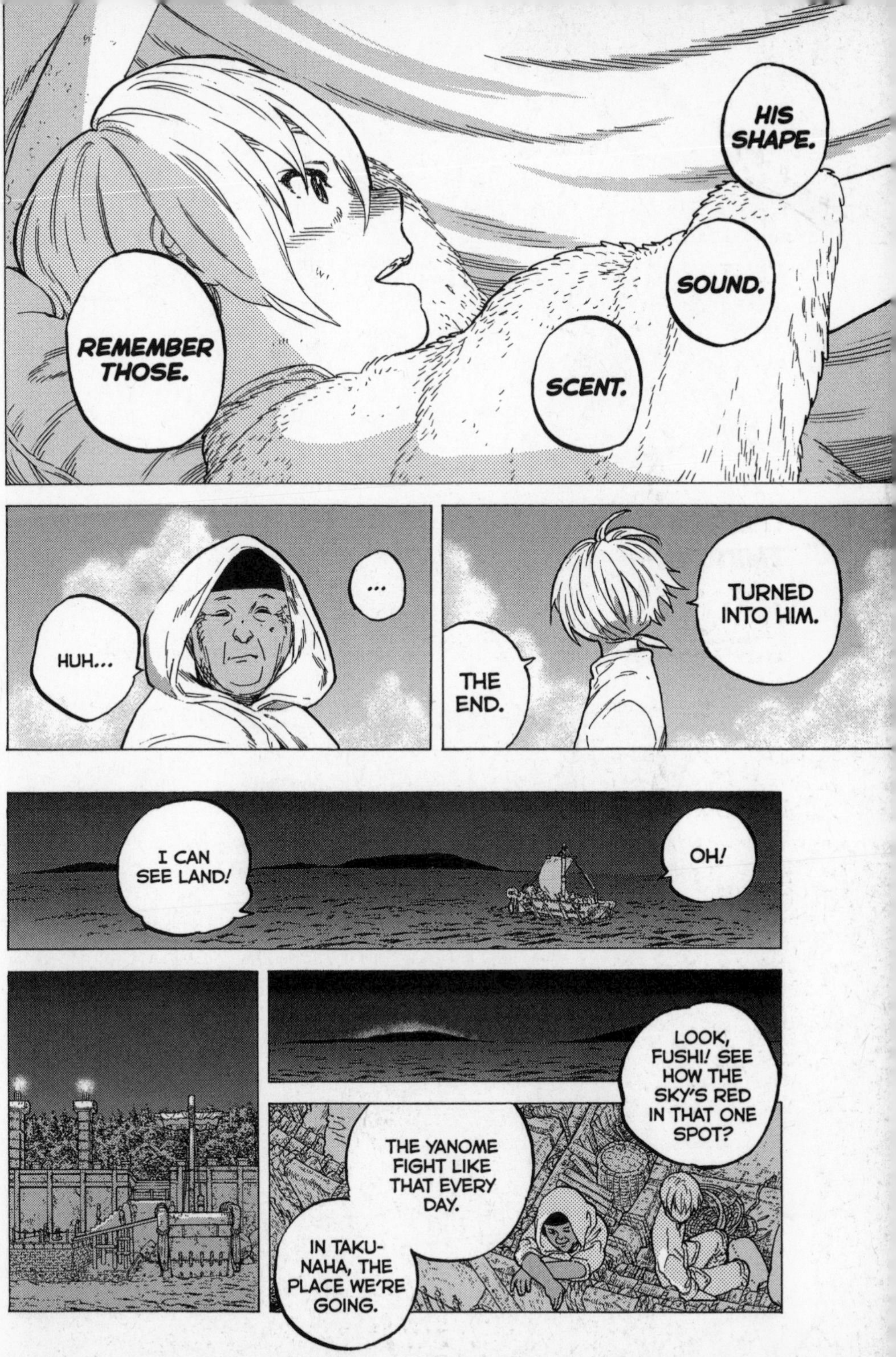
HIS SHAPE.
SOUND.
SCENT.
REMEMBER THOSE.
TURNED INTO HIM.
THE END.
...
HUH...
OH!
I CAN SEE LAND!
LOOK, FUSHI! SEE HOW THE SKY'S RED IN THAT ONE SPOT?
THE YANOME FIGHT LIKE THAT EVERY DAY.
IN TAKU-NAHA, THE PLACE WE'RE GOING.

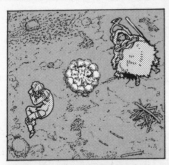

MY LOVER'S PLACE IS UP AHEAD. WE'LL GO THERE FOR NOW.

GOING WHERE?

MY LOVER'S AN INTELLECTUAL. MIGHT BE ABLE TO TELL US SOMETHING ABOUT YOU.

WE SHOULD GET THERE BY TOMOR-ROW.

OH.

IT LOOKS LIKE SOME-ONE HAS PAID MY LITTLE GARDEN A VISIT.

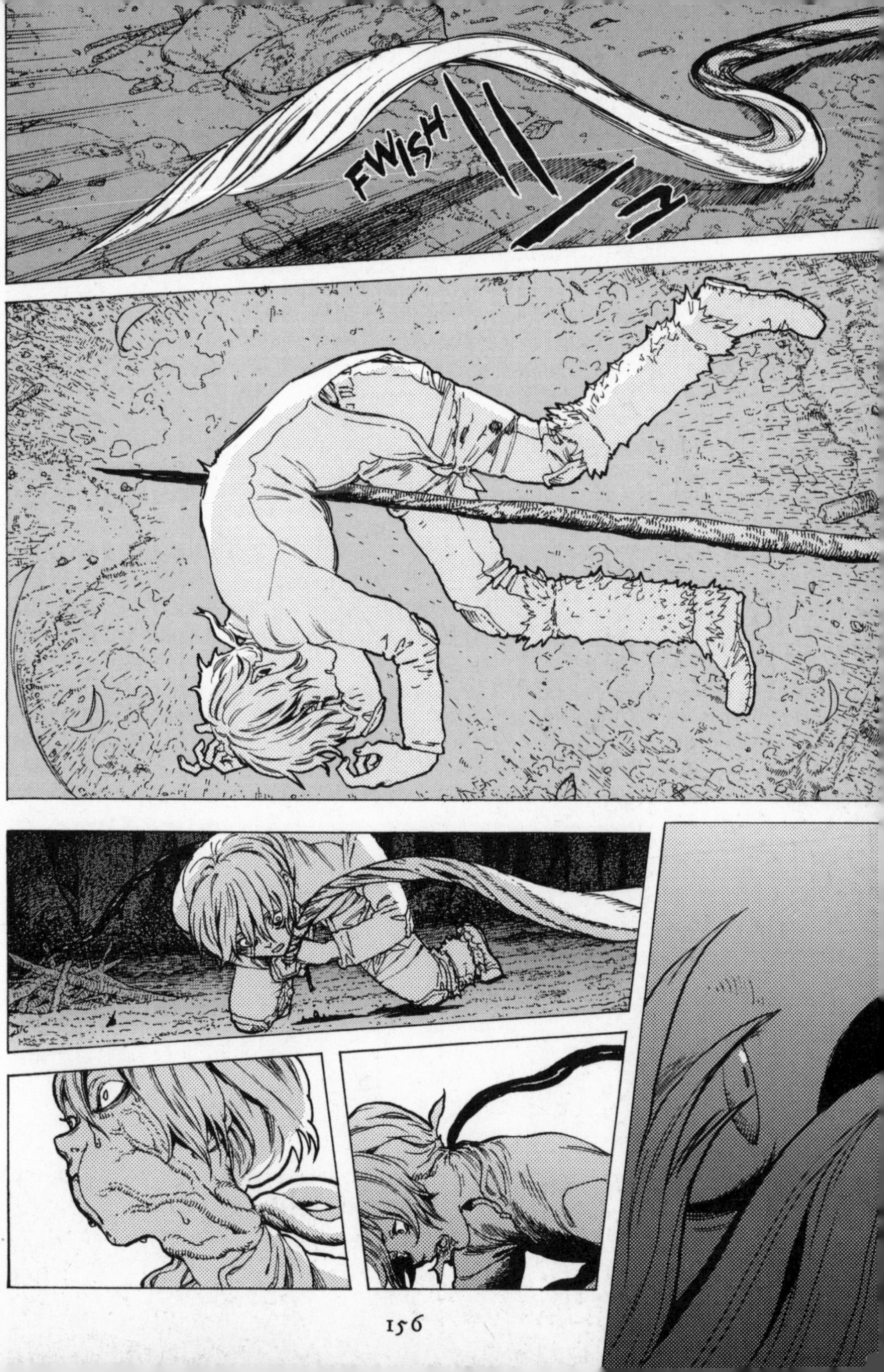
FWISH

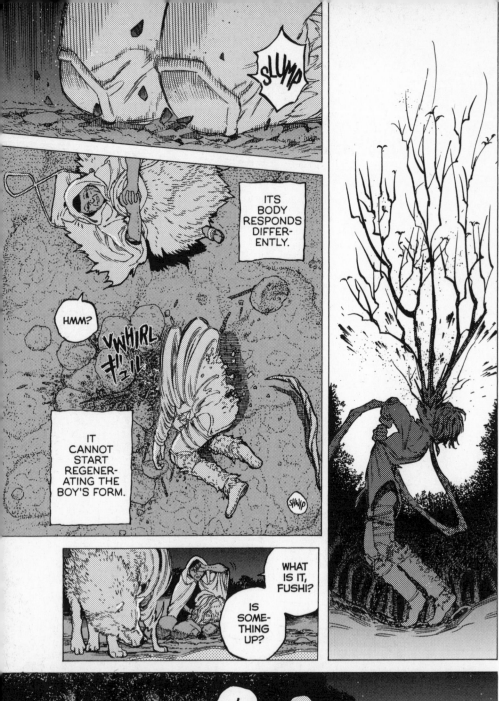

SLUMP

ITS BODY RESPONDS DIFFERENTLY.

HMM?

VWHIRL

IT CANNOT START REGENERATING THE BOY'S FORM.

SHWIP

WHAT IS IT, FUSHI?

IS SOMETHING UP?

!

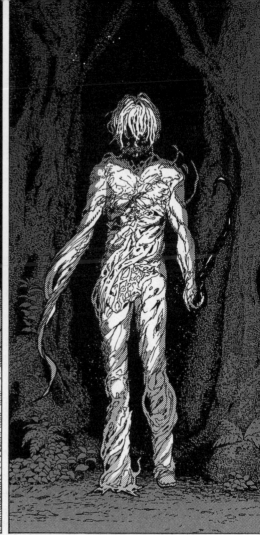

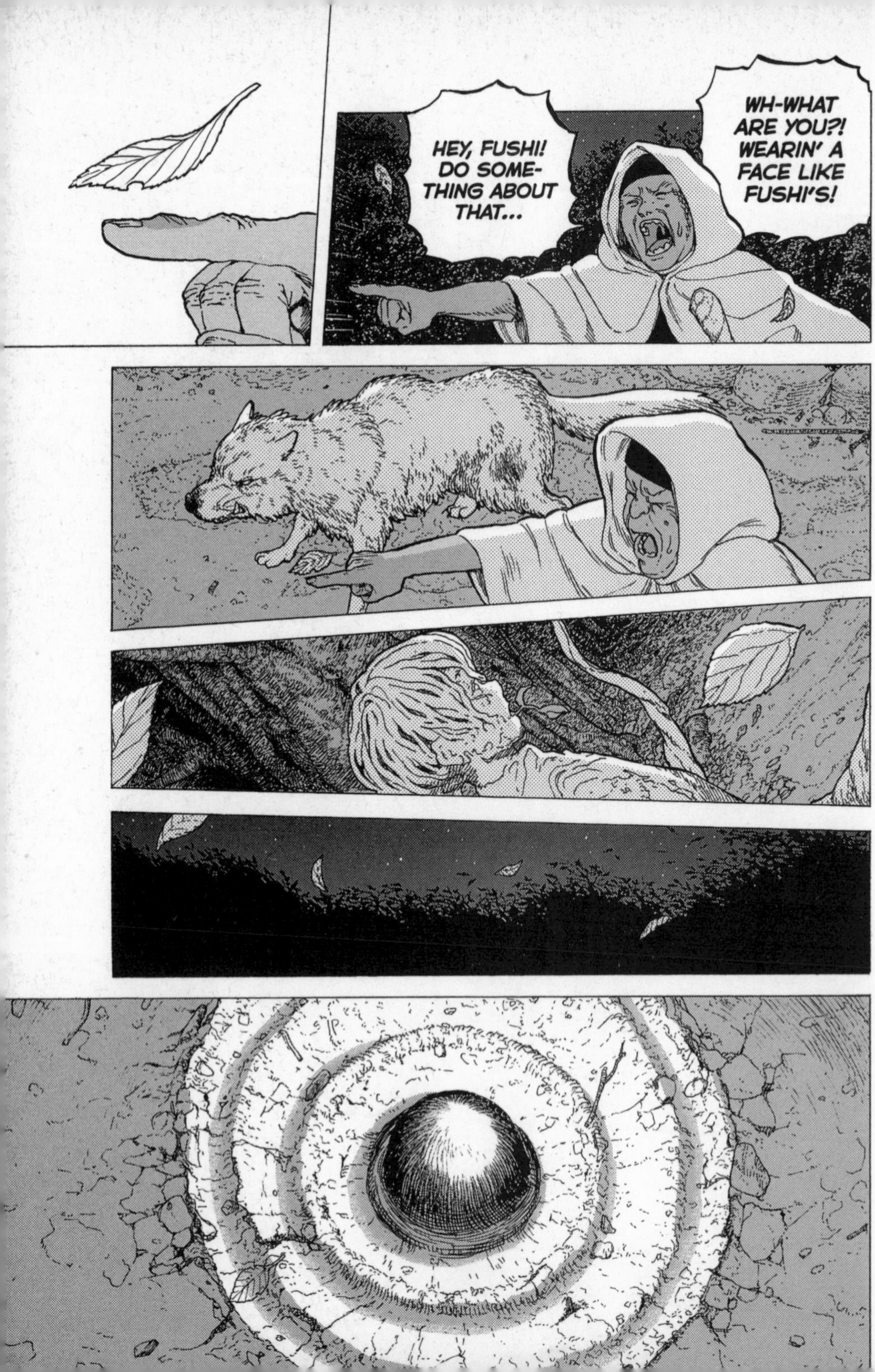
WH-WHAT ARE YOU?! WEARIN' A FACE LIKE FUSHI'S!
HEY, FUSHI! DO SOME-THING ABOUT THAT...

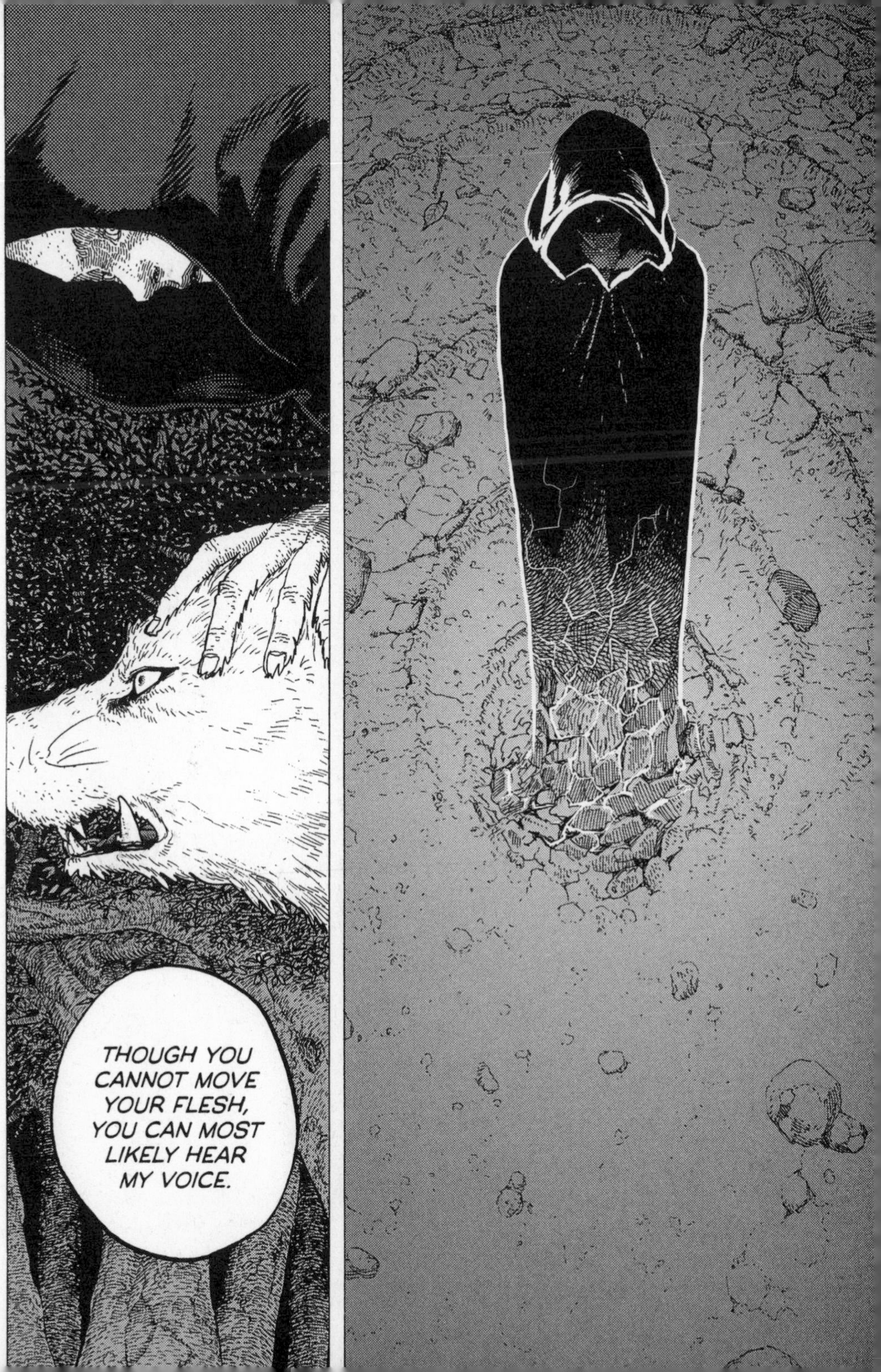
THOUGH YOU CANNOT MOVE YOUR FLESH, YOU CAN MOST LIKELY HEAR MY VOICE.

HOW DOES IT FEEL TO LOSE A PART OF YOURSELF?
THAT **THING** STOLE FROM YOU.
IT STOLE THE BOY.
HIS SHAPE.
HIS SOUND.
HIS SCENT.
AS LONG AS IT IS STOLEN, YOU PROBABLY WILL NOT EVEN BE ABLE TO REMEMBER WHAT WAS TAKEN.
BUT SURELY YOU NOTICED. THAT EMPTINESS. THAT STRANGE DISCOMFORT.
NOW, IS THAT OVER THERE SOMETHING OF VALUE?
ALLOW ME TO GIVE YOU A WORD OF ADVICE AT YOUR INTELLI-GENCE LEVEL.

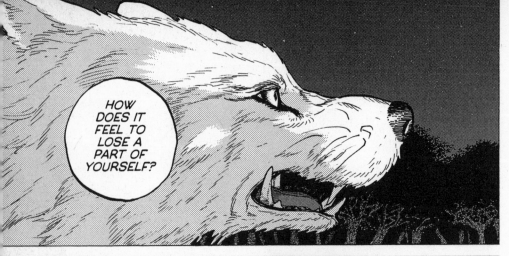

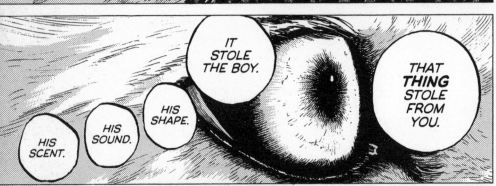

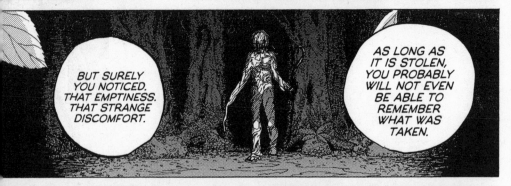

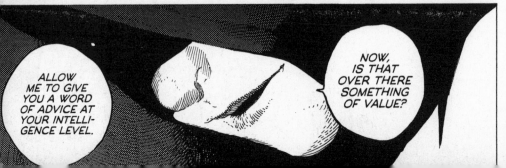

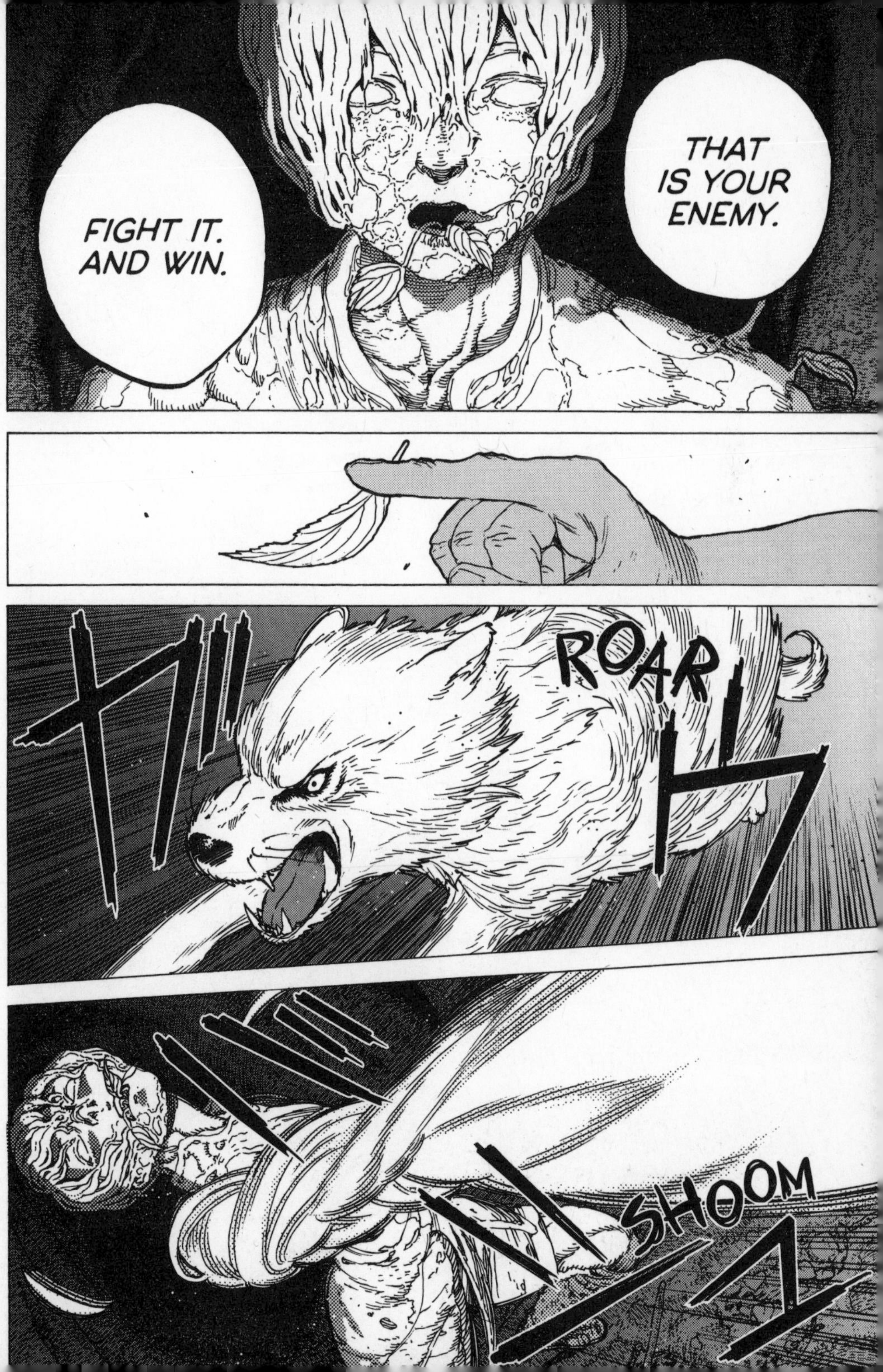
THAT IS YOUR ENEMY.
FIGHT IT. AND WIN.
ROAR
SHOOM

TO YOUR ETERNITY

TO YOUR
ETERNITY

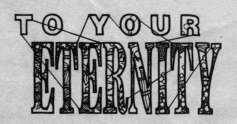

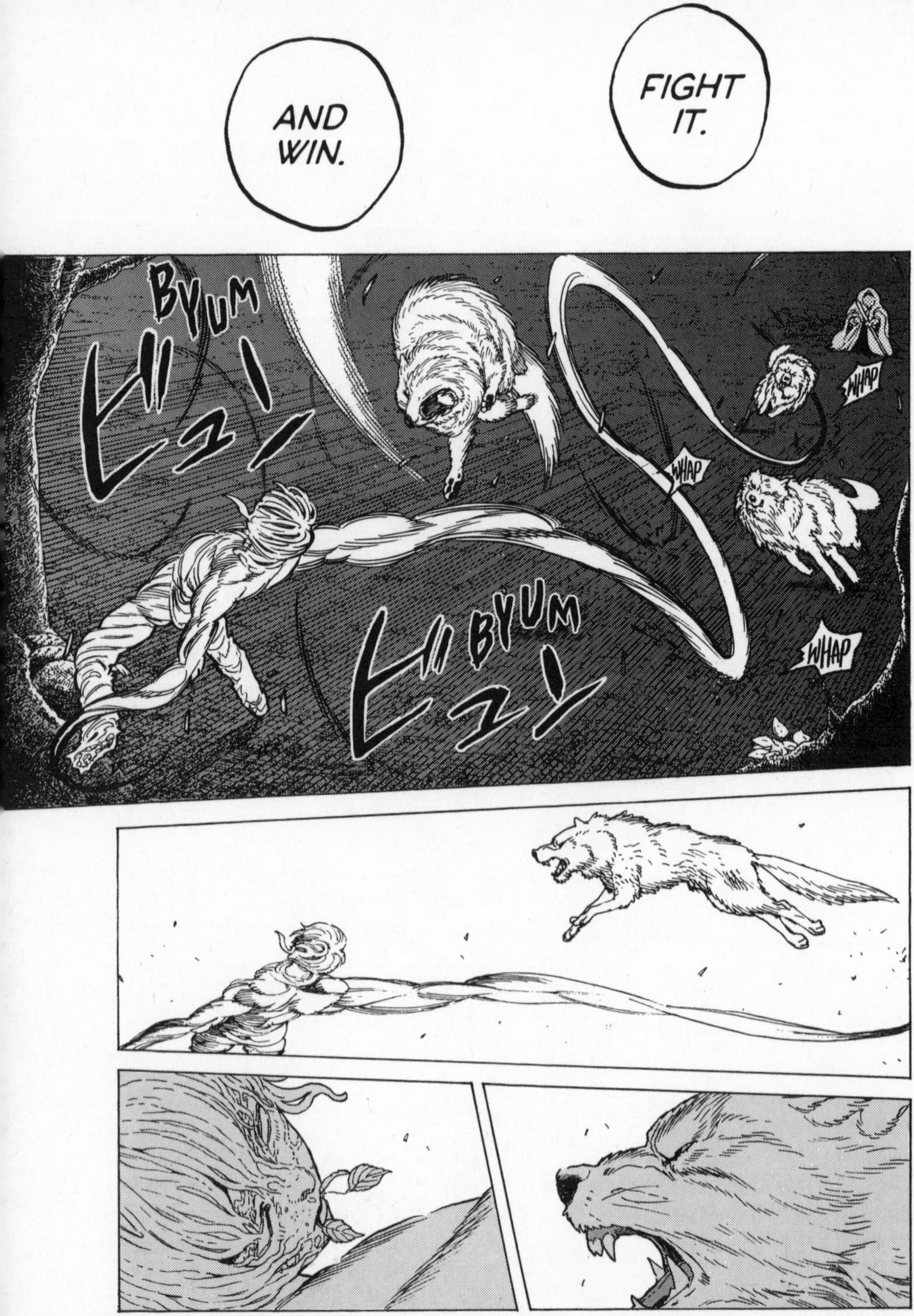
FIGHT IT.
AND WIN.
WHAP
WHAP
BYUM
ビュン
WHAP
BYUM
ビュン

#13 Our Objective

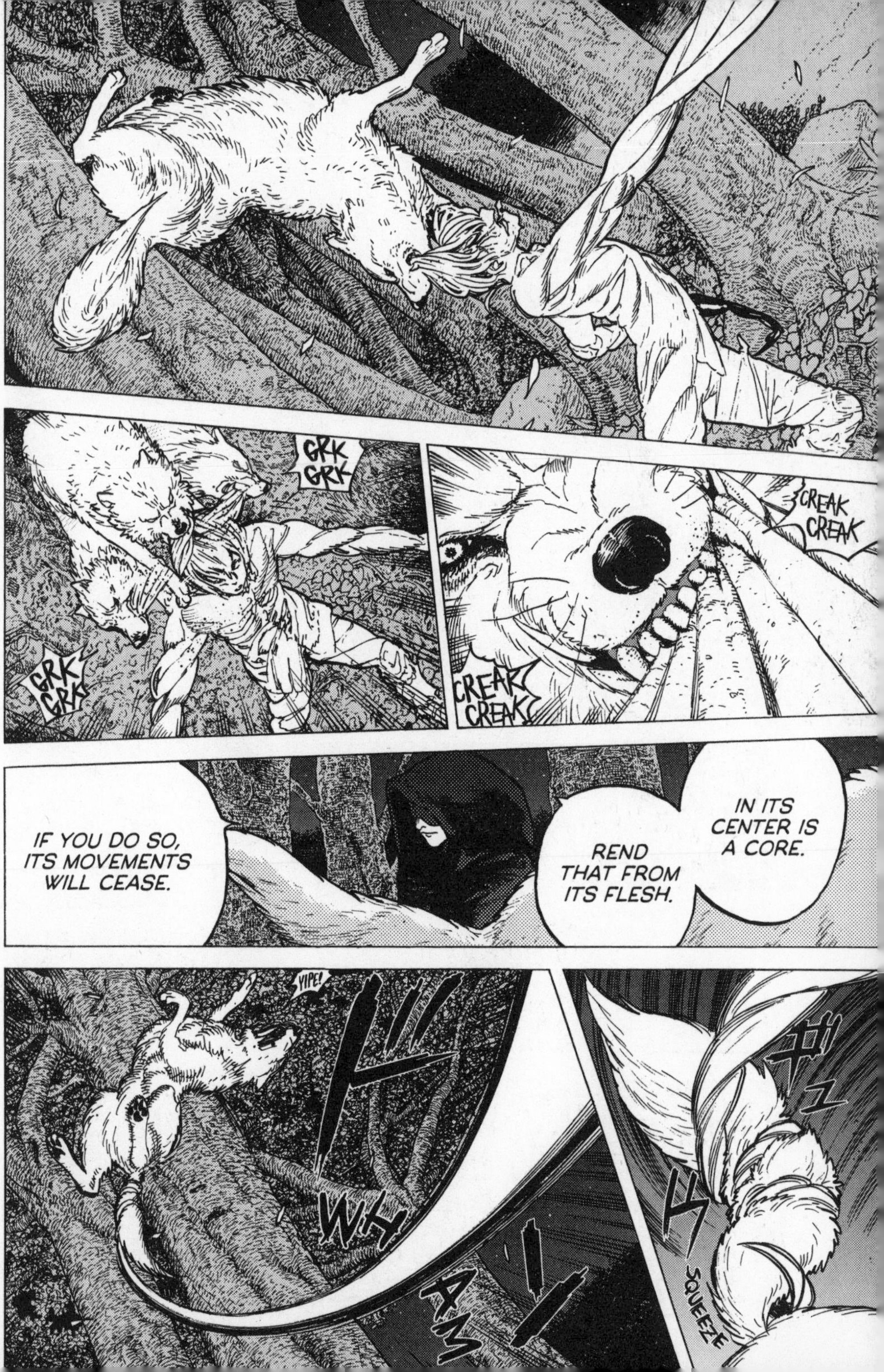
CREAK CREAK
CREAK CREAK
GRK GRK
GRK GRK
IN ITS CENTER IS A CORE.
REND THAT FROM ITS FLESH.
IF YOU DO SO, ITS MOVEMENTS WILL CEASE.
SQUEEZE
YIPE!
WHAM

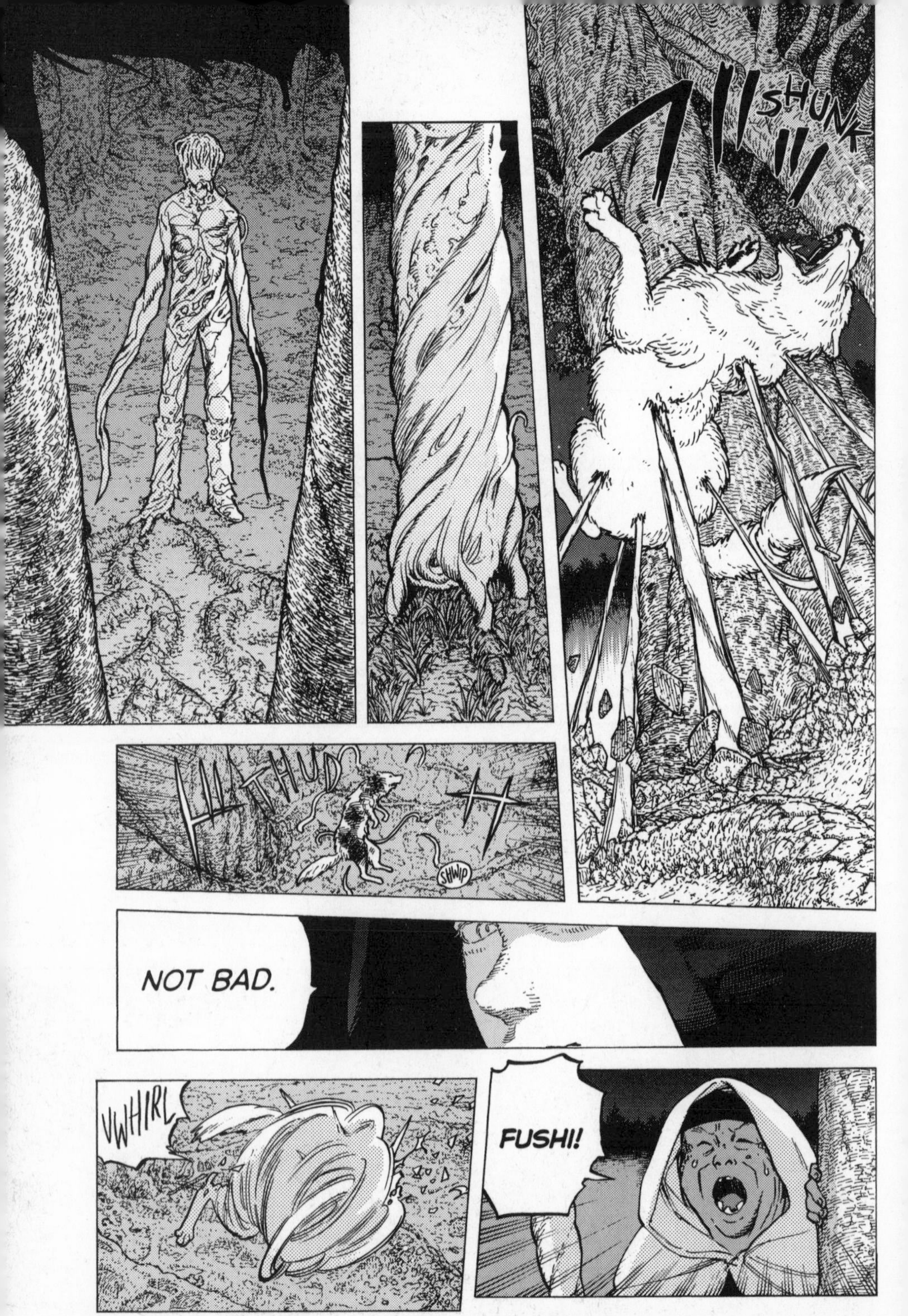
SHUNK
THUD
SHWIP
NOT BAD.
FUSHI!
VWHIRL

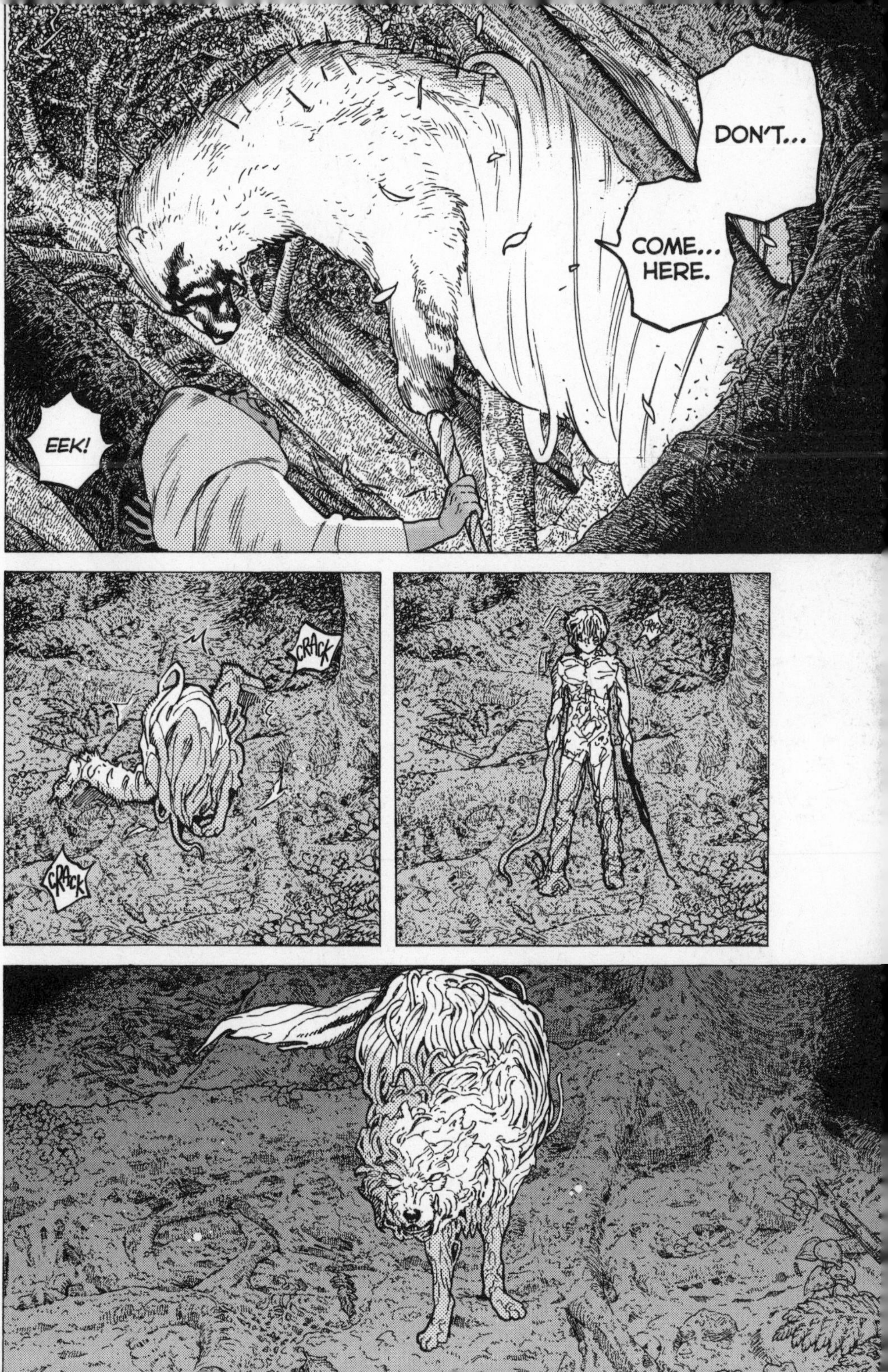
DON'T...
COME... HERE.
EEK!
CRACK
CRACK
CRACK

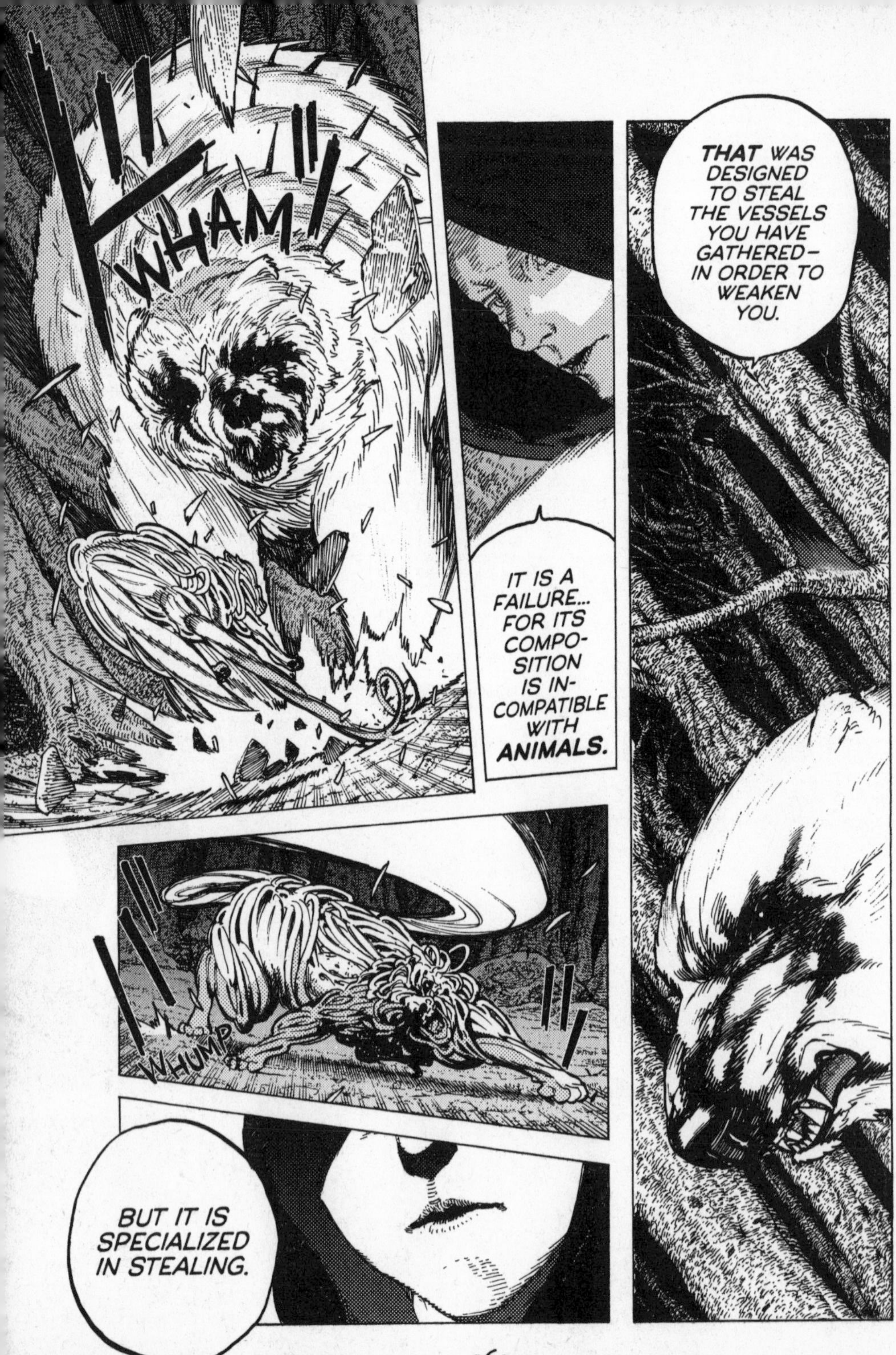
THAT WAS DESIGNED TO STEAL THE VESSELS YOU HAVE GATHERED—IN ORDER TO WEAKEN YOU.
IT IS A FAILURE... FOR ITS COMPOSITION IS INCOMPATIBLE WITH ANIMALS.
WHAM
WHUMP
BUT IT IS SPECIALIZED IN STEALING.

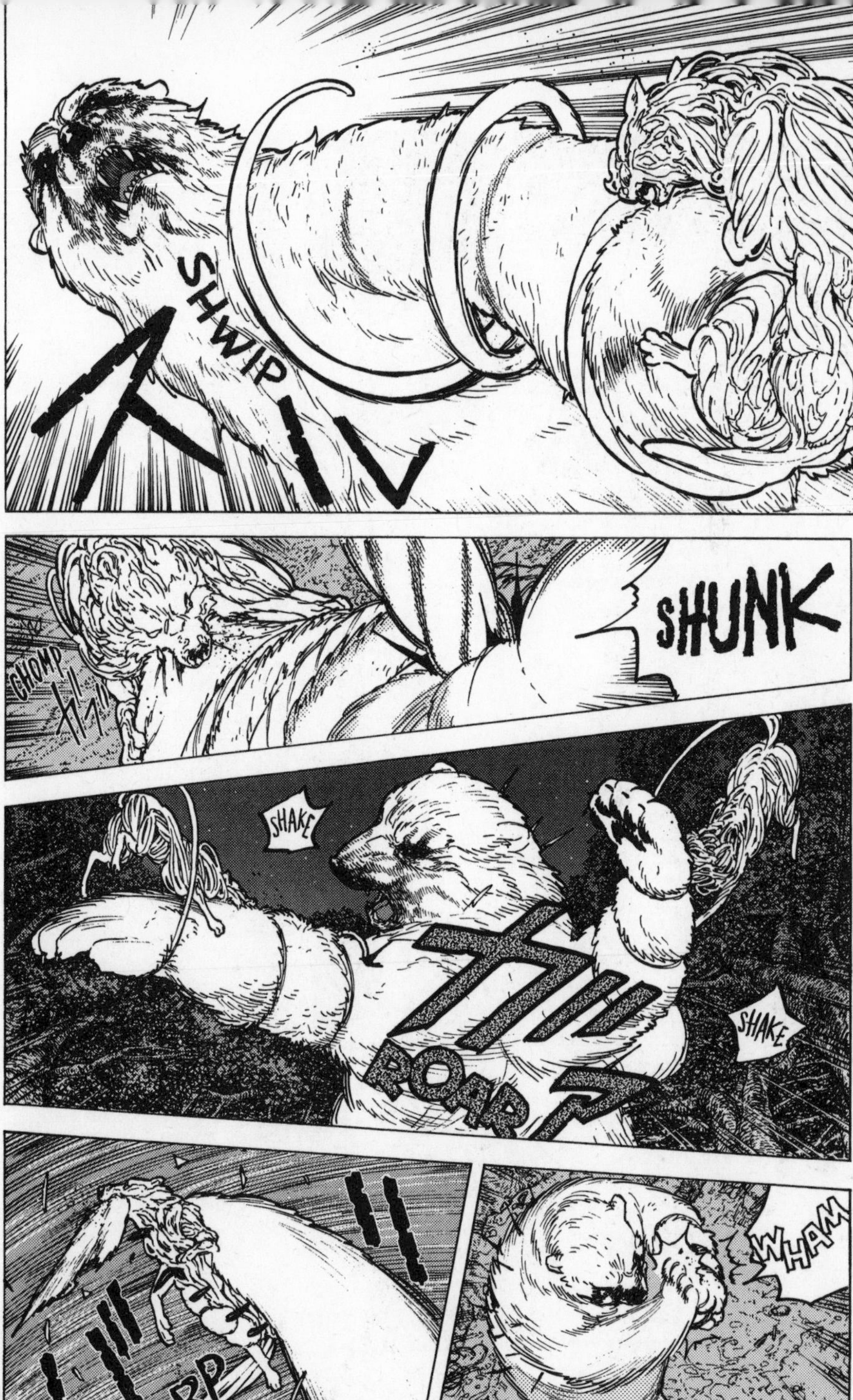
SHWIP
SHUNK
CHOMP
SHAKE
SHAKE
ROAR
WHAM
SHRP

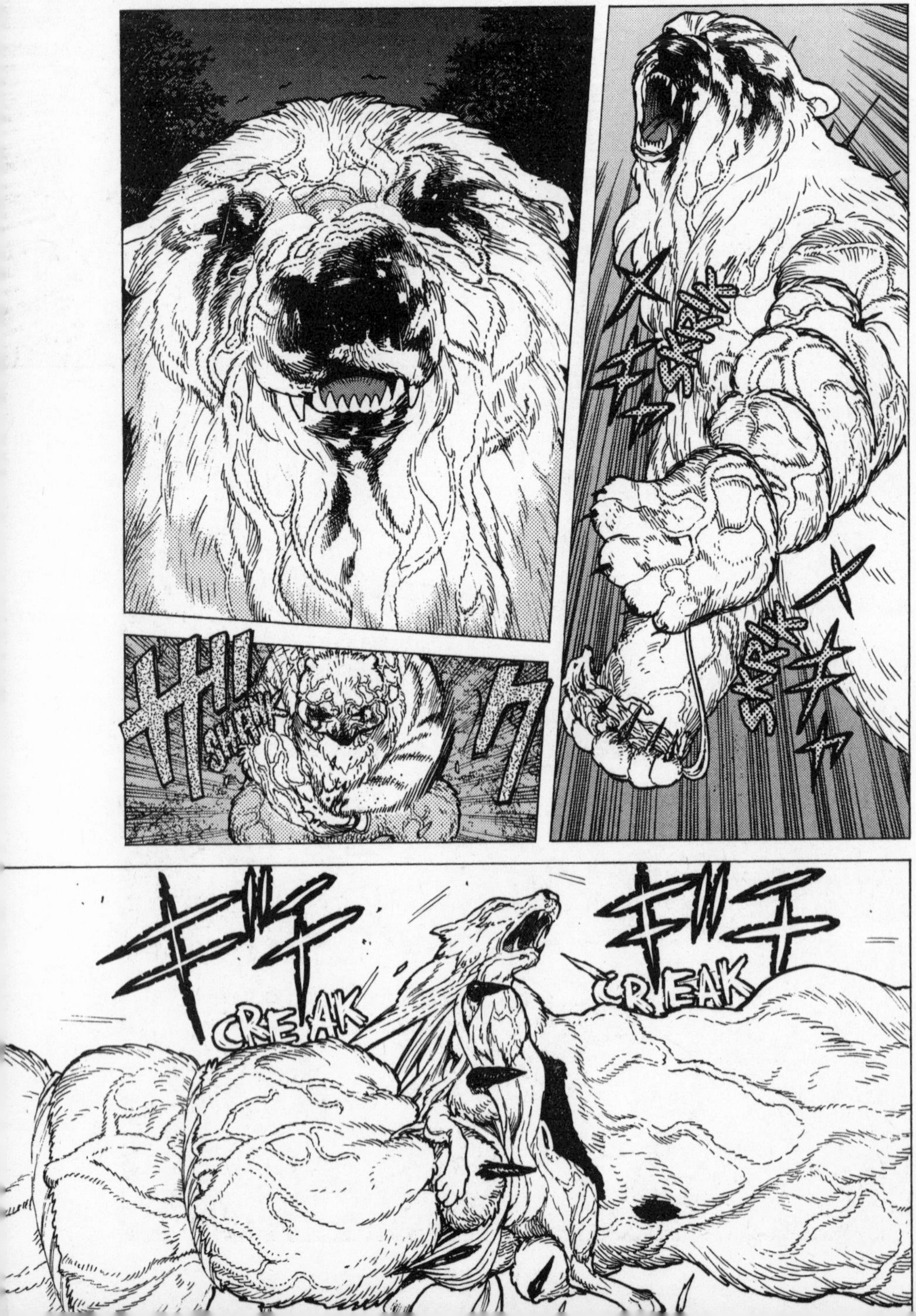
SKRIK
SKRIK
SHANK
CREAK
CREAK

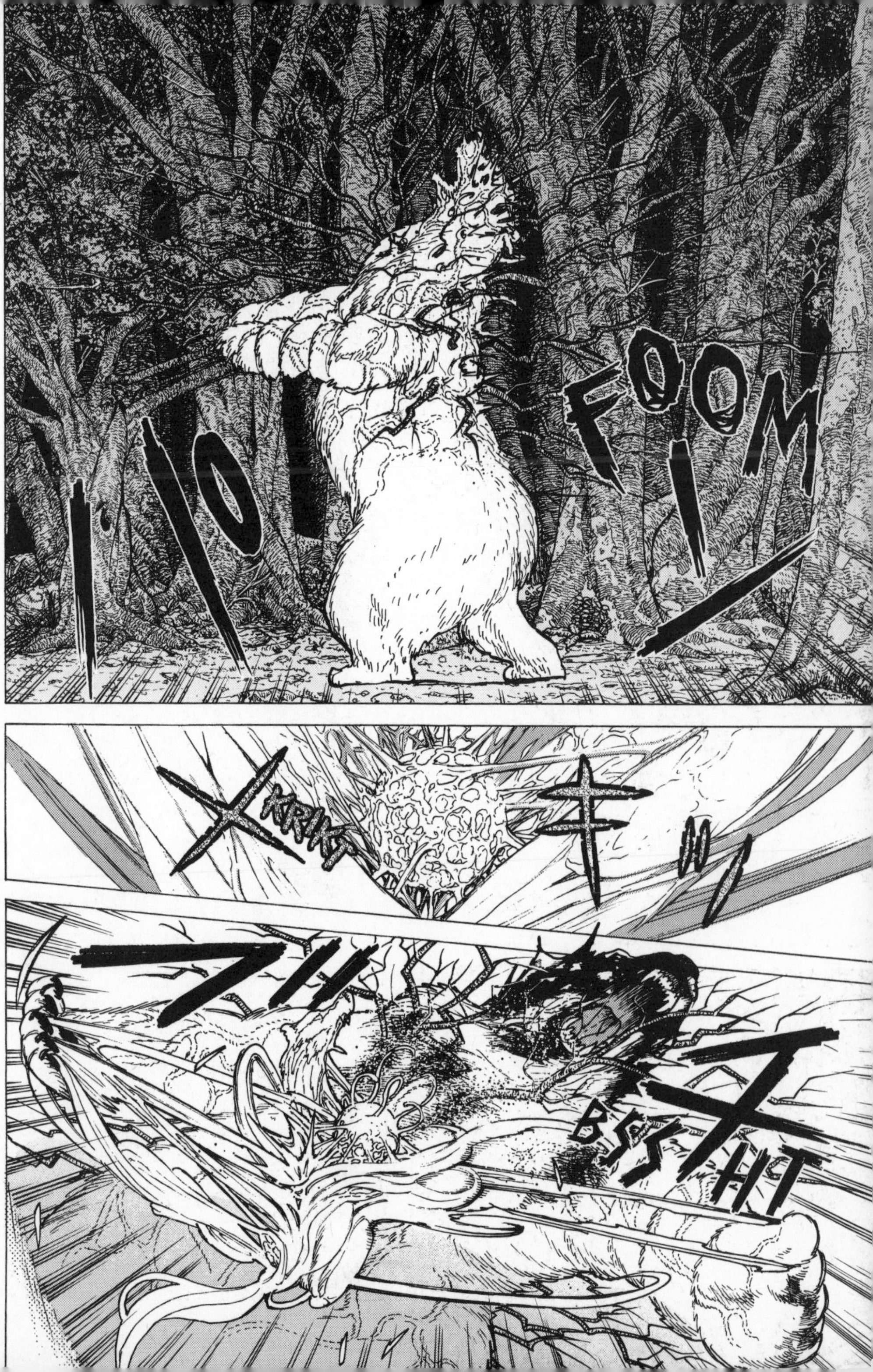
FOOM
KRIKT
BSSHIT

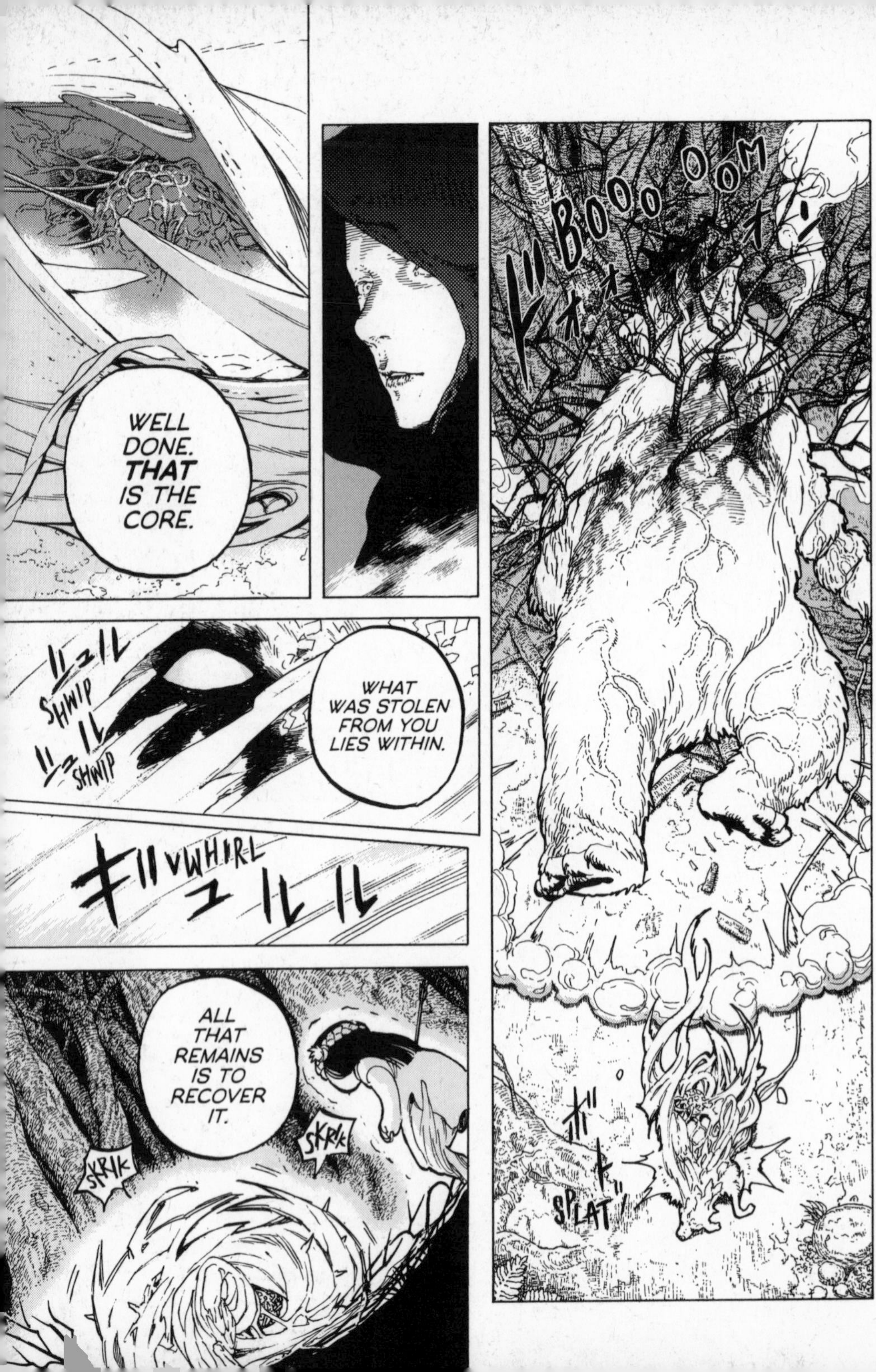
BOOOOOM
SPLAT
WELL DONE. THAT IS THE CORE.
SHWIP
SHWIP
WHAT WAS STOLEN FROM YOU LIES WITHIN.
WHIRL
ALL THAT REMAINS IS TO RECOVER IT.
SKRIK
SKRIK

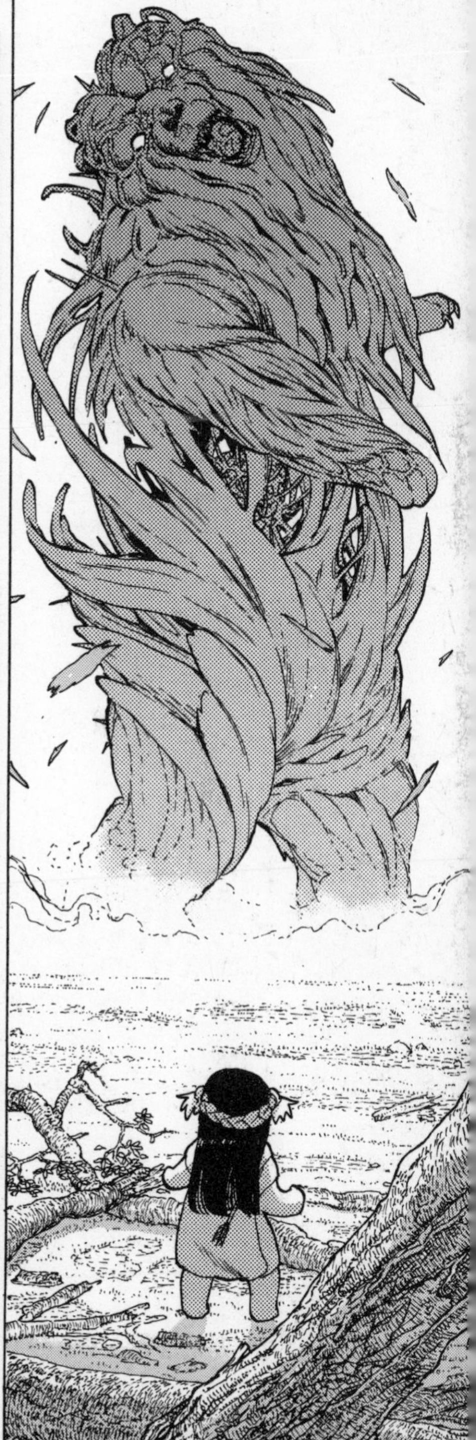

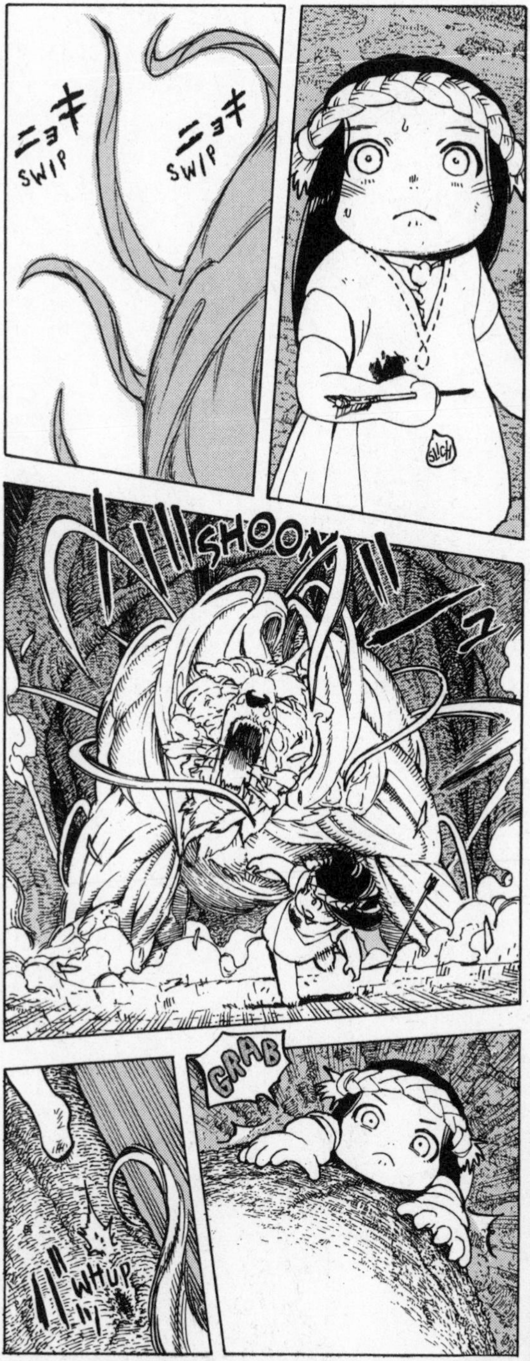
SLICH
ニョキ
SWIP
ニョキ
SWIP
SHOON
GRAB
WHUP

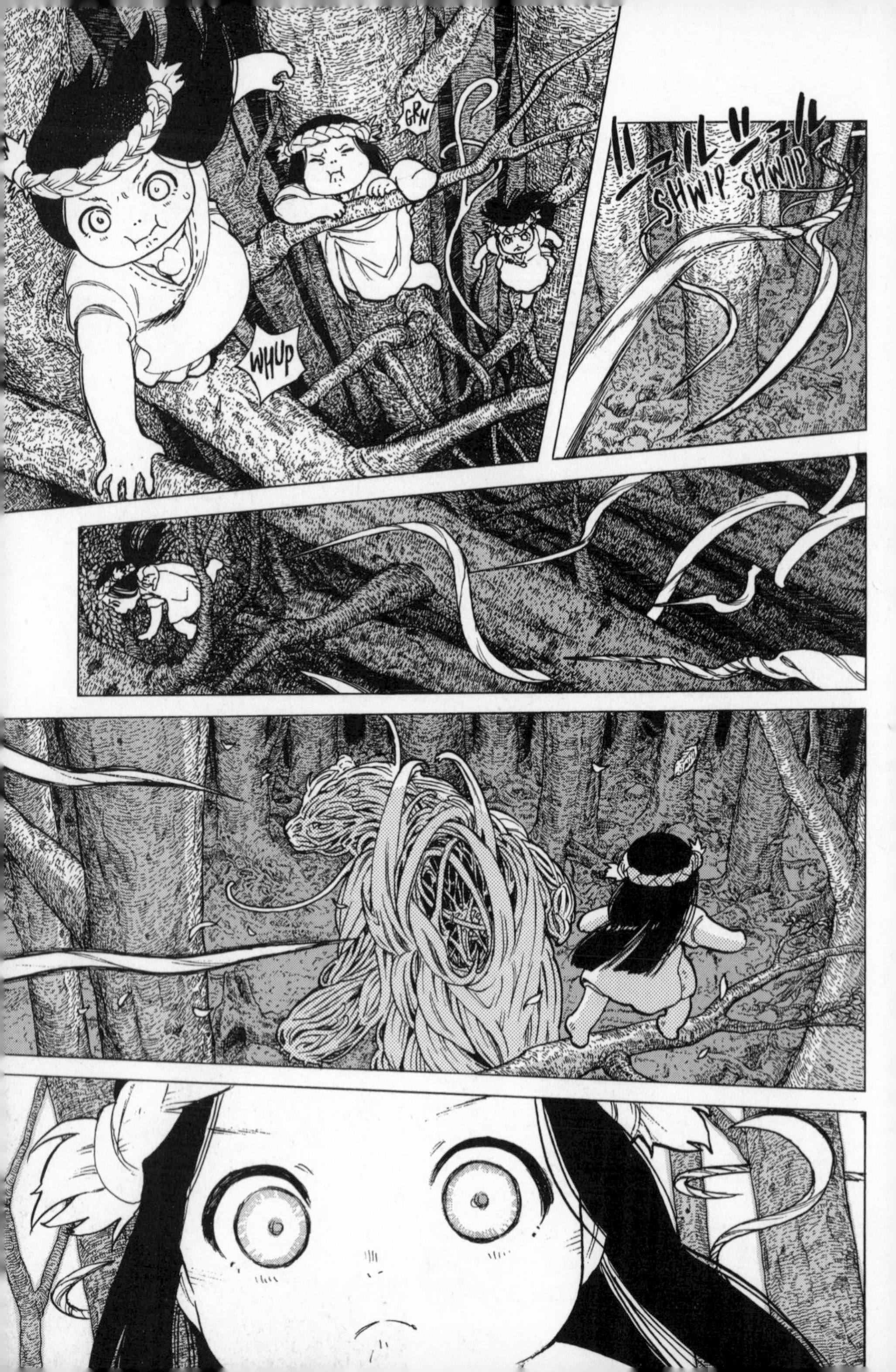
SHWIP SHWIP
GRN
WHUP

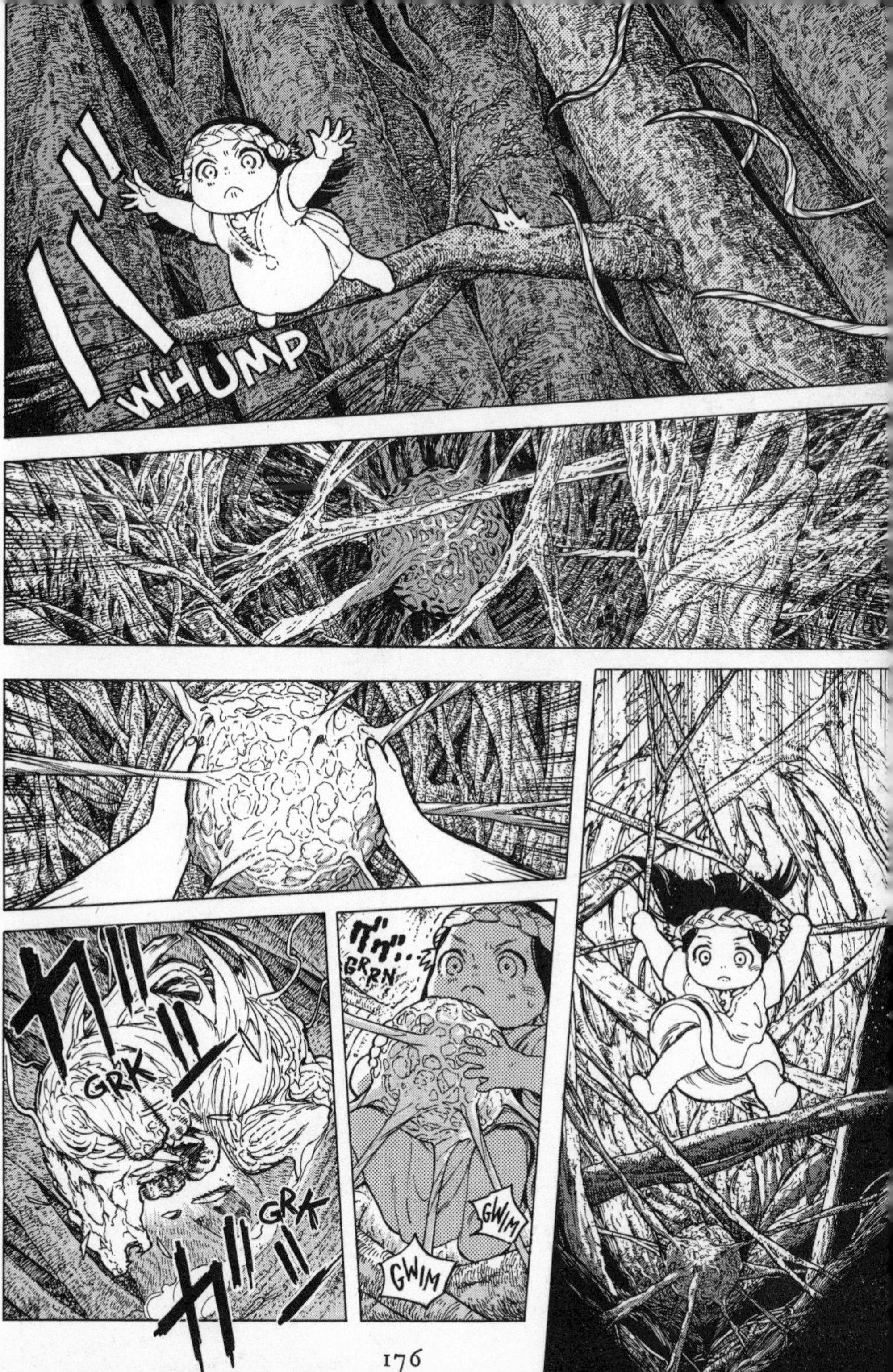
WHUMP
GRRN
GWIM
GWIM
GRK
GRK

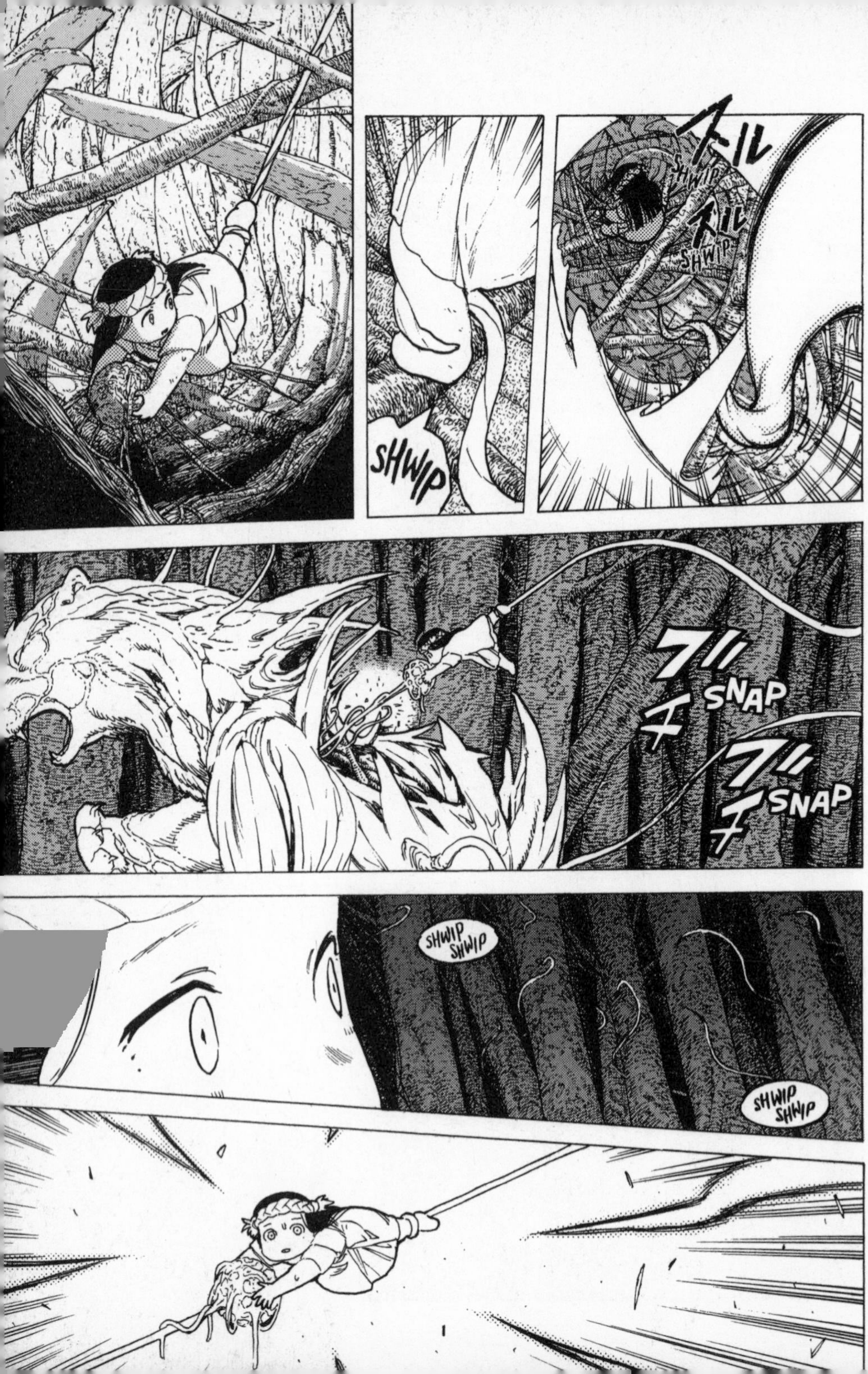
ヌル
SHWIP
ヌル
SHWIP
SHWIP
ブチ
SNAP
ブチ
SNAP
SHWIP SHWIP
SHWIP SHWIP

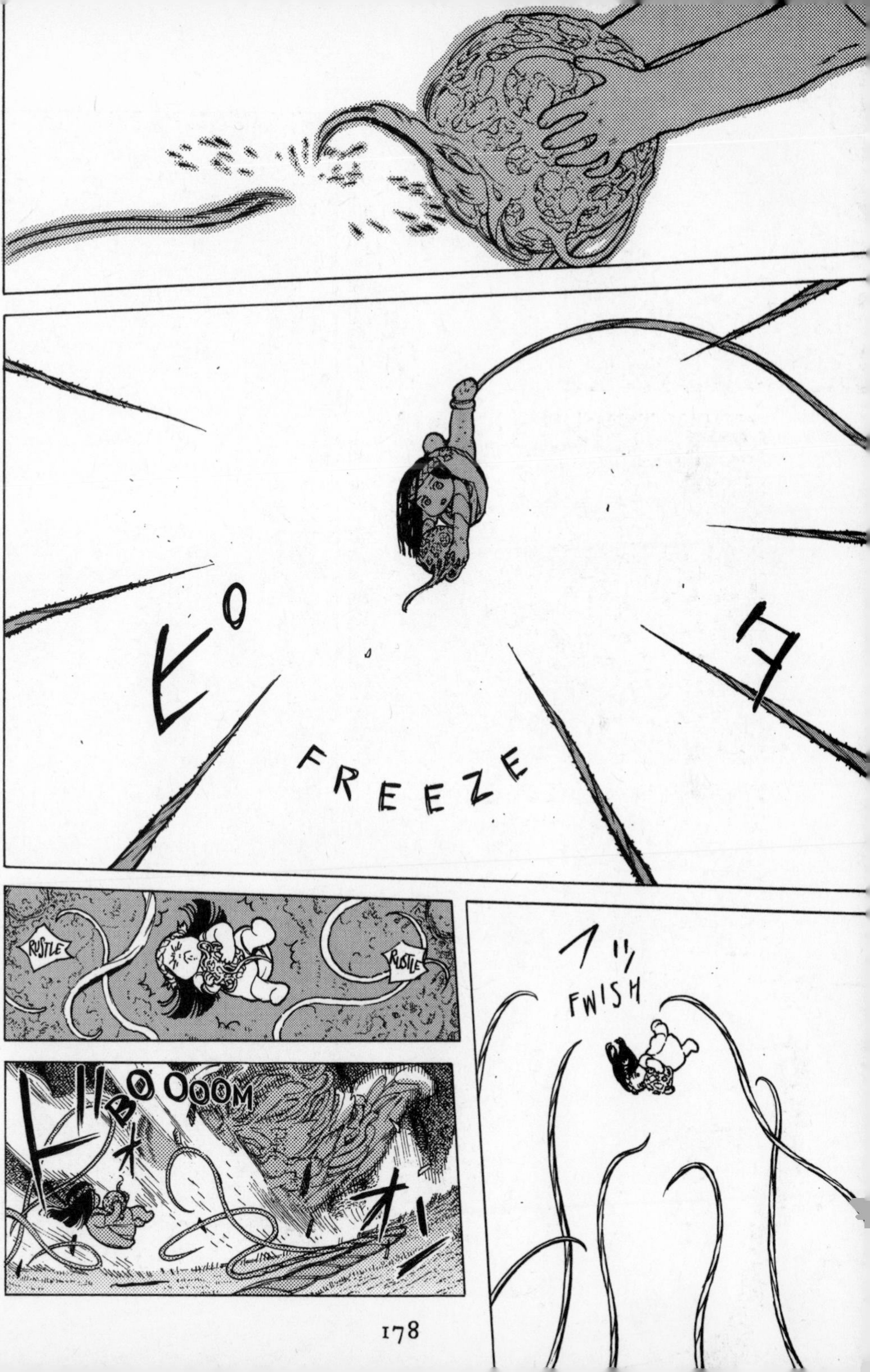
FREEZE
FWISH
RUSTLE
RUSTLE
BOOOOM

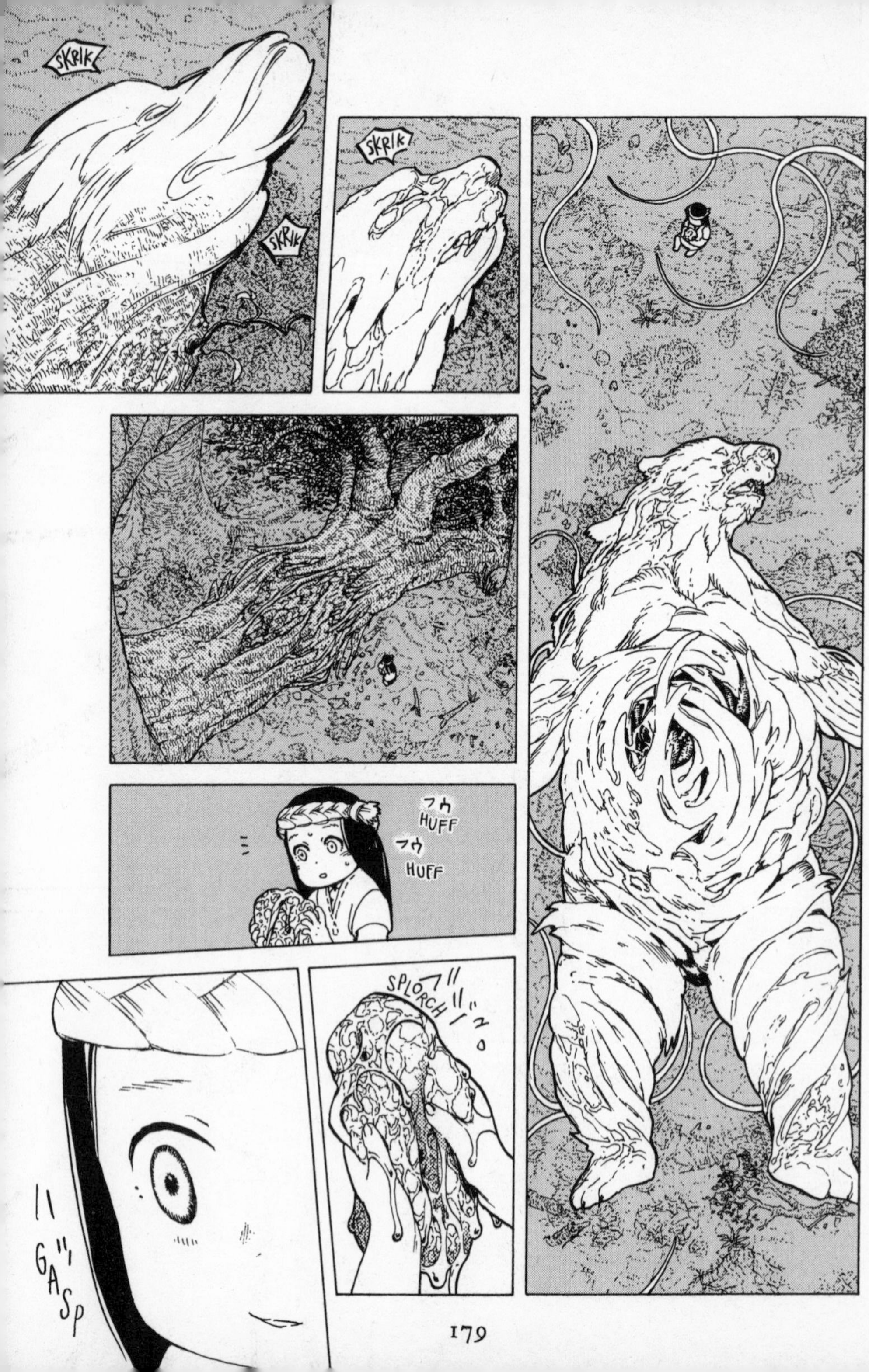
SKRIK
SKRIK
SKRIK
フウ
HUFF
フウ
HUFF
SPLORCH
GASP

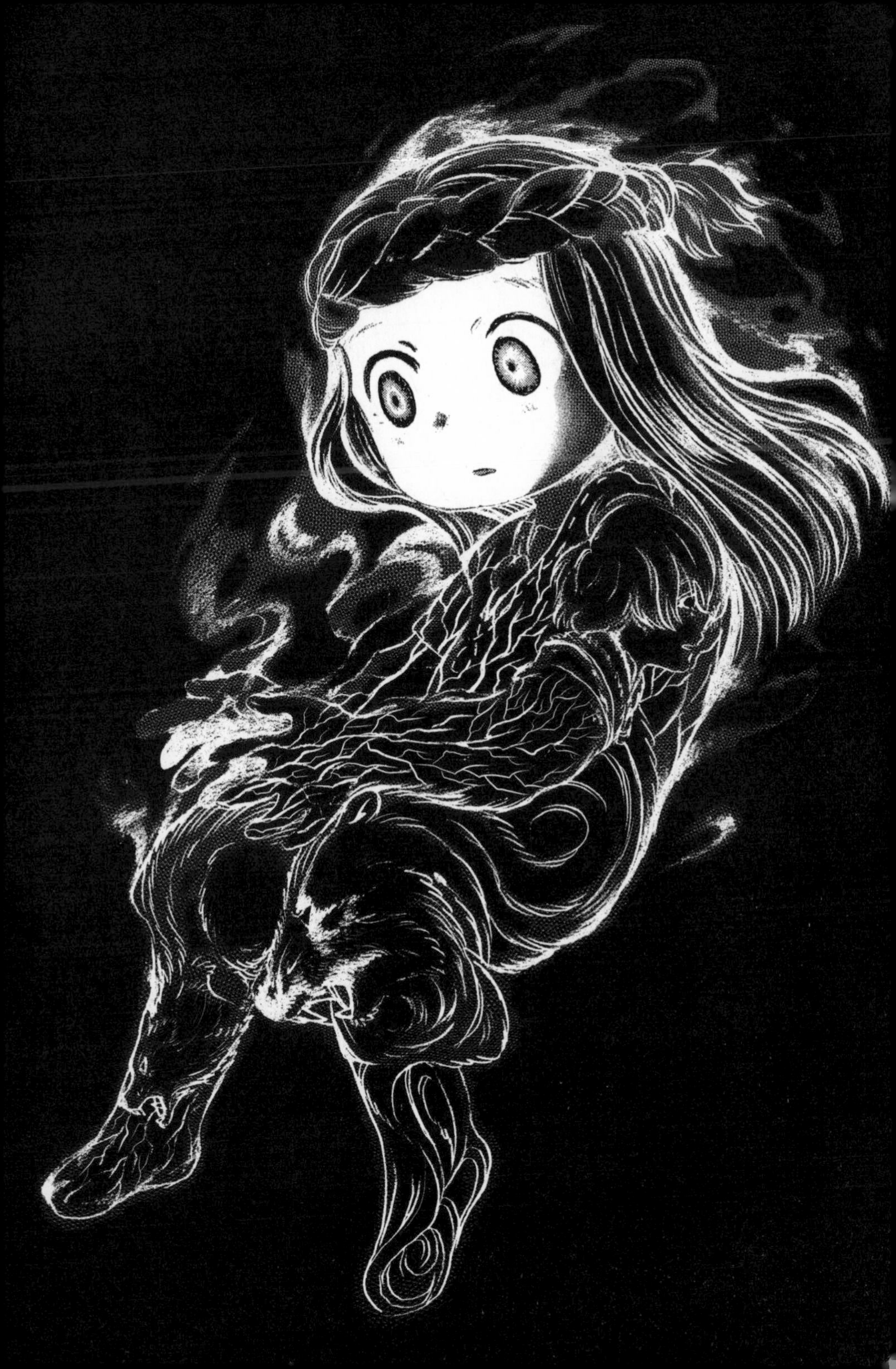

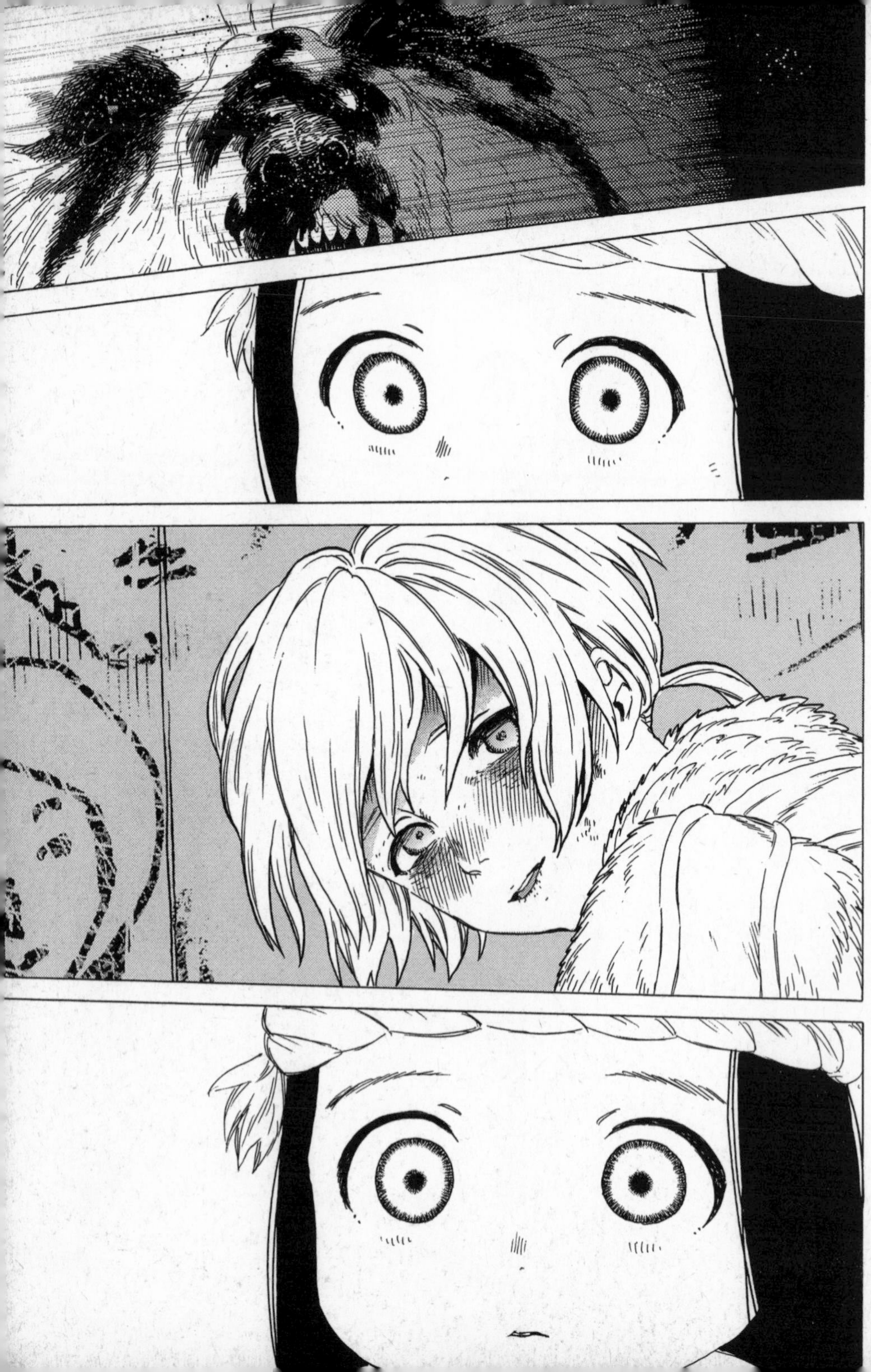

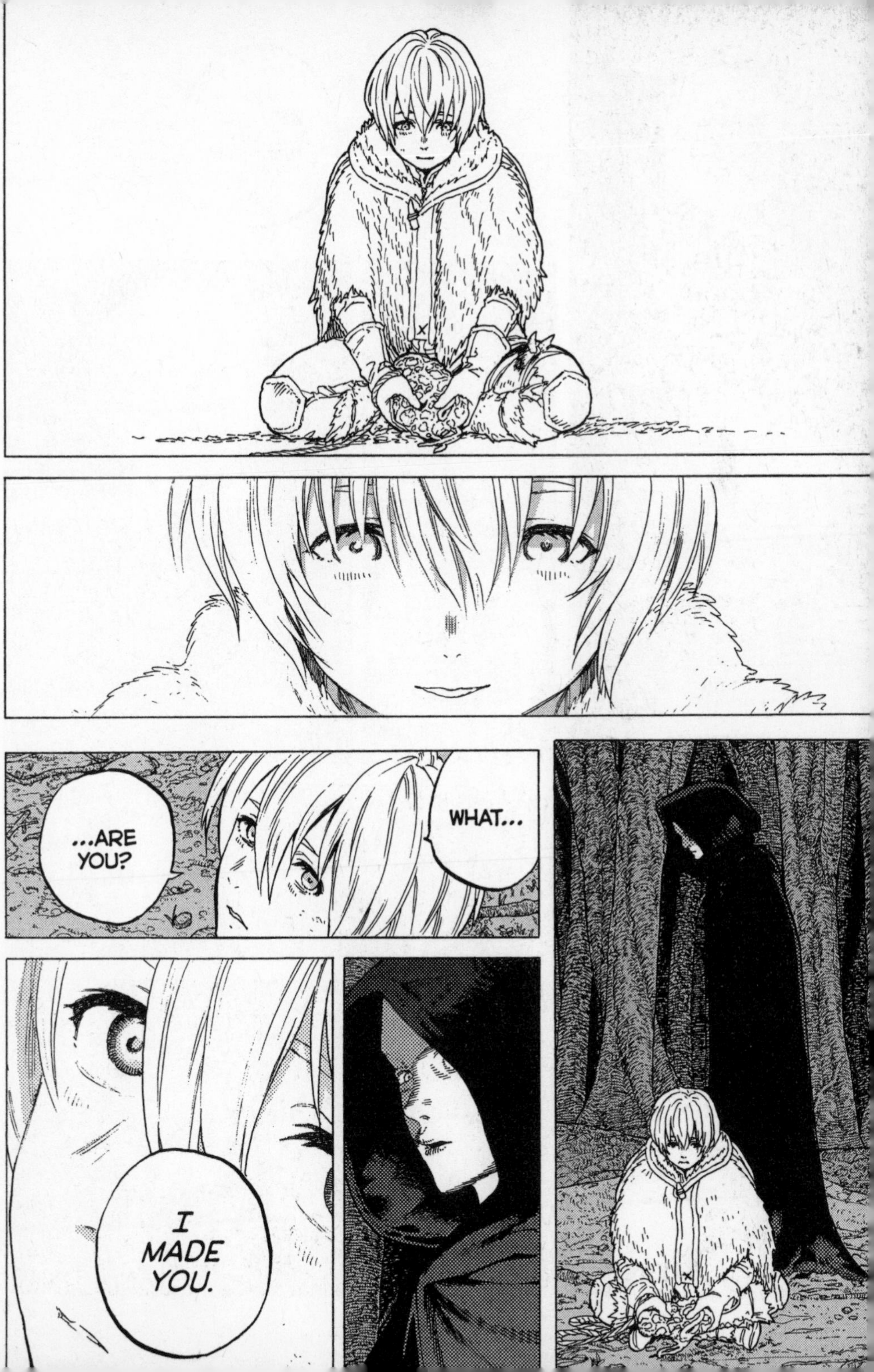
WHAT...
...ARE YOU?
I MADE YOU.

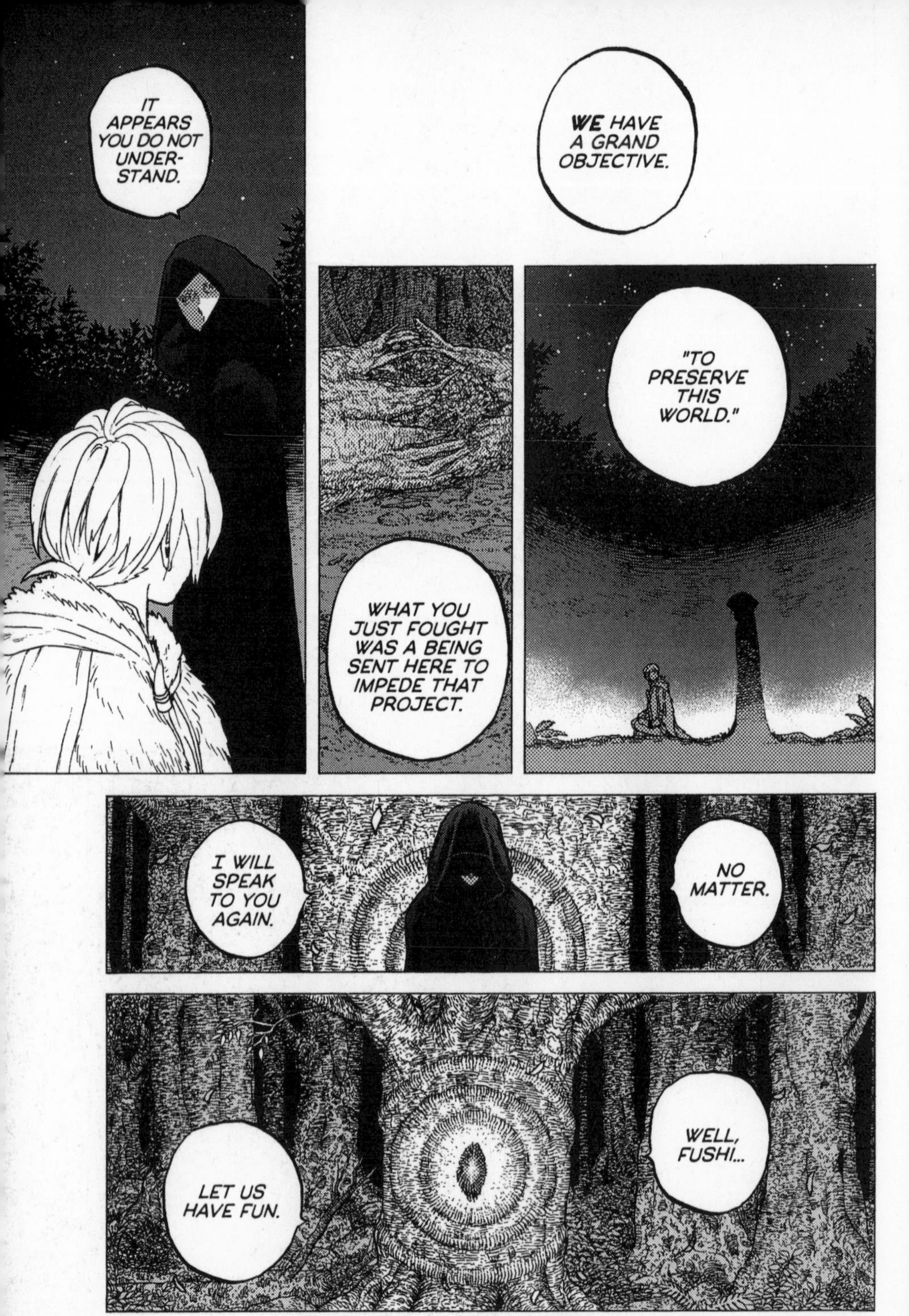

IT APPEARS YOU DO NOT UNDER-STAND.
WE HAVE A GRAND OBJECTIVE.
"TO PRESERVE THIS WORLD."
WHAT YOU JUST FOUGHT WAS A BEING SENT HERE TO IMPEDE THAT PROJECT.
NO MATTER.
I WILL SPEAK TO YOU AGAIN.
WELL, FUSHI...
LET US HAVE FUN.

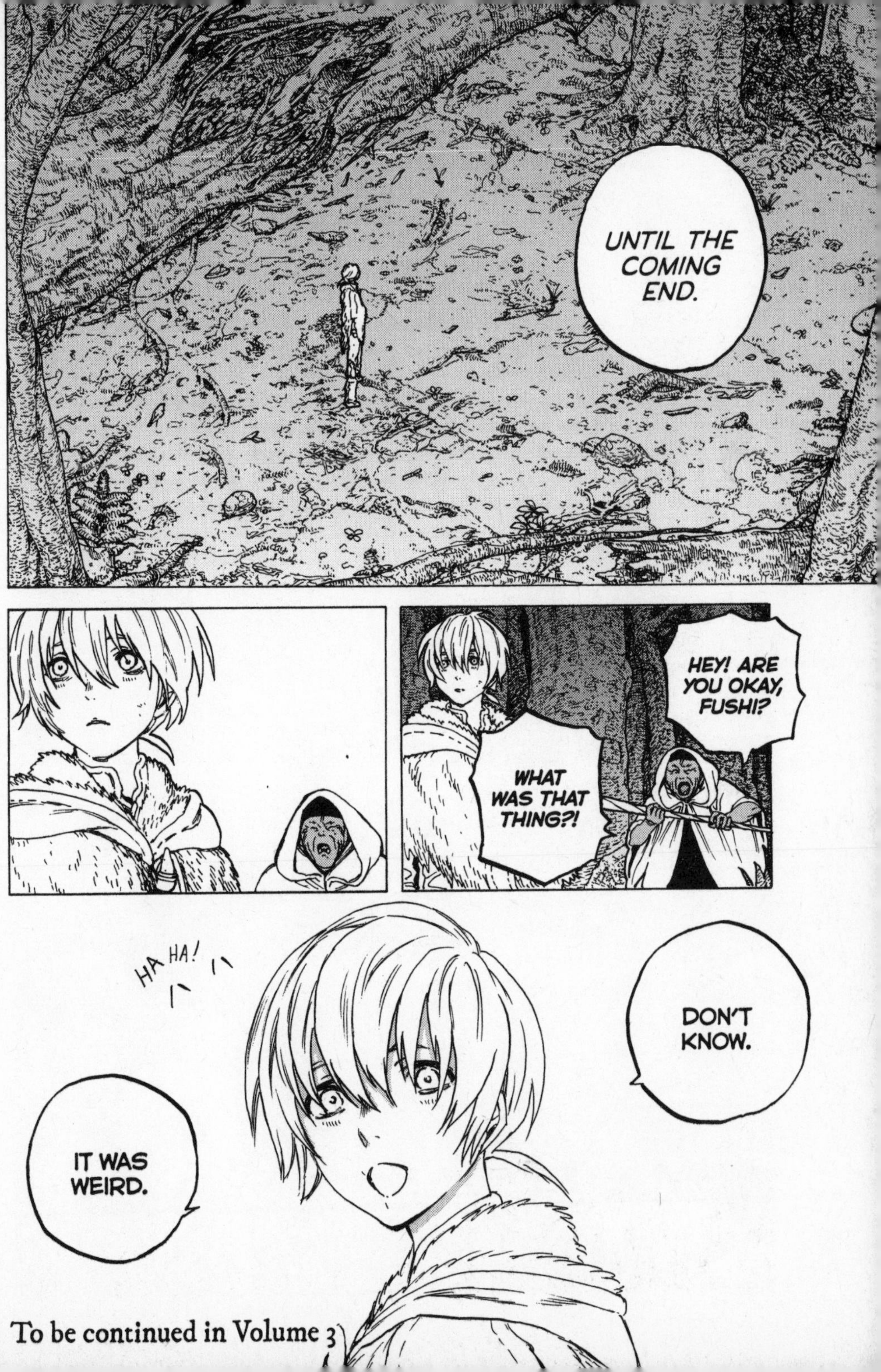
UNTIL THE COMING END.
HEY! ARE YOU OKAY, FUSHI?
WHAT WAS THAT THING?!
DON'T KNOW.
HA HA!
IT WAS WEIRD.

To be continued in Volume 3

TO YOUR
ETERNITY

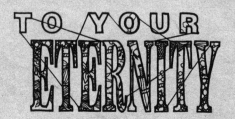

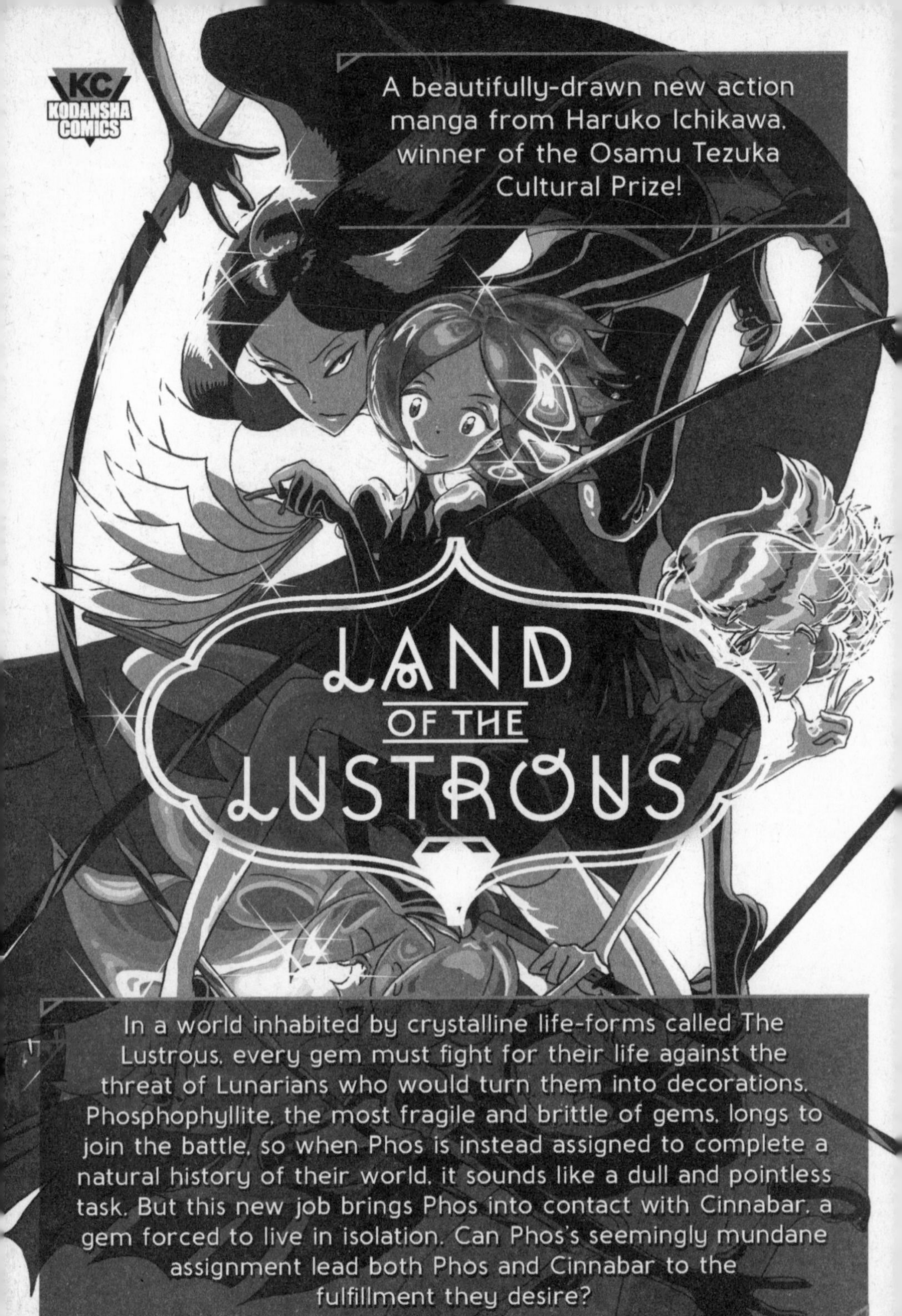

KC KODANSHA COMICS
A beautifully-drawn new action manga from Haruko Ichikawa, winner of the Osamu Tezuka Cultural Prize!
LAND OF THE LUSTROUS
In a world inhabited by crystalline life-forms called The Lustrous, every gem must fight for their life against the threat of Lunarians who would turn them into decorations. Phosphophyllite, the most fragile and brittle of gems, longs to join the battle, so when Phos is instead assigned to complete a natural history of their world, it sounds like a dull and pointless task. But this new job brings Phos into contact with Cinnabar, a gem forced to live in isolation. Can Phos's seemingly mundane assignment lead both Phos and Cinnabar to the fulfillment they desire?

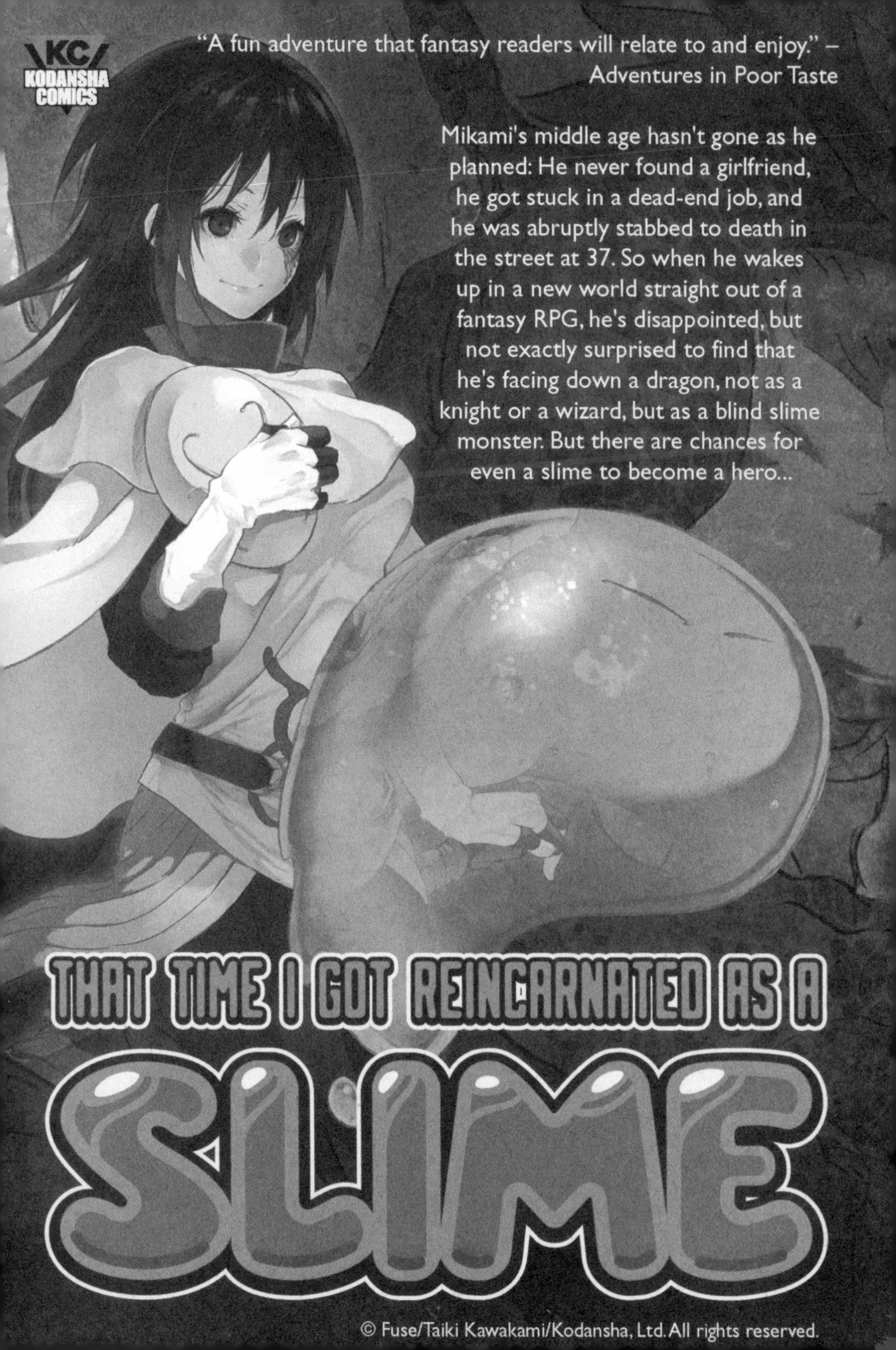
KC
KODANSHA COMICS
"A fun adventure that fantasy readers will relate to and enjoy." – Adventures in Poor Taste
Mikami's middle age hasn't gone as he planned: He never found a girlfriend, he got stuck in a dead-end job, and he was abruptly stabbed to death in the street at 37. So when he wakes up in a new world straight out of a fantasy RPG, he's disappointed, but not exactly surprised to find that he's facing down a dragon, not as a knight or a wizard, but as a blind slime monster. But there are chances for even a slime to become a hero...
THAT TIME I GOT REINCARNATED AS A
SLIME
© Fuse/Taiki Kawakami/Kodansha, Ltd. All rights reserved.

From the creator of *The Ancient Magus' Bride*
comes a supernatural action manga in the
vein of *Fullmetal Alchemist*!

More than a century after an eccentric scholar made an infamous deal with a
devil, the story of Faust has passed into legend. However, the true Faust is not
the stuffy, professorial man known in fairy tales, but a charismatic, bespectacled
woman named Johanna Faust, who happens to still be alive. Searching for
pieces of her long-lost demon, Johanna passes through a provincial town, where
she saves a young boy named Marion from a criminal's fate. In exchange, she
asks a simple favor of Marion, but Marion soon finds himself intrigued by
the peculiar Doctor Faust and joins her on her journey. Thus begins the strange
and wonderful adventures of *Frau Faust*!

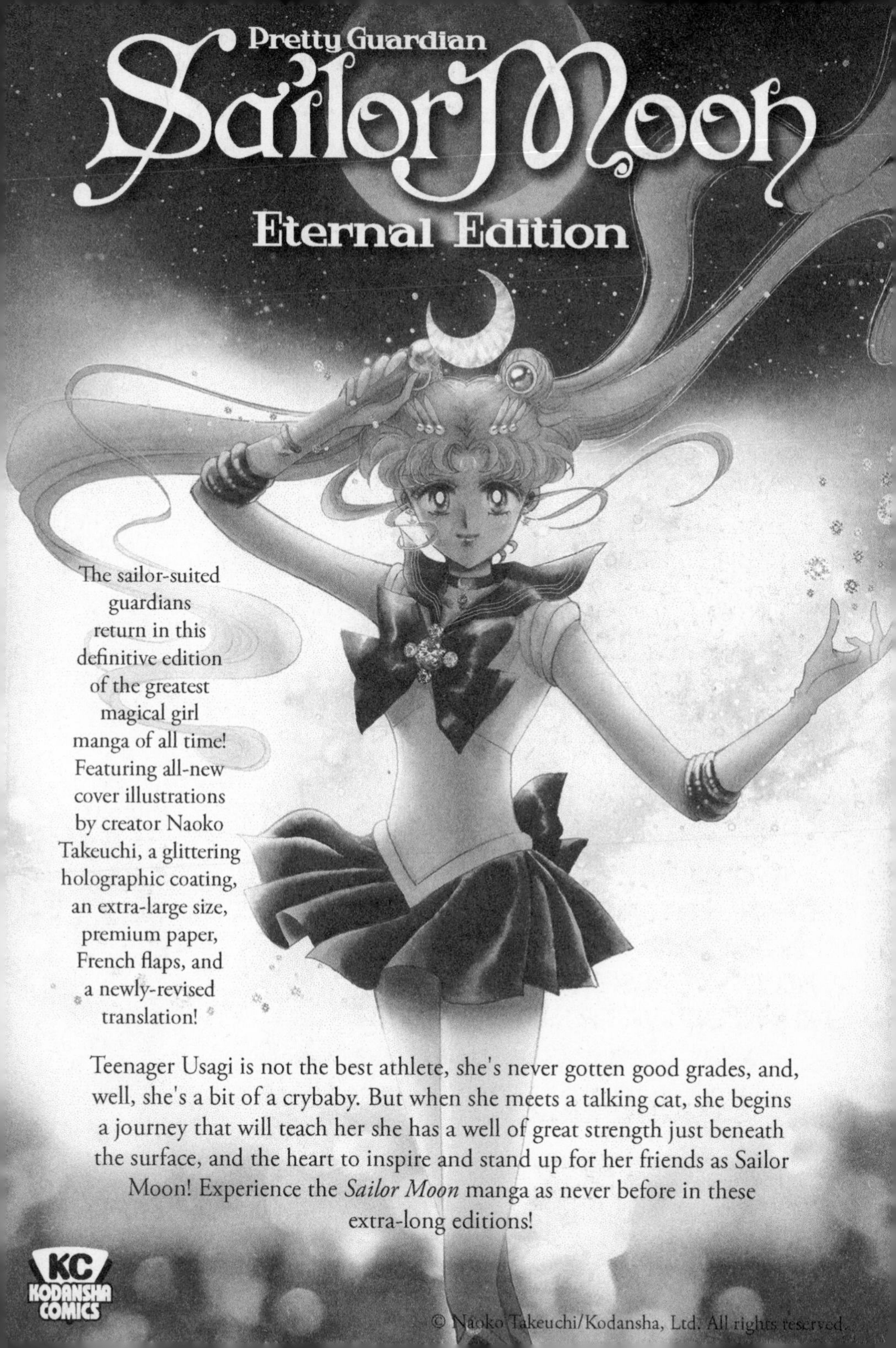
Pretty Guardian
Sailor Moon
Eternal Edition
The sailor-suited guardians return in this definitive edition of the greatest magical girl manga of all time! Featuring all-new cover illustrations by creator Naoko Takeuchi, a glittering holographic coating, an extra-large size, premium paper, French flaps, and a newly-revised translation!
Teenager Usagi is not the best athlete, she's never gotten good grades, and, well, she's a bit of a crybaby. But when she meets a talking cat, she begins a journey that will teach her she has a well of great strength just beneath the surface, and the heart to inspire and stand up for her friends as Sailor Moon! Experience the *Sailor Moon* manga as never before in these extra-long editions!
KC KODANSHA COMICS
© Naoko Takeuchi/Kodansha, Ltd. All rights reserved.

To Your Eternity volume 2 is a work of fiction.
Names, characters, places, and incidents are the products of the author's imagination or are used fictitiously. Any resemblance to actual events, locales, or persons, living or dead, is entirely coincidental.

A Kodansha Comics Trade Paperback Original.

Published in the United States by Kodansha Comics,
an imprint of Kodansha USA Publishing, LLC, New York.

Publication rights for this English edition arranged through Kodansha Ltd., Tokyo.

First published in Japan in 2017 by Kodansha Ltd., Tokyo,
as *Fumetsu no Anata e* volume 2.

Cover Design: Tadashi Hisamochi (hive&co., Ltd.)
Title Logo Design: Shinobu Ohashi

ISBN 978-1-63236-572-9

Printed in the United States of America.

www.kodanshacomics.com

9 8 7 6 5 4 3 2 1

Translation: Steven LeCroy
Lettering: Darren Smith
Editing: Haruko Hashimoto, Alexandra Swanson
Editorial Assistance: YKS Services LLC/SKY Japan, INC.
Kodansha Comics Edition Cover Design: Phil Balsman

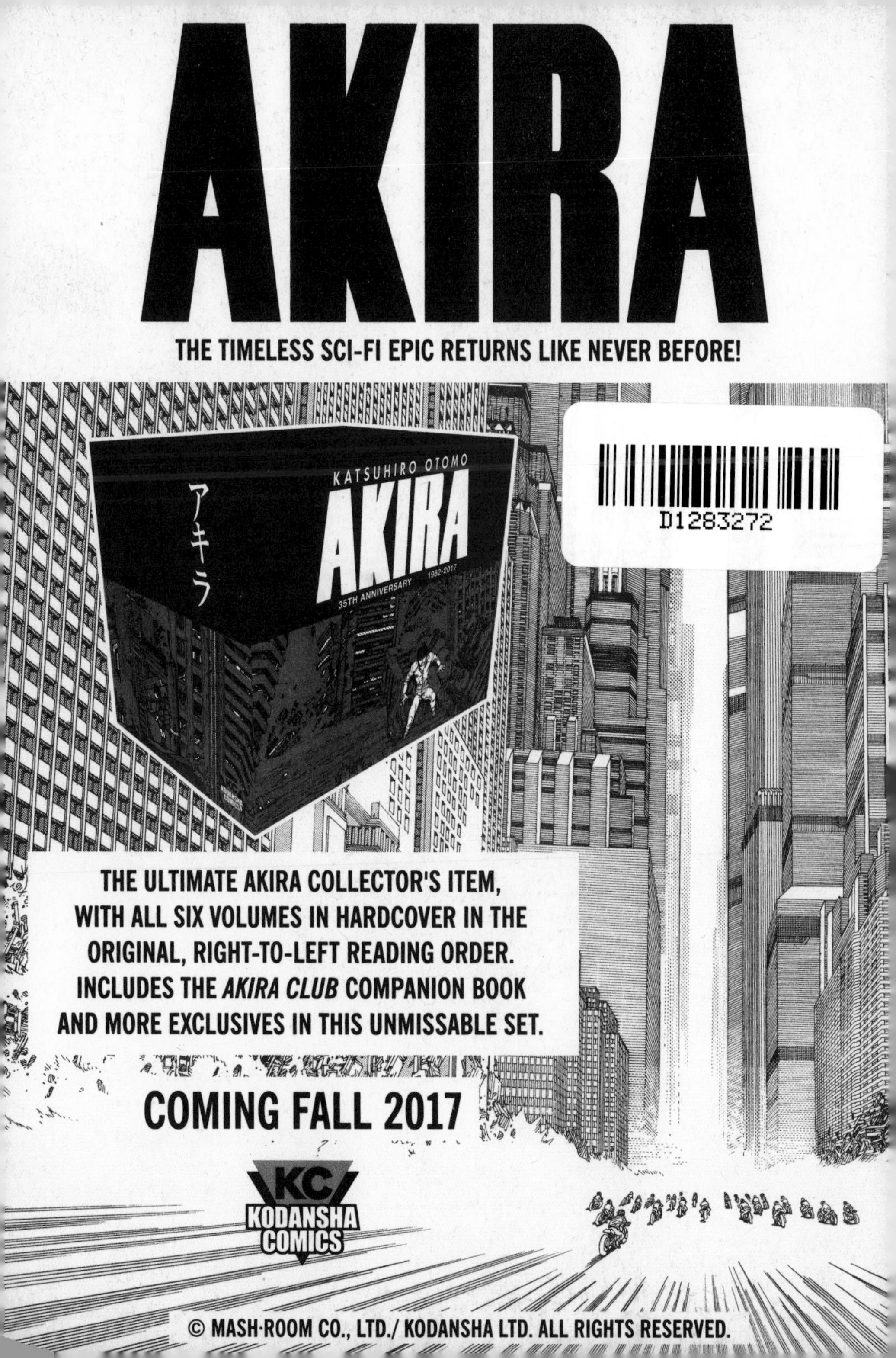
AKIRA
THE TIMELESS SCI-FI EPIC RETURNS LIKE NEVER BEFORE!
KATSUHIRO OTOMO
アキラ
AKIRA
35TH ANNIVERSARY 1982-2017
D1283272
THE ULTIMATE AKIRA COLLECTOR'S ITEM, WITH ALL SIX VOLUMES IN HARDCOVER IN THE ORIGINAL, RIGHT-TO-LEFT READING ORDER. INCLUDES THE *AKIRA CLUB* COMPANION BOOK AND MORE EXCLUSIVES IN THIS UNMISSABLE SET.
COMING FALL 2017
KC KODANSHA COMICS
© MASH·ROOM CO., LTD./ KODANSHA LTD. ALL RIGHTS RESERVED.